W9-BGQ-694

# AMERICA'S
# GILDED AGE

## ALSO BY MILTON RUGOFF

*The Beechers:*
*An American Family in the Nineteenth Century*

*Prudery and Passion:*
*Sexuality in Victorian America*

# AMERICA'S GILDED AGE

## INTIMATE PORTRAITS
*from an*
## ERA
*of*
## EXTRAVAGANCE
*and*
## CHANGE
*1850–1890*

## *MILTON RUGOFF*

HENRY HOLT *and* COMPANY
NEW YORK

Library of Congress Cataloging-in-Publication Data
Rugoff, Milton Allan, 1913–
America's Gilded Age: intimate portraits from an era of extravagance and
change, 1850–1890/Milton Rugoff. —1st ed.
p.    cm.
Bibliography: p.
Includes index.
ISBN 0-8050-0852-7
1. United States—Social life and customs—1865–1918.   2. Upper
class—United States—History—19th century.   3. Women—United
States—History—19th century.   4. United States—
History—1865–1898—Biography.   5. United States—Biography.
I. Title.
E168.R93 1989
973.91′092′2—dc19c                                      88—23556
                                                           CIP

Henry Holt books are available at special discounts
for bulk purchases for sales promotions, premiums,
fund-raising, or educational use. Special editions
or book excerpts can also be created to specification.

For details, contact:

Special Sales Director
Henry Holt and Company, Inc.
115 West 18th Street
New York, New York 10011

First Edition

Designed by Katy Riegel
Printed in the United States of America
1  3  5  7  9  10  8  6  4  2

# CONTENTS

FOREWORD                                                    vii

PROLOGUE                                                      1

**1**  *DEALER IN DAYDREAMS:*
       *Horatio Alger, Jr.*                                   7

**2**  *THE SPOILSMEN:*
       *Ulysses S. Grant, Sam Ward, James G. Blaine, and Ben*
       *Butler*                                              13

**3**  *THE MONEY KINGS:*
       *Cornelius Vanderbilt, Jay Cooke, and Jay Gould*      39

**4**  *THE PARVENUS AND THEIR PLEASURES:*
       *Leonard Jerome, Ward McAllister, Mrs. William Astor, and*
       *William H. Vanderbilt*                               68

**5**  *DREAMERS OF A GOLDEN WEST:*
       *Richard Garland, John Charles Frémont, Franklin Buck,*
       *J. Goldsborough Bruff, and Sarah Royce*              96

# CONTENTS

6  *LORDS OF THE PRESS:*
*James Gordon Bennett, Jr., Charles A. Dana, and Joseph
Pulitzer*                                                    141

7  *VIOLATORS OF THE GREAT TABOO:*
*Daniel Sickles, Jim Fisk, Henry Ward Beecher, Isaac Kalloch,
and Victoria Woodhull*                                       171

8  *WOMEN WHO BROKE THE BARRIERS:*
*Sarah and Angelina Grimké, Sojourner Truth, Ann Eliza
Young, Elizabeth Cady Stanton, Belva Ann Lockwood, and
Bethenia Owens-Adair*                                        230

9  *CRITICS AND CASSANDRAS:*
*Henry George, Charles Eliot Norton, Walt Whitman, and
Mark Twain*                                                  288

   EPILOGUE                                                  349

   SELECT BIBLIOGRAPHY                                       351

   INDEX                                                     359

# FOREWORD

In concentrating on several score lives in the Gilded Age, I have tried to fill the gap between a standard social history, consisting of generalizations and theories about issues and events, and a biography that focuses on the life of a single individual.

I chose these men and women because I believe they represent what distinguishes this period of the American past. Recent critics have objected that the term Gilded Age—taken from the title of the novel by Mark Twain and Charles Dudley Warner—emphasizes the greed and corruption of the period at the expense of its spiritual and cultural contributions. But the significant change in America was in the spread of money-oriented values and the rise of the money lords. It was this, as I see it, that made it a prelude to America today. The boom that led to the stock market crash of 1929 and, on a smaller scale, the rapid climb followed by the plunge that jolted the market in October 1987 were replays of the speculative frenzy that ended in Black Friday, 1869.

I have set the beginning of the Gilded Age in 1850 rather than, as some historians would have it, in 1865 or 1870 because, as we shall see, a multitude of forces were already transforming American life well before the Civil War.

# AMERICA'S GILDED AGE

# *PROLOGUE*

By 1868, when General Grant became president and the Gilded Age was approaching full flower, the world of the thirteen colonies and the early republic was gone forever. The America of the early 1800s had been mainly a rural world, a land of farms, hamlets, and vast wilderness areas, of handcraftsmen, homesteaders, small merchants, country lawyers, clergymen, and landed gentry. Its pace was set by the jog trot of a horse, the lurch of a two-wheeled ox cart, the drift of a canal boat; its work tempo set by a man plowing, a woman at a spinning wheel. It was no Golden Age, but life was linked to the cycle of the days and the seasons rather than to a clock, a factory machine, or a railroad timetable.

It was a world in which most Americans earned their bread by the sweat of their brow, provided their own food, made their own clothes. If anyone was not content, there was always virgin land to the west, the moving frontier where opportunity was forever renewed. There were few poor and few rich. Pleasures were simple and the material temptations were limited. In New England, life was generally narrow and hard, with much loneliness, and a harsh stifling of natural impulses. The farmer was far from being a noble husbandman—the Brook Farm dreamers notwithstanding—and his life was hardly a rural idyll. "The farmer leads the meanest of lives," said Thoreau. "He knows Nature but as a Robber." Nevertheless, very few men lived by someone else's labor. There was self-reliance, a respect for the individual, and a concern, often fearful but sometimes transfiguring, for man's soul and destiny.

Even in the eighteenth century there were those who lived opulently, especially among the planter and merchant aristocracy of Virginia, Maryland, and South Carolina. But theirs was truly a peculiar institution, based on tobacco, rice, or, later, cotton and the labor of slaves—a backwater that never entered the mainstream of American life.

In the North, America was just emerging from theocratic domination. Some citizens could still recall the spell woven by Jonathan Edwards, whose impassioned voice had exhorted man to submit to the will of an inscrutable God, to climb to heaven on a ladder whose rungs were impossibly far apart. Calvinism was still man's government, moral law, rule of behavior, spiritual guide. But there was a central paradox in Puritanism: it condemned luxury and worldliness, yet decreed that work was holy and wealth a sign of God's grace. In time the descendants of the Puritans resolved this paradox: they lost their distrust of worldliness and acquired an ever-increasing respect for prosperity.

Although vestiges of Edwards's influence were still evident, that of Benjamin Franklin in the role of Poor Richard had grown apace. Protestants and especially Quakers had always made a virtue of thrift and industry. It is ironic that Franklin, the cosmopolite, the freethinker in religion and love, and not so parsimonious himself, should have carpentered such bourgeois ideals into a code that set up a ladder leading not to heaven but to comfort and success. As early as 1808 John Adams said, with a surprisingly modern accent, "We have one material which actually constitutes an aristocracy that governs the nation. That material is wealth. Talents, birth, virtues, services, sacrifices, are of little consideration with us."

In the Revolution the colonists had gained not only political freedom but also the license to exploit their new world as they pleased. It sharpened an appetite for land that would grow until all but the remotest fastnesses would be staked out. This braving of frontiers would give those who shared in it an overweening self-confidence and aggressiveness. The heroes were Daniel Boone, Davy Crockett, and Mike Fink—trailblazers, huntsmen, Indian fighters, river giants. As the West developed, bold, buoyant, and materialistic, New England, increasingly ingrown and conservative, stagnated.

The industrial revolution brought the steamboat and the railroad to hurry men across the land; cotton gins and mechanical reapers to speed work; factories and mills to multiply the product of hands. The railroad brazenly proclaimed a new force in the world. It was the conqueror of space, iron Pegasus, tamer of wilderness, in its irresistible forward motion the perfect symbol of progress. As a man took his first ride, he passed into the age of technology. Only a few suspected that this god might be in part a demon, one that would spatter the landscape with squalid factory towns and dark imprisoning mills. It was a lonely voice that cried from Walden Pond, "We do not ride upon the railroad; it rides upon us."

Up to that time, the owner of a business had worked in it himself, had been responsible for it. Now any enterprise could be owned by unidentified men called stockholders; behind a corporate shield they could profit without producing. Just when Jacksonian democracy had completed the social leveling process, making the common man as good as a king, a new elite took over—the men of wealth.

In the years between 1840 and 1861 the dreams of the idealists— at Brook Farm, New Harmony, Fruitlands, and the other utopian communities—went out like snuffed candles, and the Concord of the Transcendentalists gave way to the Lowell of the cotton mills. The ideal of progress as envisioned by the philosophers and poets of the Enlightenment was soon appropriated by those who taught America to measure it in terms of goods and profits. Progress became the magic wand that justified every exploitation.

To the race for free land was added the scramble for gold, contributing two new possibilities: something for nothing, and luck is crucial. When Indians or Mexicans stood in the way, they were crushed. America, the young Bunyan, was something of a bully. He was the individualist, proud of his independence, scorning pomp and pretension; but sometimes lawless, violent, and predatory. By the 1850s settlements everywhere were turning into towns, and towns into cities. There Americans were no longer self-sufficient. They needed factories; factories needed workers; and in the cities workers huddled more and more in slums. Gone was the dream of a Puritan commonwealth, visions of an agrarian democracy, sons of toil amid

3

pastoral plenty. The day of the dynamo had come, and man was as unprepared to deal with it as he had been in the year 1. The preacher who had a century earlier moved in the van of colonial society was thrust aside, relegated to the role of a commentator listened to only on Sunday mornings. The Puritan had lost out to the Yankee.

Whatever youthful freshness remained in the land was burned out in the Civil War. The struggle did more than destroy 600,000 young men and maim a host of others; it wiped out a nation's innocence, the illusion that America held the secret of brotherhood. It was scarred not only by the carnage but also by the memory of the profiteers, the sellers of shoddy, the bounty-jumpers and bummers.

After the bloodletting and the mourning came a tidal desire to enjoy life and creature comforts. The centers of the nation's life shifted to the cities, and in the cities life divided into classes: at the top the rich, increasingly ostentatious, and at the bottom the poor, increasingly benighted.

It was possible now to make money without sweat or toil—in railroads, bonanza mining, petroleum, cattle, meat-packing, shipping, Bessemer steel, real estate, stocks. Soon there were fortunes to be wrung out of political power, adding graft and spoils to the blight on the blossom of American success. The plantation owners and gentlemen statesmen who had taken over government from the clergymen at the time of the Revolution gave way to the politicians and the bosses. "Failure seems to be regarded as the one unpardonable crime," Charles Francis Adams, Jr., said, "success as the one all-redeeming virtue, the acquisition of wealth as the single worthy aim of life." Where there had been inner certainties there was now a restless craving, where there had been restraint there was display. The motives written in glittering letters on the horizon were Progress, Profit, Wealth.

But to talk of the captains of industry and the masters of finance simply as robber barons and as though they served no useful purpose is both inaccurate and unjust. They were often men of immense energy, initiative, spirit, and vision. They planned and organized and they risked their fortunes in what Allan Nevins has called the heroic age of American enterprise. They made possible the building of great railroads, steamship lines, factories, and mills; of mining, lumber, and oil empires; and of banking and financial systems. And a few, such as Andrew Carnegie and John D. Rockefeller, gave back millions to philanthropic and educational enterprises.

Nor did the fever infect everyone; some men and women went their way untouched, scorning the new gods. In the closing chapters we explore the lives of some of those who defied the prohibitions, as well as of critics and dissenters, who sounded warnings or sought to stem the tide, or held up another vision of life.

# 1

## DEALER IN DAYDREAMS

Accepting the Puritan dictum that the accumulation of wordly goods was a sign of grace, early New Englanders devoted themselves almost as wholeheartedly to making money as to churchgoing. As early as 1701 Cotton Mather said that a man's work and his religion were the two oars with which he could row to the shores of eternal blessedness. The conversion of the Puritan into Yankee had begun; it would not stop until "Yankee" was a byword for sharp trader.

Similarly, in Pennsylvania the Quaker tradition permitted a Ben Franklin to create an almanac whose advice was aimed in part at the achievement of worldly success. Soon Poor Richard had captivated much of America with an arrant materialism summed up in the maxim "Time is money." Even the colleges, fountainheads of religious leadership, found a peculiar virtue in wealth. Timothy Dwight, elected president of Yale in 1795, preached, "The love of property to a certain degree seems indispensable to the existence of sound morals."

All that remained was the indoctrination of children with the respect for wealth and merchant heroes. William Holmes McGuffey's 122,000,000 books for children, published between 1836 and 1900, helped achieve that goal. McGuffey's *Reader* taught honesty, frugality, piety, and duty, not for their own sake, but as a means to success.

The *Reader* taught that the diligent do more worthwhile deeds than the brilliant, and that native talent often leads to laziness.

The gospel of success was spread even more confidently by P. T. Barnum's autobiography, published in 1854. The book itself demonstrated the shrewdness of its rules by selling half a million copies. Barnum incorporated these rules in a lecture entitled, with the brazen appeal that made him the showman of the century, "The Art of Money-Getting," and delivered it at least 100 times. It brought Poor Richard up to date, describing how "industry, perseverance, economy, and good habits," spurred by "go-aheaditiveness," could make a poor boy as rich as John Jacob Astor and Cornelius Vanderbilt. It did not seem to matter that Mr. Barnum had achieved his own success by exhibiting such curiosities as Joice Heth, a black woman alleged to have been George Washington's nurse and 161 years old—until a postmortem examination indicated that she was scarcely eighty.

It remained for Horatio Alger, Jr., to make morality the path not to heaven but to success. It is no accident that his books for boys began to appear in the mid-1860s—soon after the onset of the Gilded Age. As the most popular and respected boys' books of the time—20 million copies were sold by the end of the century, each doubtless read by a dozen boys—they had an incalculable influence. Beneath their moral cant they reveal what many young men dreamed of. With a few exceptions, what they sought, as set forth in more than 100 novels, from *Bound to Rise* and *Sink or Swim* to *Ragged Dick* and *Paul the Peddler,* was wealth and respectability. Book after book was, for its unfledged readers, a deeply satisfying working out of the American dream—of going from rags to riches, from poverty to fame and fortune.

All Alger's heroes succeed, but none of the narratives tell us how the hero fares after he achieves success. No one questions the worthiness of the hero's goal or dares to say, as some Puritan preacher might have said, that such goals may prove a snare and a delusion. Nor does anyone suggest that other goals may be more admirable. None of the heroes hope to become teachers, clergymen, missionaries, country doctors, or poets, and certainly not farmers. Indeed, Alger's farmboys dream of getting to the city, for in his books the city is full of excitement, vitality, and promise. They are undaunted by its teeming anonymity, its dangers and corruptions, the elusiveness of its glittering rewards. Gone is the Jeffersonian faith in pastoral tranquillity, the assumed goodness of the agrarian way of life. One youth does venture into journalism and another makes good as a U.S. senator, but most of them see the field of their choice as a path to one end—affluence.

Although Alger's stories are intended to show how all worthwhile goals are won by pluck, perseverance, and manly independence, by honesty, industry, sobriety, and thrift, and by such auxiliary virtues as clean living, cheerfulness, and patriotism, he is not altogether consistent. An astonishing number of his heroes achieve their goals by accident or chance. An unexpected inheritance from a long-lost father or the daring rescue of a rich man's daughter is far more dramatic than a tedious climb up the ladder of success.

Except in one early—and feeble—Alger tale, girls are slighted; in the drama of business success they are merely accessories. Sex is taboo, a pitfall for wastrels. The theory was: if you do not mention it, it is not there.

Although wealth is made to seem desirable, most of the rich men who employ Alger's young heroes are mean and unhappy. They have usually gained their wealth by being niggardly, oppressing their employees, and even cheating their customers. In the end the wicked rich men are punished, sometimes shorn of their wealth, and always worsted by the hero. But Alger's heroes are of course exempt from such corruption: they become both rich and happy.

There was so little relationship between Alger's own life and that of his heroes that we must assume his books represented the wishful dreams of his boyhood. As full of determination and courage were his heroes, so wavering and frustrated was Alger himself. The son of a perennially hard-pressed New England clergyman and a weak, submissive mother, surrounded by lofty moral standards and genteel poverty, Horatio Jr. grew up an inhibited and confused youth. Something of a weakling, with a tendency to bog down in indecision, he would throughout his life show signs of deep insecurity.

At the age of sixteen, in 1848, he was sent to Harvard, his father intending to prepare him for divinity school. A good student and a fluent writer, Horatio did well in his studies. Enchanted by the literary classics and adept at producing poems for any occasion, he began nursing an ambition to become a writer. So it was that after graduating he balked at going on to divinity school. Instead, he fumbled about, serving for a number of years in boarding schools, meanwhile contributing facile verse, humorous sketches, and moralizing stories, often about children, to various second-rate weeklies. These generally paid him little or nothing but fed his urge to write. One of the poems was addressed in amatory terms to a male Cambridge friend, and several romantic sketches betray an ambivalence about heterosexual relationships, repeatedly portraying the men as bachelors deceived by designing women. But his combined income from teaching and writing proved so unreliable that he entered Cambridge Theological School, resigned to becoming a minister. To support himself during his three years at the school he ground out, under several pseudonyms, no less than nine series full of dime-novel melodrama and sensational conflicts between good and evil, villainy and virtue. He knew they were hackwork, but they earned the money he needed.

After finishing divinity school, Alger joined two of his friends on a nine-month tour of Europe, meeting part of his expenses with letters written as a "foreign correspondent" of the *Sun*. On his return in 1861 he began preaching regularly at a part Unitarian, part Universalist church in Dover, Massachusetts. An ardent foe of slavery but physically unfit to serve as a soldier, and feeling that with his background he would be wasted as a private, Alger compensated by pouring out a stream of ballads and stories on behalf of the Union.

At the age of thirty-two, realizing that he would never achieve distinction as a writer for adults, and with a sympathy for boys that he had acquired as a teacher and tutor, he undertook a book for young readers. The writing came easily: in three months he had completed *Frank's Campaign,* a tale of a youngster who volunteers to run the family farm so his father can enlist. It would launch him on his long and spectacular career.

But just when he submitted the manuscript to a publisher, the First Unitarian Church of Brewster, on Cape Cod, called him for an audition as a preacher. His effort was so well received that he was ordained as their minister in November 1864 at an annual salary of $800. For a year the Reverend Horatio Alger, Jr., pleased and impressed his congregation. Then, early in 1866, a young boy told his aunt that the minister had approached him sexually. Almost at once other stories of "unnatural crimes" and deeds "too revolting to relate" were reported by other members of the congregation. A committee investigated and corroborated the stories. When Alger was confronted with the charges, it was reported that "he neither denied nor attempted to extenuate them but received them with the apparent calmness of an old offender." He admitted that he had been "imprudent," resigned his post, and left town on the next train. One of the parents wanted to press charges but settled for a report to the office of the American Unitarian Association in Boston, declaring, "Horatio Alger, Jr. who has officiated as our minister for about fifteen months has recently been charged with . . . the abominable and revolting crime of unnatural familiarity with *boys* . . . which is to a refined or Christian mind too utterly incomprehensible. No further comment is necessary." Alger sought refuge in his parents' home in Boston, but that was too close to Brewster. With the dreadful charges ringing in his ears, he fled to New York. He would never again serve in a church.

Desperate to repair his shattered life, Alger turned to writing again and by the end of 1866 had turned out three novels, one for adults, one for boys, and one for young women. Surely as expiation for his transgression, he filled them, as a Unitarian paper observed, with "good thoughts, pure feelings and well-developed Christian lessons." In the city Alger came upon the Newsboys' Lodging House on Fulton Street, a shelter for homeless working youths, and began gathering the material on the lives of newsboys, bootblacks, and "luggage boys" that would fill many of his books in the next ten years. Deeply attracted to the boys in the house, Alger virtually lived there himself. Like a bachelor uncle, or perhaps a maiden aunt, he gave them sympathy, candy, money, and moral lectures. He even unofficially adopted one. Seeing how gullible he was, the boys told him what he wished to hear and took from him whatever they could get. As Dixon Wecter points out, Alger, busy glorifying the newsboy with a heart of gold, was apparently unaware of the disclosure by a Sing Sing warden that a majority of 2,300 inmates had been newsboys in their youth.

It is ironic that such a disturbed man should have come to be considered a paragon of morality and a noble-souled crusader. Even more ironic, as he churned out book after book with stilted dialogue, creaking plots, and sticklike characters, he spent more time dreaming of the great American novel he would some day write.

In search of a fresh locale for his books, he went west and even tried a story of a "street Arab" resettled on the western frontier, but he soon returned to New York and his old formulas. As his reputation and income grew, his success became a legend. But as a discriminating reader, one who recognized a master novelist in Henry James, Alger grew more and more dissatisfied with his own work. In his last years, toward the close of the century, he stopped writing altogether and pathetically declared that he wanted to forget the books he had written. The victim of arrested development and neurotic obsessions, there was a double irony in his fate: he who had made wealth one of the highest goals, but had dreamed only of being a great writer, had made his way as a hack.

After his death in 1899, Alger's books continued to be read in dime-novel format, but by the end of World War I they had become outmoded curiosities, relics of the childhood of the Age of Acquisition, tales of heroes who were honest, good, and conscientious mainly because it paid off. Even his twelve-year-old readers seemed to have sensed that Alger heroes were fraudulent.

It is difficult to gauge the effect of Alger's books, but there is much to indicate that they left many youths with more of a desire to climb from rags to riches than to cultivate the virtues Alger recommended. They were daydreams for youths about to enter the empire of the dollar.

# 2

## THE SPOILSMEN

After the Civil War, Washington was a city of feverishly ambitious men and women intoxicated by the power and wealth at their disposal. Except for a few aging holdovers, such as Charles Francis Adams and Hamilton Fish, the day of the patrician statesmen, the great amateurs in the tradition of Jefferson and Hamilton and John Quincy Adams, was gone. To take their place had come the professional politicians, the bosses of "party machines," dealers in patronage, spokesmen of interests. The fever had spread through every level of government from customs clerk to Cabinet member. Businessmen, they said, are making fortunes out of the nation's resources, so why shouldn't we?

Like the age, the city of Washington was in transition. The simplicity, partly provincial, partly classical, of an earlier time, fairly well exemplified by the White House, was giving way to the overornamented marble monstrosities of the style that would come to be known as "Late General Grant." New or half-finished structures, the latter including the Capitol dome and the Washington Monument, rose amid expanses of raw ground, with here and there a cluster of shanties occupied by blacks. Streams of fine carriages as well as horsecars and hacks pounded along unpaved streets, muddy in spring, dusty in summer, frozen in winter. The population leap from 61,000 in 1860 to 110,000 in 1870 left the city a gawky, half-mature society, outgrowing its garments year by year.

With the Capital so close to Virginia, an enclave in a slaveholding empire, Washington social life had always been Southern in tone. The center of elegance, Lafayette Square, still redolent of the days of Dolley Madison and John Randolph, was dominated by the homes of Secretary of the Treasury Howell Cobb of Georgia, Senator John Slidell of Louisiana, and the cream of Virginia aristocrats, the Tayloes. The most magnificent party in the city before the war was the masquerade ball given in April 1858 by Senator William Gwin, a rich Mississippi slaveholder who had become one of the first senators from California and whose life-style was said to have cost him $75,000 a year.

Although the war turned the Capital into a huge camp ringed with barracks, hospitals, and supply depots, there was still a surprising amount of entertaining. After two and a half years of war, this became conspicuous enough to attract attention: "Gayety has become as epidemic in Washington this winter as gloom was last winter," wrote Assistant Secretary of State Frederick W. Seward late in 1863. "There is a lull in political discussion; the people are inclined to eat, drink and be merry." And a correspondent in the Springfield *Republican* of February 20, 1864, asserted:

> A soldier in the Army of the Potomac does not endure a severer strain on his constitution than a woman in "society" in Washington. . . . Think of it, shopping, dressing, calling all day; parties, dancing, late suppers, late sleep, repeated week after week. At present Washington is . . . reeling in the whirl of dissipation, before it sits down to repent in the ashes of Lent.

All this was hardly unique to the capital of the North; profiteering and profligacy were, if anything, greater in Richmond. The Richmond *Dispatch* of April 13, 1863, declared that the scramble for gain was far more shameful in the Confederacy than among the Yankees. Balls and "hops" were the order of the day, and editorial writers railed against those who gave elegant dances while want and famine knocked at the gates. Prostitutes and gamblers thrived, and diamonds, silks, and lace were in great demand. The Southern aristocracy would go down with its dancing shoes on.

As soon as peace was declared, the merrymaking burst forth like an underground river coming to the surface. The Senate was not yet the rich men's club it later became, but several members, such as William Sprague, in his early forties but already showing the effects of steady dissipation, and his wife, the accomplished Kate Chase Sprague, daughter of Salmon P. Chase, entertained on a lavish scale. The social season had never been so brilliant, the champagne flowing and the jets in the crystal chandeliers burning far into the night.

Much of the social life, unlike that of New York, was peculiarly democratic, the rich hobnobbing with the would-be rich, sophisticated easterner with bluff westerner, patrician with plebeian, and scamp with solid citizen. Swept regularly by election tides, Washington society was especially unstable. In winter the great hotels—the National, the Metropolitan, Willard's—churned with excitement. After each day's session of Congress, the halls and sitting rooms were jammed with boisterous crowds, the air hazy with tobacco smoke, and the floor spotted with tobacco juice. So detached an observer as Nathaniel Hawthorne, visiting Washington during the war, testified to the stimulating effect of Willard's: "You exchange nods with governors of foreign states; you elbow illustrious men and tread on the toes of generals; you hear orators and statesmen speaking in their familiar tones. . . . You adopt the universal habit of the place, and call for a mint-julep, a whiskey-skin, a gin-cocktail . . ."

In the lobbies senators, representatives, Cabinet officials, clerks, contractors, lobbyists, members of "rings," plain citizens and plain loafers mingled in noisy confusion. Upstairs, in the brilliantly lighted parlors, richly dressed women held court. Some were the wives and daughters of the men downstairs. Others were female lobbyists, including some of doubtful respectability; they arrived in Washington for the congressional session, rented a fine house with servant, carriage, and coachman, and entertained generously. A few even gave parties for susceptible congressmen and sundry attractive, unattached young women. These women lobbyists understood legislative procedures thoroughly, and when the more influential among them occasionally attended a session it was not unusual for them to be magically passed into the diplomatic box. At the end of the session, their work done, they packed their bags and vanished.

Despite prudery and Victorian cant, brothels and gambling houses, some of them luxurious, flourished. In the years before the war, Pendleton's gambling house on Pennsylvania Avenue, a richly furnished establishment run by a member of a leading Virginia family, was frequented by senators, congressmen, Cabinet members, editors, and lobbyists. In its outer rooms sumptuous dinners were served on gold plates; in its inner rooms large sums were won and lost. So much lobbying went on there that a contemporary chronicler, Ben Perley Poore, called it "the vestibule of the lobby."

Even though the war's end had left the nation with a staggering burden of problems—a huge public debt, unemployment, a prostrate and embittered South, a mass of uprooted blacks—the war itself had turned Washington into a magic well of contracts, subsidies, grants, and spoils. Lobbyists moved with ever greater boldness among the legislators, buying influence, currying favor, seeking privilege for the sake of profit. In one of the most cynical passages in Mark Twain and Charles Dudley Warner's *The Gilded Age,* the president of the "Columbia River Slackwater Navigation Company" explains why it cost $300,000 to get a $200,000 appropriation bill through Congress: huge sums paid to the members of both a House committee and a Senate committee, to a female lobbyist and seven male lobbyists, dinners for congressmen and gifts for their wives.

So suave and assured were the leading lobbyists that it became possible for a congressman to persuade himself that such people were simply very generous acquaintances rather than paid agents. The most famous, Sam Ward, was proud to be known as "King of the Lobbyists." Even more surprising, Ward was the son of a highly respected and cultivated banker and was himself a man of remarkable intellectual attainments. In any age he would have been a *bon viveur,* but not before the Civil War could he have become an instrument of business interests seeking to buy the favor of legislators.

In spite of all the old Puritan saws, Sam Ward proved that one could mix pleasure with study. In 1829 he had entered Columbia College, a small, undistinguished academy near City Hall, but he seems to have devoted far more time to nearby oyster cellars, billiard parlors, and dinners of quail, beefsteak, Madeira, and hot whiskey

punch in a tiny café run by two brothers named Delmonico. Summers the Wards spent at Newport. Still far from the fashionable resort
it would later become, Newport attracted a number of fine Southern
families as well as a circle of New York and Boston intellectuals. In
New York the Wards dwelt in a mansion daringly far uptown—on
Bond Street just south of Eighth.

Graduating from Columbia, Sam promptly awarded himself a year
of study in Europe. He managed to stretch one year to four, and
although he did get a degree from the University of Tübingen, his
true study was the nightlife of Paris, drinking sessions at Heidelberg,
and the management of French mistresses. Debonair, openhanded,
bright, accomplished (he studied singing and the piano), he spoke
French like a Parisian and mingled as easily with leading artists as
with the social elite.

In Heidelberg he also began the most enduring friendship of his
life—with a twenty-nine-year-old New Englander, Henry Wadsworth
Longfellow. Ward would forever after profess to envy above all things
"Longo's" life as a scholar and poet, and bemoan what he considered
his own thralldom to the world of money. Having constantly overdrawn a most generous allowance, Sam returned to New York in 1836
looking like a dandy, with a silken mustache, blond Vandyke beard,
velvet coat, and a shirt with ruffles.

Just as Sam Ward entered his father's business, the panic of 1837
struck. Even Prime, Ward & King, New York's leading bankers,
staggered, but the financial upheaval did not interrupt Sam's lavish
expenditures or interfere with his auspicious marriage to a sweet-
tempered girl named Emily Astor, the granddaughter of the richest
man in America. Suspicious old John Jacob made his son-in-law waive
all claims to the Astor estate, however, and when Emily died at the
age of twenty-two, while giving birth to her second child, all Sam
had left was grief and a little daughter. He mourned for a time, but
he was of a buoyant temperament and consoled himself with a variety
of epicurean diversions. After visiting him, Longfellow reported that
he had found Sam "as multifarious as ever; in the morning he reads
Livy an hour before breakfast . . . then hurries down to his business;
rides on horseback before dinner and sings Italian duets after."

And soon Sam was in love again—this time with Medora Grymes,
a New Orleans belle of languorous charms and improbably romantic

parentage. Her father was John Randolph Grymes, brilliant lawyer, gambler, eccentric dandy, and duelist; her mother was a Creole beauty, the widow of Governor Claiborne. Despite the fact that Medora was dominated by her mother, a scheming fortune hunter, Sam, ignoring all warnings, wooed Medora and won her.

On his father's death in 1839, Sam had become a partner in Prime, Ward & King, but where his father had considered banking a trust as well as a livelihood, Sam saw it only as an easy way to wealth. He speculated recklessly in foreign exchange and flour, and one day in 1847 he awoke to discover that Prime, Ward & King was bankrupt. In less than eight years he had lost millions.

Sam Ward was only thirty-four—and the year was 1848. The western frontier had long been a magnetic force in American life, and with the discovery of gold it became a demoralizing lure even to relatively stable men. Borrowing $600 in order to go by fast boat around Cape Horn, Ward set out with his cousin Hall McAllister, a Georgia lawyer. They arrived in San Francisco in June 1849, at the height of the gold frenzy. But Sam Ward had no intention of braving the rigors of the goldfields. He had foreseen that there would be easier ways of making money: he opened a store offering a variety of hardware and at the same time began to speculate in land. Within a few months he was worth a quarter of a million dollars. Meanwhile he had a gay time, what with gambling clubs, dances, and an occasional evening spent with explorer-adventurer John Charles Frémont and his vivacious wife, Jessie Benton Frémont, in their charming, sliding-panel Chinese-style house.

Cockier than ever, Ward returned to New York. His three sisters were also doing well. Julia Ward had married Dr. Samuel Gridley Howe, who had been, like Byron, a hero of the Greek war of independence and was now a crusader for the care of the blind in Boston. Louisa had wed the sculptor Thomas Crawford, and Annie had been captured by Adolph Maillard, a descendant of the Bonapartes. But soon Ward's San Francisco partner reported large losses, and he was forced to hurry back west. Shortly after he reached San Francisco early in 1851, a disastrous fire wiped out his second fortune. This time he went into the hills and managed to acquire shares in a mining claim. He spent a winter in a primitive frame house on the Merced River, keeping watch on the mine, running a small store, and reading

Horace. There was gold in the mine but getting it out required more patience than Sam Ward would ever have, so he sold out and retreated to San Francisco. His cousin Hall had become the district attorney, and two other McAllisters were flourishing there. With Hall's help Sam managed dinners that were a triumph of culinary passion over circumstance. Curiously, his twenty-one-year-old cousin Ward McAllister revealed the same devotion, displaying talents that would eventually make him New York society's panjandrum of lavish entertaining.

For some time Ward had heard rumors that his estranged wife, Medora, was living in Paris with an immensely wealthy Russian, Paul Demidoff, a debauchee who passed himself off as a prince. Now, returning east and finding Medora back in New York, Ward made another effort to live with her, her mother, and his two sons. But without money there was nothing left of their relationship except dissension. Hearing of his plight, his sister Julia chided him sharply:

My poor Sam, why not . . . pitch your tent elsewhere? . . . You have gathered strange views in these years, so I hear at least. . . . Come back to the old Puritan morals. . . . Wake up and find yourself all that you ever were—the honest son of an honest man. Go back to your grandfather's poverty, and dignity, and sweetness.

Of course Sam did not go back. Disdaining ordinary money-grubbing, he found excuses for trying to make money by his wits rather than by hard work. Luck and influence brought him a job as secretary and interpreter of a legation sent with a small armada to settle acute differences between the president of Paraguay and an American company trying to establish industry in the little republic. Ward found Paraguayan society cosmopolitan and charming, and he made the most of it. Shamelessly working on both sides of the fence, Ward came away with a secret commission to act as an agent for Paraguay in dealings with the American company and as its lobbyist in Washington.

Returning from Paraguay a seasoned negotiator, Sam settled in Washington in 1859 and became professionally what he had long been naturally—a lobbyist. His figure had grown opulent: large paunch, round and cheerful face, great dome bald and shining, rose in lapel, elegant goatee, diamond stud in shirt front, rings on both hands. He sublet a fine furnished house at 258 F Street, acquired a French chef, and was soon famous for matchless dinners and the eminence of his guests. Above all he brought together industrialist and financiers with the politicians they wanted to influence. Typical was a dinner party in 1860 in which his guests were the French banker Baron Salomon de Rothschild, Senators William Gwin and Milton S. Latham of California, Representative "Sunset" Cox of Ohio, and William M. Browne, editor of the *Constitution,* a pro-Buchanan newspaper. Women were not invited.

Sam Ward's success was the result of many factors: his provender was delectable; he radiated conviviality; he had been everywhere and knew everyone, from miners on the Merced River to dukes on country estates, from the president of Paraguay to England's poet laureate; he talked as easily with those who loved opera or Catullus in Latin, as he did with those who liked poker or fast horses; he could write graceful poetry, play pool, and tell the vintage of a fine wine by its taste and bouquet. Above all, his ethics as well as his political opinions were adjustable. He entertained and wooed men of every faction. When the arguments over slavery became heated, he tried to avoid entanglements by condemning both abolitionists and slaveholders. But his sympathies socially were with the Southern aristocracy. In time such sentiments became intolerable to certain Northerners, and for a while his sister Julia, whose husband had become a militant abolitionist and who would herself soon become famous, most unexpectedly, when she composed "The Battle Hymn of the Republic," no longer welcomed her once beloved brother.

But Sam Ward's contradictory allegiances undermined his credibility. A longtime friend of Lincoln's Secretary of State, William Seward, Ward decided to go south early in April 1861 to make a confidential report to Seward on Southern sentiment. His secret letters in the next few months gave a discouraging picture of the South as ready to resist forever. Perhaps because Seward realized that Sam Ward played on too many sides, his reports were ignored. To add to his distress, Ward accidentally learned that his younger son had fallen ill and died in Luxembourg; it was long before he forgave Medora for not notifying him. But his bitterness could hardly have troubled her: she soon became a part of an international coterie of wastrels on the Riviera and lived licentiously ever after.

The war's end saw at long last Sam Ward's complete fulfillment. Since President Johnson's Secretary of the Treasury, Hugh Mc-Culloch, desperately needed the support of Congress on various issues, he gladly enlisted Ward's help, which consisted mainly of exposing congressmen to more sumptuous dinners than any of them had ever known. His entertainment expenses for the first session of Congress under President Johnson are said to have amounted to $12,000—a bill that was paid, of course, by the U.S. Treasury.

Ward reigned for a dozen years. But he played such a part in the defense of President Johnson against impeachment that in retaliation a House committee charged him with using inside information to help New York gold market manipulators. Blandly Ward claimed that it was all a part of his daily business. Again, under Grant, Ward was called before the House Ways and Means Committee to explain a $3,500 fee from the Pacific Mail Steamship Company as part of its effort to get a government mail subsidy. "His eyes twinkling, his face beaming," Sam Ward kept the audience laughing constantly as he blithely defended his role.

Fame brought Sam no financial ease—if anything, it obliged him to sustain his reputation for sumptuous living. So when the depression of 1873 closed in, it was fortunate for Ward that James Keene, whom he had befriended in Gold Rush days, should turn up in New York as the most successful stock plunger ever to come out of the West. The "Silver Fox" immediately proclaimed his gratitude to Sam Ward, and when he began manipulating stocks in New York he set aside shares for Ward. Within a year, having made an estimated $7 million, Keene turned over almost a million dollars to Ward.

Now Ward's prodigality knew no bounds. Nor did his speculative bent: he financed two shady operators in promoting Long Beach, on Long Island, as a resort to rival Long Branch, New Jersey. Before he realized that the enterprise was a fiasco, the promoters had bled him of the bulk of his fortune. He had to leave the country to avoid lawsuits. The spectacle of sixty-eight-year-old Sam Ward in flight from his creditors seemed to his friends a final humiliation. But they reckoned without Sam's charms and unquenchable ebullience. In England his titled friends rallied around him. He was the guest of Lord

Roseberry (later prime minister), the Prince of Wales, and other peers, and he spent time with Henry Irving, Ellen Terry, Tennyson, and Henry James.

Approaching seventy, Ward was now bald and had a long white beard; many of his friends of other days were dead. So he went to Italy to visit his favorite nephew, the popular novelist F. Marion Crawford, who lived in an old house in Sorrento. He spent the last few months of his life there and in Rome, mingling with artists and writers and dabbling in Buddhism.

It seems cruel to break such an affable, prodigally generous and richly cultivated man as Sam Ward on the wheel of criticism. But the fact is that he was always wantonly self-indulgent and undisciplined, and took money wherever he could find it. Never once did he suffer a pang of conscience so great that a good dinner could not salve it. He coated a multitude of deals, some of them discreditable and a few of them disgraceful, with a veneer of bonhomie and elegance. In the Gilded Age he was a professional gilder.


When Ulysses S. Grant, forty-four years old, grave, dark-bearded, slightly unfamiliar in a fine dark coat, made his inaugural address on a March day in 1869, he must have seemed like the embodiment of an Alger success story: the country boy who had become President and was about to add another chapter to the mythology of democracy. Then he made his speech, and it was, as all his speeches would be, a collection of platitudes lacking in ideas or spirit. Most of his Cabinet appointments would be blundering or ill-advised. Soon, he was surrounded by a backstairs cabinet of mediocrities, self-seekers, and rascals. The myth of Grant's political potentialities died a-borning.

The fact is that Grant was not an Alger hero at all: his father owned a successful tannery; Ulysses received a good education at West Point; and, unlike any Alger hero, he failed in every career he undertook until he was almost forty. He was saved by the accident of a great war. Had he retired at the end of the war, his reputation would doubtless have remained forever bright.

His greatest mistake was in becoming President. For all his seeming modesty, he was curiously lacking in self-knowledge. The American people have again and again used the Presidency as a reward for a military hero. Generals George Washington, Andrew Jackson, Zachary Taylor, and William Henry Harrison were so rewarded; Winfield Scott, John Charles Frémont, and George B. McClellan had been nominees; and there would be others. It has never mattered whether the hero was fitted for the office or even genuinely interested in it.

The people thought of Grant as a man of decision and country-bred integrity, one who would bring dignity, efficiency, and reform to the office. "If he should throw away his opportunity to be an independent president," James Russell Lowell wrote to a friend, "he is not the man I take him to be. No man ever had a better chance to be a great magistrate than he." Such admirers would be woefully disappointed. There would be no reform, no efficiency, and precious little dignity. Grant had almost no interest in politics or government, nor had he any of the true politico's zest for dealing with human beings. He looked on the Presidency as a gift from the people in their wisdom; and he seems never to have doubted that he deserved the office or was equal to its responsibilities. Judging him only by his war record, the people did not realize how long he had been frustrated by defeat, how pinched by failure.

He had been a shy and inarticulate boy, distinguished only by a curious compulsion never to retreat. He had gone to West Point only because his father had secured an appointment for him. He himself later said, "A military life had no charms for me, and I had not the faintest idea of staying in the army." But he stayed for ten years after his graduation in 1842, rising only from second lieutenant to captain. Aside from the Mexican War, he spent his army years in posts in dreary places on Lake Ontario, in Oregon, and in northern California. Out of boredom and frustration he began drinking, and when he was sent to the Pacific Coast in 1852 and had to leave his wife behind because she was carrying their second baby, he drank out of loneliness.

On the Pacific Coast he tried out various schemes for supplementing his income—cutting tons of lake ice and shipping it to San Francisco, trading in cattle and pigs, and even joining several officers in running a club-hotel in San Francisco. His drinking finally caused his commanding officer to give him a choice of resigning or standing trial. He resigned. It was a squalid climax and it left him, at thirty-two, penniless.

Returning to Missouri, where his wife had some sixty acres and a few slaves, which her father had given her, he tried farming. To raise cash he cut firewood and carted it to St. Louis. Many later recalled seeing him drive into the city, a thin, mud-spattered figure in an old overcoat. But he could not make ends meet, and in 1858 he auctioned off his livestock and tools. He lived on borrowed money until his father took him into the family leather and hardware store in Galena, Illinois. But Ulysses was an indifferent salesman and, except with his wife and children, subdued and withdrawn.

Even after the firing on Fort Sumter he was ignored. When he went to Springfield, the state capital, a nondescript figure carrying a carpetbag and wearing a faded blue army overcoat, he was looked on as a "dead-beat military man." Then, without warning, the governor of Illinois appointed him colonel of the Twenty-first Illinois Volunteers. When he arrived at camp in his shabby civilian clothes, the volunteers, untamed farmboys, jeered at him. Thus, unheroically, Ulysses Grant climbed onto the stage of history, never to come down again.

Hardly a month later, fortune, as haphazard as misfortune, caressed him again: he was recommended by Congressman Elihu Washburne to be one of four brigadier generals from Illinois. Grant received the news with no show of feeling; it simply confirmed his fundamental belief in chance. Near the end of his life he would open his memoirs with the lines "Man proposes and God disposes. There are but few important events in the affairs of men brought about by their own choice."

As a general he was, as we know, resolute and dogged. His boyhood reluctance to retreat served him well at Shiloh and in his greatest triumph, Vicksburg. When the news went out that Grant had captured that stronghold and liberated the entire Mississippi River, he became the focus of the North's long-frustrated yearning for a military hero. Soon he was being mentioned as a potential presidential candidate. But when asked what he planned to do after the war, he answered drolly: become mayor of Galena long enough to get a sidewalk built down to the railroad station. It was not easy to make a hero out of Ulysses Grant.

In the postwar years Grant luxuriated in adulation, honors, and expensive gifts. Philadelphia presented him with a lavishly furnished mansion, practical New Yorkers gave him $100,000 in cash, and high-minded Bostonians donated a library worth $75,000. He accumulated fourteen horses and a closetful of medals, swords, and boxes of cigars. "Since Richmond's capitulation the stern soldier has spent his days and his nights," Horace Greeley's *Tribune* observed, "in conjugating the transitive verb *to receive.*" As freely as America gave, so freely did Grant accept. Starved for the easy aspects of life, he now partook of them with elementary pleasure.

As the quarrel between Congress and President Johnson became more and more savage, the more appealing became the figure of strong, silent Ulysses Grant, innocent of any stain because innocent of any declared position. Once impeachment proceedings against Johnson were launched, the radicals laid down a barrage of calumny and the Johnson camp answered with ugly countercharges. The behavior of many on both sides seemed to embody the worst qualities of the emerging age: the clutching at power, the vulgar insult, the lack of principle and self-discipline. Johnson was acquitted by only one vote. Four days later Ulysses S. Grant was nominated for President, without opposition, by the Republican party. He retired to Galena and made no statements, effortlessly maintaining the image of the simple soldier at the call of his country. The politicians and spoilsmen now took control. The Republican National Committee met in a Wall Street office with A. T. Stewart, Collis Huntington, William B. Astor, Cornelius Vanderbilt, Hamilton Fish, and William B. Dodge to get the money men to subscribe from $5,000 to $10,000 each; they assured the tycoons that Grant was safe, a "sound money" man who believed in law, order, and economy, respected property, and admired wealth.

By the close of the Johnson administration, the reputation of Congress could hardly have been lower. Henry Adams, scholarly descendant of statesmen, asserted that when he asked a member of Grant's Cabinet why more tact was not used in dealing with congressmen, the Secretary exclaimed that a congressman was a hog that could understand only a blow on the snout. It is a malicious story, but if anyone had a right to pour contempt on the new breed of public servant it was an Adams. In a period when fiction oozed sentiment and romance, Adams's *Democracy,* published anonymously in 1880, was a novel of cynicism in high places. His Senator Ratcliffe, along with such other fictional figures as Senator Dilworthy in *The Gilded Age* and Congressman John Vane in John W. De Forest's *Honest John Vane,* confront us with equally chilling examples of expediency, cant, and venality.

With the development of highly organized party machines, powerful state bosses—generally senators—had emerged, each having at his disposal a host of local and federal appointments. Chief among them was Roscoe Conkling of New York. Six foot three, handsome, with curling auburn locks and dazzling ensembles of colored waistcoats and scarves, Conkling cut a splendid figure. An arrogant man whose harsh voice slipped easily into derision and insult, he was nonetheless a consummate politician. As boss of New York State, he controlled the juiciest patronage plums. Ambitious and domineering, Conkling was politically an invaluable friend and a formidable enemy.

Hardly less influential was Senator Simon Cameron. At once an associate and a servitor of Pennsylvania's railroad moguls and ironmasters, he defined an honest politician as "one who will stay bought when he is bought." From farther west there was Oliver P. Morton, who had ruled Indiana politics with an iron hand as its wartime governor and then as a senator. Although so crippled by paralysis that he could hardly stand, he remained an aggressive speaker, and exerted so much influence on Grant that even other Republicans resented him, calling him Grant's evil genius. Another friend of Grant's was Zachariah Chandler, Republican boss of Michigan. A large man who sported diamonds and was good at drinking, cards, and telling a story, he represented the triumph of a coarse, anti-intellectual force in American political life, trailing crassness and western brag across the national scene.

Men of simple honesty and integrity such as Lyman Trumbull of Illinois, James Grimes of Iowa, William G. Brownlow of Tennessee, Charles Sumner of Massachusetts, James A. Bayard of Delaware, and William A. Buckingham of Connecticut stood out. "I believe it [the Republican Party] is today the most corrupt and debauched political party that ever existed," Grimes wrote to Trumbull in 1870. "I will no longer vote the Republican ticket."

But perhaps the most representative political figure of the age was James G. Blaine—"Blaine of Maine"—Speaker of the House, senator, Secretary of State, and five times a leading Republican candidate for President. A man of sensibilities, vibrant energy, and great personal charm, he was idolized by many people. That eminently respectable Victorian heretic, Colonel Robert Ingersoll, did not seem too grandiloquent when in a nominating speech at the Republican convention of 1876 he pictured Blaine as a "plumed knight" doing battle with wicked opponents. Unfortunately, he was referring mainly to Blaine's theatrical defense of himself against charges of most unknightly dealings with railroads. In another period a Blaine might have been content with power, adulation, and a comfortable income. But in the 1860s success plainly seemed incomplete without wealth. So Blaine hearkened to the siren song of the railroad promoters.

His venality was exposed when he became the leading candidate for the Republican nomination for President in 1876. The charge was that in 1869 the Union Pacific had advanced $64,000 to Blaine on collateral consisting of the nearly worthless bonds of a 150-mile Arkansas railroad. Blaine boldly denied the charge. But six weeks later, James Mulligan, a bookkeeper, testified that he had letters from Blaine to an officer of the Little Rock Railroad that confirmed the charges. Blaine's armor never seemed quite so shining again.

Like Grant, Blaine enjoyed the friendship of the rich. His identification with the tycoons of his time may well have defeated him in his race for the Presidency against Grover Cleveland in 1884. The climax of the campaign was a royal banquet given for him by some of the richest men in America, including John Jacob Astor III, Jay Gould, Russell Sage, A. M. Flagler, and Andrew Carnegie. His address was a paean to wealth and big business. The next day the newspapers featured it as "The Feast of Belshazzar and the Money Kings," and cartoonists contrasted the plutocrats at the heaped tables with the destitute creatures languishing in the street outside.

Historians have seen a fatal flaw in Blaine. Having joined the Republican party at its birth in 1856, when it was moved by a crusading spirit, he could see nothing wrong in any act that increased its strength. But he continued to feel this way even after it became the party of wealth and privilege and its long hold on office left it riddled with corruption. Time and again Blaine betrayed a lack of scruples. And once the struggle against slavery was over, his principal causes were higher protective tariffs, "manifest destiny," and a patriotic fervor bordering on jingoism. Much of Blaine's undoing was that he grew up, so to speak, with the spoils system, with a party organization that levied tribute on officeholders and businessmen. Any doubt that he approved of the system is dispelled by his view of those who, like Carl Schurz and George William Curtis, fought to reform it: he saw them as "upstarts, conceited, foolish, vain, without knowledge of measures, ignorant of men, shouting a shibboleth."

Like the average American of his time, newly elected President Grant harbored a solid admiration for that new breed, the captains of industry. They were, after all, men of boundless enterprise, great doers and "go-getters." And they knew how to live. Grant had long wanted to be one of them. Now, in a way, he would be. At receptions, Mrs. Grant, an unassuming, kindly woman, at first sought help from such patrician hostesses as Mrs. Hamilton Fish, wife of the Secretary of State; Grant himself simply endured the ordeal of the formal levees. One commentator, Ben Perley Poore, described the Grant social regime as a combination of Doric simplicity and vulgar ostentation. But it is easy to become accustomed to luxury: in time the Grants thought nothing of sitting down with thirty guests to a dinner of twenty-five dishes prepared by a famous Italian steward, with a different wine after every third course.

As President, Grant was neither hardworking nor conscientious. Normally, he began his official day at ten o'clock and ended it at three. He would then visit the presidential stables, visibly relaxing in the company of his favorite horses. It was undoubtedly the long years of rejection that made him an easy mark for companionable men who pleased and flattered him. Not one member of his backstairs cabinet was known for intellect or talents, and almost all of them were connivers. Again and again he turned to his fellow generals—Rawlins, Babcock, Belknap, Schenck, Ingalls, Butler, Porter, Badeau, Butterfield, Logan—and at least six of these proved utterly unworthy, if not dishonest. As though choosing an army headquarters staff, and without consulting anyone, Grant selected his Cabinet. First came the rewarding of friends, starting with his congressional sponsor, Elihu Washburne, whom he made Secretary of State. This was astonishing since Washburne was a coarse and aggressive man. Rawlins, who had been Grant's chief-of-staff, insisted on being made Secretary of War although he was plainly too ill for the task; he would be dead by fall. But before he died, he accepted $28,000 in Cuban bonds from Washington lobbyists representing the Cuban rebel junta. Most unexpected of all was the appointment of Adolph E. Borie of Pennsylvania as Secretary of the Navy. Borie had made a fortune during the war and he often entertained Grant, but he himself was nonplussed by the appointment, for he knew nothing about the navy. He resigned within a few months.

Grant did make several sound appointments. One was E. R. Hoar, his Attorney General, an urbane Massachusetts supreme court justice. Another was Jacob Dolson Cox, Secretary of the Interior, a former governor of Ohio with a desire to reform the desperately corrupt civil service. Unfortunately, neither Hoar nor Cox lasted long in Grant's service. When Washburne resigned, Grant made the only appointment that would last through his eight years in office: Hamilton Fish. Coming from a wealthy old Knickerbocker family, Fish was a conservative who had been governor of New York. He was not forceful or especially sagacious, but he was at least a man of principle and a conscientious public servant.

As private secretaries, Grant chose three of his former headquarters officers, Horace Porter, Orville E. Babcock, and Adam Badeau, with the latter permitted to spend his time writing a biography of Grant. Grant's brother-in-law, Fred Dent, became his chief usher. His father-in-law, Colonel Dent, sat around the White House with the politicians, drinking juleps and sounding off against Yankees in general and Republican radicals in particular. One of Grant's cousins, Silas A. Hudson, an Oregon cattle driver, was made minister to Guatemala, and the Reverend M. J. Cramer, a brother-in-law of Grant's, became U.S. consul in Leipzig. Other relatives, said to total forty, were scattered about in minor posts or permitted to earn remarkable fees for sundry services. As John Bigelow, New York newspaper editor and a former minister to Belgium, observed, "No President was ever 'got in the family way' so soon after inauguration."

Grant proved no more adept in matters of foreign policy. Most unfortunate was his handling of a proposed annexation of the Dominican Republic, on the island of Santo Domingo. Insofar as Grant had any opinions on foreign policy, he subscribed to "manifest destiny"—America's mission to extend its freedom and prosperity, and of course its sovereignty and mores, everywhere in the hemisphere. Santo Domingo had been wrung by savage insurrections and reduced to poverty and ruin, but it was rich in minerals, sugar, and coffee. And sheltered Samaná Bay would make an ideal naval base.

That is why Grant gave ear to Colonel J. W. Fabens when that transplanted Yankee, who had acquired large Dominican land concessions, sought to sell him the idea of taking over the Dominican Republic. Grant soon sent his secretary Babcock to make a report on the island. Babcock was bright and able but greedy. When the Cabinet next met, Grant coolly announced, "Babcock has returned . . . and has brought a treaty of annexation." An embarrassing silence followed. Finally Cox asked if it had been decided that the annexation was desirable. When no one replied, Grant flushed and went on to other business. But determined to have his way, he turned for support to Senator Sumner, the stiff-necked chairman of the Foreign Relations Committee. After hearing Grant out, Sumner said, "Mr. President, I am an administration man and whatever you do will always find in me the most careful and candid consideration." Where Grant interpreted this as a promise of support, Sumner meant only what he said. In March, Sumner opened the debate with a four-hour speech attacking the treaty unsparingly. Popular sentiment against annexing the remote, dissension-racked island mounted. On June 30 the Senate voted decisively against the treaty.

At this point Secretary of the Interior Cox resigned, intimating that the cause was Grant's neglect of civil service reform. Grant thereupon recommended various civil service reforms but soon forgot about them. Meanwhile, just before the election of 1872, Grant agreed to jettison one of the most equitable levies that had come out of the war: the income tax. Its repeal helped convince the moneyed interests that Grant was their man. As the election demonstrated, the voters cared little about such matters. To them Grant was still the hero of Vicksburg and Appomattox. But independent party members, led by several newspaper editors, rebelled and formed the Liberal Republican party. Casting about, they made the mistake of nominating Horace Greeley, a challenging and forceful editor but wildly erratic in his views. A humanitarian, a friend of labor, and personally generous, he was at the same time a strong protectionist and a foe of civil service reform. An eccentric, going about in a long linen duster and a white plug hat, he was pathetically vulnerable to ridicule; the cartoonists showed him no mercy. He suffered a resounding defeat. It was a stunning setback for such Republican reformers as Carl Schurz, and it left the party at the mercy of the so-called Stalwart bosses.

Grant interpreted his victory as a vindication of his policies, but, ironically, the major scandals of his administration were about to be exposed. The Crédit Mobilier affair was typical. It had begun when the Union Pacific Railroad had received twelve million acres and a government loan of $27 million. To prevent an investigation of outrageous dividend payments by the road's financing company, the Crédit Mobilier, Congressman Oakes Ames of Massachusetts slyly "sold" shares to leading members of Congress, whispering that they could pay for them after they had received enough dividends to cover the costs. The first dividends were handsome, and later they reached, according to *The Nation,* 1,500 percent a year.

An internal quarrel brought the story to light after the election of 1872. A congressional investigation followed: it implicated eight representatives, including a future President, James A. Garfield; a senator; outgoing Vice President Schuyler Colfax; and incoming Vice President Henry Wilson. Some admitted their participation; Colfax tried to brazen it out, but the evidence of a $1,200 check paid to him by Ames reduced him to a pathetic stammer. He retired in disgrace, but not before Grant had sent him his standard message of abiding faith: "Allow me to say that I sympathize with you in the recent congressional investigations . . . that I am satisfied . . . of your integrity, patriotism, and freedom from the charges imputed." He signed it "Affectionately yours."

No sooner had Grant begun his second term than he made clear his indiscriminate loyalty to all his associates. This included his brother-in-law, James F. Casey, an adventurer whom the President had made collector of customs in New Orleans; although a House committee had found Casey's conduct corrupt, Grant shocked everyone by reappointing him for another four years.

Perhaps the most prominent among Grant's backstairs advisers was Benjamin F. Butler. Butler was an ugly man, with a pudgy body and spindly legs, a massive bald pate fringed with oily curls, puffy eyes, and drooping mustaches. Forever clouded by rumor and charges of venality and profiteering, his reputation was scarcely more attractive. After Butler's defeat in the congressional elections of 1878, President Hayes wrote in his diary, "Unscrupulous, able, untiring, he was the most dangerous and wicked demagogue we have ever had." And although Lincoln disliked Butler, saying that he was "as full of poison gas as a dead dog," he treated him with utmost respect. Despite all this, Butler was repeatedly elected to Congress from Massachusetts, had been governor of the state, and would be nominated for President in 1884. The explanation of his success is that he was shrewd, unprincipled, aggressive, and shameless. Criticism of him has sometimes been tempered by the fact that he was privately generous, had many friends, and from time to time championed the underdog. Indeed, he thought of himself as an honest man criticized only by hypocrites.

Brought up in Lowell shortly after it had become the first factory town in the United States, what Butler saw there of the industrial revolution doubtless persuaded him to become a lawyer. By 1860 he was earning the astonishing sum of $18,000 a year. Meanwhile he had entered the Massachusetts legislature, so that by the time the war broke out he was known as one of the best lawyers and wiliest politicians in New England. As a major general sent to occupy New Orleans in 1862, his harsh policing of the city made him a target of Southern hatred. His notorious order that any female who insulted a Union soldier be treated as "a woman of the town" gained him the name among Southerners of "Butler the Beast." Far more reprehensible was the evidence that when he later commanded the Department of Virginia and North Carolina, he allowed the licensed trade with the enemy to become a large-scale enterprise—with his relatives and agents making handsome profits. Although Butler was never directly implicated in this sorry business, his fortune is estimated to have grown from $150,000 in 1862 to $3 million in 1868.

Whatever may be claimed for him as an administrator, as a field general he was a bungler. The worst of his fiascoes occurred when his Army of the James was trapped at Bermuda Hundred on its way to support Grant's advance on Richmond. No one knows why Grant did not immediately relieve him. Months later, when Grant did ask to have him replaced by General William "Baldy" Smith, Butler burst in on Grant and Assistant Secretary of War Charles A. Dana at their City Point camp and demanded, "General Grant, did you issue this order?" Noting Grant's embarrassment, Dana left. Soon Butler came out and reported that the order would be revoked. As a result, it was widely believed that Butler had had his way by threatening to spread word of Grant's drinking.

Throughout his career Butler's name was associated with so many financial scandals that one scarcely knows whether to be more appalled by his brazen turpitude or the gullibility of the electorate. As Speaker of the House, Blaine found Butler's most disturbing quality his "singular power of throwing the House into turmoil and disputation." This may explain why no one ever succeeded in making Butler admit any wrongdoing. Even the lacerating cartoons by Thomas Nast in *Harper's Weekly* and such epithets as "a moral monster" hurled at him by newspapers had no effect. Butler could afford to ignore such critics since the people of Massachusetts still voted for him, electing him governor as late as 1881, and the hero in the White House still said of him, "I like Butler, and have always found him . . . a man of courage, honor, and sincere convictions."

Again and again one wonders what Hamilton Fish's uncensored opinion of Grant's backstairs cabinet was. Throughout his voluminous journals he is a model of discretion. But once, in a letter to Assistant Secretary of State Bancroft Davis, we get a startling glimpse of what he really felt. Davis had told him how Grant's brother-in-law, "General" Dent, had become drunk while in his company and had boastfully revealed that he knew what had taken place at the last Cabinet meeting because he had been listening at the door. Fish had replied: "The little incident of eavesdropping explains some things. What a nasty crew to have about one! Drunken, stupid, lying, venal, brainless. Oh! that 'Somebody' were rid of such surroundings!"

Grant had ridden into office on a wave of prosperity. Then, in 1873, panic struck, and a depression began that was to last several years. It was the third act of Grant's career; as the end approached there was no *Götterdämmerung* but only a squalid procession of graft and intrigue. One of the most shameless episodes was that of the so-called Whiskey Ring. It had long been known that distillers evaded federal taxes. Then, in 1870, a revenue agent organized a ring and blackmailed distillers into joining in defrauding the government. A new Secretary of the Treasury, Benjamin Bristow, an eminent lawyer, using private detectives, gathered incriminating evidence against distillers, revenue collectors, and finally, Orville Babcock, Grant's secretary. Babcock, Bristow learned, had received many gifts from the ring, including a thousand dollars, a diamond stud, and even the services of a "sylph."

Eagerly Bristow brought his information to Grant's attention. Grant said, "If Babcock is guilty there is no man who wants him so much proven guilty as I do," but he made clear that he did not for a moment believe the charges. Bristow managed to have 350 distillers and government agents indicted. But when it looked as though Babcock might be convicted, Grant gave a sworn deposition asserting his full confidence in Babcock's integrity. The court had no choice but to acquit Babcock. It was not until the Secretary was implicated in the stock market's "Black Friday" and other scandals that the President dismissed him.

A stain appeared even on the good record of the State Department as a result of the activities of the minister to England, General Robert C. Schenck. A bluff, hardheaded Ohio politician, Schenck had served ably in Congress, fought bravely in the war, and become a major general. But he had a far more unusual distinction: he was an avid gambler and had even written a manual on draw poker. He no sooner reached England than he began to teach the game in the best circles—and so effectively that it became the rage. Unfortunately, he also encouraged the English in another kind of gambling—investment in the Emma silver mine of Utah. It was especially unfortunate because Schenck was a paid director of the mine. When irate English investors published evidence that the stock was a risky venture based on shady manipulations, a House investigating committee found that Schenck had received £10,000 worth of stock and a salary of $2,500 in return for promoting the stock. Schenck was recalled in disgrace—five years after his misconduct had been exposed. All he said was, "Don't send anybody here who is not rich."

So dim had Grant's luster grown that he was ignored by his party when it nominated a presidential candidate in 1876. But he earned the grudging respect of both parties by his efforts to see justice done in the fraud-ridden Hayes-Tilden election. Next to Tilden and Hayes, he once again seemed a simple and honest soul. Indeed, when in his last message to Congress he made such pathetic admissions as "It was my fortune, or misfortune, to be called to the office of Chief Executive without any previous political training. . . . Under such circumstances it is but reasonable to suppose that errors of judgment must have occurred" and "Mistakes have been made, as all can see," many were disposed to forget Grant the President and recall only Grant the hero of Appomattox.

As soon as Hayes took office, Grant prepared to go abroad. He was weary of politics and scandals, of contemptuous critics and untrustworthy friends. He and Mrs. Grant and their son Jesse sailed for Europe in May 1877. He planned to stay away a year, but it was so pleasant to be welcomed as a victorious general rather than a disappointing President that he remained abroad more than two years. In England in particular he was a popular hero—the plowboy who had become a great general and had fought to free the slaves. The English did not know that he had little sympathy for working people and was at the moment writing to his brother-in-law Corbin concerning a railroad strike in America: "My judgment is that it should have been put down . . . so summarily as to prevent a like occurrence for a generation."

American newspapers duly reported Grant's reception by kings, tycoons, and the common people everywhere, and on his return he was greeted like a conquering hero. His political friends had, moreover, been busy refurbishing his reputation in preparation for the next presidential election. At first Grant was reluctant to run for office again, but after a while he began to see in a third term the possibility of a triumphant vindication. At the Republican convention he led on the first ballot. Although the name of James A. Garfield, brilliant, erratic Ohio congressman and senator, was not even introduced until the second ballot, in the mysterious way of such conventions he gained steadily from then on and was nominated on the thirty-sixth ballot. Grant was mortified. "My friends have not been honest with me," he said. "They should not have placed me in nomination unless they felt perfectly sure of my success."

Grant now bought a mansion in New York, joined exclusive clubs, and enjoyed the company of men of wealth. But his income was woefully inadequate for the life he led. So, when his son Ulysses Jr. joined Ferdinand Ward, a young man reputed to be a financial wizard, in starting the brokerage firm of Grant & Ward, Grant was immediately interested. When Ulysses Jr. invested $100,000— borrowed from his millionaire father-in-law Senator Chaffee—in the firm, Ward promptly began paying him $3,000 a week as his share of the "profits." Soon Ward persuaded Ulysses Sr. to put in $100,000 more. So General Grant became a member of a Wall Street brokerage firm. Instead of building up a legitimate stock and bond business, Ward proceeded to get large loans from wealthy investors and promptly paid them a sizable "dividend," which actually came out of the loans. With the help of James D. Fish, president of the Marine National Bank, Ward maintained this simple swindle for three years.

Throughout, Grant remained completely ignorant of what was going on. He gave Ward his last dollar, his sister's savings, and the $1,200 inheritance of a niece. Daily he went in a fine carriage from his elegant home to his fine Wall Street office and signed, often without reading them, any documents Ward put in front of him. On May 1, 1884, he boasted that his share in Grant & Ward was worth $2.4 million. Three days later, Ward told the Grants that the Marine National Bank was having difficulties, and on May 7 the bank failed, chiefly as a result of $2 million in overdrafts by Grant & Ward. When Ward and Fish were brought to trial, it was shown that Grant & Ward had an incredible $16,792,640 in liabilities. Ward was given ten years in prison and Fish seven years. Later, Grant, never able to condemn an associate, told Mark Twain that Ward was only "an offending child."

Grant was shaken. He was humiliated as much by the thought of those who had entrusted their money to him as by the loss of all his savings. He said, "I have made it the rule of my life to trust a man long after other people give him up; but I don't see how I can trust any human being again." Perhaps he realized at last how often he had allowed himself to become the victim of unworthy men. Within a few months he developed a sharp pain in his throat. Instead of going away it became worse.

Tormented by his poverty, he let his friend Mark Twain persuade him to write his memoirs, and in February 1885 he began to dictate to a stenographer. By then he knew that he had cancer of the throat. After a month or two, his voice failed and he took to writing, gladly retreating from the wretched present into the glorious past. As he sat wrapped in shawls and blankets, floating in a sea of pain or a daze of drugs, but writing steadily, firmly, he was again the dogged soldier, the man who would die before he retreated.

It is a pity Grant did not live to see his book published, for it was a great success, the kind of commercial success he had sought all his life: it sold 300,000 copies and earned Mrs. Grant almost half a million dollars. It was also a creditable piece of writing, clear, reasonable, and assured, its impersonal manner relieved occasionally by quite unexpected touches of humor. But those who have praised it for its honesty and modesty have not perhaps noted that it scants the years of failure and never gets to the Presidency or its aftermath. By that time Grant knew where his talents lay.

Tenacious and resourceful, Grant was at his best in a practical emergency, when field expedients were in demand. The greater the pressure at such a time, the calmer and more resolute he became. Deep-rooted inhibitions smothered his hatreds as well as his enthusiasms. He lacked the power to make a total commitment; because reformers and crusaders had that power, he disliked and feared them. The most striking evidence of this inability to give himself passionately to a cause was his attitude toward war. He deplored the Mexican War as entirely unjust, and he repeatedly declared that he volunteered in the Civil War only because he felt it his duty as a West Pointer. "I never went into the army without regret," he told Bismarck, "and never retired without pleasure." His readiness to fight despite such a view arose from a kind of fatalism. Man, he had long before decided, must make the best of whatever befalls him.

Grant has been described as naïve; in a country lad this may be excusable but in the political leader of a nation it is a major liability. It was in part this quality that made him so loyal to his friends even when they were completely undeserving. At the same time he mistrusted men of high ideals, intellectual accomplishments, or rigorous ethical standards. Henry Adams, at his most corrosive in his chapter on Grant in *The Education of Henry Adams,* saw him as one of those men "whose energies were the greatest, the less they were wasted on thought . . . shy, jealous; sometimes vindictive . . . for whom action was the greatest stimulant.'' Adams's view was that of a disenchanted intellectual, but the judgment is that of a trained historian who had personally known almost a dozen Presidents.

Failure in most of his lifelong efforts to make a living left Grant with an inordinate respect for rich men, regardless of how they had made their money. Having sought and been denied material success all his life, he had come to see it as the Gilded Age saw it: as the most desirable goal.

# 3

## THE MONEY KINGS

One of the most significant results of the Civil War was the domination of American society by the money men: finance capitalists, merchant princes, captains of industry. The restraints of the old religion had grown slack, and those that would be imposed by government were still a long way off. So men were free to become as rich as they could or as poor as they might. No one except such uncompromising rebels as Henry George thought of setting limits to either extreme—and his *Progress and Poverty* did not appear until 1879. The rich were admired for what was assumed to be their enterprise, astuteness, and the blessings of the Lord, while the poor were accused of sloth, incompetence, and even sins.

The explosion of wealth in the 1850s sprang from the revolution in production that had begun in the 1820s. The development, chiefly by Yankee ingenuity, of automatic machines, standardized parts, the use of steam, and transportation by railroad and steamboat made mass production possible. Factories began to supplant the individual craftsman; by 1840 1,200 cotton spinning and weaving mills employed upward of 70,000 workers in the Northeast. By the 1850s the huge Colt firearms plant in Hartford was producing almost 25,000 revolvers a year.

Although there had long been a few rich men in America, there were probably only two or three true "millionaires" before the 1830s, when the term was first used, and they were planter aristocrats such as Charles Carroll of Carrollton or great landholders such as William Bingham of Philadelphia. By 1860 there would be about 350 millionaires and by 1880 at least 2,000, almost all of whom had made a fortune, and made it quickly, in trade, industry, finance, or land speculation.

The first great self-made millionaire whose career whetted the ambitions of a host of young Americans was John Jacob Astor, a German who had come to New York as a youth in 1784. Astor had gone into the northern wilds to gather pelts from the Indians, and he and his wife had even done the lowly work of beating and baling the hides. But soon he had become an established merchant, and by the turn of the century he was an international trader with agents everywhere. Using blankets, guns, and whiskey, Astor's men bought beaver, muskrat, mink, and fox from Indian and white trappers, shipped most of the furs to China, and brought back silks and tea for sale in Europe and America. Astor did not hesitate to let his men pick up opium in Smyrna and smuggle it into Canton, or strip the Sandwich Islands, as Hawaii was called, of all their precious sandalwood. Later, too, he was proud to make personal loans to President Monroe, but not too proud to collect the debt with interest. With the profits pouring in from every side, Astor began investing—foolishly, many thought—in farmland that seemed to be in the far north of Manhattan Island, where such streets as Forty-second would someday be cut through.

By 1811 Astor was sending agents to set up a trading-post empire, the American Fur Company, in the Northwest. How he crushed rivals, how his men in their fierce competition with the Hudson's Bay Company used rum to buy the favor of Indians, and how white trappers were sucked dry by the company is a tale of rampant individualism. Years later General Zachary Taylor, who had lived and fought in the Indian country in fur-trading days, declared, "Take the American Fur Company in the aggregate, and they are the greatest scoundrels the world ever knew."

Immigrants had long been flooding into New York, and much of the farmland Astor had bought for a trifle was soon covered with tenements. By the 1840s he was worth $20 million and without lifting a finger was receiving $270,000 a year from 470 leases on land he owned. Many years later, Walt Whitman in unforgettable detail re-called Astor as "a bent, feeble but still stout-built very old man, bearded, swathed in rich furs, with a great ermine cap on his head, led and assisted, almost carried, down the steps of his high front stoop (a dozen friends and servants, emulous, carefully holding, guiding him) and then lifted and tuck'd in a gorgeous sleigh, envelop'd in other furs, for a ride." Even when age and illness had reduced Astor to taking nourishment from the breast of a wet nurse and being tossed in a blanket for exercise, he could still become agitated by the news that someone had failed to pay the rent due him. When he died in 1848, *Hunt's Merchants' Magazine* referred to him as "perhaps the great-est merchant of this or any other age—the Napoleon of Commerce," but an old-fashioned New Englander and dedicated educator, Horace Mann, said, "Nothing but absolute insanity can be pleaded in pal-liation of the conduct of a man who was worth nearly . . . twenty millions of dollars, but gave only some half million of it to any public object."

The men who made their fortunes between 1850 and 1890 were rarely prepared for the power their wealth conferred on them. Nev-ertheless, their success set them apart: they were the fittest. Applying Darwinism to society with godlike assurance, Herbert Spencer had declared that progress was made possible by the elimination of the "unfit," among whom he included the incapable and the idle. Pre-sumably a hopeful vision of mankind's future, it seems only to have justified the view that life was a jungle. The more unscrupulous among the new lords of society were of course deplored, but by and large they were treated with deference. To some they were America's own nobility, pioneers who had earned their patents by carving out empires in the realms of commerce and manufacture. To their chron-icler, Wall Street banker Henry Clews, America was "the land of the self-made man—the empire of the parvenu. Here the accident of birth is of trifling consequence; here there is no 'blood' that is to be coveted save the red blood which every masterful man distills in his own arteries; and here the name of parvenu is the only and all-sufficient title of nobility."

Success had become magical, the Aladdin's lamp of democracy. In that faithful picture of a parvenu of the 1870s, Howells's *The Rise of Silas Lapham,* even a member of a rich old Boston family, Bromfield

Corey, acknowledges its spell: "There's no doubt but money is to the fore now. It is the romance, the poetry of our age. It's all very well. I don't complain of it." But in *A Hazard of New Fortunes* (1890) Howells had Colonel Woodburn, an unreconstructed Southerner, complain bitterly about the "virus" that has invaded American life— the worship of wealth. "The dollar," he declares, "is the measure of every value, the stamp of every success." Later he muses on how "we began as a simple, agricultural people, how the spirit of commercialism had stolen insidiously upon us, and the infernal impulse of competition . . . teaching us to trick and betray and destroy one another."

Most travelers from abroad noted the preoccupation with money-getting, and many of them questioned or lamented its effects. I. J. Benjamin, a Rumanian who sojourned in America from 1859 to 1862, wrote: "Almost every man is constrained to become a merchant, a banker, a speculator, or a manufacturer, to secure a position that will bring a sizable income. The child learns from his father, the pupil from his teacher . . . that gold commands a mighty power in every circle of society." By the 1840s those aspects of the Puritan code that had fostered rectitude, self-denial, and simple living were going by the board. The clergy had lost much of its spiritual influence and almost all of its political power. So men of wealth found themselves in the vanguard of American life with no government to regulate them and little sense of responsibility. They had been told, even by Emerson, that they could, and must, be self-reliant. Unfortunately, they had won out in a competition in which aggressiveness and cunning were the most useful qualities. Charles Francis Adams, Jr., intellectually worthy of the Adamses and yet a businessman who had risen to the presidency of the Union Pacific Railroad and the Kansas City stockyards, summed them up thus:

I am more than a little puzzled to account for the instances I have seen of business success—money getting. It comes from a rather low instinct. . . . I have known . . . a great many "successful" men—"big" financially—men famous during the last half century, and a less interesting crowd I do not care to encounter. Not one . . . would I care to meet again in this world or the next; nor is one associated in my mind with the idea of humor, thought, or refinement.

There were of course some, like A. T. Stewart, the Belfast immigrant who had become the foremost retail merchant and New York department store owner, and Peter Cooper, proprietor of a glue factory, ironworks, and blast furnace, who had made their money mainly by hard work and enterprise, more or less according to Alger's classic formula. A few, such as Cooper, had become active in public service and philanthropy, and later others began giving large sums to worthy causes. But Cooper was the exception.

Many of these fortunes were, ironically enough, made or started in the Civil War, a result of the demands of a huge army thrust suddenly into action. Overnight there was a desperate need for rails and locomotives, rifles and gunpowder, ships and tents, horses and mules, carts and caissons, uniforms and shoes, and a thousand other products, from surgical saws to bugles. The demand spurred a feverish exploitation of coal, iron, and copper; lumber, leather, and hemp; cotton and wool; corn, rice, and sugar. It demanded output on an unheard-of scale, mass production, a shift from hand power to steam and water power.

The hunger of the war machine furnished an excuse, if any were needed, for mill and factory owners to put men, women, and children to work at low wages for long hours under pitiless conditions. It concentrated workers in bleak mills and mining towns or blighted factory districts. It tolerated slovenly workmanship, the sleazy material that came to be known as shoddy, and it encouraged rigged deals and profiteering. The government contributed to the breakdown in economic values by pouring out an immense amount of rapidly depreciating currency, creating an illusion of cheap and easy money even as prices soared.

The passage of the Homestead Act in 1862, throwing open hundreds of millions of acres of public lands, including the riches beneath them, fed the fever of speculators as well as the land hunger of settlers. It inspired a race of men who dreamed, like Simon Hawkins and Beriah Sellers of Twain and Warner's *The Gilded Age,* of making a fortune from a wilderness bought for a song. Huge segments of land went into railroads, no government in history showering on a few of its citizens so much wealth in so short a time.

Even Southern plantation aristocrats, who had scorned Northern money-grubbing in antebellum days and had been left to stagnate after the war, dreamed of becoming rich overnight. Although the old Virginia colonel in F. Hopkinson Smith's *Colonel Carter of Cartersville* is a romanticized, absurdly quixotic figure who belonged to a world long gone, his own hope is that someone will put a railroad through to Cartersville and make that dying hamlet a bustling metropolis. It is a pathetic fantasy—until coal is discovered on his property. He is immediately offered a million dollars and presumably lives happily ever after.

Free land, war profits, inflation, railroads, gold, coal, oil—all these encouraged a boom-time psychology. The New York Stock Exchange, which as late as the 1830s had been made up of a handful of traders operating out of a broker's office, became a churning center of speculation. As J. K. Medbury described it in his *Men and Mysteries in Wall Street* (1871):

> Flushed with greenbacks, and influenced by the varying for-
> tunes of our armies, the whole population of the North gave
> itself up to a speculative frenzy. . . . The slang of the stock-
> board found its way to the drawing room. Everybody made
> ventures. Gold was a favorite with the ladies. Clergymen rather
> affected mining stock and petroleum. Lawyers had a penchant
> for Erie. Solid merchants, preferring their ordinary staples, sold
> cotton or corn for future delivery, or bought copper and salt on
> margins.

The fact that stocks could be bought on a margin of only 10 percent multiplied both the temptation and the risk. As soon as a stock dipped, the small speculators were wiped out, and soon the large speculators were wiped out by even larger ones.

The nation was not prepared for a war among Americans on American soil, but it was even less prepared for the ferocity of profiteers like the former cattle drover, Daniel Drew, who said: "Along with ordinary happenings we fellows on Wall Street now had in addition the fortunes of war to speculate about, and that always makes great doings in a stock exchange. It's good fishing in troubled waters.'' The country was not prepared for a shipping baron, Cornelius Vanderbilt, who sold the army a collection of rotted transport vessels; for a former Vermont peddler, Jim Fisk, who unloaded shoddy blankets on the Union quartermaster and smuggled Southern cotton to Northern mills; for a banker's son, J. P. Morgan, who sold outmoded carbines at exorbitant prices to the Union army, and even when the deal was exposed, demanded payment—and received it.

With hardly an exception, moreover, such men escaped the draft through the most undemocratic of privileges—exemption from service on payment of $300 or on providing a substitute. Some, like Judge Thomas Mellon, founder of the Mellon dynasty, looked on patriotism with open contempt. A witheringly cold man, he wrote to one of his sons:

> I had hoped my boy was going to make a smart, intelligent business man and was not such a goose as to be seduced by the declamations of buncombed speeches. It is only greenhorns who enlist. . . . Those who are able to pay for substitutes, do so, and no discredit attaches. . . . A man may be a patriot without risking his own life or sacrificing his health.

The son, James, took the advice and did handsomely in the coal business during the war. In New York, merchants opposed to war fostered a secession movement. In Boston, nursery of abolition, the sons of a rich shipowner, John L. Gardner (one of them was the husband of art patron Isabella Stewart Gardner), casually paid for substitutes when a draft was begun in 1863 and continued to attend the cotillions favored by the youth of Beacon Hill.

Of the score of millionaires in New York in 1850, Cornelius Vanderbilt comes closest to being the prototype of the robber baron. He bridges the gap between those who worked their way to the top and those who speculated their way to wealth. Son of a Dutch family, the Van Derbilts, who worked a small Staten Island farm, Vanderbilt began his career as a ferry boy sailing between Staten Island and

Manhattan. By 1810, a tall, sandy-haired, broad-shouldered youth of seventeen, he had acquired a ferry scow, called a periauger. Then, in the rough world of New York harbor and Atlantic Coast shipping, he thrust his way to the top by cunning and hard work. In the competition for passengers and freight, the "Commodore," as he came to be known, developed a technique, which John D. Rockefeller would later perfect, for squeezing out competitors and, having achieved a monopoly, raising rates mercilessly.

Although Vanderbilt was not a leader in utilizing steamboats, he was soon building and putting into service some of the finest of such vessels. With the coming of the Gold Rush he plunged into the competition for the California traffic; he undertook to get travelers across the Isthmus of Nicaragua in the face of all kinds of obstacles, ranging from deadly fevers to a Nicaraguan revolution led by an American filibusterer, William Walker. With the help of government subsidies and a huge tribute extorted from a rival line, he made no less than $10 million within a few years and was on the way to becoming the richest man in America.

Ready at last to enjoy his wealth, he decided on the eve of his sixtieth birthday to take a grand cruise. Anticipating the ostentation that would soon be the fashion for millionaires, his yacht, *North Star,* was 270 feet of satinwood, marble, jasper, and plush, with berths hung with silk and lace, and scrollwork gilded green and gold. The family party included a caterer from the Racquet Club, a doctor, and a chaplain. The London *Daily News* saw in its extravagance the justifiable pride of the self-made man. "It is time," the newspaper proclaimed, "that the millionaire should cease to be ashamed of having made his own fortune. It is time that *parvenu* should be looked on as a word of honor."

Vanderbilt's acquisitive energies were astonishing. He was well into his sixties when he was seized by the epidemic fever of the age— railroad speculation. By 1862 he was already plowing war profits into the New York and Harlem Railroad and at the same time bribing members of the Common Council of New York City to let the road extend from Forty-second Street south to the Battery. As rumors of this move spread, the road's stock rose from nine to fifty, and the "Great Bear" of Wall Street, Daniel Drew, who sometimes worked with Vanderbilt and sometimes against him, persuaded the city councilmen to join him in selling the stock short. As greedy as Drew, they decided to wait until the stock rose to seventy-five before selling it short. But Vanderbilt pushed the stock up to 150 and held it there until Drew and his fellow conspirators, outfoxed, had to buy the stock at the Commodore's price. Twice again Drew met with defeats in bear raids on Vanderbilt railroads. Ruefully, he incorporated his conclusions in a couplet:

> *He who sells what isn't his'n,*
> *Must buy it back or go to pris'n.*

A large, handsome man with a fringe of whiskers under jaw and chin, Vanderbilt is usually shown wearing a huge fur-trimmed coat, wing collar, white stock, and plug hat. In private life he was completely domineering. He consigned William, his eldest son, to managing a small farm on Staten Island until his poor, plodding heir was almost middle-aged, and when his drudge of a wife refused to leave Staten Island for a handsome home in downtown Manhattan, he had her committed to an insane asylum until she changed her mind.

Vanderbilt was the farmboy who, in the Alger tradition, works his way up to a fortune. But he had few of the Alger hero's virtues. He was tough, boisterous, and aggressive. He liked a glass of gin or beer and was never without his big cigars. He had no use for religion and he scorned charities. His chief amusements were playing whist or euchre till all hours of the night and driving fast horses, often in a rousing race with another trotting enthusiast. But Vanderbilt's most un-Algerlike pastime was the ardent pursuit of his housemaids or any other available young women. In his later years he also took a fancy to spiritualism, and he conveniently combined these proclivities by adding to his retinue two sisters, Victoria Claflin Woodhull and Tennessee Claflin, both of them free spirits as well as devotees of spiritualism.

Not all Americans admired Vanderbilt. In his diary, George Templeton Strong, lawyer and a vestryman of Trinity Church, repeatedly deplores him. When a heroic-sized, $800,000 memorial was unveiled to the Commodore, Strong's agonized cry was, "These be thy Gods, O Israel!"

Rugged, profane, barely literate, supremely arrogant, even when threatened with the law (quite early in his career he exlaimed: "What do I care about the law? Hain't I got the power?"), Vanderbilt was a holdover from the frontier period. Yet he was at the same time a frontrunner of the freebooters of business, the corporate manipulators of the Gilded Age. He made the transition from the rough-and-tumble of the shipping wars of the 1830s and 1840s to the juggling of stock and bribing of politicians in the railroad wars of the 1860s, 1870s, and 1880s. More than Astor or Drew or Gould, he was the rugged, utterly self-reliant, overbearing American.

Only Dickens would have dared to create a character like Daniel Drew. Drew was as humble-seeming and sly as Vanderbilt was brazen and aggressive. After a boyhood marked by shriveling poverty, Drew became a circus roustabout and then a drover. By dint of sharp practice ("Nobody looks for manners around the meal tub" was one of his Yankee farmer sayings, and another was, "If a cat would eat fish, she must be willing to wet her feet"), he acquired a drovers' inn on the northern outskirts of New York City. One much-repeated story describes how Drew, while driving a flock of sheep to sell to John Jacob Astor's brother Henry, a New York butcher, stopped in Harlem, fed the animals salt, and then let them fill up on water to add to their weight; whence, it is said, came the term "watered stock."

Emboldened by his success, he tried moneylending, and in time took over a Hudson River steamboat line, which he pitted, not without some success, against Vanderbilt's monopoly. By such stages he became a Wall Street stockbroker. Then, having made a large loan to New York's Erie Railroad in 1854, he gradually took control of it. He manipulated its stock so outrageously that Wall Street traders took to intoning: "Daniel says 'Up'—Erie goes up. Daniel says 'Down'—Erie goes down. Daniel says 'Wiggle-waggle'—it bobs both ways."

A lank, stooping man dressed in somewhat shabby black garments—he sometimes used an umbrella shaft as a cane—with a somber, deeply lined face, thin lips, and a whining voice, Drew was hardly an attractive figure. As illiterate as Vanderbilt, and more devious, he was, under the guise of being a frugal, devout countryman, a bold and crafty speculator. Given to churchgoing and hymn-singing, and forever affecting humility, he was a Uriah Heep, a model of the pious fraud: having offered to endow a New Jersey seminary with $250,000, he never gave the institution the sum itself but only the 7 percent interest on the money. And in moments of crisis, he would retire to wherever he was living, go to bed, wrap himself in blankets, pray, and begin drinking.

Vanderbilt and Drew were rough-hewn and primitive types; compared to them, Jay Cooke, coming twenty-five years later, was a model of respectability, civil in speech and moderate in habits. His outward conformity may be explained by his comfortable middle-class background: his father was a lawyer among the early settlers in Sandusky, Ohio, and became a congressman. At sixteen, Jay, an ambitious youth, went all the way to St. Louis to work for a trading company there and then to Philadelphia as a ticket agent in a railroad and canal shipping business. He soon shifted to E. W. Clark and Company, which had rapidly become the leading Philadelphia brokerage and banking house. So apt was Cooke at money-changing that he was made a junior partner at the age of twenty-one. For a time he also wrote a daily column on the money markets for the *Daily Chronicle*. A tall, slender, fair-complexioned youth, he dressed well and gladly took advantage of free admission, as a member of the press, to theaters and public gardens.

Young Cooke quickly sensed the change taking place in the American way of life. Along the banks of the Schuylkill he saw "palaces and castles which kings might own." Around him, in 1840, he noted an "all-pervading, all-engrossing anxiety to grow rich. . . . This is the only thing for which men live here." He also learned how to use politicians, getting advance information from them, for example, on what would happen to Texas bonds after the Mexican war. After the panic of 1857 he began investing independently. Taking over small railroads that were having financial difficulties, he reorganized them, paid off the government—which had generally subsidized them—from the proceeds of issues of bonds and stocks, and pocketed the profits.

When the Civil War started, he privately admitted that he had twice victimized the administration during the Mexican War, and he predicted that the new conflict would also prove "a grand time for brokers and private bankers.'' Volunteering to manage the sale of government war bonds, he began by raising $3 million for the state of Pennsylvania with a bond that was oversubscribed within ten days. The entire nation heard of his success, and Cooke became the Treasury Department's subscription agent for the first national war bond. Soon the Secretary of the Treasury, Salmon P. Chase, was asking him to invest his personal funds. Setting up his brother Henry as head of a Washington branch of the house, he repeatedly learned of monetary decisions before they were made public. As chief bond salesman, Cooke developed an astonishingly modern array of high-pressure selling techniques, including catchy slogans, circulars, rallies, and brass bands. He placed advertising lavishly in newspapers everywhere and gained the favor of editors and writers on finance by sending them cases of wine, game, or fish packed in ice, and the profits of a sixty-day option on $50,000 in bonds. Between July 1861 and July 1865, Cooke sold almost $3 billion in bonds.

Jay Cooke emerged from the war as the banker patriot who had financed the Union and as the head of one of the most powerful banking houses in the land. ''As rich as Jay Cooke'' became a common expression. Immediately he set about realizing his boyhood dreams. The day Richmond fell he began building a mansion, called Ogontz, on a knoll north of Philadelphia. It cost a million dollars, had fifty-two rooms, including a theater and a conservatory, private telegraph wires, and was decorated with three hundred paintings. As a host, Cooke dressed like a patriarch, with a white beard, cape, and low-crowned, broad-brimmed hat, and presided at prodigious dinners, serving wine from a cellar sometimes stocked with the entire pressing of a favorite vineyard. He entertained scores of senators, Cabinet members, and, quite regularly, General Grant.

The end of the war was also the end of Cooke's posture as a public servant. But he soon persuaded himself that raising money for the construction of a railroad—called the Northern Pacific—from Lake Superior to the Pacific was not only a rare opportunity for investors but a boon to the nation. Congress seemed to agree, for it bestowed 47 million acres on the road. The Philadelphia *Ledger,* which did not share the local reverence for Cooke's success, described these as the greatest ''robberies of public domain'' since the notorious South Sea Bubble.

Cooke marketed Northern Pacific bonds and lands with much the same devices he had used in selling war bonds. Editors everywhere were wooed with fine wines, Pacific salmon, and favors, and prominent men were sucked into the enterprise with shares of stock they could pay for when dividends made it convenient. With the help of high-pressure promoters the railway was pictured in the literature sent to prospective European investors and immigrants as passing through a region so verdant, with a climate so balmy, that critics derisively dubbed it "Jay Cooke's Banana Belt." But railroad bonds were a glut on the market, and investors everywhere had had their full of fraudulent prospectuses. It hardly helped when stories of mismanagement in the building of the Northern Pacific circulated. Cooke's very energetic partner, H. C. Fahnstock, wrote to him in June 1872 that the bonds were being sold to such innocents as widows and orphans on Cooke's word that the construction was well managed when in fact it was "inefficient . . . and extravagant to the last degree."

Despite such warnings Cooke moved forward. By late 1872 the railroad's overdrafts on its credit were mounting into the millions. Yet Cooke was so unprepared for disaster that on September 17, 1873, the very eve of the collapse of his empire, he entertained President Grant at his mansion. The following morning he learned that his New York office had had to close its doors, starting a chain reaction that led to the panic of 1873 and a long economic depression. When we learn that he had to declare himself bankrupt, give up Ogontz, and move into a crowded little cottage, we may be tempted to see a moral in his fate. But a few years later he invested $3,000 in a small Utah silver mine and then, with Jay Gould's help, took over a major share in it. Five years later he sold his share for almost $1 million.

Personally, Jay Cooke was respectable, benevolent—he liked to give away Bibles, hymnbooks, picture cards, and candies—and pious. Unlike the other Jay, he craved the good opinion of his fellows and condemned crookedness whenever it was brought to his attention. But the pressures of the age caused him repeatedly to confuse his own best interests with the public good. Perhaps, as some say, the great railroad systems could not have been assembled without the Jay Cookes. Whether or not this is so, Cooke was the prototype of the modern promoter, the operator of syndicates, the raiser and manipulator of capital.

As the war drew to a close, two men emerged as the most deviously resourceful of younger Wall Street speculators—Jay Gould and Jim Fisk. They had already learned some of Drew's tricks, and having developed a few of their own, they were ready to join him in enterprises as nefarious as any in American financial history. Great as were the differences between Vanderbilt and Drew, they were nothing compared to those between Gould and Fisk.

Both men were about thirty years old, but where Gould was a darkly sallow, black-bearded little man, low-voiced, secretive, conservative in dress, and in domestic life a proper Victorian, Fisk was a stout, reddish-blond roisterer and libertine, a lover of pomp and show, absurdly vain but likable and personally generous. Although no more scrupulous than Drew and somewhat less so than Gould, Fisk had a gift of coarsely colorful speech and the exuberance of a Davy Crockett. His antics amused and titillated the people, and in the end they forgave him even as they have forgiven other amiable despoilers.

Although Jay Gould was born to hardy, independent folk on a farm in New York's lower Catskills, he seems to have acquired none of the so-called pioneer virtues. He was small and scrawny but studious and keen. The lad who knew him best, John Burroughs, whose love of the woods and meadows would some day make him a famous naturalist, later recalled how clever Jay was in school and how crafty in play. With a precocious sense of what would be useful in business, Jay concentrated on mathematics; a young man needed, he later explained, to be "capable of speaking and acting for himself without being bargained away and deceived by his more enlightened brothers."

Leaving a local academy at fifteen, he took a job as clerk in a general store. For a working day that lasted from six in the morning to nine at night he received bed and board. This was not for him. He studied surveying books and became a helper to an engineer surveying Ulster County, New York. Soon Jay himself was soliciting subscribers for a survey he planned in his home county, Delaware.

With an astuteness staggering in one so young, he sent a contribution of five dollars to the editor of the county newspaper and followed it with his plan for a survey together with a cool request: "I want you to give me an editorial to this effect." The editor furnished it.

Young Jay did not drink, smoke, or spend time with girls. After a severe illness he decided that he preferred "self-denial" to "self-indulgence." It was not a demonstration of willpower: he simply didn't enjoy such activities. And he had already found a perfect outlet for both energies and desires: making money. Having accumulated $5,000 by the age of twenty, he was ready for bigger game. He persuaded a wealthy retired tanner, Colonel Zadock Pratt, to put up a very sizable sum to build a tannery in the Poconos. Quickly Gould hired workmen, housed them in a cluster of cottages, and then completed one of the largest plants of its kind, handling a million and a half pounds of shoe-sole leather annually. Business was so good that Gould was soon spending much of his time in New York, speculating in hide futures.

At the end of a year, after a stormy confrontation, Pratt insisted on ending the partnership, probably because he resented the younger man's independence and methods. Gould promptly came up with two new partners, a respected leather merchant, Charles Leupp, and a lawyer named Lee. Gould now plunged deeper into "The Swamp," as New York's leather market was known, and with a daring and rapidity characteristic of his later operations soon had a corner on all hides available up to six months in the future.

The panic of 1857 wiped Gould out. He took it calmly, but Leupp was totally unprepared for the news of Gould's disastrous speculations. Facing bankruptcy at the end of a long and honorable career, he went into the library of his Madison Avenue mansion and, like Edwin Arlington Robinson's Richard Cory, put a bullet through his head. The city was shocked. Although Leupp had long shown signs of mental unbalance, Gould was blamed. And years later, when Gould was accused of responsibility for the "Black Friday" crash of 1869, a mob gathered outside his offices and chanted, "Who killed Leupp?— Jay Gould!"

Undaunted, Gould tried to take over what was left of the tannery. When Lee rounded up a crew of Scranton loafers and occupied the plant by night, Gould armed a few hundred local citizens and in what was called the "Battle of Gouldsboro" drove out the defenders. But the business was ruined. Gould soon closed it down and moved to New York.

Like so many others in the years before the Civil War, Gould now turned from producing goods to speculating in stocks, especially in railroads. To learn the business he bought a controlling interest in a broken-down line that ran between Troy, New York, and Rutland, Vermont. He then performed what was to be his favorite maneuver, building up—or giving the impression that he had built up—a line, and selling it at a handsome profit. Meanwhile, he had married Helen Miller, the shy, well-mannered daughter of a prosperous New York produce merchant. He would remain a devoted husband and father until his death.

Now eager to leave the river and enter the open sea, he became a partner in the brokerage house of Smith, Gould & Martin. It is worth noting that his two partners would in time become his tools, then his rivals, and finally his implacable enemies. By the end of the war Gould had acquired an unequaled mastery of corporate finance. Operating before corporate relationships were fully understood, he undertook manipulations that would later be unthinkable. Gould now joined Jim Fisk and Daniel Drew.


James Fisk, Jr., was born in that Yankee bastion of thrift and honest toil, Vermont. But he was hardly a model Vermonter. Hopeless in school—except in arithmetic—he quit at twelve, and after a while, like Drew, traveled for a few years with a circus. Thereafter his life always had about it the atmosphere of a circus, especially the clowning, parades, and flummery. At eighteen he joined his father, a peddler. Painting his wagon like that of a sideshow and playing the merry fellow with mothers as well as children, he soon had five wagons going and was calling himself the "Prince of Peddlers."

In time his reputation reached Boston, and the expanding dry-goods house of Jordan, Marsh & Co. hired him. When the Civil War broke out he hurried to Washington, set himself up in a suite at Willard's, and spending, it is said, $1,000 a day, picked up more orders than Jordan, Marsh could handle. Finally old Eben Jordan took him in as a partner. To keep the store supplied with goods,

Fisk had immense quantities of Southern cotton smuggled to Northern mills.

By the end of the war Boston no longer held enough reward for Fisk's energies; he sold out to Jordan and moved to New York and onto Wall Street. Meeting Drew, he gained the wary old speculator's confidence, and Drew soon found a role for the brazen young man in his long-drawn-out rape of the Erie Railroad. The Erie, sometimes called the "Scarlet Woman of Wall Street," was a major road, with 7,000 employees and 773 miles of track winding northward to Buffalo from the west shore of the Hudson opposite New York City. But it had been so mismanaged and drained that its debts were huge and its trains were commonly said to run on two streaks of rust. Accidents, some disastrous, were common.

Doubtless taking a special pleasure from making money while others were losing it, Drew preferred to sell stocks short. Now, with Fisk as his broker, he sold a huge block of Erie shares short. The price dropped from eighty-eight to fifty-five, trapping many bulls, including Cornelius Vanderbilt. Drew took a huge profit. While the stock was at its low he bought back control. Foreseeing a major struggle with old Vanderbilt, he placed Fisk and Jay Gould on the Erie board to back him up. So the trio—the treacherous old drover, the flamboyant supersalesman, and the master conniver—made ready for the Commodore, tough, blaspheming veteran—he was seventy-one—of the transportation wars.

With all the pugnacity that had carried him from the deck of a Staten Island ferryboat to control of the New York Central and other major lines, Vanderbilt set out to seize control of Erie and establish a railroad monopoly between New York and the Great Lakes. The events that followed were like scenes from some early movie melodrama, with Gould, Fisk, and Drew the equivalent of western badmen. "It is something new," Charles Francis Adams, Jr., said, "to see a knot of adventurers, some of broken fortune, without character and without credit, possess themselves of an artery of commerce more important than was ever the Appian Way, and make levies, not only upon it for their own emolument, but, through it, upon the whole business of a nation."

As soon as they learned of Vanderbilt's order to buy Erie shares, Gould and Fisk hit upon a devastating countermeasure: uncovering a printing press in the basement of the Erie offices, they proceeded to print Erie certificates with unholy abandon. These, they claimed, were convertible bonds and the revenue from them would be used for repairs and new equipment. Vanderbilt's brokers bought hungrily. "If this printing press don't break down," Fisk said, "I'll be damned if I don't give the old hog all he wants of Erie." In exasperation Vanderbilt had injunctions issued by one of his kept judges on the New York State Supreme Court, George Barnard, but the Drew party got counterinjunctions from one of their own judges. Finally, on March 10, 1868, the Drew party issued 50,000 shares, worth about $4 million. The Vanderbilt men bought them up, but they reeled. Erie sagged sickeningly. Drew dumped another 50,000 shares. Vanderbilt absorbed them, but he was beaten. It had cost him over $8 million, and much of the stock he had bought was worthless.

Fisk, Gould, and Drew were about to celebrate when they learned that Barnard had cited them for contempt and that police officers were looking for them. Old Drew quaked, but Fisk and Gould, with characteristic audacity, decided on flight—across the river to Jersey City—with the loot. Drew fled to the Hudson River ferry, but Gould and Fisk, after packing millions of dollars into valises, stopped to dine at Delmonico's. By then it seemed too dangerous to take the ferry, so they hired a small steamer, adding to their larceny the touch of a bandit escape.

In New Jersey they established themselves at the Taylor Hotel, and since Jersey City was the terminus of the Erie, they made the hotel the new Erie headquarters. When reporters arrived, Fisk met them with cigars, drinks, and the blithe explanation that they had taken Horace Greeley's advice to go west. Since Fisk's wife preferred to stay in Boston, he sent for his mistress, Josie Mansfield, a well-fleshed young woman of dubious reputation and very expensive tastes.

Soon all three grew impatient in their exile, and Gould pointed out that their only hope was to get a law through the New York State legislature legalizing their "bond issue." In the postwar period New York State legislators—paid a salary of only $300 a year—could be bought by the highest bidder. So Gould left for Albany with a fortune in cash. He set himself up in the Delavan House, and agents representing the Vanderbilt forces opened up on another floor. In a frenzy of greed, the legislators scurried from one floor to the other to get the highest price. In the end Gould wrung from the legislature the bill he wanted. It is said to have cost him $500,000, and it confirmed him in his withering contempt for politicians. "In a Republican district," he later told a state investigating committee, "I was a Republican; in a Democratic district a Democrat; in a doubtful district I was doubtful; but I was always for Erie."

As Vanderbilt had developed cutthroat competition, and Cooke high-pressure salesmanship to a mass audience, Gould was a pioneer in the systematic "fixing" of politicians. Once the session was over, "Boss" Tweed, a Vanderbilt man, met Gould and, having found that he could not conquer the enemy, joined him. Meanwhile, in New York, Vanderbilt, drained of cash and thoroughly disgusted, observed: "This Erie has taught me that it never pays to kick a skunk." Knowing the weakness of the "Deacon" for double-dealing, he sent him a note: "Drew, I'm sick of the whole damned business. Come and see me. —Van Derbilt." Drew came, and they reached an understanding.

Fisk and Gould knew that Vanderbilt, with Drew on his side, would never let them return to New York. So, with their customary brass, they went straight to Vanderbilt, and after several meetings agreed that the Erie treasury—the golden goose that could not be killed—should absorb Vanderbilt's stock, his lieutenant's losses, and the demands of a group of Boston directors. Counting payments to legislators and lawyers, this "settlement" cost the Erie $9 million. Drew would be permitted to keep much of his gains if he resigned from the Erie board.

Gould and Fisk were left with only the gutted hulk of the Erie. But it was all theirs. Still in their early thirties, they had taken over a great railroad after a paltry investment. "Nothing so audacious, nothing more gigantic in the way of swindling, has ever been perpetrated in this country," declared Samuel Bowles, editor of the Springfield *Republican*. But this was only the beginning. Soon the pair "elected" Tweed to the board of directors, joining the political power of the Tweed ring to the money power of the Erie ring. They then pumped $20 million of watered stock into Erie's capital, and, as the stock fell, they and Drew sold it short. When it dropped low enough, Gould and Fisk began to buy the stock again—without telling Drew. Erie shares soared, and Drew, still selling heavily short, was trapped. Discovering who had tricked him, he came crawling to Fisk and Gould, and in tears begged them to lend him shares to cover his short sales. They spurned him.

Not trusting Drew, Gould and Fisk hurried to Judge Barnard, who, since he belonged to Tweed, was now, ironically, at the service of his former opponents. Barnard was another of the new breed. Married to a tobacco heiress, he was a man-about-town, a frequent guest of Fisk and Josie Mansfield, and at the command of whoever wielded power. An expert at obstructing justice on behalf of his masters, he declared Erie in receivership and immediately appointed a receiver—Jay Gould. Badly beaten at his own game and now an outsider, Drew ruefully observed, "To speculate in Wall Street when you are no longer an insider is like buying cows by candlelight." A few years later he declared himself bankrupt, listing as his total assets a watch and chain, a sealskin coat and other wearing apparel, a Bible, hymnbooks, etc. Of Jay Gould he had only this to say: "His touch is death."

With money flowing in from Erie, Gould and Fisk grew rich apace. Gould moved into a Fifth Avenue townhouse and acquired a 500-acre estate in Irvington-on-the-Hudson, some twenty miles north of New York City. The estate, Lyndhurst, included a forty-room, pinnacled and turreted Gothic castle. In time it also had acres of splendid greenhouses, a huge swimming pool, a private dock, and a launch in which Gould could commute to his office in lower Manhattan.

Fisk and Gould displayed their confidence even more arrogantly when Fisk purchased Pike's Opera House on Twenty-third Street at a cost to Erie of $820,000. Its upper floors served as Erie's main offices, but it also allowed Fisk to amuse himself as manager of an opera house. Occupying offices of baroque magnificence, the onetime "Prince of Peddlers" now became "Prince of Erie." In a cranny were Gould's offices—plain to the point of bareness. Apparently undisturbed by the singers, dancers, politicians, and hangers-on eddying about, or by rumors of revelry by night, Gould kept regular office hours and even came in for a few hours on Sundays. Although he may have disapproved of Fisk's more scandalous activities, he apparently never objected. Hail-fellow-well-met, always ready with a cigar and a joke, Fisk was a good "front" and a master of public relations.

Gould had something more important to think about. Having

pocketed Erie, he now pushed on to the most sensational exploit in U.S. financial history—a corner on gold. First he acquired a New York bank, the Tenth National, which permitted him to issue certified checks regardless of whether he had deposited security to cover them. Since there was only about $15 million in gold in circulation, it was not impossible for an individual or group to get control of it. What made the undertaking seem foolhardy was that the government kept almost $100 million in its vaults and from time to time sold enough for the purposes of importers and customs duties. But Jay Gould was not foolhardy. In the spring of 1869 he bought seven million dollars worth of gold. After that, the problem was to prevent the government from releasing any of its gold as the price rose. He decided that he could manage this only through one official—the President. Such was the colossal effrontery of this scheme that he must have conceived it only after he had become acquainted with a sixty-seven-year-old opportunist named Abel Corbin. Corbin, a lawyer, lobbyist, and, like Drew, a zealous churchgoer, had just married Jenny Grant, the President's middle-aged sister.

Gould began by convincing Corbin—an easy task—that it was vital for the nation and especially for farmers, who needed high prices for their crops, that gold be kept scarce and its price high. He hardly needed to add that any informed gold trader could then make a handsome profit. He sweetened his argument by setting up a $1.5 million gold account for Corbin's wife. Corbin soon reported to Gould that he had given the President the benefit of his and Gould's advice. Emboldened, Gould and Fisk, learning that the President would visit the Corbins in Boston, arranged to escort the party in a steamer of Fisk's Fall River Line and plied the President with champagne, fine food, and big cigars throughout the trip. Feigning a deep concern for the national welfare, Gould also plied him with his theory of keeping gold scarce and gold prices high. Apparently Grant did not disapprove. He returned to New York with the two speculators and sat with them in Fisk's box at the theater.

During the summer of 1869 Gould bought an additional $30 or $40 million of gold—that is, all the gold in circulation—and contracts for twice as much beyond that. Gold rose to 146 on the exchange. At the same time Gould planted stories that the administration would not sell its gold and would allow the price to rise. But gold did not rise.

Gould continued to buy, but with increasing apprehension. He convinced Fisk that Mrs. Grant had allowed some gold to be purchased on her behalf and Fisk promptly swept into the market, broadcasting the Grant story as he went. Gold climbed. It is a measure of the period that, on the word of such a knave as Fisk, almost everyone believed that the President was a party to the most rapacious assault ever made on the nation's financial structure.

Gold had climbed back up to 141 when Corbin, at Gould's prodding, rushed another letter to the President urging the administration to withhold gold. This was at last enough even for Grant. At his direction, Mrs. Grant wrote to the President's sister, "Tell Mr. Corbin that the President is very much distressed by your speculations and you must close them as quickly as you can." Corbin at once showed the letter to Gould, and the latter, holding at least $50 million in gold, and on margin, had only one hope—to sell as quickly and quietly as possible. He did not tell Fisk of his about-face but let his pudgy associate strut through the Gold Room—as the exchange was known—proclaiming, "I'll bet any part of $50,000 that gold will go over 145!" The Gold Room itself was now packed with frantic traders. When it closed, gold was at 144 and panic was in the offing.

The next day, September 24, 1869, known ever since as Black Friday, gold opened at 150. News of the raid had spread across the land, and crowds gathered as though awaiting word from a disaster area. When the indicator in the Gold Room rose to 160, the chamber began to look like a lunatic asylum, with men wringing their hands, raving, and weeping. At last, Grant, stirred out of his inertia, ordered Assistant Treasurer Butterfield to sell $4 million in gold immediately. After seeing to his own investments, Butterfield is said to have notified Gould and given him a half-hour's grace. That was enough. Gould ordered his men to "sell, sell, sell! Do nothing but sell!" One story has it that he added, "Only don't sell to Fisk's brokers." Within thirty minutes gold dropped thirty points. More than a dozen Wall Street houses went under and hundreds of firms across the country were ruined. The Gold Exchange itself never recovered.

When the Exchange closed, a mob, made up in part of ruined men hunting for Gould and Fisk, stood in the street crying, "Who killed Leupp?" and answered, "Jay Gould!" But Gould and Fisk had gone, creeping out of a back door. The mob reflected the demoralizing effect of the speculative frenzy: the only resort of the victims was to gather in the street and shout helplessly.

Some have claimed that Gould came out of Black Friday with $11 million, but others say that it left his finances in disarray. It is assumed that Gould took care of Fisk privately. Gould also came up with a solution, as insolent as it was simple, for Fisk's untold debts: the claim that they were all incurred by Fisk's brokers, who were of course bankrupt. When asked where all the money was, Fisk gave a favorite answer from his Vermont days—"Gone where the woodbine twineth." Gould's contribution was a barefaced disclaimer: "I was in no way instrumental in producing the panic." Fisk, always the court jester, drew the curtain with "Let everyone carry out his corpse."

Meanwhile the Erie wars continued. During the summer of 1869 Gould and Fisk decided they could use a little line, the Albany and Susquehanna, which connected with the Erie at Binghamton, to give them access to the Eastern Seaboard. Its builder was a tough Scot, but Fisk had Judge Barnard throw the line into receivership and appoint a Fisk man as receiver. But when Fisk arrived at the Albany office of the road he found a little army ready to oppose his taking over. Doting on such excitement, Fisk telegraphed for a force of Erie men to go to Binghamton and start toward Albany. At the same time, a Ramsey battalion entrained at Albany and headed for Binghamton. In an episode that would be appalling were it not so ridiculous, the two forces met head-on east of Binghamton. In the comic opera battle that followed, the Erie contingent was routed. Ramsey ended the war by leasing the road to the Delaware & Hudson Canal Company. Not a whit abashed, Fisk closed the affair with a quip worthy of a Restoration playwright: "Nothing is lost save honor."

Something of a reform wave now swept New York: Tweed was exposed and arrested; Barnard was impeached; and the long-suffering stockholders of Erie, led by Daniel Sickles, politician, former general, and jack-of-all connivances, literally invaded the Opera House and elected their own board of directors. Gould might have resisted, but Sickles came to him with the sly suggestion that if he resigned, Erie stock would soar and he could make a killing. The prospect of profiting from his low repute must have given Gould malicious pleasure. He agreed. The news of his leaving sent Erie up twenty points and brought him almost a million dollars.

In mighty thrusts, the railroads had penetrated the West; now they became the prime instrument of its exploitation. Gould's first venture in this larger arena was the Pacific Mail Steamship Company. He took the step along with Russell Sage, a shrewd speculator who had begun as a grocer in upstate New York. The Pacific Mail had pioneered in carrying mail and freight across the Isthmus of Panama to California, but it had been bled by manipulators. Buying and selling as they sent the stock violently up and down, the pair in a short time made, it is said, $5 million. But Pacific Mail was only a prelude. Gould had his eye on a giant—the Union Pacific.

Beginning in 1873 with a purchase of 100,000 shares, Gould and Sage were soon able to put in one of Gould's men as president of the road. But in 1877 a sharp wage cut caused violent strikes on the railroads. The moguls called state militia to put down the strikes and Gould declared that the only way to prevent anarchy in the United States was to restore Grant to the presidency. He even offered $1 million to help bring this about. The gold panic of 1869 had made Gould the villain of the money markets; he now became the social and political bugaboo of the general public. They sensed in him an impenetrable detachment that was far more menacing than the meanness of a Drew, the rascality of a Fisk, or the belligerence of a Vanderbilt.

Despite poor health and an abiding pleasure in his home life, Gould began making inspection tours of his ever-increasing number of railroads and soon showed a remarkable grasp of management practices. He now conceived a grand plan for joining half a dozen railroads in a chain that would parallel the Union Pacific and even compete with it. Unhesitatingly he bought into enough roads to give him one continuous line from St. Louis to Cheyenne. By threatening to extend his lines to the West Coast, he forced a merger between the Union Pacific and the Kansas Pacific. In this deal he cleared $10 million in less than two years.

On a trip to Europe not long afterward, he sent in his card to one of the Rothschilds. It came back with the comment "Europe is not for sale."

---

Ever since he had managed several coups on Wall Street during the Civil War by getting telegraph news of a battle, Gould had been fascinated by that new wonder of communication, telegraph lines. The great telegraph company of the day was Western Union, which Vanderbilt's son William controlled. Gould began his campaign against it stealthily; in 1875 he lured away its eastern manager, Thomas Eckert, a former general. Within two years Gould had made another company, the Atlantic & Pacific, such a powerful rival to Western Union that the latter took steps to absorb it, offering Gould close to $1 million and 12,500 shares. He accepted. But when he sought a seat on the board, he was rejected. With all the financial manipulations of which he was now a master, Gould organized a new telegraph company, the American Union. Later, before a Senate committee, he unblushingly declared that it was simply his friendship for General Eckert that had led him to organize the American Union. By this time a veteran of official inquiries, he was an imperturbable witness, prepared to offer a mockingly humble version of his activities.

Within a year the American Union had acquired 50,000 miles of lines and 2,000 branch offices. At the same time Gould conducted raids on Western Union stock, forcing it down by selling it short. He had also picked up the New York *World,* one of his most bitter critics, and used it, for the few years that he owned it, to further his views and schemes. The paper soon launched attacks on Western Union as a vicious monopoly. By the close of 1880, another Vanderbilt was ready to come to terms with the little man of the sallow face and the big beard. As soon as it was known that Gould was being appeased, Western Union soared from 78 to 114, and all insiders, including Gould, profited accordingly.

Gould now revealed that he had accumulated $30.1 million of Western Union stock and was taking control. Thus at the age of forty-five he was worth, depending on the market, between $75 million and $100 million. His hair was thin, his big beard streaked with gray, and his face deeply lined.

He was now the most popular target of abuse. The hatred of his enemies penetrated even his private life. Once he was waylaid by two fellow speculators, James Keene and Major A. J. Selover. They had joined Gould in a bear raid on Western Union but found that he was buying while they were selling. "Jay Gould," Keene had proclaimed, "is the worst man on earth since the beginning of the Christian era. He is treacherous, false, cowardly and a despicable worm." One day, Selover, a large man, confronted Gould near the Exchange and pushed him down the steps of a downstairs barber shop. Gould did not press charges, but a few years later, as Keene was about to bring off a corner in wheat, Gould moved in and broke the corner. Keene lost $7 million and went bankrupt. Thereafter, Gould never went about without a bodyguard.

Gould now mounted the last major assault of his career. His target was the New York elevated railways, the barbarously noisy and dirty trains (for many years they burned coal), which in the 1870s began to run on overhead structures along four of New York's thoroughfares. Gould had discovered that the three companies that ran the lines had been thoroughly mismanaged—were ripe, in other words, for picking. First, Gould acquired shares in one of them, the Manhattan Company, buying or wringing them from one of its directors, Cyrus W. Field. After making a small fortune in the paper business, Field had been inspired by Lieutenant Matthew Fontaine Maury, the leading American hydrographer, into organizing the laying of a transatlantic telegraph cable. So from 1854 to 1866, Field had spent much of his energies and his fortune in getting the cable built and placed. Despite his pride in his reputation as a great public benefactor, he now found himself deep in an unsavory alliance with Jay Gould.

Gould, Field, and Russell Sage delivered the coup de grace to the Manhattan when they signed affidavits declaring the company "hopelessly insolvent." The enemy breached, Gould moved in. To reward themselves for their solicitude, the Manhattan's directors authorized a $26 million stock issue, much of it going, of course, to Gould, Field, and Sage. To help pay for this, the fare on the elevated lines was raised from five cents to ten cents. The public's reaction was bitter. *The New York Times* declared: "There is no more disgraceful chapter in the history of stock jobbing than . . . the operations of Jay Gould, Russell Sage, Cyrus W. Field and their associates in securing control of the elevated railroads in New York City." To Gould such criticism meant little. But in Cyrus Field it rankled, and he pressed for a return to the five-cent fare. To Gould this was sentimental poppycock. But Field prevailed: the fare was returned to five cents and remained so until the elevated lines were dismantled more than half a century later.

Despite his twofold triumph in 1881, Gould's companies declined, and in the near collapse of the market in 1884 he yielded control of the Union Pacific, the presidency going to Charles Francis Adams, Jr., brother of Henry. The episode had a crucial result—it made Gould decide to retire from Wall Street speculation.

In the midst of all this, Gould ventured into a major political campaign. In October 1884 he and a few associates organized a dinner for the Republican presidential candidate, James G. Blaine, who was faltering badly in his race with Grover Cleveland. After the election, the *World*, owned by Joseph Pulitzer, charged that the Associated Press, controlled by Gould's Western Union, had distorted election returns in the hope of helping Blaine. A mob quickly gathered outside Gould's office—like the one after Black Friday, 1869—and chanted:

> Who buys up Presidents?
> —Jay Gould!
> Who corrupts the Supreme Court?
> —Jay Gould!
> Who are we after?
> —Jay Gould!

But Gould had long since learned to block out the cries of pain and protest from his victims.

Thus, in 1886, when he ordered large-scale discharges of Texas & Pacific employees, and the Knights of Labor, which had grown to 500,000 members, asked for a minimum wage of nine dollars a week (Gould's income was estimated at $100,000 a week), he defied them. They struck. After months of rioting and destruction, Gould, using various new methods, from strikebreakers and blacklisting to private detectives and company spies, broke the strike—and the Knights of Labor.

In contrast to the turbulence that often boiled up around Gould in his business activities, there was always peace in his home. The house itself, on Fifth Avenue and Forty-seventh Street, was a brownstone mansion. It was elegantly furnished with tapestries, gilt ceilings with huge frescoes, paintings by Bouguereau, Daubigny, Millet, and a dozen others, which Gould himself chose, a library of standard authors, whom Gould really read, and a conservatory filled with plants from the hothouses of his country estate. With a Victorian kind of solicitude, his wife, as gentle, decorous, and retiring as ever, saw to it that his home was a tower of quiet and order.

But fashionable society never completely accepted him. The Jay Goulds were not among the "Four Hundred" who could be accommodated in Mrs. Astor's ballroom or even the twelve hundred invited by the Vanderbilts to the most spectacular ball of the era. By ignoring him society gave color to the pretense that it did have a code that extended to business conduct. As Gustavus Myers, historian of America's great fortunes, pointed out, the sources of his wealth were no more tainted than those of Vanderbilt or Astor. And his forebears, ranging from respected New Englanders as far back as 1648 to a hero of the Revolution, were at least as distinguished as any of theirs.

After the death of his wife in 1889, Gould's health, never very good, began to fail. In his last weeks a ticker-tape machine was installed in a room next to the one in which he lay so that he might follow his stocks to the very end. When he died on December 2, 1892, the market reacted swiftly: Western Union, Manhattan Elevated, and the railroads all went up. Newspaper obituaries are generally merciful, but now the New York *World* declared, "Ten thousand ruined men will curse the dead man's memory." His funeral was nevertheless attended by a host of famous citizens.

The glimpses we get of Gould's home life rule out any view of him as abnormal or monstrous; in domestic and personal matters he was proper, inhibited, and reclusive. Along with the low voice, dark clothes, composure, and plain office, it was protective coloration, permitting him to concentrate all his attention on acquiring wealth and power. Gould had realized at the outset that the best way, outside of politics, to achieve power was in the manipulation of stocks and corporations. Whatever laws and codes limited freedom of action in such fields, Gould was able to nullify them by bribery, embezzlement, a matchless knowledge of financial maneuvers, and on a few occasions—as in the Pennsylvania tannery assault and against strikers—

violence. But he died with dignity, surrounded by all the symbols of power.

Whether or not Astor, Vanderbilt, and Cooke were admired, they were emulated. They did not of course introduce the profit motive, but they did make it the center of life. They used individualism to justify ruthlessness, enterprise to excuse a lack of scruple. They made a fashion of acquisition and an idol of success. America has never recovered from their influence.

# 4

## *THE PARVENUS*
## *AND THEIR PLEASURES*

So much money was being made during the Civil War and such was the urge to enjoy it that as early as the spring of 1863 in New York, and not much later in Washington, society returned to its round of parties and balls. Military debacles and high prices could hardly discourage someone like Ward McAllister, New York's foremost consultant in pleasure; he staged a weeklong party in November 1862, just before a Union army marched to death and disaster at Fredericksburg. Theaters and opera houses were crowded; prizefights were popular; horse racing for huge purses and with unrestrained betting flourished. And there was a shameless demand for diamonds, pearls, Brussels carpets, and French gowns.

Scarcely was the war over when the rich, especially the new rich, began to flaunt their wealth in every way: marble mansions, summer houses at Newport, corps of servants, gambling at Saratoga, racehorses housed in great stables, carriages with liveried coachmen, steam yachts, private railroad cars. Most of them born on a farm or in a small town, the new millionaires, descending on New York with their dollars hot in their pockets, were fascinated by the metropolis, the glitter of its luxuries and its exotic pleasures. Henry Clews, a Wall Street broker who as a youth about to take holy orders in England had visited New York and been enchanted by it, described how the parvenus were enthralled by the city's restless activity, its feverish enterprise and opportunities . . . but more particularly by its imperial wealth, its Parisian, indeed almost Sybaritic luxury and social splendor . . . the roll of splendid equipages in the "Bois de Boulogne of America," Central Park . . . scenes of revelry by night in an atmosphere loaded with perfumes of rare exotics. . . . Soon nothing remains for the wives of Western millionaires but to purchase a brownstone mansion, and swing into the tide of fashion with receptions, balls and kettledrums.

The new taste for the sumptuous and the palatial was first displayed in hotels and restaurants. Almost gone were the homely little inns or the country taverns, called ordinaries, where both sexes sometimes slept on the floor of the "long room," ate at a common table, using only fingers and knives, and washed in an outdoor basin—but, incidentally, got all the rum, brandy, and wine they wanted. The Astor House, erected in 1836 on Broadway opposite City Hall, with gaslight throughout, seventeen "bathing rooms," and black walnut paneling, was a revelation in comfort. But it was only a foretaste of the luxury of the St. Nicholas Hotel, which opened on Broadway and Spring Street in 1853. Costing a million dollars, it was a place of barbaric splendor, with gold-embroidered draperies, sofas upholstered in Flemish tapestry, Turkish rugs, scrollwork mirrors, and gilding everywhere.

Then, in 1859, the Fifth Avenue Hotel was put up on Madison Square, and overnight that square, which had seemed so far to the north, became the center of fashionable life. The Fifth Avenue offered luxurious suites, a "perpendicular railway" called an elevator, and private bathrooms. Its downstairs public rooms became the afternoon haunt of Wall Street brokers and gold speculators, and its second-floor parlors were filled with fashionable men and women bent on pleasure. One writer warned men against taking their wives and daughters to such hotels as a permanent home. "How many women," he asked, "can trace their first infidelity to the necessarily demoralizing influence of public houses—to loneliness, leisure, need of society, interesting companions, abundance of opportunity, and potent temptations!"

Just to the north of the Fifth Avenue, the marble façade of the

Hoffman House went up in 1864 and soon became notorious for the size of its glittering bar with its Bouguereau painting of voluptuous nudes dallying with a satyr. Completing the constellation of dining places in this area was Delmonico's. Following closely the growth of the city, Delmonico's, moving up from Fourteenth Street, had become a legend for elegance, rare dishes, and costliness. Its reputation was magical. When Edward Luckemeyer, a rich importer, found he could not break into the most fashionable circles, he ordered Charles Delmonico to make as magnificent a banquet as possible and invited seventy-two guests to it. The restaurateur responded by serving a matchless dinner on an oval table surrounding a thirty-foot pool with live swans in the water and cages of songbirds overhead. The banquet won Luckemeyer immediate acceptance in the most select society.

Fine homes of sober brownstone were already stretching up Fifth Avenue and by 1870 were approaching Central Park. The park itself had been landscaped and adorned with malls, boat lakes, bridal paths, and carriage drives, at a cost of $10 million, by a gifted landscape architect, Frederick Law Olmsted, and his English associate, Calvert Vaux. It provided a perfect setting for the late afternoon pageant of fashionable carriages and trotters. In good weather, along the East Drive, a shining stream of enclosed black broughams belonging to the conservative older families mingled with light phaetons driven by the bolder matrons as well as the sulkies and curricles of wealthy sportsmen.

Perhaps the most ostentatious activities among the nouveaux riches were the balls and parties. As late as 1830 an evening party started at seven and ended no later than ten-thirty. The guests would dance a cotillion or two to the music of a pianoforte, perhaps sing songs, and then sit down to a supper of shredded ham and grated cheese, followed by jellies, oranges, nuts, and coffee. The only liquor would be port and sherry. By 1865 fashionable society would have considered such a party hopelessly old-fashioned. The aim now was to do something novel or even startling. Hostesses vied to achieve the last word in extravagance—with results that were often bizarre and sometimes idiotic. One hostess, Mrs. Stuyvesant Fish, gave a banquet in honor of her pet monkey, whom she dressed in formal clothes. In a desperate effort to stimulate jaded sensibilities, C. K. G. Billings arranged a stag dinner on the top floor of Sherry's in which the guests arrived in riding habit and rode into the hall on horses that carried champagne in the saddlebags and small tables covered with delicacies.

A single ball in 1883 enabled Alva Vanderbilt to break into Mrs. Astor's inner circle, from which all the Vanderbilts had been excluded when the Astors decided that the old Commodore was not socially acceptable. Having allowed Carrie Astor, Mrs. Astor's young daughter, to join in the elaborate preparations for the ball, Alva Vanderbilt carefully failed to include Carrie or her mother among the 1,200 guests because Mrs. Astor had never visited her. Mrs. Astor, outwitted, promptly came a-visiting. The party cost the Vanderbilts $75,000. Banker-chronicler Henry Clews compared the ball to the revels of Cleopatra and of Louis XIV, and decided that, "taking into account our advanced civilization," it was superior to those historic festivities. But the great difference between the American affair and those of Rome in decline or France under Louis XIV was that postwar America was a young and exuberant society, not an old or effete one. This was the ostentation of upstarts, not the thrill-seeking of the decadent. Although society was, beneath the surface, far from being as pure as was pretended, sexual debauchery was not a part of its corruption.

In summer the scene of social pageantry and play shifted to Newport, a rocky promontory on the Rhode Island coast, and Saratoga Springs, just south of New York's Adirondack Mountains. In an earlier time Newport had been a quiet little seaside community. Such visitors as Georgia-born Ward McAllister recalled it as the favorite summer resort of well-to-do Southerners in the 1840s. They were following a pattern set in the days when Newport was a terminus in the triangular trade in cotton, rum, and slaves. Others, such as Henry James, remembered it as the haunt of such New England intellectuals as Longfellow, Bancroft, Louis Agassiz, and Julia Ward Howe.

Even before the war the rich had indulged in fancy-dress balls, and after the war, New York society, led by Ward McAllister, Mrs. Astor's grand vizier, and Mrs. August Belmont, wife of the banker and sportsman, introduced other such diversions. All summer long the city swells sailed in and out of the island-studded bay, went on garden parties by day and dances by night. On the lawns of the great houses they played croquet or a new game called tennis and vied at archery. Or they rolled up and down Bellevue Avenue in their landaus, victorias, and "dogcarts." From year to year during the 1870s and 1880s, the "cottages" and villas became more palatial, the parties more elegant, the circle of the elect richer and more exclusive.

But it was the pageant of the great sailing yachts that gave Newport much of its cachet. So when steam began to rival and displace sail, and Southampton, Lenox, and Bar Harbor offered competition, the popularity of the resort waned. Its rigid exclusiveness was chilling. It became a contradiction—ostensibly an intimate little summer colony but actually a series of vast formal houses inhabited by an increasingly staid coterie. In time, as many of its great houses were closed down or, much later, became museums, Newport settled into a kind of dowager opulence, with some old families and a few new ones clinging to its outworn glories.

Where Newport was a closed circle of private homes, Saratoga was all public hotels. It was, as such places have always been, perfect for social climbers and especially women with marriageable daughters. When Saratoga first became known for its mineral springs early in the nineteenth century, a puritanical temperance society tried to prohibit dancing, any beverage stronger than water, and orchestras that played any music but hymns. The effort failed completely; by the 1830s Saratoga was the liveliest of fashionable summering places in the land. At such hotels as the Congress Hall or the United States, the new rich from all over America—merchants from New Orleans, planters from Arkansas, landowners from Virginia, and capitalists from New York and Boston—as well as such political or literary bigwigs as Webster and Clay, Irving and Cooper, promenaded on the piazzas, drank the waters together, and at night danced in the same quadrilles.

Saratoga's popularity as a spa declined as the war approached, but after the war a crowd of spendthrift sportsmen was attracted to it, and in time its racetrack and gambling casino gave it a more gaudy life than ever. Its wide main thoroughfare, Broadway, was crowded with handsome carriages and elegant strollers—the belles in ruffles, flounces, bustles, and bonnets, brought along in round-topped "Saratoga trunks," and the dandies in striped pants, bright velvet vests, boutonnieres, gloves, and walking sticks. Not even the Vienna Prater, *Frank Leslie's Illustrated* declared, or Berlin's Unter den Linden or the Champs-Élysées could offer "a more dazzling display of fashion, beauty and wealth." At night, after a day of betting at the races, there were the roulette and faro tables, especially those at the Club-House, run by John Morrissey, former New York prizefighter and Tweed ring politician. The extravagances of Saratoga's votaries made legends: Berry Wall, the dandy, changed his clothes, it was said, a dozen times a day; "Diamond Jim" Brady arrived with twenty Japanese houseboys; and John W. "Bet-a-Million" Gates lost half a million dollars at the races in one afternoon and won back a quarter million at the gaming tables that same night.

Not everybody approved of these goings-on. "The ladies paint under their eyelids to give a more brilliant effect to the eye," *Godey's Lady's Book* observed. "What is republican America coming to? These places—Saratoga and Newport—are the Sodom and Gomorrah of our Union." And a newspaper correspondent wrote of women in Saratoga in 1865, "When earth's angels begin to paint their eyes, wear false busts and false hair in a bag behind their heads, to what extremes may we not expect the dear creatures to go!" Although its track retained a glamour, as a resort Saratoga, too, faded in the competition with other spas, other racetracks, other gambling places.

Travel abroad was another way to demonstrate one's wealth and *savoir vivre.* It was so effective for a parvenue to be able to say that she had spent the summer in London or Paris or at a German spa, and prove it with gowns from Worth or an anecdote about the waters at Baden-Baden. Equally impressive was a steam yacht. What a gesture it was to spend several hundred thousand dollars on a floating palace that would be used only in moments of leisure! Vanderbilt had demonstrated the possibilities with his *North Star,* and others followed resplendently in his wake. Gould's *Atalanta* cost $1,000 a day to run; guests at his castle on the Hudson were taken out to the vessel in a rowboat manned by ten uniformed sailors. To the average citizen an even more awesome symbol of privilege as well as wealth was the private railroad car. The Era of Opulence struck train travel with full force when George Pullman built, in 1865, the first sleeping car. It had black walnut woodwork, painted ceilings, glittering chandeliers, and Brussels carpets. Soon railroads added dining cars and smoking salons. Jay Gould's car cost $50,000; his son George, fancying himself a railroad magnate, had an entire train.

Every sport that offered an opportunity for the display of wealth and prodigality was now thoroughly exploited. In Revolutionary days horse racing had been the sport of Virginia and Maryland gentry and later of exclusive little jockey clubs in New York, Philadelphia, and Washington. Still later it had fallen into the hands of professional gamblers and other disreputable characters. Now a group of wealthy New York sportsmen led by Leonard W. Jerome, millionaire Wall Street speculator, set out to make racing, if not the sport of kings, then at least of gentlemen. Jerome, with the help of August Belmont, fabulously successful, German-born agent for the Rothschilds, and William Travers, lawyer, broker, wit, *bon vivant,* and member of twenty-seven clubs, organized the American Jockey Club and built Jerome Park, a magnificent racecourse, grandstand, and clubhouse on 230 acres in New York's northern suburbs. Its opening in 1866 attracted all the nabobs from Murray Hill to Gramercy Park, with such other connoisseurs of horseflesh as Jim Fisk, "Boss" Tweed, General Grant, and Josie Woods, elegant mistress of the fanciest house of assignation in the city.

Leonard Jerome was the American prototype of the millionaire who makes a fetish of expensive and exclusive sports such as keeping race-horses, yachting, polo, fox hunting, and trotting. The more elaborate and costly the ritual surrounding a sport, the more passionately he pursued it.

Jerome was born on a farm near Syracuse in 1818. Having managed to get a college education and read law, he established himself as a lawyer in Rochester. As western New York outgrew its frontier character, Leonard and his brother Lawrence, lively and gregarious young men, were more and more in demand in the burgeoning social life of the little city. But like the majority of parvenus and prodigals, they were country boys who yearned for the big city. So, as soon as they were able, they took off for New York and plunged into the vortex of Wall Street and the high life of the metropolis. An immensely energetic man, powerfully stimulated by Wall Street, which he himself called "a jungle where men tear and claw," Jerome easily made and lost fortunes on the Stock Exchange in the next twenty years. At the same time he bloomed in the hothouse of fashionable society. Tall, dark, with a huge, down-curling mustache, he was a dashing figure, attracted by and attracting pretty women, especially if they had some musical talent. Animated by youthful enthusiasms and strenuous pastimes, he was nineteenth-century American exuberance channeled into speculation and sport.

An appointment as consul in Trieste in 1852—a reward for services in the Whig cause—where the Jeromes hobnobbed with the local aristocracy, or what was left of it, made their tastes even richer. It gave Jerome's wife, Clara, an overweening admiration for European nobility, including their vapid recreations and their obsession with dress, gossip, and snobbery. She and her three daughters stayed on in Europe for longer and longer periods and eventually became expatriates.

Of Leonard Jerome's various love affairs, the one with horses struck the deepest. When he built a mansion on Madison Square in 1859, he ordered the stables finished first and had them furnished with carpets, plate glass, and black walnut paneling. Even on Sundays, a magnificent equipage would wheel out of the Jerome stables and roll toward Central Park, shocking respectable citizens on their way to church. But Jerome's most flamboyant gesture as a horse fancier was his revival—it was the vogue in England—of four-in-hand driving, the art of handling a coach and four horses. Along with a few other "howling swells," such as James Gordon Bennett, Jr., reckless son of the publisher of the *Herald,* Jerome organized the Coaching Club. It was not enough to be a good "whip"; style, absurdly punctilious, was just as important. The driver must wear a bottle-green cutaway coat with gilt buttons, top hat, yellow-striped waistcoat, and patent leather boots. A newspaper has left us a memorable vignette of Jerome in the full splendor of his role as a veteran whip and gay blade:

> His horses were trained to caper and rear as they turned into the street. Gay and laughing ladies in gorgeous costume filled the carriage. Lackeys, carefully gotten up, occupied the coupé behind; Jerome sat on the box and handled the reins. With a huge bouquet of flowers attached to his buttonhole, with white gloves, cracking his whip, and with the shouts of the party, the four horses would rush up Fifth Avenue, on toward the Park, while the populace said one to the other, "That is Jerome!"

There were other wonders in the house on Madison Square. At the first ball held there, two fountains were installed in the ballroom, one gushing champagne and the other eau de cologne. Over the stables was the largest private theater in the country, seating 600. Jerome had installed the theater for the benefit of the singers whom he admired—all of them female and attractive. One of the first to use the theater was seventeen-year-old Adelina Patti, who had just become the sensation of New York opera. Jerome not only placed the theater at her disposal but during the winter season drove her home nightly in a splendid sledge and attended her so assiduously that gossip said he was more than an admirer of her voice. But Jerome was not bothered by gossip. Freed by his wealth from middle-class conventions, he went at will from affair to affair.

The pace of both Jerome's market speculations and sporting activities was nothing less than feverish. The war was barely over when he organized the Jerome Park track. In 1870, when young James Gordon Bennett, Jr., accepted a challenge from a leading English yachtsman for a race from Ireland to New York, Jerome was one of the few amateurs among the professionals in a crew of thirty-seven. The American boat was beaten, but the contest became famous as the first of the America's Cup races. Like almost every other rich sportsman, Jerome bought himself a steam yacht, but when the engines gave him too much trouble and his wife decided that the interior was gaudy, he abandoned it.

Clara Jerome had more than one reason for going abroad and staying more or less indefinitely: her husband's interest in horses, music, and other women, none of which she shared, and her own predilection for titled Europeans, a preference not unrelated to her ambitions for her three daughters. Her hopes were realized beyond the dreams of the most ambitious American social climber: her daughter Jennie married Lord Randolph Churchill, younger son of the Duke of Marlborough and later Chancellor of the Exchequer and leader of the House of Commons. Their son was Winston Leonard Spencer Churchill.

Although Jerome was not a plunderer in the style of Gould, Fisk, or Drew, he could, when expedient, deal with scoundrels. Through his association with Vanderbilt in various railroad ventures, he became friendly with John Morrissey, "Boss" Tweed's right-hand man. A broken-nosed former pug, Morrissey was the leader of the dreaded Dead Rabbits, a gang of thugs that literally commanded the large

Irish vote along New York's Bowery. Vanderbilt had come to know him at Saratoga where Morrissey ran the big gambling casino; the aging Commodore had not only made the gangster his political agent but also matched trotters with him on Harlem Lane. Jerome often joined them. A powerful underworld with links to local government had already developed in America, and a member of it could fraternize openly with some of the most influential men in the community.

After 1870, Jerome found it easier to lose fortunes than to make them. The panic of 1873 nearly ruined him, and he was never again a power on Wall Street. In the 1880s, when his wife followed her three daughters to England, he closed the house on Madison Square and went to live at the Hotel Brunswick, headquarters of the so-called horsey set. While his wife entertained in her London drawing room such gentry as exiled King Milan of Serbia, Jerome went daily from his room to his club, or to one of the three racetracks where he was still an officer. Perhaps he really had, as his sister Catherine said, "much sense of honor and hardly any sense of sin." When he died, the most flattering comment that the obituaries could quote was, "One rode better, sailed better, banquetted better when Mr. Jerome was of the company." Except for the name of an avenue and a reservoir in the Bronx, Leonard Jerome is today quite forgotten, but in his passage from country boy to millionaire speculator and sportsman he realized the dreams of the age. His wife in turn realized the aspirations of a legion of socially ambitious women. Originally from an upstate New York town, she had soared through the *beau monde* of New York and into the empyrean of Europe's aristocracy.

In one area the snobbery of the men matched that of the women—their clubs. Aping English models, product of the island empire's old caste system, the Americans created little cliques dedicated chiefly to remaining exclusive. Just as when the gentlemen in a party went apart from the ladies after dinner, the clubs fostered the notion that women were too delicate and pure to be exposed to the talk of men; probably it was also a relief for the men to be freed from their disapproval. Although there were such specialized organizations as the New York Yacht Club, the Racquet and Tennis Club, and the American Jockey Club, as well as general clubs such as the Union, Knickerbocker, and Metropolitan, the primary function of all of them was the fraternizing of the males. They were patently designed to coun-

teract the leveling effects of a democratic system and frontier egalitarianism, and to establish an elite of the rich and propertied.

Part of the snobbery of men's clubs included rigid discrimination
against all who were not white, Anglo-Saxon, and Protestant. No
black would ever dream of applying, and the only Jew known to have
been accepted by them was August Belmont, who penetrated the
inner circle in the 1850s. Belmont made himself acceptable by con-
verting to Protestantism, avoiding Jews, and taking as his first wife
Caroline Slidell Perry, daughter and niece of naval heroes. Moreover,
Belmont outdid the aristocrats in *haut ton* and in observance of "the
code." He kept racehorses, drove coaches four-in-hand, played polo,
and entertained magnificently. He also brought to society a continental sophistication and a connoisseur's taste in wines, food, opera,
paintings, and porcelains. He even dueled for honor's sake, fighting
a hotheaded Southerner named Ned Hayward over the dazzling
daughter of a restaurant keeper in Water Street and coming away
with a bullet in his thigh that left him with a limp. But it was many
years before any other Jew was admitted into the magic circle.

Of the theater arts, grand opera proved peculiarly suited to the
display of wealth. For many years a handful of older families—along
with a few individuals such as Leonard Jerome and August Belmont
who showed a genuine interest in opera—had owned the choice boxes
at the New York Academy of Music. With ever increasing hauteur
they consigned the new railroad, mining, and banking barons to the
orchestra stalls, turning down as much as $30,000 for a single box.
By 1880 the parvenus, having acquired all the mansions, yachts, and
horses they could use, decided that they too would have opera. By
the time the Academy clique awoke to the threat it was too late. The
Vanderbilts, J. P. Morgan, Jay Gould, William Rockefeller, William C. Whitney, Collis P. Huntington, and others—prodded no
doubt by their wives—had joined together to erect the Metropolitan
Opera House.

To the sponsors the most interesting aspect of the new theater was
the tier of thirty-six boxes that became known as the Diamond Horseshoe. The general public was allowed into the orchestra and the upper
balconies, the topmost so remote as to afford only nominal attendance
at a performance. On the opening night the tiers of boxes, one journal
reported, "looked like cages in a menagerie of monopolies." Within

two years the Academy of Music, unable to withstand the competition, was dissolved.

The operatic standards of the Metropolitan were high, and the view of the stage from the "horseshoe" was excellent, but box owners, especially the women, considered attendance largely a social event, an opportunity to show off gems, diamond tiaras, and ropes of pearls. It was the salvation of dinner parties whose guests would have found an entire evening in one another's company intolerably boring. They often did not arrive until after the first act and did not hesitate to carry on a conversation during the performance, especially when the management, under Walter Damrosch, began to put on the strenuous music dramas of Richard Wagner.

Even more than the men, the wives of most newly rich Americans sought to escape from the heritage of democracy and equality, from the almost dead level of American social life. While men became more and more engrossed in making money, women, increasingly released from drudgery, found themselves free to indulge their social proclivities. As early as the 1830s, a visitor from Britain, Harriet Martineau, noted that in the household of a typical New York merchant the man of the family rose early, gulped his coffee, and rushed downtown to toil all day so that his wife might wear a bonnet costing as much as $100. Late in the 1830s another British traveler, James Silk Buckingham, reported that the morning parade of strollers on Broadway was made up chiefly of ladies, many of them beautiful and gaily dressed, but without the elegant male escort such ladies would have had in London; their men, he added, were fretting and slaving in offices or on the Stock Exchange.

Above all, the women itched to have their daughters make marriages that would enhance the family's social standing. Best of all was the capture of a European noble. Many upper-class Americans, mainly Anglo-Saxon, had always harbored a snobbish regard for European and especially British royalty. Paradoxically, the Revolution seems to have stimulated in them a yearning for the days when knighthood flowered and royal purple meant something. Such people made a fetish of tracing the family name back to the nobility of some remote time, acquiring a coat of arms, and presenting their daughters to the Queen. Even at the height of the egalitarianism of the 1840s, Mrs. Robert Tyler, daughter-in-law of President Tyler, wrote to a friend: "I am afraid you poor Alabamian plebeians will expire with envy when I tell you that a real live English Lord was among the guests at the President's house last week; Lord Morpeth . . . with the blood of all the Howards coursing through his noble veins!" And late in 1860 the visit to New York of a frivolous nineteen-year-old Prince of Wales created a sensation, with the aristocracy arranging a royal ball in his honor and every family with social aspirations begging for invitations.

Marriage, however, remained the shortest path to noble status. Such marriages occurred as early as the 1780s, but it was not until the 1850s, and 1860s that the financial woes of Europe's nobility combined with the rise of great American fortunes to make unions between them seem desirable to both sides. By 1909 it was estimated that 500 American heiresses had married titled foreigners. Before long, many of the remnants of Europe's royalty, some of them exiles or wastrels, and some completely bogus, were auctioning themselves off to the highest American bidder, and the wives of Ohio grain millionaires, Chicago slaughterhouse tycoons, and New York street railway magnates were trotting their daughters from Paris to London to Florence and from Marienbad to the Riviera in shameless search of some purchasable baron, count, or marquis. Plain, democratic "Mr. and Mrs." might be good enough for the average American, but for the daughters of Mrs. Leonard Jerome, formerly of Palmyra, New York, nothing less than "Lord and Lady" would do. There was no parallel tendency among the sons of rich Americans: they clearly had far more independence than their sisters. When Henry James, in *The American* (1877), one of his many probings of the differences between Americans and Europeans, has a self-made American millionaire seek the hand of a young French countess, her family, although tempted by his wealth, turns him down, with supreme hauteur, because he is "commercial."

Although there was some pretense that the family of an American heiress was important in achieving social status, the ultimate criterion was money. Since there had been so small a social aristocracy at the opening of the nineteenth century, there was little chance that someone's grandfather had been much more than a farmer, craftsman, or local tradesman. "Don't tell me all this modern newspaper rubbish about a New York aristocracy," says Newland Archer's mother in Edith Wharton's *The Age of Innocence*. "New York has always been a commercial community, and there are not more than three families in it who can claim an aristocratic origin in the real sense of the word." Whereas the first Mrs. John Jacob Astor helped her husband clean furs, her granddaughter, Mrs. William Astor, *the* Mrs. Astor, became the most autocratic leader New York society would ever know; and whereas the first Mrs. Cornelius Vanderbilt toiled in the kitchen of her Staten Island farmhouse, her granddaughter, Mrs. William Kissam Vanderbilt, would be the only woman who successfully challenged Mrs. Astor's influence in high society.

It was mainly women such as Mrs. William K. Vanderbilt and Mrs. Astor who raised snobbery to a way of life. "I know of no profession, art, or trade that women are working in today," Mrs. Vanderbilt announced, "as taxing on mental resources as being a leader of society." As for Mrs. Astor, she became the living symbol of High Society, a byword for opulence, ceremony, and hauteur. The formula for her success was determination, intimidating dignity, a fortune, and the assistance of a past master of punctilio and snobbery, Ward McAllister.

McAllister could never have risen to popularity and influence in any period before the Civil War. But by the 1860s the time was ripe for a man who would set standards of luxury that would increase the exclusiveness of the rich and surround them with an aura that wealth alone could not achieve. While other men were concentrating all their energies on business, McAllister directed his to diversion, to occupying an endless leisure, to the monstrous task of doing nothing but play. With his passionate interest in such matters as fashion, cookery, and dancing, it is not surprising that in time he was sought out by young matrons who had daughters to present and marry off. Before long he attached himself to Mrs. Astor, seeing in her a woman with the will, the means, and the talents to lead society as he thought it should be led.

It is not entirely clear what made Ward McAllister dedicate himself to so special a career. His boyhood in Savannah in the 1830s and 1840s as the son of a well-known Georgia lawyer and a New York belle doubtless gave him some idea of the livelier uses of leisure.

Summers at Newport brought him together with the family of his uncle Samuel Ward, the New York banker. Particularly interesting must have been his older cousin Sam, who had come back from Europe something of a dandy and *bon vivant*. Young McAllister went to live for a year or so with a rich maiden aunt on New York's Tenth Street. While there he was so carried away by an invitation to a fancy dress ball that he spent a legacy of $1,000 on a costume.

Returning to Savannah, he read law in his father's office and passed the bar examination. Then, excited by letters from his older brother, Hall McAllister, who had gone to San Francisco during the Gold Rush and was making a fortune there, he and his father hurried west. They prospered there. Although eggs were two dollars each and turkeys sixteen dollars apiece, Ward managed to give some memorable dinners for various European clients of the McAllisters' law firm, his development as a gourmet unchecked even by the hurly-burly of a western boomtown.

Having returned to New York and married a rich young lady, he sailed for Europe. His account of two years in London, Florence, Rome, and such fashionable resorts as Baden-Baden and Pau is a mélange of French and Italian gastronomic wonders, idle anecdotes, and worshipful backstairs impressions of royalty gained as he dined in the village inn with Queen Victoria's chef. He returned to New York in 1859 and began with missionary zeal to guide the rich to ever greater elegance and exclusiveness, especially in their dinner parties and balls. And this is all that he did for the remaining thirty-five years of his life.

He began by setting himself up in Newport and making a specialty of champagne picnics—coaching into the country with thirty or forty friends, dancing on a prepared platform, and then dining and drinking in lavish style. He would even hire sheep to complete the bucolic atmosphere of what he liked to call his *fêtes champêtres*. Just so, before the French Revolution, did the courtiers of Louis XVI, jaded by their customary dissipations, like to play at being shepherds and shepherdesses.

That there were less than a dozen chefs in private employ in New York disturbed McAllister more than the war. He was convinced that he had been chosen to rescue society from this neglect. "Fashion selects its own votaries," he wrote. "You can give no explanation of this. . . . The talent of and for society develops itself just as does the talent for art." So in 1872 he organized the Patriarchs, twenty-five men, leaders of families, each of whom would invite about ten guests to a series of balls. Armed with a professional knowledge of cookery, wines, and royal etiquette, he remained for many years the ringmaster of the Patriarch Balls, society's social secretary and arbiter of elegance.

McAllister also organized the Family Circle Dancing Class for the younger generation of the socially chosen, including his own daughter. Preening himself as "The Autocrat of the Drawing Room" and growing cocky with age, despite an increasing paunch, unimpressive face, thinning hair, and a wispy beard, McAllister grew more and more snobbish, reaching a climax in his revelation to a newspaper reporter, "There are only about four hundred people in fashionable New York society." The statement created a minor sensation, "the Four Hundred"—allegedly the number of guests that could be accommodated in Mrs. Astor's ballroom—becoming the catchword for the haughtiest of the idle rich.

By that time the older generation had learned all that McAllister could teach and the younger generation found him dated and a bit ridiculous. Cartoonists such as Charles Dana Gibson caricatured him as a goose girl leading geese. McAllister had lived on into an age of Pullman strikers, Haymarket rioters, unionists, anarchists, and socialists, of such rebels and critics as Eugene V. Debs and Thorstein Veblen, to whom a Ward McAllister was a parasite on parasites, an object lesson in conspicuous consumption, and a master only of waste. McAllister's occasional articles and his autobiographical *Society as I Have Found It* confirmed a growing realization that he was only a shallow hanger-on of the rich and titled, his head filled with little besides memories of extravagance, pomp, and glitter. He had not even substance enough to be genuinely wicked or decadent. Although dedicated to gaiety and the sensual pleasures, he was a genteel Victorian in his respect for propriety, property, rank, and tradition. Next to an Oscar Wilde, he appears boring and pathetic—without wit or true talents. A century later he would have been just another playboy. The Puritans would have predicted damnation for one who had lived so giddy and frivolous a life; all that McAllister suffered was eclipse. He is significant mainly as a measure of the vanity of the social elite to whom he pandered.

Perhaps the most intimate view of the people to whom McAllister devoted himself is given in Edith Wharton's novels of New York in the 1860s and 1870s. Her own background—a family of lawyers and bankers, an education by tutors, marriage to a rich Bostonian, homes in New York, Newport, Lenox, and, in her later years, Paris— peculiarly qualified her to interpret life in the upper crust. As a writer who understood the values of artists, she could appreciate the narrowness of the standards the social elite used to protect its status. Her best-known novel, *The Age of Innocence* (1920), is a consummate picture of the cruelty with which society dealt with those of its members who flouted its conventions. Its main characters, a young lawyer named Newland Archer and his childhood friend Ellen Mingott, who has married a Polish count, Olenska, are both victims of that cruelty. Archer is about to make an approved marriage to May Welland, a beautiful young woman but with almost no character of her own, when the Countess Olenska returns from Europe and shatters his plans and his complacency. The countess has broken a major taboo by fleeing from an unhappy marriage. Surrounded by the rich aura of her European experience, Ellen Olenska challenges and arouses Archer. In the light she casts, the figures in his circle seem pitilessly exposed.

It is a milieu in which the traditional functions of its members have withered away: most of the young men, having inherited fortunes, go through the motions of being busy at an office or in the stock market. The wives, with homes run by maids, governesses, and cooks, concentrate on sumptuary pleasures or a round of inconsequential activities. The daughters grow up with one aim: capturing a rich, socially acceptable husband. The "double standard," that creation of Victorian hypocrisy, keeps most of the daughters more or less innocent until they marry, while it allows the sons to "sow wild oats." The reward for conformity is a life of ease and privilege.

Archer, stirred to his shallow depths, offers at last to go off with the countess, but he backs down when she warns him that running off and living outside the pale may require tawdry maneuvers and painful readjustments. The neutralized product of overbreeding, he resigns himself to marriage with May and a lifetime of wistful memories.

It was in their mansions that the parvenus expressed most completely their baronial aspirations. There had been stately homes in America from the 1740s on, such as John Tayloe II's Mount Airy (1758) on the Rappahannock, Jefferson's Monticello (1770–1809) at Charlottesville, and Gore Place (1806) in Waltham, Massachusetts, to name only a few. Mainly adaptations of the Greek Revival style, they were elegant and patrician, and in the South, especially in such centers as Charleston, part of a way of life that freely embraced gaiety and pleasure. Indeed, a straitlaced New Englander, Josiah Quincy, declared, after enjoying the lavish hospitality of Miles Brewton, a Charleston merchant, early in the 1770s:

> State, magnificence, and ostentation, the natural attendants of riches, are conspicuous among this people: the number and subjection of their slaves tend this way. Cards, dice, the bottle, and horses engross prodigious portions of their time and attention: the gentlemen (planters and merchants) are mostly men of the turf and gamesters. Political inquiries and philosophical disquisitions are too laborious for them.

Nevertheless, such homes as Brewton's would seem neither magnificent nor ostentatious by the standards of the 1870s. In the 1780s Puritan New England had only just begun to thaw, and there was still far from enough wealth to foster the suppliers and the taste needed for the homes the rich would require by the time of the Civil War.

Palatial homes began to appear as soon as the industrial revolution produced the first great fortunes of the 1840s and 1850s. Americans, living in a new world, most of it lacking in mystery, color, and splendid history, discovered the uses of the past. They seized especially upon the rich periods of history opened up to them in the writings of Scott and Byron, Irving and Longfellow. Reacting against Puritan austerity and colonial provincialism, their novelists, poets, and essayists, from Charles Brockden Brown through Poe and Hawthorne, and their architects led them back to an exotic past. The architects seem to have been attracted most of all by the trappings of the Gothic romances of Ann Radcliffe and William Beckford. Beckford was a wealthy English eccentric who had transposed his bizarre fantasies into Fonthill Abbey, a monstrous pseudo-Gothic pile on his country estate.

Encouraged by a spreading abundance, Americans began to abandon the old strictly utilitarian standards. The pride of the self-made man in his success was not to be hidden. The parvenu leather dealer, silk importer, carpet manufacturer, real estate speculator, mill owner, local banker, or shipper of ready-made suits to the forty-niners in California wanted to acquire as rapidly as possible the aura of wealth and power that had surrounded the lords of other days—Renaissance princes, Norman barons, Turkish and Persian potentates. New experts turned up to serve men who had become rich so fast they did not yet know how to live up to their wealth. Foremost among these were the architects, and outstanding among the architects from 1830 to 1850 was Andrew Jackson Downing. Downing favored Gothic castles precisely because they had been the bold expression of a master class. "There is something wonderfully captivating," he ingenuously declared, "in the idea of a battlemented castle, even to an apparently modest man, who thus shows to the world his unsuspected vein of personal ambition." Although he added that the inhabitant must be equal to such a virile abode "warranted by feudal times and feudal robberies," he evidently thought that more than a few American merchants would qualify. For the many who did not live in suitably wild and rocky glens, there was a tamer mode called "rural Gothic" and a presumably democratized and cozy American style known as "Gothic cottage."

One of the earliest homes in full-blown Gothic was Lyndhurst, a castle designed by Alexander Jackson Davis—an architect as influential as Downing and even more addicted to romantic Gothic—for a wealthy merchant, William Paulding, at Irvington-on-the-Hudson. Although outwardly it was—and still is—a graceful structure in gray stone, Philip Hone, mayor of New York City, former auctioneer, and an inexhaustible diarist, described it in 1841 as "resembling a baronial castle, or rather a Gothic monastery with towers, turrets, and trellises; minarets, mosaics . . . and pinnacled roofs, and many other fantasies . . . the whole constituting an edifice of gigantic size, with no room in it; great cost and little comfort." Hone's sarcastic comments notwithstanding, Jay Gould took over Lyndhurst late in the 1860s and flourished in it. To the flat, colorless lives of newly rich clients, Davis lent a perspective of romance and grandeur.

But most of the prewar houses were modest compared with those built after the war. By 1867 builders were offering their clients a choice of Gothic castle, English manor house, Tuscan villa, "suburban Greek," Chinese casino, or Persian pavilion. The urge to grandeur was hardly limited to New Yorkers. In the Chelten Hills outside Philadelphia, Jay Cooke built Ogontz. At about the same time, Leopold Eidlitz was creating in Bridgeport, Connecticut, a bastard-Persian conglomeration of domes and minarets, Iranistan, for that master purveyor of the exotic and the fake, P. T. Barnum. The Great Fire delayed Chicago builders for a while, but they caught up rapidly in the 1880s, beginning with the feudal castle erected for Potter Palmer. San Francisco entered the competition with the gaudy Crocker mansion on Nob Hill; and Cleveland, Milwaukee, and Denver were not far behind.

Handsome, agreeable, and superbly trained in the most rigorous French architectural tradition, Richard Morris Hunt was the ideal architect for the new plutocracy. A few years after his father, a congressman, died, his mother, a talented painter and independent spirit, carried off her two sons to Europe. While the older son, William Morris Hunt, studied painting in Paris and Dusseldorf, fifteen-year-old Richard entered the atelier of Hector Martin Lefuel, prominent Paris architect, and in 1846 became the first American to enroll at the celebrated École des Beaux Arts. After completing his studies and traveling as far afield as Turkey, Palestine, and Egypt, he became an assistant to Lefuel, who was designing additions to the Louvre for Napoleon III.

Hunt returned to America in 1856, but the climate was not yet quite right for a connoisseur who surrounded himself with Venetian glass, medieval missals, wrought metalwork, faience, and all manner of "strange and costly toys of every era of civilization." After a few years Hunt went back to Europe. When he returned to America again, in 1868, the Age of Opulence had arrived. Craving the old, the original, the new rich tricked out their homes in finery appropriated from the families of Europe's distressed nobility: vases, chests, tapestries, silver, stained glass, marble and bronze statuary, paintings, porcelains, and even entire staircases and ceilings. Whether such objects were appropriate, pleasing, or had intrinsic merit did not matter. More than one would-be Maecenas accumulated a houseful of almost worthless "art treasures" and fifth-rate "masterpieces"— the *disjecta membra,* as Matthew Josephson called them, of dead civilizations.

Hunt soon acquired a reputation for splendor of conception and delicacy of detail, so it was inevitable that when the third-generation Vanderbilts began their assault on the heights of ostentation, Hunt should be their architect and arbiter of ornament. He was called on in 1879 by William Kissam Vanderbilt and his redoubtable wife, Alva, to build them a mansion on Fifth Avenue and Fifty-second Street. Scorning the dun dignity of the brownstones rising on all sides (of brownstone, Henry James said that even time could do nothing for it, and Edith Wharton added that it gave New York a "chocolate-colored coating of the most hideous stone ever quarried"), Hunt came up with a French late-Gothic château in pleasing gray-white limestone. It had a two-story dining room and banquet hall, a gymnasium, a billiard room in Moorish style, and a bathroom cut from solid marble. It cost $3 million. Louis Sullivan, prophet of functionalism in architecture, and sometimes a bitter critic of those who craved the appurtenances of wealth, jeered:

> Must I show you this French château, this little Château de Blois, on this street corner, here in New York, and still you do not laugh? . . . Must I tell you that while the man may live in the house physically . . . he cannot possibly live in it morally, mentally, or spiritually, that he and his home are a paradox, a contradiction, an absurdity, a characteristically New York absurdity?

But Vanderbilt did not want a house suited to his needs or his time; he wanted a house that would proclaim that its owner had joined the aristocracy.

The Vanderbilt mansion launched Hunt on his greatest period. He designed the Astor Library, a new façade for the Metropolitan Museum, and the administration building for the 1893 Chicago

World's Fair. He built mansions on Fifth Avenue for Mrs. Astor and John Jacob Astor, and near Asheville, North Carolina, laid out for George Washington Vanderbilt probably the grandest house ever built in America, Biltmore, on a tract of 130,000 acres.

Late in the 1880s Hunt helped transform Newport into the most exclusive resort in the United States. Each of the homes he provided there for Robert Goelet, Belmont, and the Vanderbilts was more monumental, theatrical, and cold than its predecessor. Utterly destructive of the intimacy and informality a summer resort should create, many of Newport's grandest homes were in time closed up or converted to other uses—monuments not to the greatness of their owners but to their vanity. Hunt saw architecture not as the peculiar expression of a people and a place but as a utilization of the best that had been built in the past. He considered originality almost presumptuous, the indulgence, so to speak, of a whim. He encouraged the finest craftsmanship and he was endlessly ingenious in blending styles, but he remains only an anthologist, a consummate eclectic. A phenomenon of the Gilded Age, his influence died with the coterie that had fostered him.

While the rich had Gothic castles and begilded interiors strewn with objets d'art, the less than rich had clapboard cottages in "carpenter Gothic" with gingerbread ornaments, interiors crowded with overstuffed furniture, bric-a-brac, and gimcrackery. The relative bareness of the typical household ended in the 1840s when mass production made all kinds of furnishings, from wallpapers and carpets to chairs and statuary, available to the average family.

For 200 years such families had toiled and sweated and "gone without"; now that money came a bit easier, they wanted comforts and little adornments, the "pretty coxcomalities," as Frances Trollope called them, that had begun to come within reach. Cheap goods, rising incomes, and the weakening of the old Puritan strictures against luxuries combined by the time the war ended to produce the typical Victorian interior: portieres at every door, wallpaper with large floral designs, huge easy chairs, tufted ottomans scattered with embroidered cushions half hidden under "Persian" tidies, marble-topped tables, carved sideboards, footstools, large clocks, plaster casts, wax flowers under glass domes, filigreed fireplace screens, coal scuttles in repoussé and wrought-iron firewood holders, odds and ends of shellwork mottoes in petit point, a radiator covered with a Japanese screen, knick-knacks festooning a mantelpiece or overflowing a whatnot in the corner. The windows were large but completely overhung by blinds, draperies, and tasseled valances, creating what art historian Oliver Larkin called "a ponderous plush gloom." Full of clues to the Victorian mind, such an interior was romantic, conservative, comfortable, insulated, and stifling.

The impulse to flourishes and scrollwork was evident everywhere: in ironwork, needlework patterns, poster lettering, Spencerian handwriting, and even mustaches. Wherever someone could afford it, there was gilt; even teeth were capped with gold.

Flamboyant spendthrifts among the children of the rich are hardly rarities, but in the Gilded Age the number of these was remarkable. Some wealthy parents ruined their children by indulging them shamelessly or by setting them an example of wanton prodigality, others by dominating their offspring and denying them any responsibility.

Although John Jacob Astor's heir, William, came of age much before it was fashionable to live extravagantly, he acquired a mansion in New York and a country estate, and after his marriage into the Dutchess County clan of the Armstrongs and Livingstons he mingled with older New York families such as the Brevoorts and Schermerhorns. But he was an unsociable man who, as the "landlord of New York," spent his life collecting rents from much of the city's rapidly growing slums. At his death in 1875, he left more than $40 million, with virtually no philanthropic bequests. *Appleton's Journal* declared: "The wealth of the late Mr. Astor was not won *by* him, it was conferred *upon* him. . . . He made no experiments . . . contributed no results, set no needed example even in the domain of house building, into which his wealth ever steadily went." And reformer Henry Demarest Lloyd in the *Independent* asked, "Has any man the *right* to leave his eldest son 20 or 30 millions of dollars?"

Untouched by such criticism, Astor left the bulk of his fortune to his two elder sons, John Jacob Astor III and William Astor. Although John, as the eldest, served faithfully in the Astor empire, coping with leases, taxes, and rents, he and his brother lived in unabashed splendor. But it remained for William's wife, Caroline, to make the Astor name synonymous with princely magnificence. Caroline Webster Schermerhorn became not only *the* Mrs. Astor, but the high priestess of America's *haute monde,* the bespangled divinity of the latest aristocracy. Married to a man with no interest in society, who much preferred to sail his yacht into far-off waters or busy himself with his horses on his 80,000 acres in Florida, she moved into the gap and took charge. But for such delicate matters as guest lists, menus, and floral decorations, she relied heavily on Ward McAllister and a fop named Harry Lehr. Mrs. Astor was not beautiful, witty, or especially charming; her dinners were impeccable but boring; her circle included almost no one of talent or intellectual distinction. But she was regal, resourceful in her sphere, and dedicated. She made a cult of social life, with a mystique of leadership, rituals of the most ceremonious kind, a fetish of loyalty, and banishment from the inner circle for anyone who violated the code.

Although she was committed to the totally undemocratic proposition that only the wealthy older families (hers was old but her grandfather Schermerhorn had been a ship chandler) were eligible for the aristocracy, her life represented for a vast number of Americans the ultimate reward of the democratic system of free competition. She was America's substitute for grand duchess and queen. Women all over America, frustrated by Victorian middle-class restraints, read with fascination and vicarious pleasure, in the society columns beginning to appear in newspapers, of the ball she gave annually, like a holy rite, on the third Monday in January, of how she stood under her flattering, full-length portrait by Carolus Duran, receiving her thrice-sifted, caste-proud, bluest of blue-blooded guests—Iselins, Goelets, Rhinelanders, Roosevelts—and such anointed outsiders as the British minister, an Italian baron, and General Grant. Readers reveled in descriptions of her satin gown embroidered in pearls and gold, of diamonds glimmering in her hair, at her throat, and on her arms. They read of gold dinner plates worth $300 apiece and delicacies heaped so high that the table legs had to be braced to bear the load.

They read of guests strolling through the art gallery in the ballroom. Curiously, almost all the paintings plucked the chord of pastoral simplicity: sheep by Troyon, geese by Millet, peasants by Jules

Breton, cattle by van Marcke. Perhaps Mrs. Astor, like Ward Mc-
Allister with his *fêtes champêtres,* craved some relief, even if only painted,
from the glitter and pervading artifice of her life. Unlike the celebrated French *grandes dames* who often presided over both society and
a salon, Mrs. Astor and her steward had no interest in gifted people.
As Mrs. Winthrop Chanler, a more enlightened member of the clan,
said, "The Four Hundred would have fled in a body from a poet, a
painter, a musician or a clever Frenchman." Artists, like art, were
considered articles to be bought for display. Typical was the leading
hostess who asked the Polish soprano Marcella Sembrich to sing at a
dinner party. Mme. Sembrich set her fee at $3,000, but when the
hostess requested her not to mingle with the guests, the singer
promptly replied that her fee would then be only $1,000.

Mrs. Astor continued to give her annual ball until 1905, and although the affair was as resplendent as ever, she had outlived her
age. Her husband, William, her chamberlain, Ward McAllister, and
many of her old associates were gone, and she herself was aged and
wrinkled. The new generation looked on her as a museum piece, a
gilded relic, and on all the older society as stuffy and outmoded.
Everywhere, moreover, there were parvenus with money to burn and
no respect for breeding and the old aristocracy. And finally there were
the socialists and other radicals who had for decades been using the
Astors, Vanderbilts, and their like as examples of all that was para-
sitical and undemocratic in the American system.


Several of Jay Gould's six children bear out the charge that a goodly
number of the parvenus' offspring were wastrels. His eldest son,
George, was chiefly interested in polo, riding to hounds, and amusing
himself with actresses. In business he was a blunderer who eventually
lost control of Western Union, Missouri Pacific, and the New York
elevated railways, dropping $25 million in the process. He married
Edith Kingdon, a young ingenue, and had seven children by her, but
he also had three children by another actress whom he kept on an
estate in Rye, New York. Another son, Frank, showed some promise
as a manipulator of power companies but soon turned to the pleasures
of life abroad, especially fast cars, women, and Riviera casinos.
Gould's eldest daughter, Helen, alone showed character and a sense

of responsibility, devoting herself to a vast miscellany of minor charities. A younger daughter, Anna, a spoiled, unattractive girl, acquired an insolent French count who squandered no less than $5 million of her inheritance before she divorced him and married his cousin, a marquis.

Although Cornelius Vanderbilt did not indulge any of his children, within a dozen years after his death the Vanderbilts had become the embodiment of pharaonic wealth and power. Taking the dynastic view that his nine daughters were no longer Vanderbilts once they married, he ignored them in his plans for eternalizing his name. But his three sons were hardly the answer to his dreams of family grandeur. The youngest, George, died in Paris at the age of twenty-five. His second son, Cornelius Jeremiah, was an epileptic; even more unfortunate, he was pathologically irresponsible, gambling uncontrollably and passing bad checks everywhere. Repeatedly his father committed him to an insane asylum—a common way of dealing with epileptics—but he was soon released because he was not insane but simply without scruples or shame.

Because William H. Vanderbilt, the eldest son, was a heavy-bodied boy with a sluggish disposition, the Commodore treated him with disdain. William was clerking in Daniel Drew's brokerage office when a nervous disorder caused him to retreat to the family farm on Staten Island in New York Bay. But he had a kind of cunning under the clodlike exterior, and eventually his father rewarded him by letting him manage the bankrupt Staten Island Railway and then the more valuable Hudson and Harlem lines. He developed into a methodical executive; at last, at forty-eight, he was made manager of the vast network of Vanderbilt roads.

Like his father, William enjoyed driving fast trotters and soon joined in the impromptu races on Harlem Lane. He was not a man of fashion, but as head of the Vanderbilt clan he learned to play his part. In a sense he was led into it when his son, Willie K., built a mansion on Fifth Avenue. William Henry thereupon commissioned the grandest of triple mansions for himself and his two married daughters on the next block. Employing 700 workmen, including sixty foreign sculptors and carvers, the builders raised a palace in a style they called "Greek Renaissance." In its furnishings it was an object lession in ostentation and clutter. The drawing room was littered with objets d'art ranging from cloisonnées, lacquers, and a royal Polish drinking flagon to glass-doored bookcases containing untouched sets of books bound in the finest leather. The house had its own telephone system and an electrically controlled refrigerator. Adjacent to it was a stable with a glassed-over courtyard where horses could be exercised in any weather. William Henry commissioned a three-volume work about his home: with supreme disingenuousness, the author declared that it was a "typical American residence" and "nothing but what a reasonable and practical family may live up to." No one knows what princely fee he was paid to treat one of the most extravagant mansions of the period as though it were a modest little cottage.

William Henry soon began to collect paintings. He was attracted by the obvious and banal: superficial elegance, as in Boldini's *Ladies of the First Empire,* and matronly voluptuousness, as in Bouguereau's *Going to the Bath.* Typical was his admiration for a painting by Constant Troyon showing oxen turning away from a plowed furrow—just as he had seen them on his Staten Island farm. In such directions he spent about $1.5 million.

The year of the Commodore's death, 1877, was a dark one in the annals of American railroads, marking a radical change in the attitude of laboring men toward their masters, the captains of industry. The trouble began with a strike resulting from a wage cut on the Baltimore and Ohio and spread swiftly westward, engulfing Pittsburgh, Chicago, St. Louis, and San Francisco in train-burning and pitched battles. The strikers lost on every front except one: it was the beginning of a militant labor movement in the United States. The insolence of the Vanderbilts and Goulds gave rise, moreover, to a new image in American life—that of the "bloated plutocrat," a man who had reached the top by craft and ruthless drive. Suddenly the bright doctrine of unrestricted competition seemed not so bright. There would forever after be an ambivalence in the common man's view of the captains of industry, resentment mixing with envy, skepticism tainting respect.

Lacking the personality that made his father's arrogance seem colorful, William Henry's disdain for his employees and the public seemed merely offensive. Once, during a newspaper interview in 1882, he was caught in what became a classic expression of the money lord's contempt for hoi polloi. When he explained that the only reason he kept the New York Central's Chicago Limited running was the competition of the Pennsylvania Railroad, the reporter asked whether he hadn't also considered the public. "The public be damned!" was William Henry's reply. In the same interview he said of the anti-monopoly movement: "It is a movement inspired by a set of fools and blackmailers. . . . When I want to buy up any politician, I always find the Anti-Monopolists the most purchasable." His attitude toward the public was a cynical distortion of the pioneer credo of individualism. Not until the Interstate Commerce Act of 1887 and the Sherman Anti-Trust Act of 1890 would there be any official disclaimer of this predatory view.

At his death in 1885 William Henry left an estate of $200 million. He was laid to rest in the family mausoleum, a Romanesque chapel that is said to have cost $5 million.

The progression from uncurbed fortune-making to uncurbed extravagance had taken only fifty years, or little more than two generations. Capitalism and democracy had not yet learned to live together. Men of wealth found themselves with a power to which all men bowed. They could corrupt public officials, flout the law, demoralize business practice, ignore religion, oppress their employees, and exploit the nation's resources almost at will. Unlike elected officials, they had power without responsibility. And unlike the best of the European nobility, they had not even a tradition of *noblesse oblige*.

# 5

DREAMERS
OF A GOLDEN WEST

There is an old belief that man in his migrations moves ever westward. Europeans long dreamed of finding a western passage to the Indies. The New World was discovered in the West and became the Promised Land for Europe's millions. And Americans from the earliest days of the Republic saw the West as a gateway to endless opportunity.

There was much that was romantic and almost mystical in the attitude toward the western wilderness. As early as 1780, St. John de Crèvecoeur, a French nobleman's son, described the American frontier as an Arcadia and the American farmer as a nobleman of the soil. Influenced, however indirectly, by such views, Americans acquired a faith in what Henry Nash Smith called the regenerative powers of the virgin land. Thoreau, adding the twist of a New England individualist, went so far as to say, "in wildness is the preservation of the world"—an antidote to the dead tameness of civilization. Paradoxically, the pioneers who shared this view were the first to tame the wild and begin its domestication.

Americans have always been movers. Cotton Mather decried the tendency almost 300 years ago, and as soon as the colonies had achieved independence, the movement became a stream. Soon the frontier of the United States was across the Missouri, and the "West" was anywhere from western New York to the Mississippi. When the westering impulse invaded an eastern region, it spread irresistibly, carrying away the prosperous even more often than the poor, the practical men as well as the dreamers. It struck especially hard among the rocky hill farms of New England, leaving whole districts scarred by deserted farmhouses and moldering barns. And once a man moved, it was unsettlingly easy, especially after a crop ruined by drought, gale, or chinch bugs, to move farther west, to another place with fresh promise. Farmers went from Massachusetts or Connecticut to Ohio, then to Illinois, Wisconsin, or Missouri, then to Iowa and Minnesota and finally to Kansas, Nebraska, Dakota, and Utah. How wishful the urge could be is illustrated by the pioneer who in 1818 wrote of the rich country he was passing through: "This is a land of plenty but we are proceeding to a land of abundance." By the 1830s the urge was so strong that Alexis de Tocqueville saw it as "a game of chance" pursued for "the emotions it excites, as much as for the gain it procures."

Always there was another farmstead where the soil would be blacker, the grass greener, the wheat taller, the springs more plentiful, the weather more agreeable, the game fatter, and the pests more merciful. So after five, six, or seven years the meager furniture, the chipped dishes, the patched clothes, the tools, the old keepsakes would be packed, the neighbors bade good-bye, and the huge covered wagon would roll bravely down the rutted roads into the West. If a settler stayed on, he did so because he found the land tolerable or he had survived disasters long enough to take root or he lacked the strength to move again. But some moved as many as four and five times in the years between 1850 and 1880.

Such a mover was Richard Garland, father of Hamlin, famous in afteryears as a pioneer of realism in American fiction. Hamlin later described his father's life in *Trail-Makers of the Middle Border* and in his autobiography, *A Son of the Middle Border,* poignant evocations of a man who had forever to be on the frontier.

Richard Garland began life as the American farmboy of tradition. Born in Maine in 1830 when it was the northeast frontier of New England, his father, a grim deacon of the church, put him out to work for wages at the age of nine. Driving a team of oxen over the harsh and hilly land of a neighbor, Dick earned a dollar a week— which went to his father—and meager board. After a few years he

ran away for a season to help build what was in the 1840s the eighth
wonder of the world, a railroad. Then, at seventeen, with no more
education than a few months of schooling yearly, he went off to Boston, the Big City, to work as a teamster. A strong and willing lad,
he was prospering, loved the city and especially the theaters, when
news came in 1848 of the discovery of gold out West.

In a moment the entire East crackled with the fire of immigration.
Many set out for California; others headed for the unploughed prairie
country, the boundless level Eden, free of steep slopes, crops of rocks,
and stone bruises. Word came to Richard that an uncle had gone off
to Wisconsin and that other hill farmers were following. So Richard
threw up his job in Boston and along with a small band of Maine
farmers took the train over the mountains, an Erie Canal boat from
Troy to Lake Erie, a steamer across the lakes to the little frontier
port of Milwaukee, and finally a covered wagon over tortuous roads
to a raw settlement in Brownsville, Wisconsin.

Garland was only twenty and craved something more exciting than
a farm all year round. Each winter for seven years he went up to the
north woods to fell trees and do the dangerous job of piloting a raft
of logs down the rapids of the Wisconsin River into the Mississippi.
In 1858, when his family and friends moved west to the valley of the
La Crosse River, near the Mississippi, he finally tried to settle down.
He married, bought a quarter section in a coulee, and raised a tiny
frame house—although log cabins were still common—for himself
and his bride. His wife, Isabel McClintock, was a gentle, sturdy
young woman from a family of men known for their huge size,
strength, a love of their fiddles, and what Hamlin describes as Celtic
melancholy.

The site was pleasant but not easy to clear. While Garland toiled
like a field slave, his wife worked harder than any Southern house
slave: she carded wool, spun yarn, knit socks, and made jackets,
trousers, gowns, bonnets, rag carpets, quilts, candles, sausages, and
sauerkraut. She churned butter, dried fruit, plucked chickens, kept a
vegetable garden, and bore three children.

Surrounded by New Englanders with Free Soil sympathies—
although Norwegians and Germans were moving into the valley—
and unable to forget how in Boston he had heard the great Wendell
Phillips rage against slavery, Richard Garland was ready to enlist

soon after the Civil War began. But three young children and a wife·
kept him on the farm till he had paid the mortgage. Finally, in the
dark days of 1863, he joined Grant's men on the approaches to Vicksburg. For six months he served as a scout and courier; then typhoid
laid him low and he was mustered out. He arrived home emaciated,
but harvest time drove him back to work at once. In the seasons that
followed he toiled backbreakingly in field and stable, but even before
he had cleared the last acres he was dreaming of the level land he
had seen in his travels farther west. He reminisced sometimes of the
wonders of Boston, but whenever the McClintocks gathered on
family occasions and took out their fiddles after dinner they sooner or
later sang,

> *Then o'er the hills in legions, boys,*
> *Fair freedom's star*
> *Points to the sunset regions, boys,*
> *Ha, ha, ha-ha!*

But to Garland's wife it was a song of sad augury, prophesying parting from friends and relatives, tearing up roots, and starting over
again in a strange land.

So they moved—to a log cabin on a farm in Iowa. It was sheltered
by white oaks and had a clear spring and plum trees. But in a season
or two Garland sold it for cash and a chance to move out onto the
true prairie. This time they came to rest in a pine shack on a treeless
plain. Now even eleven-year-old Hamlin was expected to take his
turn at the plow, rising at five and turning over two acres of stubble
by nightfall. The house had only the rudest furniture, and much of
the family's clothing was still homemade.

The schoolhouse that the children attended for a few months each
year was a drab box on the bare prairie. Inside it had crudely plas-
tered walls and hacked benches. The only schoolbooks were a Mc-
Guffey *Reader,* an arithmetic, and a geography. But the McGuffey
was enough to give Hamlin a lifelong passion for the English poets
from Shakespeare to Byron. Outside of school, Hamlin traded Bea-
dle's dime novels and wandered, enchanted, from Westerns to historical romances.

The spring after the Garlands arrived, the neighbors helped them put up a plain pine house with a few rooms below and a garret above. It was furnished with several worn pieces, a lone chromo on the wall, a clock with a picture on its face, and a printed portrait of General Grant. The only books were a Bible, a Sunday-school book, Franklin's *Autobiography,* and *The Life of P. T. Barnum.* Later, there would be a rag carpet on the floor and a tiny reed organ, called a melodeon, in the corner.

The summers were very dry, with a fierce sun day after day and often with smoke rising from disastrous prairie fires. Reaping was a cruel task for it had to be done even when the temperature was ninety-five degrees in the shade. And there were heartbreaking accidents, as when a spring gale blew the soil away just as the wheat was sprouting. But when the growing had been good, the abundance of wheat at harvest time was a thing of joy and wonder. Winter was a bleak time punctuated by blizzards that lasted for days, the wind shrieking, the snow drifting ever higher, and the thermometer sometimes at thirty below zero. The only break in the dreary monotony was such homely recreation as an hour or two of singing songs, with sister Harriet playing simple tunes on the melodeon.

In time, the trees near the house became a grove, and sheds and granaries lent an air of permanence to the homestead. Houses sprang up nearby and the farmers started a grange with its social activities— "oyster suppers," picnics, and debates. Revival meetings and quilting bees had become old-fashioned; now there was a county fair with its trotting races, the hypnotic spiel of patent-medicine vendors, and the excitement of booths and crowds.

Convinced of the need for cooperation among farmers, Garland accepted the job of buyer for a newly organized grain elevator in Osage, the county seat, and for a year the Garlands lived in town. To fifteen-year-old Hamlin, it was a revelation in its sidewalks, one or two fine lawns and flower gardens, an "opera house," the Merchants Hotel, a drugstore, an ice cream parlor, saloons, and square dances in the church. Abruptly he was elevated from the rudest of prairie schoolhouses to a seminary that served a good part of the state. The seminary was hardly more than a high school, but its teachers were called professors and it had a chapel, debating society, dramatic group, and visiting lecturers such as Wendell Phillips. Young Garland blossomed into intellectual and social maturity.

For a few years the harvests were good; then, in 1879, the chinch bug swarmed in the billions and destroyed the crops. For Garland there was still only one solution—moving west. It infected even Hamlin at school: the theme of his commencement oration was "going west." Before long, the Garlands, having moved for the fifth time in twenty years, were putting up a shanty in the James River Valley of the Dakota Territory, a vast plain beginning to swarm with land-hungry Scandinavians, Scots, English, and Russians. As the settlers staked their claims, there was a holiday spirit among them, and when sowing began they were possessed by the elation of men seeding their own piece of earth. Then the summer came, with days of fire shriveling all green things. Many abandoned their claims and fled back to the older settlements. The Garlands held out, but after a winter of prairie blizzards young Hamlin turned his back forever on the pioneer life and went east to become a writer. His parents remained on the plains for eight years, years of good crops and bad ones. In the end, the bad years, along with falling prices for wheat, high freight costs, and mounting debts, defeated them once again.

For a time the elder Garland joined in the radical protest movement of Populism, driven by the realization that the pioneer farmer was as subject to the politicians and the economy as the city dweller. Although he was no longer young and the frontier lands were gone and only desert—"irrigation country"—remained open, he was ready to push westward once again. Only when his wife, Belle, exhausted at last, suffered a stroke, did he allow his son to persuade him to retreat. The old couple went back, numb and confused, to a little house not far from the Wisconsin coulee where they had started their life in the West.

Richard Garland had failed. It is difficult to say whether he failed because he had been a pioneer or whether he remained a pioneer because he had failed. What is certain is that he deserved a kinder fate. He had toiled incessantly, was frugal, did not drink, was as God-fearing as any Alger hero, and a model of self-reliance, fortitude, and honesty. But he spent most of his last years on a four-acre plot bought for him by his son with money earned as a teacher and writer in the big cities to the east.

When Richard Garland retreated eastward in 1893, it was the end of a century of restless, compulsive westering, the end of a blind faith in the land. It was the beginning of the end of the United States as a country of independent farmers. (In 1860 there were 6 million farmers in a population of 30 million; over a century later there were still only 6 million but in a population of 240 million.) The Middle Border had become largely a world of small towns and burgeoning cities.

It often took shrewdness and toughness, if not rapacity, for a farmer to prosper. Even as a boy, Zury in Joseph Kirkland's *Zury: The Meanest Man in Spring County* is a sharp trader. Seeing that his father's farm on the Illinois prairie in the 1830s needs hogs if the best use is to be made of the corn his father has planted, he persuades his father to mortgage several quarter sections to get more young pigs. By the time his father dies, the Prouders have a hundred acres in corn, as well as wheat, sheep, and a sea of fat hogs. Zury is not only as rugged and tireless as Richard Garland; he is also hard and crafty. He invests in mortgages and land and although he does not lie or cheat, he drives hard bargains. He marries partly to get his bride's share of her father's farm, and when she dies he marries her sister to get another share. He is uneducated and crude, but because he is a success and a master of all practical matters his neighbors elect him assessor of property and finally a state legislator.

*Zury* is one of the earliest realistic novels of midwestern farm life. But it is even more interesting as a product of the view that success is often achieved by sharp dealing and, if necessary, ruthlessness. The ending of the book, with Zury about to leave for a vacation in Europe, neatly brings to a close, in one man's life, the cycle from pioneer farmer to rich farm capitalist. If one may trust the portrait by Kirkland—he had spent his boyhood in backwoods Michigan and traveled as a railroad auditor throughout Illinois in the late 1850s—Zury's career suggests that the money mania infected countrymen as well as city dwellers. In time, as the clusters of farmsteads on the Middle Border grew into towns, and towns into cities, the life-style and standards of the latter, for better or worse, prevailed. The traditional images of country life, whether on farm or in village, reflected in Currier & Ives prints and in popular novels, were chiefly of a vine-covered cottage complete with happy youngsters, buxom maidens, and fat cattle. The barn is charming, the pigs quaint, smiling yeomen pitch hay merrily, and splendid blacksmiths shoe magnificent horses.

It is always spring—except in gay sleighing scenes—and kindness, humor, and sentiment abound.

It was not until after the Civil War that a few writers started to note the more disagreeable realities of life on the Middle Border, beginning a tradition that would lead directly to Edgar Lee Masters's *Spoon River Anthology,* Sherwood Anderson's *Winesburg, Ohio,* and Sinclair Lewis's *Main Street.* One of the earliest of such novels, Edward Eggleston's *The Hoosier Schoolmaster* (1871), concerns a young teacher in a back-country Indiana town who is accused of a series of local robberies. The characterizations are crude but the comment on small-town men and mores is keen and irreverent. The townspeople emerge as an uncouth lot, not wicked but mean-spirited. They are willing to believe the worst about the new teacher because he is an outsider, and they resort repeatedly to mob law. The biggest boys in the one-room schoolhouse—there are seventeen-year-olds among them—thrash each new schoolmaster; the gentle Hannah, a "bound girl," is treated like a slave by her mistress; and pious women support missionaries in the South Seas while the local almshouse remains a hell on earth. There are some noble or simply good souls, such as the old maid Nancy Sawyer, but the community does not cherish them. The town has, in short, all the crudeness of a backwoods settlement with little of the charming simplicity or country freshness reflected in popular prints. Eggleston had the experience to be a competent recorder: he spent his childhood in frontier Indiana and later served as a Methodist circuit-riding preacher.

There is a much somber cast to E. W. Howe's *The Story of a Country Town* (1883), a novel of northwestern Missouri after the Civil War. The central figure, Jo Erring, an inordinately ambitious youth, destroys himself and the girl he marries through the conviction that an earlier infatuation with another man has sullied her forever. We see an even more bitter residue of the Calvinist tradition in the Reverend Westlock, the narrator's father, around whose church the town springs up. Westlock uses his religion as a levee against the flood of his instincts. The levee bursts and the preacher runs away with the widow Tremaine, who had continually launched offensives against vice. Thus the two who warn most earnestly against temptation prove to be the most vulnerable to it.

It would be misleading to use such fictional characters as evidence of life on the Middle Border did we not know from Howe's autobiography, *Plain People,* that the Reverend Westlock closely resembled his father, an austere Methodist minister. The Reverend Howe was apparently as entangled with women as his fictional counterpart, marrying five times and divorcing three of his wives. Like Westlock he was ousted from his church for unseemly intimacy with a widow who, like Mrs. Tremaine, is a zealous church member.

In the few other novels or autobiographies of the Middle Border that are not bound by pious clichés, religion is often as much a source of dread and guilt as of solace or inspiration. The most dynamic religion in the early Middle West was summed up in revival meetings that swept recurrently across the land, stirring a fervor that sometimes amounted to hysteria. What the circuit riders brought to lonely, overworked men and women in Indiana, western Pennsylvania, Ohio, Illinois, Kentucky, and Tennessee was not so much dogma or creed as emotional release, drama, and hope. Primitive, long-buried impulses surged to the surface when thousands gathered in fields or groves and submitted to the shamanlike preachers. The speakers lashed their listeners till they moaned and wept, and then swept them into exultation with glorious visions and heavenly promises.

The first Methodist circuit riders, usually without formal training, churches, or possessions, rode from place to place, delivering as many as ten sermons a week. As the frontier coalesced into villages and towns, small-town ministers in their frame churches became the central figures in each community. The average Methodist minister of the Middle Border was sobersided and devout, but just as the frontier encouraged ruffians among the settlers, so it gave rise to primitives among the preachers. With Dickensian bite, Eggleston describes Mr. Bosaw, the "hard-shell" Baptist preacher in an Indiana village, as a sniffling, nasal-voiced illiterate. He is a backwoods grotesque whose doctrine is a caricature of Calvinism: "If you're elected, you'll be saved; if you a'n't, you'll be damned. God'll take care of his elect. It's a sin to run Sunday-schools, or temp'rance s'cieties, or to send missionaries. You let God's business alone. What is to be, will be, and you can't hender it."

By the 1860s, however, a new type of minister was emerging here and there. In his novel, Howe's own sympathies lie not with the

Reverend Westlock but with his successor, the Reverend Goode Shepherd, who thinks religion should make men happy, not miserable, and believes in angels more than in devils. "The right kind of religion will," he says, "let sunlight in at the window, and fill the house with content and happiness. I became a Christian man because I longed for heaven, rather than because I feared the dreadful abode of the wicked, and it is my intention to introduce this gospel here." A kind and gentle man, he represents a giant step away from Calvinism and its camp-meeting mutations.

Much the same kind of shift is recorded in Hamlin Garland's memories of his youth. Although revival meetings were waning by the end of the Civil War, the first winter, 1870, of the Garland's sojourn in western Wisconsin was made memorable for eleven-year-old Hamlin by a revival held in the schoolhouse. An evangelist, already "old-fashioned," who hurled threats of fire and brimstone at his transfixed listeners, cast a pall of puritanical gloom over the community. Yet everyone went to hear him night after night because he broke the monotony of village life with dramatic and occasionally nightmarish visions. The sight of sober citizens sobbing hysterically was one that Hamlin Garland could never forget.

But in time Garland's own sympathies were stirred by a warmer, gentler doctrine preached by a few young ministers. He never forgot the rapture inspired by a very unorthodox young Methodist minister who pleaded for a faith in beauty. "We have been taught that beauty is a snare of the evil one," he said, "but I say that God desires loveliness and hates ugliness. He is not a God of pain, of darkness and gloom; he is a God of delight and consolation." But that was late in the 1870s and the Middle Border was changing. To those who had moved farther west, the communities of Indiana, Ohio, and Illinois already seemed as settled and staid as any in old New England.

Although a great many emigrants still continued to stream into the Middle Border, the goal after 1849 was more often the Far West— the Eldorado across the Rockies rather than the imagined Eden of the prairies. The trans-Missouri had been gradually penetrated by explorers, and as early as 1820 Senator Thomas Hart Benton of Missouri announced that it was the destiny of the United States to reach from sea to shining sea. At the beginning of the century Lewis and Clark had shown that it was possible to push across prairie and scrubland, over the Continental Divide, and down the rivers to the Pacific Coast. Men who sailed the Pacific—whalers from New Bedford and Yankees who sought the fur of the sea otter—reported that California was a benign land occupied by picturesque Franciscan missions and indolent Mexican-Spanish settlers. But getting there required a six-month journey around Cape Horn or a fever-fraught mule trip across the Isthmus of Panama. So the task remained for men to chart the trails across the 1,800 miles between the Missouri and the western Sierras.

Zebulon Pike, Benjamin Bonneville, and other explorers had made forays into that vast *terra incognita,* but the wilderness had soon closed around their paths. Mountain men—trappers, fur traders, voyageurs such as Jedediah Smith, Jim Bridger, Kit Carson, Joe Walker, and Bill Williams—had lived in it, but they were hunters, fighters, guides, caring little about maps or records, or locating places for settlement. A few pioneers such as Marcus Whitman, the missionary who led a wagon train to Oregon in 1836, were their own pathfinders, but they were rare.

In the 1840s the trans-Mississippi remained the last great outlet for American enterprise and energy, the last refuge for fugitives from settled lives, for lovers of solitude and untamed wilderness—and for fortune hunters. Even a Boston Brahmin, the historian Francis Parkman, who made a trip west for his health, testified: "To him who has once tasted the reckless independence, the haughty self-reliance, the sense of irresponsible freedom, which the forest life engenders, civilization thenceforth becomes flat and stale . . . and often he upon whom it has cast its magic . . . remains a wanderer and an Ishmaelite to the hour of his death." For some, especially the young men, the West offered pure adventure—fighting Indians, hunting buffalo, defying blizzards, scaling great peaks, spending days in the saddle and nights around a campfire under the stars.

Into this vast arena moved John Charles Frémont, craving glory. He had all the equipment of a hero—courage, dash, gallant manners, a darkly handsome face—and he did everything a hero should do. The western frontier had burst on the national consciousness as early as the 1830s, and by the presidential campaign of 1840, as William

Henry Harrison demonstrated, a log cabin, hard cider, and a coon-skin cap had become talismanic objects for a candidate. Frémont led his first western expedition in 1842, and by 1854, the year of his last expedition, the West had been won. Now came the day of the settler, the exploiter, and the speculator.

Of patrician Virginia stock, Beverly Whiting, fleeing from a love-less marriage to an old man, had eloped with a penniless French émi-gré, Charles Frémon, and in 1813 bore him a son, John Charles, out of wedlock. Such a beclouded birth may explain why John Charles would seek, sometimes rashly, to prove his worth over and over again.

Although Frémon died when "Charley" was seven and left him a poor widow's son, his boyhood in Charleston was not unpleasant, and he made his way easily. With characteristic impulsiveness he became infatuated with a Creole girl and so neglected his studies that the authorities at Charleston College expelled him a few months be-fore graduation. But his very eagerness won him the sponsorship of several influential men. The first of these, Joel R. Poinsett, first U.S. minister to Mexico, found him a post teaching mathematics to mid-shipmen aboard a sloop-of-war on a South American cruise. Poinsett then secured him a place with a party surveying a railroad route in the South. After that came a reconnaissance for the U.S. Topograph-ical Corps of the strip beyond the Mississippi to which the Cherokee Indians were being transferred. In this rugged country Frémont learned the crafts of camp and trail.

Again through Poinsett, Frémont was commissioned a second lieu-tenant in the Topographical Corps and appointed assistant to Joseph Nicollet, distinguished French mathematician and geographer, on an expedition to the West. He joined Nicollet in St. Louis. The French-man was not only a savant but a man of the world, and he soon introduced his young assistant to the cultivated French society of the city. But St. Louis was even more interesting as a springboard to the West. From there and nearby Independence, Missouri, the great wagon trails fanned out. Its population was under 10,000, but it was alive with emigrants preparing to push westward, weather-beaten trappers in buckskin, Indian braves and their squaws, voyageurs, keelboatmen, French nuns, Germans and Mexicans and black slaves. Across the river, the country was wide, unfenced, and full of promise.

On this first trip the expedition went up the Minnesota River to the Lac Qui Parle trading post of the French-Canadian Joseph Renville, who controlled the Indian tribes of a vast domain. Returning to St. Louis for the winter, the travelers set out on their second journey in April 1839. Taking several mountain men, including Étienne Provôt (for whom Provo, Utah, would be named), they rode one of the crude new steamboats 1,300 miles to Fort Pierre on the upper Missouri. Here, in the middle of Indian and buffalo country, they took on a well-known guide, Louison Frenière, and explored the Red River of the North.

The importance for Frémont of these expeditions was great: apprenticeship under a trained scientist and exposure to such masters of the wilderness as Provôt, Frenière, and Renville. Back in Washington early in the 1840, Frémont joined Nicollet in making a report in person to President Van Buren. Nicollet credited him generously, and Frémont came away with an ambition that would consume him for the next fourteen years—glory as an explorer.

An old friend of Nicollet's, the Swiss-born scientist Ferdinand Hassler, who headed the Coast Survey, invited Nicollet and Frémont to live and work in the rambling house he owned in Washington. Among the best known of their visitors was the senior senator from Missouri, Thomas Hart Benton. Benton had been in the Senate since 1820 and had long been the most ardent American expansionist, harboring a vision of the United States as stretching from coast to coast. An immensely forceful personality, he was pontifical and conceited, an eloquent but interminable speaker, and a harsh antagonist. Frémont later declared that he was immediately struck by Benton's vision of the West as essential to an "American empire." The hero had found his epic. In Benton, Frémont acquired his most powerful sponsor, and in Benton's daughter, Jessie, his future wife and zealous champion.

Jessie Benton, although not yet sixteen, was already known as one of the loveliest, most intelligent and independent young ladies in Washington society. She was, as Senator James Buchanan put it, the square root of Tom Benton. Benton had treated her as an intellectual equal, making her help him with his speeches and reports, and reading the Greek and Latin classics with her. At the age of eight she was already visiting the Senate gallery to hear him proclaim manifest destiny and the need for a national road from St. Louis to Santa Fe. At fourteen she was sent to the most fashionable boarding school in the Washington area. It was there that Frémont met her.

It was love at once. She was eager and brimming with bright talk. He was eleven years older, the charismatic young lieutenant just back from exploring Indian country. Mother and Father Benton protested that she was too young. Senator Benton went further: to Frémont's amazement he was notified that he would replace the ailing Nicollet in completing the mapping of the Mississippi-Missouri system. Great as Frémont's frustration may have been at being parted from Jessie, he did not hesitate to accept. By fall he was back in Washington. The separation of the young couple only sharpened desire, and when the Senator and his wife still firmly opposed the union, the couple eloped. Benton, a veteran of political wars, knew when he was defeated.

The senator also knew that the West was in need of someone who would not only map the trails but describe the countryside—the safest fords, the best passes over the mountains, the available wood, game, and drinking water, and the temper of the Indians. So he pushed through an appropriation for an expedition to chart that rudimentary path of empire, soon to become the greatest emigrant route in history, the Oregon Trail. Later, Frémont declared that the expedition had had broader implications—not only to aid emigration but to indicate "the best positions for military posts." When Nicollet proved too ill to lead the expedition, Benton decided that Frémont must take over. It was a matchless wedding gift.

In St. Louis, Frémont took on the master hunter Lucien B. Maxwell as well as nineteen Creole and Canadian voyageurs. Then, in a boat going up to Westport Landing, present-day Kansas City, he met Christopher "Kit" Carson, who was, at thirty-three, on the way to becoming the most famous of mountain men. Despite his fearsome reputation as an Indian fighter and a hunter, Carson was, unlike Frémont, quiet, calm, and completely reliable—which is undoubtedly why they were able to get along together for many years. Frémont immediately offered him $100 a month to join the expedition. Carson accepted.

On all his expeditions in the next twelve years Frémont was able to secure the services of so many legendary mountain men because the beaver they had relied on had been all but trapped out. Supreme individualists, intoxicated by wilderness, and endlessly resourceful,

these men were true trailblazers of the West. They lived for the moment and the physical challenge—trapping beaver in icy waters,
hunting their daily food, coping with storm and thirst and savage
attack, contenting themselves with Indian women, coming once a
year to a post to sell their pelts and spend their money in a grand
debauch.

Frémont's first expedition went only to the foothills of the Rockies.
The trail had been traveled by emigrant trains for seven or eight
years, but what made Frémont famous was his 120-page report—which
Jessie rewrote freely and skillfully. It told emigrants not only about
the trail, weather, water, grass, fuel, game, and such, but was infused
with a sense of discovery that captured the imagination. It exploded
forever the legend that much of the West was godforsaken desert. It
acknowledged that there were harsh and barren places, but it also
made clear how much of it contained broad rivers and swift streams,
stands of beech and cottonwood, rich bottomlands, and buffalo, elk,
and antelope. A stirring description of a buffalo hunt ends: "Indians
and buffalo make the poetry and life of the prairie, and our camp
was full of their exhilaration." Frémont's report immediately made
him one of the heroes of the westward movement. When Jessie gave
birth to a girl a few days after his return, his triumph seemed
complete.

Benton quickly secured orders for Frémont to survey the remainder of the Oregon Trail. By late spring of 1843, Frémont was ready
in St. Louis with the best-equipped expedition ever assembled in the
United States. Besides a grand array of chronometers, barometers,
and sextants, Frémont had borrowed a howitzer from the St. Louis
arsenal, planning to use it in fighting off Indians. Instead, it almost
ended his career.

While Frémont and his men were at Westport Landing, he received
a startling message from Jessie: *"My dearest: Do not delay another day.
Trust me, and start at once."* Frémont promptly led his men far enough
into the prairie to be out of touch with the town. It was fourteen
months before he learned the reason for the message. Jessie had
opened a letter to Frémont from Colonel Abert, head of the Topographical Corps, ordering him to return to Washington to explain
why he was taking a cannon on a "peaceful" scientific survey,
and informing him that he would be replaced. With staggering high-

handedness Jessie, guided by "intuition," had sent her husband the message and then written to Abert explaining why her husband would need the howitzer in Blackfeet country. Senator Benton wrote to Washington hotly demanding an explanation. Abert, a reasonable man, saw that it was too late to stop Frémont, and never answered Jessie or the senator.

Frémont went on his way. At the foot of the Rockies, he was joined by Carson and another redoubtable mountain man, young Alexis Godey, a Creole. After struggling for weeks to find another pass farther south, they finally went through the South Pass and followed the Oregon Trail to the Great Salt Lake region. (Frémont's description of this region, especially of a fertile river valley, led Brigham Young four years later to make it the Zion of the great Mormon trek from Nauvoo, Illinois.) Late in October the expedition reached the Columbia River. To return by way of the Oregon Trail seemed much too tame to Frémont. So he moved south into Nevada and then abruptly announced that he would cross the High Sierras into California.

Despite the Mexican order banning Americans from entering California, Benton had undoubtedly encouraged Frémont to make a reconnaissance into that most tempting land. But Frémont's men and animals were so exhausted that the decision to scale that uncharted mountain barrier in midwinter was extremely rash. Within ten days the going became so rough that they had to abandon the howitzer and were reduced to eating their mules. Weak and emaciated, they straggled into the Sacramento Valley and up to the thick-walled adobe enclosure known as Sutter's Fort. Sutter, a gentle-mannered German-Swiss, greeted them most hospitably. A penniless immigrant on his arrival in California in 1839, Sutter had bought a trading post, become a Mexican citizen, and received a huge land grant. Soon he had made himself lord of 150,000 acres and hundreds of Indians, Mexicans, and Pacific Islanders.

Here the travelers feasted on venison, smoked tongue, fruits, and Rhine wines. Frémont noted the richness of the country and the prosperity of the American and European settlers. He heard how lax Mexican rule was but how high the taxes were. He probably did not hear that the native "Californios" were an affable people who made an art of living pleasantly. His appetite for adventure still unsatisfied,

Frémont started south. His description of the band as it moved through the San Joaquin Valley is self-consciously romantic: "Our cavalcade made a strange and grotesque appearance . . . guided by a civilized Indian, attended by two wild ones from the sierra, a Chinook from Columbia; and our own mixture of American, French, German." In the south the expedition cut eastward and made its way back to St. Louis.

In an impressive 300-page report, Frémont and Jessie spread before a fascinated public the wonders and oddities, human, animal, vegetable, and mineral, of the Columbia Valley, the Great Basin, and California. It was a tremendous success, presenting Frémont as heroic yet modest, decisive yet sensitive. It took an Emerson to detect the flaws in the spirit that moved Frémont. In his *Journal* for 1846 he wrote that Frémont continually remarks on "the picture . . . which we make," and that his "passion for seeming, must be highly inflamed if the terrors of famine and thirst . . . Arapahoes and Utahs . . . could not repress this eternal vanity of *how we must look.*" But Frémont was the hero of the hour, the President making it official by giving him a double brevet promotion, first to lieutenant and then to captain.

Soon a third expedition was in the making. National events helped. Polk, an expansionist, became President in 1844. Texas, independent for nine years, was annexed in 1845. War with Mexico seemed inevitable. So Frémont was authorized to explore the Cascade Mountains, the Sierra Nevada and the Great Basin—all of them possible avenues into California. "My private instructions," Frémont claimed in his *Memoirs,* "were, if needed, to foil England by carrying the war now imminent with Mexico into the territory of California." Unfortunately, such instructions came not from his superior, Secretary of War Marcy, but from his self-appointed advisers, Benton and Secretary of the Navy Bancroft. Frémont was plainly convinced that the expedition had a political mission, the acquisition of California.

Quickly Frémont recruited more than sixty men, a dazzling array of famous guides and hunters. In the late fall of 1845, they moved through the Rockies and went on to the wretched little town of Yerba Buena, soon to become San Francisco, and south to Monterey. The Mexican commander, Don José Castro, was deeply mistrustful of the American intruders, but Frémont insisted that his aims were purely scientific. However, instead of going north, he swung southwest, straight through settled areas. Although Frémont had no right whatever to do so, he built a log fort in the Gabilan Mountains and ran up the American flag. "If attacked we will fight to the extremity," he sounded off, "and refuse quarter, trusting to our country to avenge our deaths." Castro's answer was to brand them a band of robbers. After three days, Frémont withdrew. On the surface, the exchange was something of a comic opera, but it really had much more significance, for it brought about an open break between Americans and Mexicans.

Frémont was pushing north when a Marine Corps officer, Lieutenant A. H. Gillespie, gave him a dispatch from Secretary of State Buchanan urging him to conciliate the Californians and aid them in achieving independence. Whether Gillespie also brought secret instructions encouraging Frémont to take an aggressive stand has been a matter of harsh controversy. The only alternative, moreover, was to turn back, and perhaps be reproached for lacking boldness and enterprise. If there were any qualities that Frémont had in full measure, it was these. Late in May he marched back into California in a move that was—as he long afterward sadly, dimly remembered—a turning point in his career.

Many of the 800 Americans in northern California were hardworking ranchers, but a number were drifters or adventurers. Mainly Anglo-Saxon and Protestant, rugged and energetic, they looked on the easygoing Californios, all of them Latin and Catholic, as a shiftless breed, and dubbed them "greasers." The Californios in turn looked on the Americans as largely boorish intruders. Since some of Frémont's men shared the settlers' view, there was much pressure on him to take action. He gave way: hearing that Castro was inciting the local Indians, a wretched people, he rode roughshod through every Indian village in the area.

Then, at Frémont's instigation, thirty-four settlers led by Ezekiel Merritt, a rough frontiersman, and William Ide, a fuzzy-minded farmer-teacher-carpenter, took over the so-called military post of Sonoma. To dignify the mob action, they hoisted a flag made of a strip of petticoat on which someone had painted in pokeberry juice a star and a bear with the words "California Republic" under it, thereby giving the episode the name of the Bear Flag War. In Sonoma, on

July 4, 1846, amid much speechmaking, Frémont organized 234 men into the "California Battalion." At that point Commodore Robert Stockton, politically ambitious, tactless, and a braggart, sailed in and assumed command. He promptly took the California Battalion into the naval service, with Frémont as its major. At the same time, Brigadier General Stephen Watts Kearny, leading a few hundred dragoons, set out from Santa Fe to occupy California. Within a month he and Stockton, with 600 men, occupied Los Angeles. So ended the "war" in California.

Frémont and his "battalion" had meanwhile started south. Made up of voyageurs, ranchers, and adventurers, they were a rough-looking crew—sunburned, with untrimmed beards and long hair, low-crowned felt hats, buckskin trousers, moccasins, and belts hung with pistols and bowie knives. Frémont, spare and wiry, went about in a flannel shirt, leggings, old moccasins, and sometimes with a bandanna around his head. Everything about them proclaimed that they were irregulars not too concerned about the difference between self-defense and aggression.

Not far from Los Angeles they learned of the victory there; when Frémont marched in it was for him a moment of triumph, of vindication after a year of uncertainties. Exultantly Jessie wrote of his promotion to lieutenant-colonel. "So your merit had advanced you in eight years from an unknown second lieutenant to the most talked of and admired lieutenant-colonel in the army." A few months later he would be a prisoner facing court-martial.

The instrument of his casting down was General Kearny, an old-style officer, able but domineering. On reaching Los Angeles, Kearny demanded that Stockton stop organizing a civil government. Stockton rejected the request and proceeded to appoint Frémont governor of California. Kearny summoned Frémont and asked him whether he intended to obey orders. Frémont handed him an icy statement that concluded, "Until you and Commodore Stockton adjust between yourselves the question of rank . . . I shall have to report and receive orders from the Commodore," thereby making an enemy who would never again show him mercy.

For a month or two Frémont was accepted as the civil governor. Then the Secretary of the Navy ordered his officers to turn over all control to Kearny. When Kearny sent a Colonel Mason to Los Angeles to take command, Frémont's stiff-necked reaction ended with Mason threatening to put him in irons and Frémont challenging Mason to a duel. Kearny intervened and started east, with Frémont accompanying him as a virtual prisoner.

Months earlier, Kit Carson had arrived in Washington with the ugly news of the quarrel in California. As the daughter of Senator Benton, Jessie knew what she must do: she went straight to President Polk. The President's diary clearly reveals what he thought of her visit: "I consider that Colonel Frémont was greatly in the wrong when he refused to obey the order issued to him by General Kearny. It was unnecessary, however, that I should say so to Colonel Frémont's wife, and I evaded giving her an answer."

The trial of Frémont, beginning on November 2, 1847, and, involving a general, a famous explorer, the Bentons, and sundry mighty mountain men, was the major news of the day. The charges against Frémont were mutiny and disobedience. Frémont's defense was based chiefly on the conflicting orders issued by the government. On January 31, 1848, the court brought in its verdict: guilty on all charges. The sentence: dismissal from the service. The sentence was excessively severe and for once justified Frémont and Benton's belief that the West Point men were persecuting them. Polk set aside the punishment, but Frémont would have none of it. Angrily he submitted his resignation. All at once, at the age of thirty-four, his career in the army was over. Jessie took it even harder; she began to suffer fainting spells, and the baby she bore in July had a defective heart.

Inevitably Frémont was driven to counter defeat with a stunning exploit; he would cross the Rockies in midwinter—without the support of the army. Benton saw to it that the undertaking had a practical purpose—proving that a railroad through the mountains could be used in winter as well as in summer. So the Frémonts were soon on their familiar journey to St. Louis, the explorer strange in civilian clothes, with cropped beard and hair already streaked with gray. While in California Frémont had given the American consul Thomas O. Larkin $3,000 to purchase some old orchard land overlooking the sea near San Francisco. The consul instead bought a vast tract, fully seventy square miles, in the wild Mariposa area a hundred miles from the sea.

In the eyes of the public Frémont was still the intrepid pathfinder, so he had no difficulty recruiting thirty-four able men. Obviously many joined him in the hope of making their fortunes in California, already known as the land of milk and honey. Although snow was falling heavily by the time the expedition reached Bent's Fort, Frémont decided to cross the Colorado Rockies near the Thirty-seventh Parallel—one of the most inhospitable regions in the United States. Always an impetuous man, he was now also a desperate one.

The expedition paused at Pueblo, Colorado, a cluster of adobe huts occupied by some former mountain men. There Frémont persuaded "Old Bill" Williams to come along as pilot. Brought up on a frontier farm, Williams had become a backwoods Baptist preacher, but in doing missionary work among the Indians he had found it easier to adopt their way of life than to get them to follow his. So he married an Osage woman and lived like an Indian.

In person he had become a caricature of "nature's nobleman," a gaunt heron of a man, dressed in a greasy buckskin shirt tricked out with barbaric beadwork and a blanket cap with two points like wolf's ears. His talk, like an Indian's, combined a few words with gesticulations. Williams was ethically as well as physically no paragon, resorting, when pressed, to stealing herds of horses and even cheating members of his adopted tribe. He was frontier individualism gone to seed, but was considered unmatched in wilderness lore.

Heading across the Sangre de Cristo range and into the San Juan Mountains, with peaks over 14,000 feet high, the expedition entered the gap in the mountains made by the Rio Grande. Then a storm swept down on them and with it, in Frémont's words, "sudden and inevitable ruin." It snowed for three days. Their fires burned great pits in the snow and they shivered and dozed in the bottom of the pits. The starving mules gnawed rawhide ropes and finally one another's manes and tails. Then they froze to death.

On Christmas Day, Frémont dispatched Captain King, Old Bill, Tom Breckenridge, and the botanist Frederick Creutzfeldt to fetch relief from the New Mexico settlements 160 miles to the south. When sixteen days had gone by without word from the relief party, Frémont and four other men set out after them. After Frémont had gone, nine of the remaining twenty-four men died. Within a few days, Frémont caught up with the first relief party. Breckenridge described how he had killed a deer and Old Bill had torn off "great mouthfuls of the raw flesh." But all the early accounts indicate that the meat that sustained the three men came not from a deer but from King, and that Frémont found King's body "horribly devoured." Frémont had the three men brought down to the nearest settlement and then went on to Taos, washing his hands of any further responsibility for them. Automatically Frémont resumed the attitude of the dauntless leader. By some mental alchemy, he was even able to announce: "The result was entirely satisfactory. It convinced me that neither the snow nor the mountain ranges were obstacles in the way of the road."

It was April 1849 and as he passed along the Gila Road to California he heard astonishing news. From a horde of Mexicans on their way to "Alta California" he learned of the discovery of gold. As the owner of a vast Mariposa tract he was as much excited by the news as were the Sonorans. Nothing is more fascinating in Frémont's career than the abrupt alterations in his fortunes. He should have arrived in California a broken man; instead, he rode back on a wave of jubilation. Eighteen months later he would go back to Washington a millionaire and a senator from California.

After a harrowing journey across the Isthmus of Panama, Jessie arrived, exhausted and ill. With his mines yielding gold and his exploration reports in great demand, Frémont was soon on fire with ambition again. After a visit to the ranch, Bayard Taylor, then a young correspondent for the New York *Tribune,* wrote of Frémont's hawklike eyes, thin, weather-browned face, and a strength combined with refinement, and hailed him as "the Columbus of our central wilderness."

For a time Frémont sent gold down from the Mariposa mines in bags estimated at $25,000 each. But thousands of prospectors had drifted onto the tract, and he also saw that the surface gold was nearly exhausted and that he would need heavy machinery to mine the quartz veins. California had acquired over 80,000 immigrants in one year, and a number of citizens began to clamor for more and better government. A constitutional convention was held in Monterey, but Frémont took little part in these proceedings. This was typical of his political activities in the next fifteen years—never truly committing himself, yet willing to accept high office as though it were an accolade. The first California legislature elected him and William Gwin senators. But when he drew lots with Gwin, he won only what remained of the short term. After a month in Washington he had to return to California to run for reelection. A poor politician, he was decisively defeated.

He was not too disappointed for he had already plunged deeply into gold mining. Partly because of complaints about a devious agent whom he had authorized to raise money for mining equipment in London, the Frémonts now went to Europe themselves. By April 1852 they had moved from Sierra mining camps to London's Hotel Clarendon. Jessie had always had an affinity for the society of the high-placed and well-born, and she now indulged it to the full, including, in Paris, a villa on the Champs-Élysées, a carriage and footmen, governesses for the children, and entertaining in grand style. Frémont paid for all this with utmost prodigality.

The Frémonts were drawn back to America by financial problems but even more by word that Congress, awakened to the need for a transcontinental railroad, had authorized the exploration of five possible routes to the Pacific. To Frémont's bitter disappointment, army officers were appointed to lead the various expeditions. Again Frémont reacted with a bold gesture. With Benton's backing he organized another expedition. Since the government favored a southern route, he decided that he would once more follow a central route and, to establish its feasibility, again do it in winter.

This time he took only twenty-one men and no guides. He crossed the Continental Divide by way of Williams Pass and struck across Nevada to the Sierras. Finding the latter impassable because of snow, the expedition turned south, cut through Walker's Pass, and entered San Francisco on April 16. Frémont hurried back to New York and tried to make a case for the route he had followed. But no one heeded him. So the expedition, his fifth and last, failed in its purpose. But it undoubtedly did help to thrust Frémont, most unexpectedly, into the political spotlight.

For thirty years the Missouri Compromise had kept a lid on the simmering slavery issue. Then, early in the 1850s, the lid was jarred loose by the Fugitive Slave Law and in 1854 it was blown off by clashes in Kansas. By 1855 the movement toward a new party, called Republican and dedicated to opposing the spread of slavery, was well under way. It made its appeal not only to anti-slavery elements in the Whig and Democratic parties but also to the violently anti-immigrant and anti-Catholic Know-Nothing, or Native American party. In this highly charged atmosphere all parties cast about for a politically fresh presidential candidate, one free of all alliances and fixed positions. They turned to Colonel Frémont—born in the South, famous in the West, a hero in the North.

The Frémonts had moved to New York, into a fine new brick house on Ninth Street, west of Fifth Avenue. Before long it became the scene of important political conferences. After a while a friend of Frémont's, Representative Nathaniel P. Banks of Massachusetts, convinced him that his place was in the new Republican movement, and that winter Banks drummed up support for him. By the time of the first Republican convention in June 1856, Frémont was a leading candidate. He was backed by an assortment of Northern reformers, from abolitionists to women's rights advocates, all imbued with evangelical enthusiasm. The convention nominated Frémont for President, and the nomination was ratified at the huge Broadway Tabernacle with wild jubilation and the brave slogan "Free Speech, Free Press, Free Soil, Free Men, Frémont and Victory." A presidential candidate was expected to maintain a dignified reserve and simply stand on his record, but Frémont had no political record and therefore the electorate never knew what opinions or plans he had, if any.

The campaign began promisingly for Frémont with huge rallies in New York and Philadelphia. Frémont's lack of political experience did not matter; he was a hero, he was against slavery, and he had a wonderful young wife. Indeed, it sometimes seemed as though people planned to vote for Jessie rather than her husband. But soon the Democratic offensive began. It charged that Frémont was secretly a Catholic—because his father had been one—but the vilest attack was on the circumstances of his birth. "Tell me," the governor of Virginia, Henry Wise, cried, "if the hoisting of the Black Republican flag . . . over you by a Frenchman's bastard, while the arms of civil war are already clashing, is not to be deemed an overt act and declaration of war?" How Frémont, so proud and headstrong, tolerated all this, no one can say.

Since the South had threatened to secede if Frémont won, it is perhaps just as well that he lost. He showed little emotion at the outcome. He had looked on the Presidency as a reward rather than a responsibility and evidently considered the result only a game lost. He was still the hero who did not win.

Quickly he turned his back on politics and sharply expanded his mining operations. He later claimed that the mines yielded $3 million in quartz gold alone between 1850 and 1862. But the cost of development, taxes, and litigation continued to outstrip income. The Frémonts now moved to a small estate on a headland on San Francisco Bay. In the nine years since they had left it, the town had become a prosperous city with many well-built houses, horsecars, and even a full season of opera. Soon literary and political celebrities were frequent visitors at the Frémont place.

Beset by debts, Frémont again went to Europe to raise money. While passing through New York in January 1861 he met Lincoln. The new President still hoped to avoid war, but Frémont did not, and he offered his services, anticipating a conflict. Frémont was right. He was in France when news came of the firing on Fort Sumter and of his appointment as one of the first major-generals. His star rising again, he left for America immediately. Jessie wrote to their estate manager: "Mr. Frémont was called to his old first love and duty, and I have not been so happy in years for him. . . . I am so glad I am going into an atmosphere where dollars and cents are not the first object."

In Washington, Frémont conferred with Lincoln and came away in command of a newly created Department of the West. He later declared that Lincoln had said, "I have given you *carte blanche,*" and he went off to St. Louis convinced that his power was almost unlimited. The task that faced him in the West was staggering: to clothe, feed, arm, train, and deploy an army already numbering 25,000 men, many of them enlisted for only ninety days, in a state that was half Southern and half Northern. It required administrative ability, discretion, and good judgment, especially of people—in all of which Frémont was notably deficient.

St. Louis was muted and sullen, with a Confederate flag flying from secessionist headquarters. The Unionists, led by Frank Blair, Jr., and General Nathaniel Lyon, had forced Governor Claiborne Jackson, a secessionist, to flee. But the rebels rallied and moved to

confront General Lyon's troops at Springfield. Lyon called on Frémont for aid. Frémont, harried by frantic pleas from General Benjamin M. Prentiss, the Union commander at Cairo, advised Lyon to
fall back. Stranded, Lyon attacked. He was killed and 1,300 of his
5,400 men were put out of action. Coming less than three weeks after
the defeat at Bull Run, the battle at Wilson's Creek shocked the
North and loosed a blast of criticism against Frémont. Although he
worked tirelessly, he was tactless and haughty. He—or rather Jessie,
for she was virtually his chief-of-staff—rented a mansion and surrounded himself with a bodyguard of foreign soldiers who wore gaudy
uniforms and screened visitors with Prussian rigor; next to the
average Missouri recruit, they seemed outlandish dandies.

Stung from every side and especially plagued by reports of guer-
rilla raids supported by secessionist sympathizers, he and Jessie decided that he could stop the guerrillas and their supporters by
confiscating their property, including all slaves. So on August 30, 1861,
without warning, he issued his own emancipation proclamation—a
policy-making act of the most momentous kind. As soon as the nation
had recovered from its astonishment, many in the North hailed the
proclamation, but Lincoln and all those who had been trying to conciliate the undecided border states were dismayed. Lincoln wrote to
Frémont ordering him to modify the proclamation. Frémont resisted
stubbornly, forcing Lincoln to modify the proclamation himself. Lincoln now sent Montgomery Blair to investigate Frémont's administration. Frémont quickly passed from arrogant independence to the
bitter conviction that he was being persecuted. As always, Jessie—
General Jessie, some called her—shared his view, and once again she
went directly to the President.

Arriving in Washington, she at once sent a messenger to the President, requesting a hearing. By the same messenger she received a
card saying *"Now, at once, A. Lincoln."* The President, recalling the
episode two years later, said:

> She sought an audience with me at midnight, and tasked me
> so violently with so many things that I had to exercise all the
> awkward tact I have to avoid quarreling with her. She surprised
> me by asking me why their enemy, Montgomery Blair, had
> been sent to Missouri. She more than once intimated that if

General Frémont should decide to try conclusions with me, he could set up for himself.

Jessie reported that Lincoln was hard and unfriendly. Plainly tried to the limit, Lincoln is said to have exclaimed, "You are quite a female politician."

It was a most inopportune moment for a quarrel with a member of the influential Blair family. In northwest Missouri, Colonel Mulligan, confronted by General Price's troops, begged Frémont for reinforcements. No help came, and Price attacked and overwhelmed Mulligan. Adjutant-General Lorenzo Thomas, sent to investigate Frémont, handed in a scathing report. One hundred days after he had taken charge in the West, Frémont was relieved of his command.

On the surface Frémont bore it all almost gaily, convinced that he was the victim of spite. Many newspapers praised him, and he was guest of honor at a dinner given in New York by Henry Ward Beecher. But astute Sam Ward wrote to Secretary Seward: "There is nothing of Frémont save a capacity to endure privation and fatigue. . . . He is so great a humbug that anything like ordinary contact with the people would betray his vapidness and wear out the prestige which he only sustains by the mystery of silence and invisibility." Bowing to Frémont's admirers, Lincoln gave him another chance, appointing him commander of a newly created Mountain Department in western Virginia and eastern Tennessee. But when he failed to produce results within three months, the President placed the department under the Army of Virginia, commanded by General Pope. Frémont at once asked to be relieved, convincing Lincoln once and for all that he was unreliable and intractable.

With his careers as frontier path-marker, political figure, gold mine operator, and general behind him, Frémont rode more brashly than ever into another arena of great risks and glittering rewards—railroads. With deficits at Mariposa piling up uncontrollably, he had put the estate into the hands of speculators and sharp lawyers, and by the close of the war it became apparent that he had been bilked of almost all his holdings by a string of swindlers.

Frémont was still rich enough to buy a one-hundred-acre estate with a gray stone mansion overlooking the Hudson River near Tarrytown. With a French chef, servants, tutors for the children, horses, and a large library, the Frémonts lived at "Pocaho"—or occasionally in their New York townhouse—in quiet luxury. Jessie impressed distinguished guests and a few adoring protégées with her wit, bold opinions, and broad sympathies. As a railroad magnate, Frémont played the role of a man of substance.

Yet at fifty-two he was as rash and driven as ever. He now put his entire fortune into a projected Memphis and El Paso Railroad and was made its president. Having acquired franchises from several western states, Frémont soon had visions of a road from coast to coast. Arrangements were made to start building westward from Arkansas and eastward from San Diego. By 1869, millions of dollars in bonds had been sold, a good part of it in France, mainly by means of outrageous claims that the "Transcontinental Memphis Pacific" was already in operation from Norfolk to Memphis, with good progress being made on other sections. The agents also claimed land grants, federal subsidies, and a government guarantee of 6 percent interest on the bonds.

Frémont later argued that he knew nothing about these representations. But his disavowals were tardy and inadequate. Hardly had work started on the road than it was staggered by every kind of difficulty—landslides, steep grades, and unanticipated costs. Disaster followed fast. The road went into receivership. French authorities brought criminal charges against Frémont and the agents. When Frémont failed to appear in a Paris court he was condemned; it was only a judgment by default but it left a stain on his reputation.

It also left him, at the age of sixty, almost penniless. The townhouse in New York went, and then Pocaho, gradually, pathetically. The Frémonts moved across New York harbor to a small cottage on Staten Island. Jessie turned to writing to help support them, doing scores of small pieces during the next fifteen years, most of them nostalgic and chatty—the causeries of a *grande dame*. Frémont was thus inordinately pleased when in 1878 he was appointed territorial governor of Arizona at $2,000 a year. As their train crawled through the western mountains, bittersweet memories crowded in on the aging man, and he wrote a poem, of which one stanza read:

> *The buoyant hopes and busy life*
> *Have ended all in hateful strife and baffled aim,*

*The world's rude contact killed the rose,*
*No more its shining radiance shows*
*False roads to fame*

The couple rented a small house in Prescott, but after a year Jessie returned to Staten Island, and Frémont rejoined her in 1883. A harsh but haunting view of the Frémonts in their Staten Island cottage has been left by Josiah Royce, only thirty years old but already on his way to eminence as a scholar. He had undertaken a history of the conquest of California and, convinced that Frémont had been the villain in that drama, he unfeelingly decided to test his theories by exposing them to the Frémonts themselves. After one interview he reported, "Mrs. F. is, I grieve to say, none the better for old age— very enthusiastic, garrulous, naïvely boastful, grandly elevated above the level of the historical in most of what she either remembers or tells of the past." After another interview he added: "I cherished . . . a hope that, now all his official secrets were out, he might have some revelation to make, that would show Benton's plans more clearly. . . . But no; cordial he still was, dignified and charming as ever . . . but alas, he lied, lied unmistakably, unmitigatedly, hopelessly." Frémont was untouched, protected by a lifetime of denying error or guilt.

When Frémont fell ill and a doctor recommended a warmer climate, Collis P. Huntington, who had built the Union Pacific over the site of many Frémont campfires, gave the Frémonts a pair of tickets west. In Los Angeles, Frémont recovered and, restless to the end, left Jessie and came east to attend to what he still called his business affairs. On a hot July day in 1890 he overtaxed himself and within a few hours was dead. He was buried, as he had directed, in a plain suit in a pine box, with nothing to indicate that this had been a famous explorer, senator, presidential candidate, general, railroad president, millionaire, and hero.

John Charles Frémont's talents and energies found their perfect expression in his first three expeditions; they made a contribution. But at the height of his fame, he became an opportunist on an unprecedented scale, trying field after field, regardless of lack of training, experience, or aptitude. Having once commanded, he was never again able to obey. It became more and more difficult for him to acknowledge his mistakes: in disobeying Kearny, in crossing mountains in midwinter, in not reinforcing Lyon at Springfield and Mulligan at Lexington, in alienating Lincoln, in using rascals to sell railroad bonds. And in all of these Jessie Benton supported him unqualifiedly, encouraging him in his intransigence and the belief that he was the victim of persecution. She brought out the best in him—and the worst. Although his illegitimate birth may not have been, as some have seen it, the hidden springs of his entire career, it was a wound that could be healed only if he could prove himself the best of the breed.

The age itself contributed conspicuously to his undoing. As other paths were closed to him, Frémont's hopes turned more and more to business, and he betrayed, like the era, an increasing indifference to the line between astute promotion and fraud. But he had choices, and those he made were the result of his temperament. Just as surely as his courage and impetuosity, his will and his vision, led to the moments when he was truly a hero, they led to others when he was merely a gambler who lost.


The Gold Rush is often seen as an outburst of young men craving adventure as well as fortune, a response to all the exciting legends of a Golconda in the West, an explosion of American enterprise. It was all these, but it was something more. The revelation, in 1789, that in a democracy any youth could become President was now supplemented by the revelation that he could also become a millionaire. Men and women came from everywhere to share in the new way to get rich quickly. Had anyone accused some of the more respectable forty-niners of risking their lives and sometimes their families to play in a lottery, they would have been shocked. On their way back, disillusioned and exhausted, many would admit their folly: wagons that had gone west marked ''Pike's Peak or bust'' came back marked ''Busted, by God!''

Some of those who joined in the rush were genuine pioneers—farmers, craftsmen, or merchants more or less prepared, if they found no gold, to settle on the land, open a store, or work at their craft. Often they were older men who took their families with them and went by the overland route. That way was the cheapest and seemed best suited for a family and its possessions. The fastest route was by sea to the Isthmus of Panama, thence overland by mule, and up the West Coast by boat. But travelers crossing the isthmus were subject to deadly fevers, a fierce sun, and long delays in getting passage on the Pacific Coast. The voyage around Cape Horn was often pleasant, but it was long and expensive. The time required by each route— eight months overland, six months around the Horn, and two months across Panama—was a major problem in itself.

The response to the news of the discovery of gold was explosive. The find was made at Sutter's sawmill in January 1848 and by summer almost every able-bodied man in California was in the fields. In the East there was at first skepticism, but when the news was confirmed by President Polk at the end of the year, it immediately became the chief topic of conversation and fantastic rumors. By December the New York *Herald* was describing the Gold Rush as a mania that was "carrying off its victims hourly and daily." At every report of a new "strike," those who were about to leave were filled with panic lest they be too late. Along the East Coast thousands began clamoring for a place aboard the few steamers bound for the Isthmus of Panama or around Cape Horn, and in the spring, wagons from all over the Midwest converged on Independence and St. Joseph for the journey over the Oregon-California Trail. When Frémont had marched through California in 1846 there had been only a few thousand American and European settlers there; by 1852 there were 250,000, with 80,000 arriving in 1849 alone.

If the great majority of the forty-niners were young men, it was only because they were freer to roam. But the number of older men as well as women and children that were swept into the westward stream is astonishing. It was, as someone said, as though the continent had suddenly tilted, sending tens of thousands tumbling westward. The range of types is equally astonishing—lawyers, doctors, bricklayers, clerks, farmers, carpenters, and cooks, as well as ruffians and misfits, refugees from the revolutions of 1848 and the Irish potato famine, ex-convicts from Australia's penal colonies, English noblemen, long-queued Chinese in black linsey-woolsey pantaloons and slippers, Chileans, and brown-skinned kanakas.

The range is illustrated by Stephen J. Field and James Stuart. Field was a brother of Cyrus and David Dudley Field, the latter already a well-known lawyer. A precocious youth, Stephen at the age of thirteen had been taken to the Levant by his brother-in-law, a missionary, and had studied Greek and Turkish there. After returning to the United States and graduating from Williams College, he entered his brother David's law office in New York. In 1848 he was thirty-two and fairly well established. Chagrined at having ignored his brother's suggestion, in 1846, that he should settle in California, he quickly set out and after a rough trip by way of Panama arrived in San Francisco in December 1849.

In a memoir many years later Field recalled that the atmosphere of expectation in San Francisco's streets was so exhilarating that although he had little money and no plans, he went around proclaiming, as did everyone else, that it was glorious country. He soon moved on to Sacramento and the Yuba City area. When a land salesmen urged everyone to buy lots for a town site, later named Marysville, while they were still available, Field put in his name for sixty-five lots, worth about $16,500, without paying a cent down.

As the only lawyer on the scene, Field helped draw up the deeds for the site of the new town, was promptly elected *alcalde,* and began functioning as both magistrate and town supervisor. Within ninety days his lots were estimated to be worth $150,000 and he was collecting $1,000 a month rent on several "frame and zinc" houses he had arranged to have shipped from San Francisco. Although he soon lost all his money in other speculations, he had already begun a career that would carry him to the state legislature, the supreme court of California, and, finally, in 1863, as one of President Lincoln's appointments, the Supreme Court of the United States, where he served for thirty-seven years.

If Stephen Field represents the forty-niner who made a career in California, "grew up with the country," and contributed richly to the state, James Stuart is representative of those who came to prey on it. Frontier cities, especially where gold or silver has been found, whether in Australia, South Africa, or the Klondike, have always been magnets for outcasts and desperadoes not only because such places are outside the pale of law but because everyone in them is scrambling for money beyond the limits of normal wages or profits. It is a poignant fact that before the Gold Rush, California had been almost free of crime and the money fever.

Born in England in 1820, James Stuart had at sixteen committed a forgery and, in the merciless code of the time, had been banished to Australia's New South Wales for life. In time he was emancipated, and as soon as he heard of the discovery of gold in California he made his way across the Pacific and reached San Francisco in 1850. A handsome, well-dressed young man of deceptively frank manner and smooth speech, he moved into the mining country beyond Marysville and hired a man to work his claims. As he later confessed, he soon wearied of the quiet life, and after losing heavily at gambling, he rifled the tent of a man who had won money from him and came away with $4,300 in gold. But he was suspected and fled to escape being hanged by a mob of miners.

In San Francisco he fell in with assorted Australian criminals known as the "Sidney ducks" and launched into a career of crime, including housebreaking, selling stolen horses and mules, holdups, assault, and murder. Arrested for a minor theft, he was identified; and because he had repeatedly escaped punishment by bribery, breaking jail, and the help of clever lawyers, the newly formed Vigilance Committee of 1851 kept him hidden from the regular authorities.

Hoping perhaps to escape the death sentence, Stuart made a complete confession of his crimes, implicating a score of accomplices. But he was convicted of murder by a grim "jury" consisting of the 400 members of the Vigilance Committee assembled at their headquarters. Stuart was hanged on the Market Street wharf before a huge throng on July 11, 1851. The Vigilance Committee, the crowd, and Stuart himself all represented the contribution of the Gold Rush to the western theme of violence. Vestiges of this violence, in the form of both outlaws and vigilantes, would be found throughout the West for a long time. But the forces of law and order were already emerging in the person of men like Stephen Field.

For some young men in 1850, the Gold Rush looked like a perfect pretext for sowing wild oats, a license to the life of a prodigal son. But even for right-thinking, stable youths it seemed like a good excuse for exploring the exciting world beyond the control of those who preached only duty, prudence, and nose-to-the-grindstone.

Young Franklin Buck was of the latter strain. Coming from an old and distinguished family in Bucksport, Maine, he graduated from Phillips Academy in Andover and went to New York in 1846 to work as a clerk for commission merchants. After stagnant, narrow, small-town New England, he delighted in New York, finding it even more cosmopolitan than Boston. In letters to his sister Mary in Maine—to whom he would write devotedly for almost forty years—he boasted of the freedom and pleasures of city life, of going to the theater—in the heyday of those idols of the stage Macready and Forrest—concerts and the opera, of picnics and parties, and of women who wore daring, low-necked dresses and ate with kid gloves on. A tall, red-headed, agreeable youth, he was so mortified at never having been taught to dance that he was soon taking lessons in the polka and the waltz.

Then, in the fall of 1848, came the stories of gold in California. By December, Frank was writing to his sister: "You need not be at all surprised to hear of my going. . . . If only I had about $1,000 to invest in goods, wouldn't I sail! (Oh, Poverty, thou art a crime!)" Two weeks later he described how unsettling it was to pass docks where twenty to thirty ships bound for California were filling up with merchandise and passengers, including friends of his, some of them leaving good jobs: "There is something about it—the excitement, crossing the Isthmus, seeing new countries, and the prospect of making a fortune in a few years—that takes hold of my imagination, that tells me, 'Now is your chance. Strike while the iron is hot!' " Soon he was on his way, sharing a cabin in a brig headed around Cape Horn. The voyage took more than six months but it had its compensations, especially when they went ashore at Rio de Janeiro and later at Lima, where the promenades, orange gardens, splendid Catholic cathedrals, and the dark and lovely women enchanted him.

As soon as he arrived in San Francisco, Buck was caught up in the excitement. He wrote home, like every other newcomer, of the staggering prices everyone paid without a murmur, of buildings that sprang up overnight, of the gaudy saloons and gambling houses. He and a partner had had the foresight to bring with them the framework of four houses, which had cost them $600 and which they immediately sold for $4,000. When they were paid in gold dust, a pail full of it, Franklin's dreams of fortune soared dizzily. But he and his partner soon saw men coming back from the gold fields empty-handed, and decided that trade was the work for them.

So they opened a store in Sacramento and proclaimed their westernization by donning red flannel shirts—they didn't need washing—buckskin pants, and broad-brimmed hats, and growing beards. But in November the rains came and flooding rivers drove them out. For a few months they tried trading in Marysville, a rough town, with shootings every night, and Frank was called on at least once to join a posse hunting cattle thieves. Soon it was May, and what could be more exhilarating, at twenty-four, then spending half one's time on horseback, "scouring over the prairies free as air!"

On his return to Sacramento, Buck found the city flourishing rankly, especially with gambling saloons such as See's Exchange, which was 120 feet long, had splendid chandeliers, fine paintings, an orchestra, two bars, and a score of monte, roulette, and faro tables. Tiring of his store, Buck sold out at the end of 1850 and went on a trading voyage to "the islands." For four months he sailed through the Marquesas—as beguiling, he agreed, as Melville's *Typee* had said—and Tahiti, where he dined on coconuts, breadfruit, and roast chicken with the royal family, watched the wahines dance the hula-hula from noon to dusk, and dreamed of settling there forever.

But instead he went back to California and up to Downieville only twenty miles from the summit of the Sierra Nevada. There he finally tried mining. He labored for five months from dawn to nightfall and when he was through he had only $100—less than when he had begun. Realizing that he was not going to get rich quickly, he decided to settle down. For this solemn purpose he chose Weaverville, a town of 1,200 inhabitants near the headwaters of the Sacramento, and opened a store. There were many respectable families all around, but on Saturday nights the miners still celebrated by drinking, fighting, and shooting, and Sunday was a day of pleasure rather than prayer. Buck himself retained his taste for the theater—brave traveling companies turned up constantly—and for reading, following *Harper's* and Dickens religiously, and filling in with classics such as *Plutarch's Lives* and the *Iliad*.

When business dwindled, he tried mining again and then a partnership in a sawmill, starting each venture with enthusiasm, and abandoning it sadly, reluctantly. After a while he stopped promising his sister that he would come home as soon as he had "made his pile," and it was not until 1858 that he took his first trip back east.

Although the visit was a pleasant one, he had no desire to stay in Maine. He did find a wife there, but after visiting New York, going to all the theaters, and hearing Henry Ward Beecher preach, he took his bride back to Weaverville. The town had churches now, two schools, gardens and orchards, and other signs of settled respectability.

With all the optimism of the moment, Buck opened another store, but soon left it and turned to raising hogs. Despite the frustration he suffered in towns that blossomed for a few years and then withered, he remained content with the western way of life. A child of Maine, he never ceased to wonder at the early spring, the almond trees, the rich growth of plums and pears and grapes. And he continued to point out that in the West it did not truly matter whether a man was rich or poor. "There is no caste in society here," he wrote, "and the miner and the man who works for wages live in just as good houses and eat and drink and wear the same things as the merchant." He failed to realize that this condition was temporary, that as the town grew, social castes would develop, as they already had in San Francisco.

The threat of war remained far from California, but the animosities reached it rapidly. In spite of his New England origin, Buck misliked the abolitionists, predicting that they would bring on a civil war. And when the new Republican party in its antislavery zeal nominated Frémont in 1856, Buck wrote to his sister that everyone in California knew he was a "humbug" and an "unmitigated fraud." But the insolence of the Secessionists exasperated him increasingly and by January 1863 he was describing himself as ready to do his part till the South was "conquered, annihilated, and made a desert of."

After the war, the opening of mines in Idaho, Montana, and British Columbia began to drain Weaverville of its life. Buck, now in his forties and the father of four children, began once again to look for a new venture. He found it in another "rush"—this time for silver in Nevada. So in 1869 he took "the cars" over the mountains and then rode horseback 500 miles from tunneled hillside to hillside, through jerry-built towns, often only streets of shacks fringed with canvas houses and tents, all crowded with miners, tradesmen, speculators, Indians, gamblers, and prostitutes.

In the end, using money advanced by John Benson, a relative who had made a fortune in San Francisco, he bought shares in a silver mine in southeastern Nevada and settled nearby in the town of Pioche. While waiting for the mine to make him rich, he sold lumber and marketed chickens and eggs. Unstable as the life was, he still found it, as he wrote to his sister, preferable in its informality and tolerance to its New England counterpart:

> You are right in thinking that we live here just as we please. If we want a hot whisky toddy we have it. If we choose to lay abed late, we do so. We come and go and nobody wonders and no Mrs. Grundy talks about it. We are free from all fashions and conventionalities of Society. . . . I like this. About one half of the community are thieves, scoundrels and murderers and then we have some of the best folks in the world and I don't know but what our lives and property are as safe as with you. You can go up town and get drunk and get shot very easily or you can live peaceably. I don't have any trouble.

Franklin Buck was obviously one of those who lived peaceably. He still went through *Harper's* each month and was discriminating enough to note that Bret Harte had "gotten his reputation in the East . . . but never created a furore in California. He throws a kind of charm around California life and mining camps, bars, etc. Very pleasant to read about but which I never experienced while living in them." Within a few years most of the mines around Pioche reached water and became too expensive to work. Once again the townspeople began to drift away and business languished. By the end of 1875 he was writing, "We are like Micawbers here, waiting for something to turn up, which means finding a bonanza in our mines." He clung to Pioche until it was, as he said, completely "gone in," petered out. He made one more effort to edge his way into the magic circle of the moneymakers, building a tiny hotel—"21 × 40, two stories," he wrote—in Mammoth City, 9,000 feet up in the Sierra Nevada, and renting it out for $150 a month. But when his benefactor John Benson asked him to act as manager of a 300-acre farm in California's Napa Valley, which Buck thought of as "a paradise," he accepted the offer. The decision, as he told his sister, was not easy: "We have gotten so used to this life of excitement, speculating in stocks, rich strikes. . . .

It will be a humdrum slow business to go to picking grapes and milking cows and raising chickens; but . . . we are getting along in life and we had better take a certainty on having a good living than the uncertainty of making money.''

When Buck and his wife passed through San Francisco in August 1880 on their way to the Napa Valley, they were amazed at the mansions Leland Stanford, Charles Crocker, and other western barons had raised on Nob Hill. "It was a kind of melancholy satisfaction for Jennie and me," he wrote, "to stroll around and gaze upon those splendors and try and guess which house our twenty-dollar pieces went into . . . for here is where it all gets to. These magnates own the mines, the State of Nevada, and all the people in it."

At the age of fifty-five, after more than thirty years in the West, he had almost nothing to show for his labors as storekeeper, miner, speculator, hog raiser, and lumber merchant. If he was more rueful than bitter, the explanation is that he himself had been enough of a gambler to see his fate as a matter of luck—and having had scruples. It was not the miners who had made the fortunes but the promoters and the merchants, especially those who had not hesitated to profiteer.

But it had been, as Buck said again and again, exciting: he had taken part in the building of a new world, shared in the shaping of another American type and tradition. It had given him, he was convinced, a freer life, released him from the cold hand of New England. Rich or poor, he, like Richard Garland, never dreamed of going back east. "If I were younger," he concluded in his last letter before he left for the Napa Valley farm, "I would take the mining camps."

The career of no forty-niner illustrates more vividly than that of J. Goldsborough Bruff the power of the Gold Rush to uproot even the most settled men. In 1848 Bruff was forty-four years old and a family man with a responsible government job as a draughtsman and designer in Washington. His father had been a doctor and an inventor of dental instruments, and he himself was known for his efforts to start a national art association and for several exhibitions of drawings and lithographs.

It is true that in his youth Bruff had had an urge to see the world.

He attended West Point, but after a fight with a classmate he went off to sea as a cabin boy and was gone for over three years. He was still only twenty-three years old when he married and began a career mainly in the Bureau of Topographical Engineers in Washington. Except for the twenty-seven months spent in the search for gold, he remained in the same government division for sixty-three years.

Despite such a background, Bruff was tempted as soon as the rumors of the gold discovery were confirmed. He was doubtless tantalized by such reports as that of the Reverend Walter Colton, *alcalde* of Monterey, which appeared in the Washington *Daily National Intelligencer* in the late fall of 1848: "At present the people are running over the country and picking it [gold] here and there just as a thousand hogs let loose in a forest would root up the ground nuts." Then Colonel E. F. Beale arrived in Washington with a nugget that had been found on the banks of the Mokelumne River. It weighed twenty-four pounds and was worth $5,000.

As an expert cartographer, Bruff had been assigned to make duplicates of Frémont's maps and charts. These revived in him, he later admitted, "the spirit of adventure so long dormant." He mentioned his urge to friends, and by spring the Washington City and California Mining Association had been formed as a semi-military organization, with Bruff, probably because of his West Point experience, as its captain. On April 2, 1849, the sixty-four members of the company, each in uniform forage cap, gray frock coat with gilt eagle buttons, and pants with a side stripe, and each with a rifle, pair of pistols, knife, canteen, blanket, and tools, left by train for Missouri. Most of the men were under thirty, but all were ready to pay $300 to cover the cost of mules, wagons, and provisions and to entitle them to one share of the profits. At St. Joseph they were dismayed to find so many wagons waiting to cross the Missouri on the single ferry that it would be two weeks before their turn came. So they crossed at Fort Kearny. The journey along the Platte River to Laramie and through the South Pass of the Rockies was unexciting. After that there was pathetic evidence of the tribute the trail had levied—abandoned chests, clothing, tinware, dead oxen, a brand-new "Gothic bookcase." Increasingly there were signs of desperation and tragedy— slabs of meat and sacks of beans and salt, wagons, and graves with crude markers, like the one that was inscribed

> Jn. Hoover, died June 1849
> Aged 12 yrs. Rest in peace,
> sweet boy, for thy travels are over

There were pleasant moments, of course, as when they camped in a bottomland along with other parties and at night the campers played old songs on sundry instruments and sang. But the traveling grew more and more exhausting, especially when they reached the Sierra Nevada and took the more northerly route through the mountains. On October 3 they reached the top of the pass. A passage in his journal describes the scene on the slope behind him:

> In the centre of a very broad, sandy, and dusty road, men urging their heavy ox-trains up the steep hill with lashes, imprecations, and shouts . . . clouds of blinding dust and sand flying . . . an old man on a jaded horse; a mattress covered the horse, the sick man astride and laying over it on his breast, with a coverlid thrown over him. . . . He was afflicted with the flux and scurvy. . . . Some small boys, not over ten years of age, were leading jaded animals up. Women were with the trains, occupied at chocking the wheels. . . . One wagon with women and children in it, when near the summit, became uncoupled and down hill it ran—*stern foremost,* with great rapidity. The women and children screamed, men shouted, and . . . there was a great clamor. A dead ox . . . brought up the backing-out vehicle, luckily without damage to anyone.

The trail become so rocky that although they were only thirty-five miles from an outpost of the California settlements, Bruff decided to send the company ahead on the remaining mules while he camped with the wagons. After seven months and 2,000 miles of travel he was weary of the selfishness of many of his men, and he was not surprised when none of them came back to help him. When he fell ill and began to run out of food, a stranger, an old hunter named Clough, helped him for a while. He himself did his best to assist exhausted families that straggled over the mountains just before winter closed in. Some were grateful but others stole his food and clothes, and one shameless fellow abandoned an ailing six-year-old boy in his cabin. Soon old

Clough disappeared and the ailing boy died. Reduced to chewing old bones and weakened by fevers and dysentery, Bruff in desperation started down the mountain and managed to reach "Lassen's rancho"—a year after leaving Washington.

For Bruff, as for many of the forty-niners, the period spent in California was an anticlimax. He took part in a futile hunt for a "gold lake" and then in bluffs along the coastal beaches. After a brief stay in San Francisco, he returned home by way of Panama, reaching Washington in July 1851. He had found not a single ounce of gold.

Bruff returned to his designer's board and remained there for forty years, dying a respected citizen known chiefly for the length of his government service. In the end his Gold Rush adventures became a cluster of strange and turbulent memories encapsulated in a humdrum past. How could he believe in 1885 that he had once nearly died of fever and starvation among the winter storms of a Sierra Nevada mountaintop? He had heeded the siren's call, risked everything to pursue her, and had nothing to show for the risk except the experience. In any earlier period the escapade would have marked Bruff as unstable; in 1850 it was accepted without question as a sign of what P. T. Barnum called "go-aheaditiveness."


Because the violence and vice of early California were so sensational, it is hardly surprising that histories have neglected the speed with which traditional values emerged and triumphed. Just as remarkable as the turbulence of the mining camps and the sinfulness of San Francisco were the development of conventional towns and the conversion of San Francisco into a cosmopolitan city, proud of its elegance and the trappings of culture.

The same wave of pioneers that brought the sinners brought the virtuous. Such was young Sarah Royce. In 1848, not long after her marriage, she and her husband and baby daughter left a comfortable home in the Genessee Valley in western New York and moved to what Sarah later wistfully described as "a pleasant village in Iowa." They had been there only a few months when word came of the discovery of gold in California. Although, as Sarah noted in her "Pilgrimage Diary," they were "utter strangers to camping life" and were "guided only by the light of Frémont's *Travels*," they loaded a covered wagon, hitched three yoke of oxen to it, and started for the "Golden Gate" on April 30, 1849. Sensitive, devout, well-educated (she took along her lap writing desk as one of her dearest possessions), Sarah Royce nonetheless seems never to have questioned the wisdom of leaving friends and a settled community for a perilous journey into unknown country in search of gold.

As they approached the Missouri River at Council Bluffs, they learned that cholera was raging among the emigrants waiting to cross the river and that the grass along the trail on the plains beyond had been consumed by those who had gone before, but they pressed on, caught up in the excitement of the rush. Soon they were moving out across the prairie, enduring storms, sickness, quicksand, menacing Indians, a stampede of cattle in a camp. When they crossed the Continental Divide, Sarah gave thanks in a primitive biblical gesture, raising a cairn of stones in gratitude to God.

After a brief rest in Salt Lake City, they moved out over the desert, one of the last parties on the trail west that year. But they lost the trail and had to turn back for water and grass. The second time they set out over the salt waste, they crossed it. But then came the Sierras, and the cold of October creeping up on them. Throughout, a profound, almost mystical faith carried Sarah Royce through every crisis; so she saw it as a demonstration of divine Providence when two men, sent out by the U.S. Government Relief Company to succor straggling parties, rode down the trail toward them. The men made the Royces abandon their wagon and go forward as quickly as possible with only their oxen, mules, and a horse. Thus it was on muleback with her child in her arms that Sarah Royce rode into the Promised Land, almost six months after leaving Iowa and only ten days before snow blocked the mountain passes and the stormiest winter in years set in.

The Royces spent their first months in California in a tent in the mining town of Weaverville amid a horde of men feverishly panning for gold. Royce, preferring business to mining, opened a store stocked with merchandise sent up from Sacramento City. Although the camp was primitive and the prospectors all seemed rough, a surprising number of them turned out to be men of education and breeding, and all of them, recognizing in young Mrs. Royce a woman of character and intelligence, treated her with great respect. For her part she saw how lonely and wretched many of them were, working in icy streams, living on salt meat and hardtack, sleeping in their clothes, falling ill with dysentery and fever. She saw, too, how disappointed they grew and the desperation with which they rushed off, chasing across the mountains every rumor of a great new "strike."

After the Royces had themselves suffered from illness and fevers, they resolved to move down into Sacramento. At the time they had left Iowa in April, Sacramento had had only four houses; when they entered it in December it had a population of more than 10,000. Butter was a dollar a pound, and a quart of milk, obviously watered, twenty-five cents. And they had reckoned without the Sacramento and American rivers: floods marooned them for days until they finally escaped by boat to San Francisco.

After a few months in a tiny, flimsily partitioned room in a "hotel" in San Francisco, the Royces managed to get into one of the tenements of cloth and paper springing up all over the city. There, Sarah Royce saw with dismay the standards of men and women brought up according to what she considered unquestionable, God-given tenets, disintegrate amid the bewildering realignments, the greed and license of a city created by a gold rush. Putting down her memories for the benefit of her distinguished son Josiah, she later wrote:

> Any newcomer into San Francisco in those days had but to seek, in the right way, for good people, and he could find them. But in the immense crowds flocking hither from all parts of the world there were many of the worst classes, bent upon getting gold at all hazards, and if possible without work. These were constantly lying in wait, as tempters of the weak. A still greater number came with gold-getting for their ruling motive, yet intending to get it honestly, by labor or legitimate business. They did not at all intend, at first, to sacrifice their habits of morality, or their religious convictions, but many of them bore those habits, and held those convictions too lightly; and as they came to feel the force of unwonted excitement and the pressure of unexpected temptation, they too often yielded, little by little, till they found themselves standing upon a very low plane, side

by side with those whose society they once would have avoided. It was very common to hear people who had started on this downward moral grade, deprecating the very acts they were committing . . . saying, "But *here* in California we *have* to do such things."

Without bitterness, and unshaken in her idealism, she told how women accepted or even sought expensive gifts from men who had made a "strike," and then moved step by step into adultery and desertion. One dissatisfied woman whose husband had given her everything she wanted repaid him by getting control of much of his property and then divorcing him. Two neighbors, both beautiful women, wrecked their homes for the sake of other men. Men, too, were infected. One friend of theirs at first talked of the wife and children he had left in Illinois but in time referred to them less and less, and finally revealed, with little sign of regret, that his wife was divorcing him.

In the fall of 1850 the Royces, now with three children, moved to a mining town about twenty miles from Sacramento. Their home, a frame building covered with cloth, contained a single large room curtained off to create a bedroom, a kitchen, a dining room, and a parlor. The furniture was rude, the "ottomans" made of rough boxes that Mrs. Royce stuffed and covered with plush. Her particular pride, a sign of her loyalty to the tradition in which she had grown up, was a shelf of books and—like the Garlands on the Wisconsin frontier—a melodeon, said to be the first to be brought to California. But soon the San Francisco speculators who owned the engines that furnished water for the mining work decided to close the operation.

The Royces settled down at last in Grass Valley, a mining town in the Sierras. Grass Valley was an established community with a good-sized school, two social and benevolent societies, and, most important to Sarah Royce, several churches. The Royces lived there for twelve years, and it was there, in 1855, that their fourth child, Josiah, was born. Although the town was still occasionally unsettled by word of new discoveries—such as those on the Frazer River or at Washoe— that sent men scrambling frantically over the high ridge, Grass Valley demonstrated how quickly the old values could reassert themselves.

Whatever the limitations of the old religion, it could lead to the strength of character and almost mystic idealism of women like Sarah Royce.

Mrs. Royce taught such values to her son Josiah and they help to explain his lifelong dedication—beginning at the newly founded University of California in 1871 and continuing through his great days as a professor of philosophy at Harvard—to the world of ideas and the power of the ideal. Royce was proud that he was the son of forty-niners, and his devotion to the life of the mind was testimony to the spiritual tradition his mother had kept glowingly alive amid the materialism of the pioneer world. In his history of early California, Royce himself wrote:

> Our true pride, as we look back to those days of sturdy and sinful life, must be . . . that the moral elasticity of our people is so great, their social vitality so marvelous, that a community of Americans could sin as fearfully as . . . the mining community did sin, and could yet live to purify itself within so short a time, not by a revolution, but by a simple progress from social foolishness to social steadfastness. Even thus a great river for an hour defiled by some corrupting disturbance purifies itself merely through its own flow over its sandy bed.

No single factor was more significant in the development of the United States, especially between 1850 and 1875, than the free land that lay always to the west, adding boundless economic promise to political and social liberty. The Gold Rush literally gilded the American dream.

# 6

## LORDS OF THE PRESS

When James Gordon Bennett started the New York *Herald* in a Wall Street basement in 1835, he was a lean, hardheaded man of forty with a sardonic view of the world. His view was doubtless the result of his upbringing in Scotland—mainly education in a Catholic seminary, which he later mocked almost blasphemously—and fifteen years of newspaper work in the New World, much of it onerous and not well rewarded. Whatever the sources of his personality, he emerged a bold, original, and resourceful editor. He represented in newspaper publishing what Vanderbilt represented in steamships and railroads, Stewart in merchandising, Astor in furs—an aggressive, dynamic, and egocentric force. Like them, he was a logical response to a society that was expanding explosively—from a population of 3 million in 1790 to over 30 million in 1860—and greedily exploiting the most magical of all magic querns, the machine.

Up to the 1830s newspapers were printed on primitive presses, subscription rates were high, and the average circulation was little more than a thousand copies. In editorial policy most newspapers were the bought servants of one of the two political parties. They showed little interest in news and often relied heavily on scurrility and slander. The change had been heralded by a New England journalist, Benjamin Day, when he founded the New York *Sun* in 1833. Paying no attention to politics, he concentrated on crime, vice, and fires—and charged only a penny. The *Sun's* circulation rose swiftly. Imitators sprang up on every side. Bennett completed the revolution.

Bennett was made for the age of the mass audience. Not for him the sixpenny journal sold to a handful of prosperous subscribers. When his drive for mass circulation succeeded, he had the delusions of grandeur that gripped most of the giants of the era of personal journalism: Bennett and Bennett, Jr., Dana, Medill, Pulitzer, Hearst. Such men had a double motivation: making a fortune and capturing a huge audience for their opinions. The newspaper that Bennett gave readers was not only readable and informative but also impudent. In the news columns he splashed racy accounts of big-city sin and evil, and in the editorials he mocked sacred cows in a way that delighted the frustrated and envious. The paper recorded the high life as well as the low; at first it treated fashionable society half contemptuously but later it began to flatter the rich, Bennett obviously realizing that they were rapidly becoming the new elite.

The *Herald* reported Wall Street expertly, wooing the small investor with exposés of swindles. It also covered the courts, racing and other sports, foreign news, and the theater. Bennett set up bureaus in Washington and Europe, and hired fast cutters to meet inbound vessels bringing the latest news from abroad. He immediately recognized the value of the telegraph and was able to publish reports on the Mexican War before news arrived by mail. In the Civil War he sent no less than forty correspondents into the field, and the *Herald's* coverage of the conflict was unmatched. Within half a dozen years it was the most successful daily in the United States. Aroused by the sensationalism of the paper and Bennett's insolence, sundry clergymen, abetted by Bennett's competitors, launched a "Great Moral War" against Bennett. He reacted contemptuously. The fact is that he was the vanguard of the coming America, the embodiment of free enterprise shouldering and elbowing its way forward.

The other great editor of the period, Horace Greeley, was equally sure of his own opinions, but he was a reformer, an incorrigible optimist, persuaded that he could right all the wrongs in American life. In the place and time of his growing up—he was born in rural New Hampshire in 1811—Greeley was a part of that flowering of idealism, moral earnestness, and faith in man's perfectibility that resulted in so many utopian communities throughout the North in the

1840s. Greeley himself was in close touch with Brook Farm and was very sympathetic to the life of high ideals and hard work pursued there by such brave explorers as George Ripley, Charles A. Dana, Nathaniel Hawthorne, and, briefly, Margaret Fuller. Indeed, Ripley, Dana, and Fuller would at one time or another be associated with him on the *Tribune*. But perhaps because Greeley's family had been so poor that his father had gone to debtors' prison and Horace himself had left school at fourteen to become a printer's apprentice, he had had to forgo such noble experiments. He had, instead, plunged head-first into the world: at twenty-one, with all his belongings in a bandanna slung over his shoulder, he came, like a true Alger hero, to make his fame and fortune in the big city.

Greeley had an exceedingly keen but quirky mind, one that ranged with equal enthusiasm from great causes to queer fads—from abolitionism and socialism to vegetarianism and the wonders of graham bread. He poured out convictions inexhaustibly but without system or consistency. Thus he abominated slavery but hated the war against it, supported Lincoln but abused him, championed the slave but forgave the South, opposed laissez-faire but fought for the rights of the individual.

In the end, carried away by thirty years of being accepted as oracle and conscience by a vast audience, he persuaded himself in 1872 that he could defeat Grant. He was wrong: the people preferred the hero, however commonplace or tarnished. With his round pink face framed in scraggly white whiskers, shapeless coat, battered hats, and absent-mindedness—in his office he went about with galley proofs pinned to his lapels—and his fetishes, Greeley was the perfect target for caricature and jest. He was beaten overwhelmingly.

But Greeley demonstrated that a newspaper could combine a vigorous style, moral purpose, and unorthodox opinions and still be successful. The weekly edition of the *Tribune*, distributed nationally, reached a peak circulation of 200,000 and is said to have been the most influential paper of the century. In his high-minded if eccentric way, Greeley bridged the gap between the newspaper as the purely personal and often irresponsible expression of its editor and a more or less public service.

James Gordon Bennett and Horace Greeley lived into the postwar period—both died in 1872—but new men to match the new age were already emerging. In 1868 the elder Bennett turned the *Herald* over to his son, and Greeley's former chief associate on the *Tribune,* Charles A. Dana, bought the New York *Sun* and began to make it famous for brilliant editing, deadly use of ridicule, and defense of the rising gods of profit and patriotism.

The almost pathological arrogance, lifelong self-indulgence, and willfulness of James Gordon Bennett, Jr., were surely the result of a mother who spoiled him and a father who gave him all the money he wanted, and nothing else. Because his father was too busy to care about him, his mother, a pretty Irish girl half her husband's age, carried him off to Paris. There the boy was brought up by tutors and governesses who left him convinced that all men were his servants or footstools. Young Bennett returned to New York a cosmopolite, fluent in French and experienced in sex and drinking. His wealth and wildness made him even more interesting to the emerging younger social set in New York. At the age of sixteen he was the youngest person ever admitted to the exclusive New York Yacht Club. His father, having already given him a sloop, now bought him a 160-ton yacht, with a famous sea captain, "Bully" Samuels, to act as skipper. When the Civil War was declared, young Bennett offered to join the navy if he would be permitted to serve with his yacht. Strings were pulled as high up as the President, and Bennett spent almost a year on blockade duty.

Theoretically he now began his training on the staff of the *Herald,* but since he had seen that editors could be had for a pittance, he paid little attention to business. Instead he flung himself into the increasingly hectic sporting and high life of the city, joining those who spent their time looking for novel and exciting forms of dissipation and play. If these involved a wager, a gamble, a contest, or danger, all the better. For the first time the nation, or at least the North, had a group that pursued pleasure without disguise and worried not at all about their immortal souls.

Having come by his wealth without effort, Bennett Jr. was not only extravagant but reckless to the point of lunacy. When ordinary coaching proved insufficiently exciting, he simply drove with breakneck abandon. Along with equally wild friends he would drive into New England, pushing on furiously for weeks on end, buying new teams when the old ones gave out, displaying the urge to move faster than anyone else that would mark so many Americans in a later age. "I want to be able to breathe," he would say. This presumably explains his wildest habit—throwing off his clothes and careening stark naked across the countryside, shouting like a madman.

Only Leonard Jerome, much older but almost as obsessed about horses and racing, was not shocked by his behavior. Bennett was among those who encouraged Jerome to launch the American Jockey Club and build Jerome Park. Ten years later Bennett took the lead in the horse cult when he introduced polo into the United States. Indian army officers had brought the game to England in 1859. Bennett saw it there in 1875, quickly learned to play it from a Captain Candy, and carried back to America not only mallets and balls but also the captain. He soon taught the game to August Belmont and others who could afford to own a string of trained ponies, and established the Westchester Polo Club. The one title Bennett truly earned is "father of American polo."

But Bennett's addiction to horses was as nothing to his devotion to yachting. Out of it came the first sensational episode of his career. Starting with an argument between Bennett and two other yachtsmen concerning the merits of various yachts, it led to a $90,000 wager by the three men and a race across the Atlantic in midwinter. Bennett not only won the race but was the only one of the three who actually sailed. The recklessness of the exploit—six men were washed overboard from one of the vessels—was forgotten in the acclaim from sailing enthusiasts everywhere.

Late in 1867 young Bennett began to take a more active interest in the *Herald* when Bennett Sr., at seventy-two, began relinquishing control of the paper. When the old man formally turned over command to his son, Bennett Jr. ran the empire with the willfulness of an Oriental potentate. Because the *Herald* had grown too tame for him, he soon launched another newspaper, the *Evening Telegram,* that was printed on pink paper and featured murders, scandals, and sports. A notable forerunner of the Hearst papers and other sensational sheets, it was blatant, vulgar, and, Victorian standards notwithstanding, for a time popular. Soon Bennett Jr. moved into the company of some of the most distinguished editors in American newspaper history—such commanding figures that readers automatically referred to their papers as Greeley's *Tribune,* Dana's *Sun,* Pulitzer's *World,* and Bennett's *Herald.*

Bennett's cockiness, unchastened by experience, served him in at least one respect. He had no editorial policy, socially or politically, but he had a keen sense of what would fascinate, titillate, or astonish readers. With his taste for adventure and a willingness to go to any expense to get what he wanted, he developed techniques for forcing news or even creating it. A tall, stiff-backed man with a strong jaw, sweeping mustaches, and a chillingly haughty expression, his combination of baronial contempt and generosity reduced those who worked for him to puppets or slaves. Not one of them knew when he might be fired, given a bonus, or within a few hours be sent overseas for a news story. And yet Bennett could, like many whose lives have been carefree and undisciplined, be charming and debonair. Long afterward, Joseph I. C. Clarke, a *Herald* night editor, wrote, "Unstable in many things, in others whimsical to the point of extravagance, close and generous, optimist and pessimist, unrelenting and forgiving, sparkling with joy or deep in the blues, he was a constant puzzle to everyone about him, yet endowed with the perception of great things."

The paper's style soon grew terse, Bennett banishing leisurely exposition along with other old-fashioned modes. By making much use of the transatlantic cable as well as the telegraph, he repeatedly scooped other editors on both foreign and domestic news. At the same time he gave more space to society news, realizing that the middle-class reader, most oppressed by the taboos of the day, was enthralled by revelations of the elegance in which self-made Americans could live. And Bennett also realized that the newly rich liked publicity.

Within two years of his taking over he launched the most remarkable newsmaking exploit of the age—Henry Morton Stanley's search for David Livingstone. The plan could have occurred only to a man with a passion for bold action, no concern for cost or danger, and a matchless sense of drama. Bennett's choice of a man with the drive and toughness to carry out the assignment (Stanley would come to be known in Africa as *Bula Matari,* "Breaker of Stones") was mostly luck. And when the results made Stanley even more famous, especially abroad, than Bennett or the *Herald*, Bennett became so jealous of him that Stanley finally left the fold.

Another remarkable correspondent nurtured by the *Herald* was an Ohioan, Januarius Aloysius MacGahan. An engaging and talented young man, MacGahan had fallen in love with life abroad and become a roving correspondent—one of the first—for Bennett. In 1873 Bennett, sensing a Russian threat to British India, assigned him to follow a czarist military expedition sent to subdue Khiva, the last great Moslem stronghold in Central Asia. MacGahan's 1,700-mile ride across steppes and deserts into Turkestan made him world-famous, and his dispatches—as well as his lively book, *Campaigning on the Oxus, and the Fall of Khiva*—made Americans aware of worlds they had never even heard of.

After missions in Cuba, Spain, and the Arctic, MacGahan proposed to investigate rumors of Turkish massacres in the Balkans. As envious of MacGahan as he had been of Stanley, Bennett's response apparently led to a violent quarrel, and MacGahan promptly went over to the London *Daily News*. His reporting of Turkish atrocities in Bulgaria made him a Bulgarian national hero and is said to have led to the Russian attack on Turkey. While covering the war that followed, he was stricken with typhoid and died at the age of thirty-four. So great was his reputation that his body was brought to America by a U.S. battleship and lay in state in New York and in Ohio.

By the mid-seventies the editors of other newspapers, regardless of their opinions of the *Herald*'s editorial policies, had developed a great respect for its news-gathering powers. Oswald Garrison Villard, who joined the staff of the *Evening Post* in the 1890s, recalled a time when no rival journalist dared to go to bed before picking up a copy of the early edition of the *Herald* to see whether it contained another scoop.

Bennett's behavior reached a climax of boorishness on New Year's Day, 1877. After long confining his wenching to actresses and women of easy virtue, he became engaged, at thirty-five, to a Maryland belle, Miss Caroline May. Rounding off a cycle of New Year's Day tippling, he arrived at the Mays' home on West Nineteenth Street. Staggering into the crowded drawing room, he downed a few more drinks and then did something as addle-brained as it was offensive:

he unbuttoned and urinated—in the fireplace, it is said. Miss May broke off the engagement. The following day her brother horse-whipped Bennett in front of the Union Club; and a week later the two men went through the formalities of a pistol duel on the Maryland-Delaware state line, neither firing carefully. Had Bennett been guilty of mayhem or embezzlement, polite society would probably not have held it against him, but he had flouted its code with a most contemptuous gesture; so he was ostracized.

As furious as a spoiled child punished for a tantrum, he left for Paris and remained an expatriate until his death more than forty years later—the prodigal who never returned. For such a shameful reason did Bennett join the small company of Americans—it already included James McNeill Whistler, Henry James, banker James Still-man, and novelist F. Marion Crawford—who had found Europe more congenial than the United States. In Paris, Bennett was among those Americans who scorned foreign standards of conduct and behaved as they pleased. His sprees were monumental, and several times his coach-driving while drunk—and sometimes naked—were almost fatal. Whether on his estate at Versailles, his villa near Monte Carlo, or his grouse-shooting retreat in Scotland, Bennett entertained like a manor lord. His three American homes, one on Fifth Avenue, another in Manhattan's Washington Heights, and a third in Newport, were kept in constant readiness for his arrival. On board his yacht his eccentricities reached psychopathic proportions. He insisted that every man who came aboard be clean-shaven, that no one address him until he spoke first, and that no vessel be permitted to cross his boat's bows. Although each of these decrees caused agonizing scenes, he never relaxed them. But he always had a crowd of guests aboard, many of them evidently willing to accept any indignity for the sake of an interlude of luxury.

Despite such recreations, Bennett managed to keep surprisingly tight control of his newspapers. He often worked from sunup to sundown, and he made up for his absence from New York by sending so many cables that an executive was on duty day and night to receive them. He also summoned staff members to Paris as though they were in the next office—sometimes simply for the pleasure of firing them.

In the mid-eighties Bennett's fortunes ebbed. Angered by exorbitant cable rates, he joined John W. Mackay, one of the "Silver

Kings,'' in a struggle to break Jay Gould's stranglehold on American telegraph and cable facilities. The battle was bitter, inconclusive, and costly. This, together with the effects of Bennett's unremitting abuse of his editors, proved the *Herald's* undoing. By 1914 it had only 60,000 readers left. The world was sobering up after fifty years of capitalist sprees and colonialist orgies, and Bennett, now in his seventies, was sobering up along with it. The million-dollar-a-year income had long since shrunk sadly, the yachts had vanished, the carousals had petered out.

Like a man purged of all wild humors, James Gordon Bennett, Jr., at the age of seventy-two, married a mild-mannered, middle-aged American woman, widow of Baron de Reuter, founder of the news agency, and spent the last five years of his life as a decorous husband. He would end his life not with a bang or a whimper but with something like a purr.

If James Gordon Bennett, Sr., was a good example of a self-made success of the pre-Civil War period, his son was an even better example of a youth of the postwar era who inherited everything he owned but plainly believed that his wealth made him a privileged human being. His whole life was a mockery of the American ideal of equality; like most rugged individualists he could not tolerate individualism in anyone around him. The fact that he remained a man of influence despite his raw use of money power, his profligacy, and his contempt for ability and talent is striking evidence of the decline in community standards. Nor did he make any lasting contributions to journalism; for better or worse his father had been the true innovator.

Bennett also left politics and the great social issues to others. While the Tweed ring plundered New York City and Grant's administration fell prey to grafters and spoilsmen, the most the *Herald* contributed was a pinprick here, a gibe there. While Greeley smote the enemy, and Henry Raymond in the *Times* published the exposés that toppled Tweed, other editors averted their eyes. Or perhaps they were blinded by the glitter of gold: the *Post* received $5,000 a month from Tweed, and Bennett's *Evening Telegram* enjoyed a large share of municipal advertising.

James Gordon Bennett, Jr., never displayed any desire to improve morals, purify government, or achieve justice; Charles A. Dana started out with just such ideals.

Dana never became a mogul on the order of Bennett Jr., Pulitzer, or Hearst, nor was he a spendthrift, a roisterer, or an eccentric; he was a man of learning, with a love of languages and literature, a master of editorials, and probably the most able newspaper editor of his time. He was liked and respected by his associates and his private life was irreproachable. That is why the development of his views from the time he reached maturity in 1840 to the postwar years is such chilling testimony to the opportunism and shallow expediency fostered by the age.

Dana's was a classic early American boyhood. He was born in 1819 in a small town in New Hampshire, and his schooling ended at twelve when he was sent to clerk in an uncle's general store in the frontier city of Buffalo. A remarkably bright youth, he studied Latin, Greek, and English literature by himself, and even helped to form a literary society, so that within two years after his uncle's business collapsed in the panic of 1837 he was ready for college. He entered Harvard and, according to his letters, enjoyed two wonderfully stimulating years before severe eyestrain and lack of money forced him to leave. The extent of his idealism can be gauged in a passage written just before he went back to Harvard for his second year:

> I look forward to the time when I shall breathe the air of Cambridge and Boston . . . where one would never guess that there are such things as money and money-getting in the world. And indeed, I hold it an evidence of human depravity that there are such things, and dream . . . of the time when the cycle of humanity shall be completed and it shall not be said "God makes man, and man makes money."

Among the new doctrines that excited him during those years was a philosophy called Transcendentalism, preached by the Reverend George Ripley, Ralph Waldo Emerson, and Amos Bronson Alcott. So when Dana learned that Ripley was putting the doctrine into practice at Brook Farm, near Boston, he decided to join the group—as much for the sake of his eyes as of his soul. Soon he was writing to his sister that he had moved in with "some friends who have associated themselves for the purpose of living purely and justly and of acting from higher principles than the world recognizes.''

With more business experience than most of his elders in the group, he became a principal member of the association: he acted as its secretary, taught German and Greek, milked cows, served as a waiter in the dining room, sang in the choir, and wrote reviews and poems for its publications, *The Dial* and *The Harbinger*. Contemporaries describe him as a handsome youth, slender but masculine, with a firm, expressive face, a scholar's forehead, auburn hair, and a full beard. Kind in manner, he nevertheless gave an impression of force— qualities that characterized him throughout his life.

Dana stayed for five years in the Brook Farm Institute of Agriculture and Education—a nest of Yankee visionaries and an improbable mélange of German idealism, cooperative association, joint-stock capitalism, and dedication to hard work. His companions included such luminaries as George Ripley and his wife, Sophia, Nathaniel Hawthorne, George William Curtis, and, from time to time, Ralph Waldo Emerson and Margaret Fuller, as well as farmhands, domestics, a baker, a grocer, a valet, and a pressman. Dana and his wife remained to the very end of the experiment, leaving only after fire had destroyed the farm's buildings and its hopes. Although his views as an editor after the war denied utterly the spirit and hopes that animated Brook Farm, he never repudiated the experiment; as late as 1895, he declared that it had not proved its applicability but had nonetheless been a valuable experience.

After an interval on a Boston newspaper, Dana joined Greeley as city editor on the New York *Tribune*. Although his salary was soon raised to fourteen dollars a week, only one dollar less than Greeley's, news of the revolutions breaking out in Europe made him decide to go abroad. Having arranged to make an impressive forty dollars a week by writing a weekly letter to the *Tribune* and four other papers— probably the first example of syndicated correspondence—he sailed for Europe in the spring of 1848.

Charles Dana's reports from the social battlefronts of Europe, and especially France, were as boldly sympathetic to the working-class revolutionaries as any by an American. Indeed, the *Tribune* prefaced his first letter with an apology for its ''undisguised sympathy with the misguided laborers who were driven . . . into so dreadful a rebellion." In that letter Dana pointed out that just as the "old Revolution" in France had accomplished much good in destroying the old feudalism and laying the foundations of political liberty, so "the new Revolution had also its work to do. It is to destroy the moneyed feudalism and lay the foundation of social liberty." He did not shrink from the conclusion that if there was violence, it would be the fault of the moneyed classes who resist change.

Learning that the discontent had spread to England, he wrote, in terms that Marx and Engels (their *Communist Manifesto* had just appeared) would have approved:

> The majesty of England is after all fragile at the base, the feet of the statue are of clay. Its day will come. . . . A feudal aristocracy monopolizing the materials and implements of industry, are both things that cannot stand before the spirit that is abroad. Nor will they disappear peacefully by a gradual and harmless process.

Although bred in the doctrines of Brook Farm, with their faith in human nature, he saw, as soon as he faced the reality in France, that the middle class would resist stubbornly:

> The bourgeoisie have as firm a faith in their cause as the nobility had in theirs in '89. . . . They regard the people with the same contempt levelled on themselves. They think the innovation is foolish and impracticable; just so thought the aristocracy. They . . . hate the masses that cry out against their privileges . . . just so did the aristocracy.

In the fall, when the National Assembly passed a bill offering the workers paternal aid and charity, Dana rejected it as a shameful compromise. "The Right to Labor is the Right to Live," he wrote. As high hopes waned, he insisted that his sympathy for the people would survive their errors and defeats.

After returning in 1849 to the *Tribune* as managing editor, Dana continued for a while to champion the revolutionary movements in Hungary and Austria, but he was soon occupied with American issues—the Missouri Compromise, squatter sovereignty, slavery in the territories. An expansionist, he believed in almost unlimited aid to the builders of transcontinental railroads, seeing no danger in vast grants to small groups of ambitious men. Like Greeley, Dana was active in organizing the Republican party in 1855, but his great confidence in the party's first presidential candidate, Frémont, was a blunder. That was only the first of a number of his misjudgments of prominent men, leading him sometimes to excessive admiration but more often to merciless abuse.

He attacked the slave power unsparingly, but he believed that under the Constitution the South had a right to keep its slaves, and he rejected Greeley's notion that a dissatisfied state should be allowed to secede. When Greeley's high-flown response to threats of secession, "Erring sisters, depart in peace!" began to appear regularly in *Tribune* editorials, it was surely not with Dana's approval. As the threat of secession increased, so did the gap between the views of the two editors. Once Fort Sumter had been fired on, Dana's attitude of course prevailed, and the battle cry, "Forward to Richmond!" began to be used almost daily in the *Tribune*. Despite Dana's increasing disagreement with Greeley, it came as a shock when he was abruptly dismissed in March 1862.

Dana was now forty-three years old and had a wife and family to support, so he began taking special assignments from the War Department. Because the North, badly in need of cotton, permitted traders to buy cotton across the Rebel lines, Dana decided to try this open speculation in contraband. It was very profitable but he soon saw that the South was getting much the better of the bargain, and that, even worse, every captain and quartermaster was in league with the traders. Returning to Washington, he urged Lincoln and Stanton to stop the trade and let army quartermasters buy any needed cotton at fixed prices. The suggestion was adopted.

Impressed by Dana's competence, Stanton now sent him on an important mission: to obtain information that would "enable Mr. Lincoln and himself to settle their minds as to Grant . . . against whom there was some complaint." Dana accepted and arrived at Grant's headquarters in April 1863. According to his *Recollections of the Civil War,* he found the general the most modest and honest man he had ever met, "not an original or brilliant man but sincere, thoughtful, deep and gifted with courage," and possessing "a judgment that was judicial in its comprehensiveness and wisdom." Dana's impressions were doubtless colored by the fact that rumor had pictured Grant as a sullen, bumbling drunkard. Dana's reports did note that since Grant was "neither an organizer nor a disciplinarian himself, his staff is naturally a mosaic of accidental elements and family friends." Dana's reports, trenchant and vigorous, earned him the post of Assistant Secretary of War.

On his return to civilian life, Dana managed, with the backing of leading Republicans and sundry businessmen, to buy the New York *Sun*. In 1868 all the major figures of the great age of personal journalism were still alive—Henry Raymond of the *Times* and William Cullen Bryant of the *Evening Post* as well as Greeley and the elder Bennett. Raymond had founded the *Times* in 1851, and perhaps because his family had been well off and his path smooth, he had declared from the outset that he would try to "get into a passion as rarely as possible." Despite the furies loosed in the next two decades, he kept his promise; by the time he died in 1869, the *Times* was known for its moderation and reliability. If it sometimes seemed tame or colorless, that may have come as a relief in an age of dogmatic opinions violently expressed.

The reflection of Bryant's personality in the *Evening Post* was equally distinct. A lesser, weaker Wordsworth, mining a narrow, somewhat didactic vein of nature poetry, he had in his twenties achieved a considerable reputation as a poet. Discouraged by an unrewarding law practice in the Berkshires, he turned to journalism and in 1825 went down to New York to become editor of the *Post*. But he remained a New Englander, reticent and austere, strong in integrity and conscience. Born in 1794 and old enough to remember another way of life, he was never taken in by the gospel of success; he kept the *Post* staunchly liberal. By the end of the war he had become a patriarchal figure, a monument, and the *Post* reflected his dignity and literary refinement.

Trained in a tradition of newspapers dominated by such individualists, Dana took it for granted that a paper should be an expression of its editor's personality, however eccentric. When it was suggested, a few years later, that this tradition was dying out, he answered:

A great deal of twaddle is uttered by some country newspapers just now over what they call personal journalism. They say that now that Mr. Bennett, Mr. Raymond, and Mr. Greeley are dead, the day for personal journalism is gone by, and that impersonal journalism will take its place . . . a sort of journalism in which nobody will ask who is the editor of a paper . . . and nobody will care.

Whenever, in the newspaper profession, a man rises up who is original, strong, and bold enough to make his opinions a matter of consequence to the public, there will be personal journalism; and whenever newspapers are conducted only by commonplace individuals whose views are of no consequence to anybody, there will be nothing but impersonal journalism.

This view had its dangers: it led to the irresponsibility of the younger Bennett and the sensationalism of Dana himself and of Joseph Pulitzer and William Randolph Hearst. In the end, personal journalism would die of its own excesses.

The first major demonstration of Dana's personal approach was his change of heart concerning Ulysses Grant. In the very first issue that he edited, in January 1868, Dana endorsed Grant for the Presidency. He also collaborated on an adulatory campaign biography of the general. Hardly had Grant been inaugurated when the *Sun* began its assault. Before long it had descended to such gratuitous insults as "It is announced that 'Mrs. Grant will receive every Tuesday afternoon during the winter.' President Grant will receive anytime and anything whenever anything is offered." Many believed that the *Sun's* special virulence resulted from Dana's chagrin at not being appointed New York Collector of Customs after learning that he had been recommended for the post.

Dana was soon pouring contempt on every member of Grant's Cabinet, accusing most of them, including Hamilton Fish, of venality. In the election of 1872, the paper, ostensibly supporting Greeley, used any and every device to defeat Grant. It coined the slogan "Turn the rascals out!" It accused Grant of drunkenness, nepotism, taking bribes, low moral standards, and involvement in fraud. It claimed he was anti-Negro, anti-Catholic, and anti-Semitic—and a boor to boot.

After the second inauguration, the *Sun*'s attacks continued unabated. And when it appeared that Grant might run for a third term, the editorials became frantic, warning the nation that it would saddle itself with plunderers, grafters, and a family dynasty forever. Although many of Dana's attacks on public officials were justified, his criticism was often malicious or vindictive. American newspapers had discovered that one of the pleasures of the common man in a democracy was seeing the mighty "put in their place"; the more frustrated the reader, the more he would relish a devastating attack on some satrap.

By the close of Grant's second term, Dana, disgusted with the Republican party, was aiming his fire at Rutherford B. Hayes. After the fraud-ridden elections of 1876, he invariably referred to the "fraudulent President" and the "fraudulent Cabinet," and he called Hayes infamous. As briefly as Garfield served, the *Sun* was already recommending his impeachment. But it reserved for Grover Cleveland some of its ugliest abuse. While Cleveland was governor of New York it often referred to him as obese, dull, and a moral humbug. When he ran for President, it stooped to supporting the unprincipled Ben Butler, thereby suffering a drastic loss of respect. Finally when Cleveland, before his election, accepted responsibility for a child born out of wedlock, Dana declared that he was "a coarse debauchee who might bring his harlots to Washington," a man "leprous with immorality." Other newspapers charged that Dana had turned against Cleveland after Cleveland had failed to appoint a friend whom he had recommended for office. But one also gets the feeling that Dana simply did not want to believe that any political figure could be as honest and serious of purpose as Cleveland seemed to be.

But political figures were not the only targets of Dana's rich store of prejudice. His criticism of other newspapers was unbridled: he described the *Times* as revolting and salacious, the *Herald* as without principle or character, the *World* as stupid, and Whitelaw Reid, who succeeded Greeley on the *Tribune,* as incompetent. But most of all he vilified E. L. Godkin, the Anglo-Irishman who edited the *Nation* and later the *Evening Post,* calling him "totally depraved" and a "stupendous humbug." Perhaps the reason for Dana's bitterness was that Godkin was what Dana might have been—a keen intelligence addressing itself to the best minds of the time, and a champion of progressive causes.

If Dana's opinions of his contemporaries indicate how wrongheaded and spiteful he could be, his positions on the great issues of the day reveal, in particular, a rabid faith in expansionism. In this, Dana shared the cockiness of a young nation that has discovered its muscles: jingoism would always be a staple of the more sensational American newspapers. Dana subscribed to the doctrine of America's manifest destiny and at one time or another urged the annexation of Cuba, all of the Antilles, Canada, Mexico, Venezuela, and Hawaii.

Dana's views of the problems of industrialization—unions and strikes, monopolies and trusts—were marked by an extreme form of laissez-faire. At first the *Sun* seemed to sympathize with striking workmen, but as labor unions and farmers' granges burgeoned after the panic of 1873, the paper took the position that a man had a right to strike but not to prevent anyone else from taking his job. When violence broke out in a strike, the *Sun* blamed it on anarchists, communists, and "crazy Socialists." By the late 1880s the Knights of Labor ranked the *Sun* as the most contemptible of all newspapers.

As for westward expansion, the *Sun* had at first supported the huge government subsidies to the railroads. Later it deplored the greed of the railroad barons. But its view of trusts remains a classic defense of uncontrolled monopoly: "The objects of trade being to buy as cheap as possible, to sell as dear as possible, and to get control of the market as far as possible, the formation for these purposes of these gigantic and widely extended partnerships is just as natural and regular as the partnership of two shoemakers or of two blacksmiths." Perhaps the strongest statement of this view was an editorial entitled "May the Better Trust Win!" It was the Darwinian theory of survival of the fittest used to rationalize unlimited greed.

Given his perfervid nationalism, it was logical that Dana should believe in a high tariff not only as protection for American industry but as a magical source of revenue. As a corollary, he inveighed against the income tax, declaring it "a betrayal of the country into the preliminaries of communism." A champion of rugged individualism, Dana opposed government aid to less successful citizens, control of interstate commerce, pure food laws, government street cleaning services, and a free city college. He was also witheringly contemptuous of all government efforts at civil service reform, charging that they were pure hypocrisy; he preferred, in effect, the spoils system. He dismissed reformers as windbags.

In contrast to the younger Bennett, Dana surrounded himself with the most competent journalists and treated them with respect. Newspaper men everywhere admired the *Sun*'s boldness and bite and its vigorous reporting even when they deplored its lack of principle. The more critical observers thought it owed its success to its sensational features: stories of the traffic in women, of ministers charged with immorality, or murder, rape, suicide, and opium addiction. Certainly many of its readers turned to it mainly because it entertained them and exercised so irreverently the democratic right to criticize political leaders. Apparently they were little influenced by its opinions: they ignored its opposition to Grant, Hayes, Garfield, and Cleveland as presidential candidates; they rejected its campaigns to get the United States to annex its neighbors; and they accepted income taxes, civil service reform, social legislation, and the right to strike.

Dana, rich and successful, with a fine home on Madison Avenue and an estate on an island off Long Island, developed into an epicure. He enjoyed the company of musicians, writers, and artists, became a gourmet and a connoisseur of wines, gathered one of the first and finest collections of Chinese porcelains, cultivated exotic trees and flowers, and led groups in the study of Dante and other classics.

Between the 1840s and the 1880s, the United States and Charles A. Dana came a long way on much the same road. While the nation was changing from an agrarian democracy into an industrial autocracy, Dana was developing from a youthful idealist into a malicious cynic. By 1880 he was light-years away from the lad who had joined Brook Farm or the journalist who had championed revolutionary French workingmen. Dana had turned from an optimist, convinced that man could perfect himself and society, into a scoffer who derided reformers and crusaders. In a time of agrarian democracy he had milked cows, eaten with farmhands, and rested content; in a plutocracy he had enlisted in the newspaper circulation wars and become a success. Having triumphed in free competition, he decided that the losers must be lazy or incompetent.

Charles A. Dana died in 1897, a man of means, a force in the world, a pillar of American journalism. But as the Gilded Age wore on and the era of overconfidence gave way to self-examination, it became evident that beneath the sparkle, the clever thrusts, the icon-oclasm of the *Sun,* there had been mainly prejudices, opportunism, irresponsibility. Shortly after his death, the *Nation,* weighing various newspapers, went to the chilling heart of the matter when it declared:

> One paper struck out in the novel line of abusing and ridiculing everybody whom the community considered good and respect-able, highly eulogizing the persons whom the community con-sidered criminal or depraved. . . . The success of this was great for twenty-five years. The paper circulated among thousands of people who enjoyed its paradoxes, its satire, and found its in-difference to truth amusing; and the editor . . . preserved a reputation for wit, scholarship, and general editorial "great-ness." A generation grew up under his influence which natu-rally learned to doubt the value of everything but money, the sincerity of all reformers, and the utility of patriotism for any-thing but war.

A curious combination of circumstances made Joseph Pulitzer per-haps the most unusual character to emerge from the personal jour-nalism of the Gilded Age. He was born in Hungary, the son of a Jewish grain merchant and a well-bred Austro-German Catholic mother. A brilliant student, especially of languages and literature, but excitable and headstrong, he left a comfortable home to go off to America in 1864. He arrived in time to serve briefly in the Union cavalry. A tall, scrawny youth of seventeen, with poor eyesight and only a smattering of English, he was occasionally the butt of jokes by his fellow soldiers but he brushed off these gibes. At the war's end, penniless but with immense self-confidence, Pulitzer made his way to St. Louis, attracted by word of the number of Germans there. He found it a bustling city of 300,000, a mixture of well-kept residential districts and shantytowns, of theaters, gambling joints, and riverfront warehouses, of proper, well-groomed ladies and boisterous, rough-clad cowboys. Pulitzer worked at such odd jobs as waiter and deckhand while studying law in the office of a friendly attorney. Soon he was admitted to the bar and soon, too, he attracted the attention of Carl Schurz, that role model for every liberal-minded foreigner.

Schurz had fled to America after taking part in the revolutionary uprisings in Germany in 1848. Plunging into politics, he had supported Lincoln in 1860 and had been appointed minister to Spain but had hurried home to serve as a general in the Civil War. Now, as co-editor of an influential German-language newspaper in St. Louis, the *Westliche Post,* he gave Pulitzer a job as a reporter, starting him, at twenty-one, on his remarkable career in journalism and politics.

Often working sixteen hours a day, Pulitzer soon acquired a reputation for uncovering abuses in public office and, in the Schurz tradition, pushing for reforms. Although some of his fellow reporters mocked him as "Joey the German" or "Joey the Jew," he won the confidence of leaders among the reformers and, with his rich variety of interests, the cultural circles of the city as well. Still emulating Schurz, who had been elected a senator from Missouri, he became active in the Liberal Republican party, and in 1869 he was chosen, much to his surprise, to fill a vacancy in the state legislature. It was testimony to the cosmopolitan makeup and democratic atmosphere of St. Louis that it chose as a representative a twenty-two-year-old who had been in America less than six years.

Even though Schurz and Pulitzer failed in an attempt as Liberal Republicans to stop Grant's reelection in 1872, Pulitzer was tremendously stimulated by his growing recognition in both journalistic and political arenas. Having established himslf as a key figure on the *Westliche Post,* he persuaded Schurz to let him buy, on generous terms, a controlling share in the paper.

He now began to display a taste for elegant living that would grow ever stronger. He moved from a modest hall bedroom to the glittering new Lindell Hotel and dined regularly with well-placed friends at the Planter's House. A discriminating lover of music and literature, he attended plays and musicales, quoted Goethe and Shakespeare at length, and studied Plato and Aristotle in the original Greek. Almost six foot three, with thick, black hair, a reddish beard and pince-nez, and impeccably dressed, he was a striking figure at social gatherings. And when Schurz and a partner bought back control of the newspaper for the handsome sum of $30,000 in 1873, Pulitzer toured Europe and vacationed on what would become one of his favorite resorts, the Riviera.

On returning to St. Louis, he cast about for a newspaper that he could buy, meanwhile practicing law and making some profitable investments. Disgusted by the corruption and profligacy of the national administration, he joined other reformers in organizing a People's party. But when it compromised on its demands, he abandoned it. Craving political independence, he also broke with Schurz and the Republicans and went over to the Democrats. He would remain an independent, and sometimes very critical, Democrat for the rest of his life.

In the bitter presidential race of 1876, Pulitzer campaigned for Tilden while Schurz backed Hayes. In a remarkable tribute to Pulitzer, the St. Louis *Times* declared that Schurz would not dare to debate with his rival because Schurz was "immeasurably the inferior of the other in nimbleness of intellect, in practical knowledge and available requirements." So markedly had Pulitzer's reputation grown that he was invited to New York to meet Tilden and other Democratic leaders; while there he was also called on to address a major rally at Cooper Union. Just as important for Pultizer was his meeting with Charles A. Dana. Perhaps Dana remembered that Pulitzer had once written to him praising the *Sun* as "the most piquant, entertaining, and, without exception, the best newspaper in the world." Dana was so impressed by Pulitzer's grasp of both politics and journalism that he asked him to go to Washington to cover the presidential election for the *Sun*. Serving as a privileged recorder of the Washington scene at such a time proved an invaluable experience for Pulitzer.

It was also memorable because Pulitzer, now thirty years old, met and fell in love with Kate Davis, the intelligent, lively, and attractive daughter of Judge William Worthington Davis and a distant relative of Jefferson Davis. Since Pulitzer knew by then that only the ownership of a newspaper would satisfy his mounting ambitions, it was obviously his meeting with Kate Davis that persuaded him to tarry in Washington, filling in the time with practicing law. As for Kate Davis, she was clearly swept off her feet by this brilliant, many-talented man. Although her parents disapproved of Pulitzer because he was unidentifiably foreign-born and had no settled career, the couple was soon married. The ceremony was performed in a prominent

Episcopal church; we can only imagine how shocked Pulitzer's wife and her parents were when they learned that he was a nearly unthinkable fusion—half Jewish and half Catholic.

The couple's long honeymoon in Europe was financed in part by articles on conditions in Europe that Pulitzer wrote for the *Sun*. In them, he assailed Europe's monarchies for their callous exploitation of the common people. But he also rejected socialism, mainly because it would do away with private property and individual initiative. He opposed both extremes because he believed that both limited the freedom to fulfill all of one's potentialities.

Soon after Pulitzer brought his wife back to the United States he took over a bankrupt St. Louis newspaper, the *Dispatch,* and a small new journal, the *Post;* merging them, he launched the St. Louis *Post-Dispatch*. It would become, and remain, one of America's outstanding newspapers. Convinced that a large circulation was the only way a newspaper could achieve influence and reforms, Pulitzer soon began to mix sensational stories and lurid features with a succession of crusades against political and social abuses. For the sake of what he considered worthy causes, he did not hesitate to cater to not-so-worthy tastes. He presented his case as a reformer in the plainest, crudest terms:

> What is the great demoralizer of our public life? Of course, corruption. And what causes corruption? Of course, the greed for money. And who offer the greatest temptation to that greed? Corporations. . . . Money is the great power of today. Men sell their souls for it. Women sell their bodies for it. . . . Others worship it. . . . It is the glowing dark cloud to our free institutions . . . the irresistible great conflict of the future.

Pulitzer was now a strange blend: Central European intellectual, muckraker, Gilded Age high-liver, and intense individualist. Pursuing exposés and reform campaigns with a revivalist's fervor, he persuaded his readers that he was their devoted defender and the foe of all special privilege. Aware of the danger of suits and ridicule if his charges were not well-founded, he insisted on accuracy and reliable evidence and was sharply critical of his editors when a case proved unwarranted or weak.

On the sensational side the paper featured graphic accounts of protected prostitution, abortionists, opium dens, and the sins of supposedly respectable citizens. Such attacks, not to mention those against lottery rackets, insurance frauds, tax dodgers, and wide-open gambling houses, brought threats and even blows—St. Louis was not long past its frontier days—and eventually led Pulitzer to carry a pistol. Fiercely competitive, he drove his employees as hard as he drove himself, but he paid them well, bestowed gifts on them when they pleased him, and took a personal interest in their affairs.

Although he was sympathetic to the basic aims of unions, he fired employees who tried to organize his shop, brooking no interference in the management of his business. He and his family—there were now two children—lived in fine style, enjoying a large, richly furnished home, servants, vintage wines, and vacations at the most fashionable resorts. At their parties, the talk, in several languages, of music, literature, and politics was like that in a European salon.

Pulitzer's capacities as a publisher were soon demonstrated: within three years he increased the circulation of the *Post-Dispatch* from 2,000 to 20,000 and its annual profit to $85,000. But attacks by more and more enemies made him and his wife increasingly uncomfortable in St. Louis. This as well as his success spurred him into seeking a grander arena for his efforts. He saw his chance when he learned that the New York *World,* owned by Jay Gould, who had acquired it as an incidental part of a railroad deal, was for sale. The paper, faced by increasing competition, had lost circulation. But Pulitzer believed that all the New York papers were too sober and unimaginative. Aimed at educated and chiefly Republican readers, and unconcerned with reform, they lacked, he felt, appeal for the metropolitan masses. So he bought the *World,* paying the formidable sum of $346,000, and moved into the major stage of his career.

In his announcement of ownership in May 1883, Pulitzer declared that the *World* would be cheap, bright, and truly democratic. It would, he said, be "dedicated to the cause of the people rather than that of purse-potentates" and would expose "all fraud and sham, fight all public evils." What he did not say was that he wanted above all to sell millions of copies. He admired the high standards and discriminating readership of Godkin and Schurz's *Evening Post*—Schurz had joined Godkin in 1881—but he preferred "to talk to a nation not to a select committee."

So he cast off dignity and loaded the front page of the daily edition with provocative headlines and spicy stories of crime and sin, and the Sunday edition with bizarre tales of human sacrifice in religious sects, life in Sing Sing, and cannibalism at sea. Aiming at the tens of thousands of foreigners settling in the city, he insisted that the writing be lively and direct and do its work with short sentences and "active verbs." At the same time he pounded away at the irresponsible rich and what he described as a "sordid aristocracy . . . ready to sell their daughters, for barren titles, to worthless foreign paupers." Most radical was his call for a tax on large incomes, luxuries, inheritances, and corporations, although he himself would be fully subject to such taxes. Within a few months his publishing formula, and doubtless the fact that the *World* was the only eight-page paper selling for two cents, doubled the circulation.

Encouraged by his journalistic success, Pulitzer now plunged into the political wars. After much consultation with Democratic bigwigs concerning a candidate for the presidency in 1884, he came out for Grover Cleveland. When Dana, angered by personal slights from Cleveland, deserted the New York governor, Pulitzer and the *World* suddenly assumed major political importance. Pulitzer was promptly rewarded with a nomination for Congress from New York's Ninth District. After a campaign marked by much mudslinging, Cleveland won. Pulitzer also won and the *World* became overnight the largest Democratic newspaper in America, with a circulation that had risen from 15,000 to more than 200,000 in eighteen months. Anti-Semitism, which would shadow Pulitzer throughout his career, now raised its repulsive head: a trade paper, *The Journalist,* observed that as the manager of a clothing establishment on New York's Chatham Square, "Jew Pulitzer would be an honor to his race and a glory to his surroundings."

The industrialization that was creating more and more millionaires was also leading to the unchecked exploitation of labor. Even as the new rich were lining Fifth Avenue with French châteaus and Italian palazzos, noisome slums were spreading across sizable sections of New

York and other cities. The promises held out by Alger's tales and McGuffey's *Reader* seemed not to apply to the vast majority of immigrants in the new Babylon. With a range that some may have thought demagogic, Pulitzer attacked the "vulgar wealthy" and welcomed immigrants, meanwhile feeding the dreams of the lower classes with accounts of the lavish balls and other extravagances of the rich. Now a millionaire himself, Pulitzer moved his family, including five children, to a handsome home on Fifth Avenue's "Millionaire's Row." The paradox in Pulitzer's assaults on the "snobocracy," while he himself associated with its members and shared its privileges, may be explained in several ways: his belief that, having begun as a poor immigrant, he had earned his rewards; the hope, shared by his wife, that they could avoid the hostility that had made them leave St. Louis; and most of all, the conviction that his association with the wealthy in no way affected his support for social justice.

When Pulitzer went to Washington as a congressman late in 1885, he apparently hoped, despite poor health, that he could perform his congressional duties and still manage his newspapers. But he was soon spending most of his time in New York. So, after only four months, he gave up his seat and, with it, all aspirations to public office.

Pulitzer had meanwhile made new enemies among the wealthy and powerful. Although he was not radical and believed that the great hope of democracy lay in an enlightened capitalism, his foes labeled the *World* a fraudulent, proletarian, and revolutionary sheet. Surprisingly, in view of his earlier admiration of Dana and his rewarding service with the *Sun,* the ugliest attack came when the rise of the *World* and the decline of the *Sun* touched off a ferocious rivalry between the two men. It culminated in 1887 when they supported opposing candidates for the office of New York district attorney. Dana began by charging that Pultizer's candidate was the captive of a publisher who had fled from St. Louis after using his influence to help his managing editor escape a murder conviction. The *World* retorted that Dana was a "mendacious blackguard" and a "broken-down calumniator," whereupon the *Sun* called Pulitzer a "renegade Jew" who "exudes the venom of a snake." Beside himself with rage, Pulitzer described Dana as "poor, despised, disgraced old Ananias." When a Jewish newspaper declared that Pulitzer was a Jew who denied being a Jew, the *Sun* quoted the statement time after time, adding such comments as "His face is repulsive, not because the physiognomy is Hebraic, but because it is Pulitzeresque . . . [stamped by] cunning, malice, falsehood, treachery, dishonesty, greed and venal self-abasement.'' All of it illustrates how tame our libel laws have since made our publications.

Pulitzer's candidate was defeated. Ten days later he complained of failing eyesight—a condition that would in time lead to virtual blindness. He also began, or continued, to suffer from asthma, insomnia, nervous exhaustion, a psychopathic sensitivity to sound, and fits of depression—ailments mainly psychological in origin. All of his many doctors would advise the one remedy he could not achieve— complete rest and relaxation. In desperation he went off to Europe with his wife and two of his children, beginning twenty-two years of almost constant journeying in search of health.

Long subject to sudden shifts in mood, Pulitzer now often swung unpredictably from elation to dejection, from amiability to rage— sometimes accompanied by outbursts of blistering profanity—and from surges of energy to apathy. Made doubly irritable by his ailments, he wore out his physicians, many of his editors, and an endless succession of secretary-companions. Alternating between benevolence and sharp criticism, he reduced his children to submission, real or feigned, and his employees, with few exceptions, to hasty compliance. But blindness alone, in one so dependent on being able to read, makes almost any degree of exasperation or rage understandable. His afflictions, combined with his disappointment in Cleveland on the national scene and disgust with the power of the Tammany bosses in New York, may well account for his growing impatience with politics and the pace of reform.

Despite Pulitzer's absence from his newspapers and his dependence on lengthy messages to and from his editors, his papers prospered and his income soared. In 1890 the golden-domed Pulitzer Building was completed, its twenty stories making it the tallest in New York. In the next few years Pulitzer bought a $100,000 yacht, wintered on Jekyll Island, a Georgia resort limited to millionaires, and built a magnificent summer home among the social elite at Bar Harbor, Maine. Nevertheless, some of his more snobbish neighbors on Jekyll Island and elsewhere still refused to associate with him. He was doubtless thinking of this while dining in London with Alfred Harmsworth, later Lord Northcliffe, another newspaper tycoon, when he said, "I am the loneliest man in the world. People who dine at my table one night might find themselves arraigned in my newspaper the next morning."

In 1895, young William Randolph Hearst, son of a California millionaire, began, much like Pulitzer in 1883, to make a major place for himself in the New York newspaper world. He used much the same tactics—a low price, vigorous campaigns against corporations and monopolies, and sensational features. He went Pulitzer one better, hiring away the entire staff of the Sunday *World*, including R. F. Outcault, the creator of the first comic strip, and featuring lavishly illustrated accounts of scandal and crime and staging publicity stunts. Critics were soon referring contemptuously to both papers as the "yellow press," and churchmen were deploring their lurid reporting.

Pulitzer had supported the Democrats because they seemed closer to the people. But in 1896 when they nominated William Jennings Bryan, whom Pulitzer despised as the Pied Piper of the silver-coinage craze, he refused to go along. He also distrusted the radical Populists, considering them a collection of misfits and cranks implicated in the deadly violence of the Homestead and Pullman strikes. But he did not campaign for the Republican candidate, William McKinley. The result was that Hearst, who remained loyal to Bryan, became the Democrats' only champion among New York's newspaper publishers. Even though McKinley won, the circulation of Hearst's *Journal* rose while that of the *World* fell.

Rubbing salt into Pulitzer's wounds, Hearst mocked the *World* as well as other newspapers as has-beens practicing an outmoded journalism. With a gall that left Pulitzer furious, Hearst declared that his rival was a journalist who "made his money by pandering to the worst tastes of the prurient and horror-loving by dealing in bogus news, such as forged telegrams from eminent personages, and by affecting a devotion to the interests of the people while never really hurting those of their enemies."

Frantic at the way Hearst was beating him at his own game, Pulitzer slipped into a circulation war with his foe and into equally unconscionable practices. The most shameful episode was Pulitzer's part in fomenting war with Spain over Cuban independence. Although Hearst surpassed Pulitzer in concocting bloodcurdling reports of Spanish atrocities against Cubans and in clamoring for a declaration of war, both papers were soon spending fortunes for famous correspondents and faked "eyewitness" horror stories calculated to whip up war hysteria and, of course, boost circulation. Spain made all kinds of conciliatory gestures toward the United States, but the feuding newspapers achieved their aim when the battleship *Maine* exploded in Havana harbor in February 1898. The response of the *Journal* and the *World* was so inflammatory that Godkin, editor of the *Evening Post,* wrote: "Nothing so disgraceful as the behavior of these two newspapers in the past week has ever been known in the history of journalism. . . . A yellow journal is probably the nearest approach to hell in any Christian state." In that week the *World* sold a total of 5 million copies. But the shooting war—Hearst proudly called it "the *Journal*'s war"—lasted only two months; at its end the circulation of both papers dropped sharply.

Now in his fifties and almost totally blind, Pulitzer still traveled compulsively, surrounded by a cordon of secretary-companions and provided everywhere with soundproof rooms. His bookkeepers reported that his Bar Harbor summer place fed a daily average of fifty-three servants, secretaries, and guests, and stabled thirty-five horses at a cost of $15,000 a year. His latest New York mansion, designed by Stanford White, included a ballroom, a music room, paintings by Titian and other old masters, a swimming pool, and a vaultlike sanctum with double walls and triple-glazed windows.

To his children Pulitzer was sometimes a tyrant and sometimes indulgently generous. Although his wife rarely traveled with him and they saw little of each other, they evidently remained staunchly attached. A sociable, luxury-loving woman, she occasionally exceeded an allowance for family expenses of $7,000 a week—in a period when clerks earned from four to eight dollars a week and when an ad for a night watchman to work seventy-two hours a week for a salary of $10 brought 725 responses.

Pulitzer had forbidden any member of his staff to write for outside publication under his own name. So David Graham Phillips, a talented young writer whom Pulitzer had taken into his confidence and made a foreign correspondent but who was annoyed at being denied a byline, published a novel under a pseudonym. When the author's identity became known, Pulitzer immediately had the book read to him. We can imagine his mortification when he realized that it was based on the *World* and, entitled *The Great God Success,* portrayed a publisher who begins as a reformer but is corrupted by success and wealth. The climax comes when the publisher, Howard, avoids exposing the crooked practices of a railroad in which he has a large investment. Phillips drove home the indictment by describing Howard as exposing corruption and advocating reform mainly to gain circulation and advertising. But the picture of Howard as later haunted by remorse because he had betrayed a trust is overdrawn: he is too purely idealistic at the outset and too selfish and venal at the end. Yet *The Great God Success* remains an impressive attempt to show how the goal of financial success in the Gilded Age undermined social ideals. Six months later Phillips left the *World* and went on to become famous for his novels on social problems and his articles in the muckraking tradition.

Perhaps goaded by Phillips's novel, Pulitzer resumed his attacks on corruption in high places. In 1908 the *World* assailed the way the United States, under Theodore Roosevelt, had gained control of the Panama Canal project. Perhaps because Pulitzer envied Roosevelt's popularity as a reformer and his rise from police commissioner of New York City to the Presidency, he had sometimes challenged and even mocked Roosevelt. But when the *World* asserted that a sizable part of the $40 million due the French government for the canal properties had gone to American financiers such as J. P. Morgan and Roosevelt's brother-in-law, the President branded the charge an "abominable falsehood." In a virulent editorial the *World* retorted that the President's statement was full of "flagrant untruths" and "reeking with misstatements." Enraged, Roosevelt labeled the editorial "criminal libel" and ordered the Attorney General to sue. Although badly shaken, Pulitzer announced, "The *World* cannot be muzzled." A grand jury indicted Pulitzer and the *World,* but they were triumphantly vindicated when the Supreme Court ruled in the *World*'s favor. The actual disposition of the canal money remained a mystery, but the decision was generally considered a major victory for freedom of the press.

Pulitzer now spent most of his time on his newest yacht, one of the largest of its kind. It was a private kingdom, with a crew of sixty and six secretary-companions. The secretaries, screened for everything from their classical education to their table manners, took turns guiding Pulitzer on his walks, talking to him, and reading to him from newspapers, magazines, and as many as two books a week. Although drained by his demands and criticism, they were all dazzled by his learned discourse, his recall of the classics in four or five languages, and his observations on politics, government, and journalism.

Although Joseph Pulitzer was only sixty-four when he died, he was already one of the legendary giants of personal journalism. Even such a foe as Hearst, conveniently forgetting their bitter rivalry, eulogized him as ''a great power uniformly exerted in behalf of popular rights and human progress.'' Pulitzer left an estate of $8 million, including a million dollars for a school of journalism at Columbia University, scholarships, and, reflecting the diversity of his interests, funds for the Pulitzer Prizes in journalism, drama, literature, and music.

After his death, the St. Louis *Post-Dispatch,* run by his sons, maintained its reputation and influence, but the *World,* outdone in sensationalism by the new morning ''tabloids,'' lost ground. Even though it abandoned Pulitzer's opposition to bylines and became known for such columnists as Heywood Broun, Walter Lippmann, Franklin P. Adams (''FPA''), and Alexander Woollcott, it declined steadily. In 1931, with the onset of the Depression, it was merged with an undistinguished unit in the Scripps-Howard chain.

Joseph Pulitzer was a man of paradoxes, most of them traceable to forces loosed in the Gilded Age. He mounted campaign after campaign to root out corruption and bring about social reform, but he was convinced that he could achieve such ends mainly by increasing circulation and advertising. He pledged his reporters to truth and accuracy but sometimes allowed the news to be distorted dangerously. He disparaged the social elite but titillated readers with reports of their diversions, and he castigated the plutocrats while indulging in much the same luxury. He was a benevolent despot at home and a paternal autocrat in his office. In temperament he could be both kind and harsh, both independent and in need of sympathy. He was at once a critic of the age and a product of it.

# 7

## VIOLATORS
## OF THE GREAT TABOO

The prudery of Americans in the middle of the nineteenth century was a rearguard action covering the slow retreat of Puritanism. With each decade after 1840, the stirrings of resistance, clandestine as well as open, spread a little farther. At the same time, virtue became increasingly a matter of appearances. The intensity of the Puritan opposition to sexuality was being replaced by the middle-class belief that sexuality was disreputable and vulgar. The Puritans damned it because they believed the body was vile, the senses a trap, and worldly pleasures wicked; the Victorians decried it largely because it was improper and hurt one's reputation. The Puritans bore down on it with the wrath of God and the fires of hell; the Victorians treated it with suppression, euphemisms, and silence.

This does not mean that mid-nineteenth-century prudery was a mask for sexual indulgence. It does mean that genuine innocence was confined chiefly to young ladies of good family, and even in them it was valued in part for its usefulness in capturing a husband. Before 1750, if New Englanders sinned they went in fear of divine punishment; by 1860 they had to cope mainly with conscience and the opinion of their neighbors. And it was of course easier to conceal a transgression from the latter than from God. Mrs. Grundy had taken the place of Cotton Mather.

So a bourgeois concern for respectability joined with a residue of the Puritan distrust of the instincts to suppress all signs of sexuality. Even the relatively liberal-minded opposed it as an appetite not governed by reason. John Stuart Mill observed that in his father, "Logos was forever engaged in slaying *Eros.*" The sexuality of men was considered animalism, and the ideal was to sublimate it. Young men were exhorted to subdue desire by means of exercise, cold baths, hard beds, religion, and avoiding French novels. Even married men were advised, according to such an influential medical work as Sir William Acton's *The Functions and Disorders of the Reproductive Organs* (London, 1857, and often reprinted in the United States as well as in England), not to indulge in sexual relations with their wives more often than once every week or ten days. Another medical authority, Sir James Paget, went so far as to assert that "nocturnal emissions" signified impurity and would arouse deep feelings of guilt. Acton even suggested tying a cord around the penis at night. Masturbation was invariably described as dangerous.

Little or no attention was paid to sexuality in women because it was assumed, or pretended, that normal women did not experience desire. Even William W. Sanger, a New York physician whose *History of Prostitution* included a remarkably thorough report on what was called "the commerce of the sexes," declared in the 1850s:

> But it must be repeated, and most decidedly, that without these or some other equally stimulating cause [destitution, drink, or seduction and abandonment], the full force of sexual desire is seldom known to a virtuous woman. In the male sex, nature has provided a more susceptible organization than in the females, apparently with the beneficent design of repressing those evils which must result from mutual appetite equally felt by both.

Incredibly, this suggests that some nameless immorality would result if the two parties, even if married, were equally passionate. It was assumed that wives merely submitted to their husbands and did so only for the sake of procreation. So Victorian women, deprived of the right to full sexual expression as well as many other rights, became what the Reverend Theodore Parker described as drudges, good only for housekeeping, or dolls, good only to look at.

The facts concerning sexual activity in any earlier era are difficult to come by, especially when, as in the Victorian period, they were suppressed, glossed over, or distorted. But we can filter revealing evidence from a variety of tangential sources: statements on divorce reform, contraception, and free love; accounts of prostitution and abortion; novels; sermons; reports of scandals and adultery trials; medical works; and even pornography.

As always, the prime deterrent to free sexual activity in or out of wedlock remained the fear of pregnancy. Contraceptives were known as far back as ancient Egypt, but Christianity made them unthinkable in Europe. Doubtless *coitus interruptus* had always been practiced, but few found it satisfactory and some thought it unnatural. In the eighteenth century, Englishmen who went a-wenching, as Boswell tells us, sometimes used a sheepgut sheath, called a condom after the British doctor who is supposed to have invented it. And Casanova, certainly an authority, tells of using "English overcoats" made of "very fine, transparent skin." But they used these mainly to ward off venereal diseases. It was largely Frenchwomen in the seventeenth century, having separated intercourse for pleasure from intercourse for procreation, who turned to such preventive devices as a vaginal sponge.

English social reformers, bent on helping the poor reduce the size of their families, introduced these practices into England. One of them, Robert Dale Owen, who helped his father, the famous Robert Owen, establish a cooperative colony at New Harmony, Indiana, spread the information in America, describing sheaths, sponges, and various techniques in his *Moral Physiology* (1831). Apparently intimidated by harsh criticism, he omitted most of this information in later editions; but 25,000 copies of the book were sold in the next forty years. Another pioneer of contraception in America was Dr. Charles Knowlton. Although a New England farmer's son who remained a rural Massachusetts physician all his life, he early became a freethinker. In 1832 he published, under the innocent title of *Fruits of Philosophy: or the Private Companion of Young Married People,* a reliable guide to what he called "the anti-conception art," particularly recommending various douches and syringes. He was immediately accused of providing a "complete recipe" for "the trade of a strumpet," arraigned and sentenced to three months at hard labor. Nevertheless, 277,000 copies of his guide had been sold in the United States and Britain by 1880.

By the end of the Civil War, observers noted a sharp decline in the size of families and agreed that this was the result of a conscious effort to avoid having children. A few added startling details on the availability of contraceptive information. In his *Serpents in Doves' Nests* (1867), the Reverend John Todd declared, "There is scarcely a young lady in New England . . . whose marriage can be announced in the paper, without her being insulted by receiving through the mail a printed circular offering information and instrumentalities . . . by which the laws of heaven in regard to the increase of the human family may be thwarted."

Soon even a woman dared to offer advice on the subject. Condemning other practices as unhealthy, Mrs. Eliza Bisbee Duffey in 1873 recommended the use of the "safe period" to women whose monthly cycle was regular. A way was thus opened for an evasion of the "laws of heaven" that doubtless satisfied even the most hypocritical Victorians. If the spread of such preventive practices, despite all the taboos, seems surprising, the prevalence of that far more drastic measure, abortion, will come as a shock. The practice had become so open that the Reverend David Macrae, a visitor from Scotland in 1869, felt compelled to discuss the subject in his book, *The American Home:*

> The papers swarm with advertisements of the requisite medicines; and books and pamphlets . . . in this diabolical art are openly advertised and sold. . . . A medical man in one of the large cities of the North enumerated thirty practitioners in that one city who . . . devoted themselves to this species of murder. In all these cities there are establishments called by such names as "Invalids' Retreat," but well known to be reserved almost exclusively for cases of this description.

The clergyman was not exaggerating: a formidable mansion on Fifth Avenue was widely known to belong to a "Madame Restell," queen of New York abortionists. Born Anna Trow, she had come from England in 1831 and, setting herself up as a "Professor of Midwifery," was soon prospering. After a jail term early in her career, she reestablished herself, and spending, it was said, $20,000 a year advertising "infallible French pills for female complaints" and "a cure at one interview," she became rich. Vigorous efforts were made to close her down or jail her, but she had too much money as well as political influence and, as she made very clear, secrets that would shake some of New York's best families. Far from being ashamed of her calling, Madame Restell felt that she had saved many women from ruin and not a few respectable families from great shame. A dark-haired woman with hard features, neither desiring attention nor shrinking from it, she would come out of her house each day and, entering a magnificent carriage attended by two footmen, go for a ride in the park. Her patients, often shrouded in veils, preferred to come at night. No one knows how many women she attended or how many did not survive her ministrations.

Madame Restell's fate was perfect for sermons. In 1878, Anthony Comstock, a young man who would in time become the leading "vice crusader" and censor in New York history, decided to trap her. Not hesitating to play the *agent provocateur,* he repeatedly visited Madame Restell, pretending that he had to help a woman end a pregnancy and protect her from conceiving again. Madame Restell supplied him with medicines and syringes. On his last visit he had her arrested and carried off to the Tombs. She is said to have offered him $40,000 to let her go, but he refused. Released on bail, she was found dead in her home—a suicide, her throat slashed. Comstock supplied a blood-curdling epitaph: "A bloody ending to a bloody life."

Comstock was in his way as warped as Madame Restell. Entering the scene in the 1870s, he embodied the neurotic distortions produced by mid-Victorian repression. He is the mirror image of the most extreme pornographer of his time; and he was so clever at apprehending such men because he had exactly the same interests. Like the author of *My Secret Life,* an autobiography by an outwardly respectable Englishman who spent all his days in sexual adventures and his evenings recording his accomplishments, he gloated over his exploits. He stopped at nothing to lure his victims into the most incriminating acts. Without any shame he publicly testified that he and his associates had entered a brothel and paid three women to parade in the nude before he arrested them for indecent exposure. In the decade after the founding of the New York Society for the Suppression of Vice, Comstock confiscated 65,000 "articles for immoral use" and 27,000 pounds—a curious way of measuring—of "obscene books."

That pornography did flourish throughout this period we know from the huge collections and the staggering bibliographies assembled by fanciers of such material. In fact, the eighteenth and nineteenth centuries have been called the Golden Age of pornography. This is not entirely surprising: the more rigorous the suppression, the greater the demand for substitute outlets. There is little doubt that the range of sexual experience described in the 4,000 pages of *My Secret Life,* and the ease with which the author seems to have made many of his conquests, could be paralleled in New York. Even if we disallow many of the thousand-odd escapades he records, the remainder constitutes a picture of women, particularly in the lower classes, whose scruples were weak, whose favors cheap, and whose sexual desires, supposedly nonexistent, were easily aroused.

Such desires obviously help to account for the number of unwed mothers, especially among the poor. The Victorians were so intolerant in this regard that the image of a Victorian father righteously ordering his "fallen" daughter never to darken his door again has long been a favorite target of parody. The implications of this tableau are worth noting: first, it apparently occurred so often as to become trite; second, the daughter was banished not so much because she had sinned as because she was socially ruined; and last, it ignored Christ's example of mercy and forgiveness. It was so cruel that—like other aspects of Victorian inhumanity such as the mistreatment of the destitute, the insane, and orphans—it aroused the first community efforts to care for unwed mothers and their babies.

Prostitution is of course another significant clue to the moral standards of an age. The Puritans, experts at dealing with all the emissaries of Satan, managed at first to keep out whores by means of sensational public punishments and confessions, in themselves a form of voyeurism and sexual release, but in time "bawds" were included in the undesirables shipped to the colonies by the mother country. By the early part of the nineteenth century, the influx of immigrants with other standards, along with corrupt city officials and police, permitted the spread of professional prostitution. According to the Magdalen Society, a group devoted to the rescue of "fallen women," there were 20,000 prostitutes in New York City in 1830. If they received only three visitors a day, the reformer Robert Dale Owen pointed out, this meant that they were visited 10 million times annually.

In the years before and during the war, moreover, the number of women in the profession increased so rapidly that by 1866 Bishop Simpson of the Methodist Episcopal Church asserted that there were as many prostitutes in New York as Methodists. Superintendent of Police John A. Kennedy protested that this was a fearful exaggeration but blandly admitted that there were 621 houses of prostitution, ninety-nine houses of assignation, and seventy-five concert saloons of ill repute. He also conceded that he had no way of knowing how many other women roamed the streets or haunted the bars. What every aware person did know was that in New York any man with the means could enjoy any vice at any time.

The vileness of the dives frequented by the brutalized poor was not half so surprising as the elegance of the bordellos patronized by the rich. The most luxurious was The Seven Sisters, a "parlor house" that occupied no less than seven august brownstones in a row on West Twenty-fifth Street. With patrician ceremony the madam left engraved invitations for men registering at the best hotels, and the patrons sometimes came in formal dress. Even more exclusive was Josephine Wood's house on Clinton Place (later Eighth Street), west of Broadway. It welcomed only the elite, and every visitor had to identify himself to the satisfaction of the butler. The parlors where patrons waited were furnished with crystal chandeliers, velvet carpets, paintings, gilt-framed mirrors, and sofas upholstered in satin and brocade. The girls, chosen for their accomplishments as well as attractions, wore evening dresses and were models of decorum. Only champagne was served, and it was said that a girl could earn as much as $200 on a busy night. Josie Woods, still beautiful, was herself a sophisticated hostess. A familiar figure at Saratoga as well as in New

York, she was known for her rich clothes, diamonds, and splendid carriages and horses. In clothes and manners she was certainly indistinguishable from the most fashionable women of the day.

Equally notorious were some of the larger "concert saloons." Perhaps the most curious was John Allen's dance hall and "fast" house on Water Street. Allen was a tough, wiry little man who made his girls wear short, low-necked scarlet dresses and sometimes spurred them on with blows and curses. The chief duty of the girls was to persuade the customers to buy drinks after each dance. Allen is particularly interesting because he had been a student at Union Theological Seminary, came from a well-to-do upstate family, and had several brothers in the clergy. He left religious tracts on the tables in his dance hall, put a Bible in the rooms to which the girls took their customers, and sometimes preached a sermon to his employees. One night when a group of evangelists descended on his place—they found him drunk—and conducted a prayer meeting there, Allen was so impressed by the publicity that he let the clergymen continue to hold meetings in his hall. After a few months the hall was closed, and it was announced that Allen himself would lead revival meetings. Then a newspaperman uncovered the facts: the clergymen had rented both Allen's place and his cooperation. The only lesson that might be learned from this was that Allen was a fraud and that clergymen would go to any lengths to make converts.

Even more revealing were the so-called houses of assignation. Many of these were located in the best neighborhoods, including Fifth Avenue. They guaranteed privacy and discretion, the man entering by one door, the woman by another. The busiest time, according to Dr. Sanger, the New York physician who investigated the "commerce of the sexes" in the 1850s, was during the promenade hours on Broadway, approximately from noon to five o'clock. The couples who met in these houses made appointments through the "Personals" column of newspapers. The men were often, Dr. Sanger reported, from the most respected walks of life, and the women "exclusively from our fashionable society." He suggested that in the preceding fifteen years a looseness in morals had been induced by easy money, theories of "free love," foreign influences, and such fashions as "the low-necked dress and the lascivious waltz."

It is generally agreed today that poverty and the wretched conditions and pitiful pay of working women were the main causes of prostitution—that and the idea that a man had a vital need to "relax his vessels" by sexual intercourse. These conditions were hardly peculiar to New York. They were duplicated in Boston and Washington; and in the West whores flourished in every mining camp, and ranged in San Francisco from sophisticated courtesans in the larger gambling casinos to "white slaves" in Chinatown.

In the South, the plain fact is that men who had access to slave women had a convenient outlet for their sexual urges. This was demoralizing not only to the black women who were used like concubines and the black men who stood by helplessly but also to the white men with their feudal sexual code and the white wives who had to share their men with their slaves. This is not a conclusion reached only by outsiders. One of the most revealing journals of the period (it was not published until 1905), that of Mary Boykin Chesnut, daughter of a South Carolina governor and wife of a Confederate brigadier general, had this entry in March 1861:

> Under slavery, we live surrounded by prostitutes, yet an abandoned woman is sent out of any decent house. Who thinks the worse of a Negro or mulatto woman for being a thing we can't name? God forgive us, but ours is a *monstrous* system, a wrong and an iniquity! Like the patriarchs of old, our men live all in one house with their wives and their concubines; and the mulattoes one sees in every family partly resemble the white children. Any lady is ready to tell you who is the father of all the mulatto children in everybody's household but her own. Those, she seems to think, drop from the clouds. . . . My disgust is sometimes boiling over.

Besides this domestic license, there were in such places as New Orleans unique concentrations of organized licentiousness. A modern authority on prostitution describes New Orleans as "the greatest brothel city of all time—a veritable Mecca of whores." Large areas of the city were occupied by Creole prostitutes who openly invited passing men with obscene gestures and offers. Quadroons and octaroons were preferred both as whores and as mistresses, and according to one study, some masters forced female slaves to submit to impregnation by white men in order to secure mulatto young. The easiest path to freedom and relative comfort was to become a prostitute or a concubine. There were even elaborate balls at which the male guests, all white men, negotiated for the purchase of the female guests, all quadroons, with the mothers or aunts who accompanied the girls.

It was therefore distinctly a case of the kettle calling the pot black when *DeBow's Review,* published in Louisiana, declared in 1857: "In eighty years the social system of the North has developed to a point in morals only reached by Rome in six centuries. . . . Already the priceless gem of chastity in women has been despoiled of its talismanic charm with men. . . . [The rule is] so long as exposure is avoided, no wrong is done."

If a man was rich he could make light of his transgressions or even flaunt them. It was, so to speak, the American version of *droit du seigneur.* In fashionable society it was not taken amiss if a youth had an affair with an older woman—as Ben Franklin had recommended to a young correspondent a century earlier—as long as he was discreet.

We have already seen Leonard Jerome playing mentor to adoring young singers, George Gould siring three children by a kept chorus girl, and Commodore Vanderbilt pursuing housemaids. Add to these Russell Sage, the parsimonious millionaire who was three times brought to court by women who testified that he took sexual liberties with them. One even claimed that he was the father of her child, and the marchioness Gregorio D'Adjuria charged that he had beaten her when she had refused to undress and submit to his embraces. Two of the suits were thrown out of court because of the statute of limitations, but Sage never denied his guilt in either case.

Others found release in the tolerant atmosphere of Europe. Young Sam Ward learned about women as well as wine in Paris in the 1830s, not to mention his wife, Medora, who went to live with a "Russian prince" in Paris in the 1860s. The orgies of James Gordon Bennett, Jr., remained the talk of New York long after he had gone abroad and made them the talk of Paris. American travelers, carrying their taboos abroad with them, rarely commented on sex relations in such countries as France, scandalous though they must have seemed. Henry Wikoff was an exception. The ward of a wealthy Philadelphian, Wikoff went to Yale but was dismissed for spending more time at play than study. A tall young man who dressed like a dandy, he returned to Philadelphia and divided his time between the theater, "female society," and studying for the bar. Like Sam Ward, he went to Europe in 1834 and was so enchanted by European society that he eventually spent most of his time abroad. Relying on *savoir-vivre* and certain small talents, he was the intimate of dancer Fanny Elssler and gained notoriety in 1852 when he was jailed in Genoa after an attempt to force Jane Gamble, a forty-two-year-old English heiress, to marry him.

Wikoff's *The Reminiscences of an Idler,* written many years later, is interesting for the frankness with which he describes his surprise in the 1830s at the boldness with which Frenchwomen of all classes entered into relations with men. He had known that it was common for a man of the upper class to take a mistress while his wife took a lover, but he had not realized that "the middle and lower strata were not a whit more prudish than their betters." Thus an unmarried woman who supported herself could, without loss of respectability, establish a temporary liaison with a man and, similarly, a workingwoman might move into a room with a workingman in a so-called *mariage de St. Jacques,* which would endure "at least as long as their lease." As for students in the Latin Quarter, everyone knew that they consoled themselves with *grisettes,* and often shared lodgings with them. Wikoff concluded that although all this may have constituted "libertinage," it did not lead to depravity. Describing the "universal jollity" of Sundays in France, he observed that "the rigid notions of our Puritan fathers would have been regarded, not merely as fanaticism, but downright insanity." Men like Wikoff and Ward were uncommon in the 1830s but by the 1870s they were an American type, one that no longer heeded puritanical disapproval.

There was precious little sexual realism in American novels of the mid-nineteenth century. Fiction had been taken over by a race of female novelists and ladies' magazine contributors who, with the exception of a few remarkable regionalists, turned out sentimental or pious stories of contemporary life or idealized historical romance. Rejecting the tradition of sexual candor from Chaucer and Shakespeare through Defoe and Fielding, they suppressed the sensual and with it a vital aspect of the relationship of the sexes.

But the novels of John W. De Forest and, later, of Edith Wharton lift a corner of the veil on forbidden relationships. Wharton's novels of upper-class life in the 1860s and 1870s make clear that it was not uncommon for a young man, such as Newland Archer in *The Age of Innocence,* or an older, unmarried man-about-town, such as Henry Prest in *New Year's Day,* to have an affair with a married woman. Although under the double standard an unmarried woman was denied any such freedom, married women who had an affair would be sharply criticized but not ruined. Of this curious dispensation Wharton says: "It was easier, and less dastardly on the whole, for a wife to play such a part toward her husband. A woman's standard of truthfulness was tacitly held to be lower: she was the subject creature, and versed in the arts of the enslaved." Along with other feudal ordinances, such attitudes reduced women of the upper class to the status of attractive retainers, suitable for display or as an aspect of conspicuous consumption.

The hypocritical concern for appearances is illustrated in *The Age of Innocence* by the treatment that upper-class society accords Ellen Mingott when she marries a Polish count but deserts him because she finds him "a brute." She is accepted back into New York society but is prohibited, on pain of ostracism, from divorcing the count. The opposition of the patricians to divorce was summed up by Mrs. John King Van Rensselaer. Recalling the 1870s, she wrote, some fifty years later:

> That domestic troubles should ever end in a divorce court was unthinkable; so families remained intact, whatever happened, and the most outrageous conduct was accorded no further publicity than the whisper of gossip. . . . The much deplored, frequently assailed morals of current society are no bit worse than they were in the prim and prudish half century ago. In that day the woman who obtained a divorce was a Pariah.

By the late 1860s the opposition to divorce was already beginning to give way. The Reverend David Macrae reported in 1869 in his *The American Home* that divorce mills had sprung up in several cities. Certain Chicago lawyers, he said, would arrange an immediate divorce if one party made charges and the other "confessed" to them. By the 1890s divorces were more or less frequent in fashionable society, one of the most publicized being that of Willie K. and Alva Vanderbilt.

A novel by John W. De Forest, *Miss Ravenel's Conversion from Secession to Loyalty* (1867), dealt far more frankly with illicit relations between the sexes than any work by any other well-known American novelist. Although the transgressors in the book, Colonel Carter and Mrs. Larue, are hardly of the Wharton breed, their uninhibited sexuality indicates that in certain circles the common Victorian taboos were beginning to be ignored. Colonel Carter, member of an aristocratic Virginia family and a graduate of West Point, is an able officer but a hard-drinking, loose-living spendthrift who is eventually driven to swindling the government in order to cover his debts. His virility captivates young Lillie Ravenel, and Lillie's sprightly innocence captivates Carter. They marry, but when the war takes Carter to New Orleans and he meets Mrs. Larue, a youngish widow whose desires are as strong as his—partly explained by the fact that she is French— he has an affair with her. In several remarkable passages, Mrs. Larue declares that she believes in taking love whenever she is moved to do so and expects every normal man to do the same. De Forest presents her not as a thoughtless wanton but a mature and tolerant woman who wants little from Carter except his embraces.

It is scandals with their newspaper publicity, courtroom confrontations, and bitter charges that light up glaringly what went on behind the closed doors and drawn shades of some Victorian homes. Many newspapers and magazines paraded intimate details of private life with as much zest as any paper of our day; they seized even more hungrily on sexual scandals than do we who are exposed to far more frank and clinical disclosures on stage and screen and in books.

One of the first major scandals to reveal a marked sexual sophistication and no concern for sin or propriety was the Sickles-Key affair. The son of a New York patent attorney, Daniel Sickles had moved up from Tammany politics to Congress. His friends attributed his rise to energy and a dynamic personality; his enemies thought it was his pugnacity and lack of conscience. All agreed that he was constantly at the center of controversy or scandal. Something of a rake, Sickles was known for such outrageous exploits as turning up at a session of the New York State Assembly with Fanny White, a young woman he had plucked from a Mercer Street brothel. Even when he married Teresa Bagioli, sixteen-year-old daughter of an Italian musician of some renown, it was whispered that he had seduced not only the daughter but also the mother.

Elected to Congress in 1856 as a supporter of Buchanan, Sickles arrived in Washington as an influential friend of the President. He leased the Stockton mansion on patrician Lafayette Square and began entertaining on a grand scale. Ironically it was Sickles himself who introduced his wife to tall, handsome, thirty-eight-year-old Philip Barton Key, son of Francis Scott Key and a widower with four children. Key soon began to escort Mrs. Sickles to the weekly hop at Willard's whenever Sickles was busy. And Sickles was often busy, not only with politics and legal work but with other women. It was soon apparent to everyone but Sickles that Key was acting as more than an escort to Mrs. Sickles.

The first tremor of disaster came when a friend of the Sickleses, a young government clerk, asserted that he had repeatedly seen Teresa and Key ride to a house outside the city and tarry there. Sickles at once confronted Key with the charge. Key challenged the clerk to repeat the accusation, whereupon the frightened youth fled to New York. Having thus easily disposed of Sickles's suspicions, Key returned to his trysting with no more prudence than before. Soon Sickles received an anonymous letter informing him that Key was meeting Mrs. Sickles in a rented house on Fifteenth Street. Distraught, he confronted his wife; she broke down and admitted everything. Sickles forced her to write out a confession. It declared in part: "I have been in a house in Fifteenth Street with Mr. Key. How many times I don't know. . . . I did what is usual for a wicked woman to do. . . . Was there on Wednesday last. . . . I undressed myself. Mr. Key undressed also. . . . I do not deny that we have had connection in that house . . . in the parlor, on the sofa."

The following day Sickles called in Samuel Butterworth, an old friend, to advise him. As Butterworth was warning him that a scandal would wreck his career, Sickles suddenly saw Key waving a handkerchief at the house from the square outside. Sickles, armed with a pistol, dashed out of the house, shouted, "Key, you scoundrel, you have dishonored my bed—you must die!" and fired twice. Screaming, Key fell dead.

The shock waves from Sickles's act reached the President; bumblingly, Buchanan tried to suppress the story. Some Southerners were troubled only by the fact that Key had been unarmed; gallantry apparently prescribed that Sickles should have given Key an opportunity to kill as well as cuckold him. At the trial Sickles pleaded temporary insanity—said to be the first use of such a plea—resulting from the "defilement" of his marriage bed. The prosecution, fearing Buchanan's displeasure, made no attempt to show that Sickles had defiled that bed time and again. The trial was thus perverted from a prosecution of Sickles for murder into a condemnation of Key for adultery. Sickles was triumphantly acquitted and 1,500 admirers gathered to congratulate him. To the dismay of his supporters, he rejoined his wife a few months later.

For a time Sickles was ostracized. But when war came he quickly raised a full brigade, qualifying him as a brigadier general, and soon became known as a cocky commander. The gay dances and lavish banquets he gave during the winter encampment were the talk of Washington. But the gaiety was short-lived. At Gettysburg, early in July, Sickles thrust his troops too far forward, lost 4,200 men in four hours, and was himself carried from the field with a shattered leg. He was convinced that he had saved the day, but General Meade is reported to have said that if Sickles had not lost his leg he would have been court-martialed.

Recovering amazingly from his amputation, Sickles was soon undertaking missions for President Lincoln. After the war, President Andrew Johnson appointed him military governor of the Carolinas. He was, however, too hot-tempered to tolerate unreconstructed Southerners, and Johnson was forced to replace him. Sickles's response was to move into the Grant camp. Always quick to reward a supporter, Grant made him minister to Spain, ignoring his record of shameless and headstrong conduct. In Spain he was soon deep in plots and counterplots. Meanwhile, he entertained the elite of Madrid in the style of a grandee. Since poor Teresa had died suddenly at age thirty-one, he was more than ever free to pursue his amours. His most spectacular conquest was Queen Isabella of Spain, who lived in exile in Paris, a triumph that gained him the title, among cynical Frenchmen, of the "Yankee King of Spain." Some even said that his abrupt marriage, at fifty-one, to a very young niece of a Spanish marquise was only a blind for his affair with Isabella.

After an interlude in New York he returned to Spain and joined in overthrowing the king and establishing a republic. Late in 1873, when a Spanish gunboat captured the *Virginius* as it was running arms to Cuban rebels and shot many of the Americans in the crew, Sickles protested violently. He was already threatening war when Secretary of State Fish settled the dispute. Sickles immediately resigned in protest, and suddenly, at the age of fifty-five, he was not only out of office but out of favor.

For a few years he lived in Paris. Although his wife and two children were with him, he engaged, as always, in intrigues and amatory adventures. In 1874 he returned to America alone, restlessly seeking to realize unsatisfied ambitions. He tried politics again, returning briefly to Congress when he was seventy-four years old, practiced law, and speculated on Wall Street. He still pursued the ladies, sending a diamond to every woman who struck his fancy. In time, spending and speculation wiped out his fortune. He died penniless—but as peppery and unrepentant as ever.

It is impossible to classify Daniel Sickles. He was capable of warmth, pride, courage, and resolution, but again and again he canceled out these qualities with a fatal combination of rashness and vanity. Just as in practical matters he was often ruled by passion, so in love he was guided entirely by appetite. He made a mockery of many of the Alger virtues, but his fate hardly serves as an object lesson: he lived to the age of ninety-five, often in posts of honor and responsibility, and constantly enjoying sinful pleasures to the full.

The Key affair betrayed a confusion and hypocrisy amounting not to a double standard but to a triple standard. Sickles assumed a right to philander but felt impelled to murder a man who made free with his wife. For Teresa Sickles there was no punishment mainly because she was considered a subject creature too helpless to be blamed for what any man did to her.

In 1859 the nation was shocked by the Sickles-Key affair, but eleven years later the Fisk-Stokes affair was simply another scandal. Jim Fisk was a knave whom decent citizens deplored—as much for being a vulgarian as for being a libertine. Soon after he bought Pike's Opera House, gossip told of orgies in the Erie vice president's office and of chorus girls who doubled as concubines. At the same time, Fisk, keeping his wife ("a plump, wholesome big-hearted commonplace woman," as Fisk described her) in a mansion in Boston, installed his mistress, Josie Mansfield, in another mansion down the street from the opera house. Daughter of a California newspaperman, Helen Josephine Mansfield was endowed with a voluptuous figure, luxuriant black hair, lustrous dark eyes, and a soft voice. Easily seduced at an early age, she quickly learned to rely more on her charms than her talents. After a tenuous marriage at age seventeen to an actor, she turned up in New York and was soon friendly with a Miss Annie Wood, who ran an elegant bordello. Through Miss Wood, Josie met Jim Fisk. Before long, he had set her up in a four-story townhouse, with servants, a carriage and coachman, Paris gowns, diamonds, and sables, and had entered with her on a life of pleasure that was the talk of the city. Regularly he took her riding in one of his six splendid rigs, with a pair of black footmen in front and a pair of white footmen in back. He could never take her to the finest restaurants or hotels, but this was a trivial restriction because at Josie's place she and Fisk entertained some of the best-known figures in the worlds of politics and entertainment.

At his opera house, after achieving a noisily advertised success with *The Twelve Temptations,* a musical extravaganza featuring a regiment of beautiful girls and a rousing can-can, Fisk concentrated on the lightest *opéra bouffe,* simply putting on the stage what he constantly put into his life. He often played two full-blown light opera characters in real life: an admiral and a colonel. First he took over the Fall River Line, which operated some of the finest sidewheelers in America and dominated the run from New York to Boston by way of Long Island Sound. With all the gusto of his peddler-wagon days, Fisk decorated two of his new steamers, the *Bristol* and the *Providence,* with lavender paddleboxes and yellow smokestacks, and furnished them with thick carpets, grand staircases of mahogany, gaslit saloons 300 feet long, and a large orchestra. Decked out in a dress uniform like that of an admiral, he would station himself at the gangway of the Chambers Street wharf to oversee the afternoon departure.

Fisk's role as an army officer was just as outlandish. As one who had worn silk underwear and patent leather shoes throughout the war, his instant rise to the colonelcy of the Ninth Regiment of the New York State Guard can be explained only by the fact that the regiment had fallen on evil days. That Fisk was a flabby bag of a man who ached at the very thought of riding a horse did not matter at all. In an age of money lords, even a famous regiment had to have a promoter. Fisk entered enthusiastically into his new role. He ordered the most colorful colonel's uniform in U.S. military annals (it is said to have cost $2,000), outfitted every man at Erie expense, and entertained them at a performance of *The Twelve Temptations*—with free champagne for all. Such antics soon gained the Ninth the names of the "Opera House Army" and "Fisk's Footmen." But it also tripled the roster.

By this time, Josie Mansfield's unfaithfulness to her fat lover was known widely enough to make Fisk seem a fool. The deceiver was Edward Stiles Stokes. Fisk had met him on Wall Street and was engaged in a few business ventures with him. Ned Stokes was young, handsome, as lithe as Fisk was flabby, and a dandy. Although both his own and his wife's parents were affluent, and he shared with Fisk a Brooklyn oil refinery that was showing a profit because Erie bought its oil, he was a reckless spender, especially at racetracks and sporting saloons.

Shortly after Josie met Stokes she began showing dissatisfaction with her lot as Fisk's mistress, insisting that since he could not marry her, he should settle enough money on her to make her independent. At last, in the summer of 1870, Fisk learned that Stokes was seeing Josie whenever he himself was away. The ruptures and reconciliations between Fisk and Josie became more and more violent. Nettled, Fisk ended Erie's connection with the Brooklyn refinery. Stokes, facing bankruptcy, collected a $27,500 company debt and kept the money, whereupon Fisk had him arrested for embezzlement. Forced to spend a weekend in jail and deprived of his daily manicure and scented

Florida water, Stokes swore vengeance. He and Josie began to threaten to expose Fisk's "Erie secrets." Armed with Fisk's letters to Josie, Stokes demanded $200,000 from Fisk. At the same time Josie sued Fisk for $50,000, which she claimed he owed her. When the suit came to court, the whole tawdry relationship of the trio became public. It was what George Templeton Strong, respected lawyer and caustic diarist, called "a special stinkpot." Even Jay Gould decided that Erie could no longer afford to be associated with such shabby rascality. So Fisk resigned as vice president of Erie.

At this point Fisk won several victories in court, including a grand jury indictment of Josie Mansfield and Ned Stokes on a charge of blackmail. For Stokes these reverses were disastrous. He already owed $38,000 to lawyers. And now he was revealed as helping a scheming harlot cheat a bountiful lover. A vain and foolish man, Stokes drove to a new hotel on Broadway, the Grand Central. Waiting at the top of the stairway, he shot Fisk twice as the latter started up the stairs. Fisk lingered until the following morning. Boss Tweed—himself free on bail and facing ruin—came to sit at his bedside. Jay Gould sat in a corner and wept.

The reaction of the city was astonishing. In the preceding months the newspapers had taken to ridiculing Fisk mercilessly, but the circumstances of his death evoked sympathy and sorrow. The funeral was, like Fisk himself, a charade of falsehoods. First came the coffin draped in the Ninth Regiment's Civil War battle flag (for a man who had traded with the enemy), followed by Fisk's riderless horse (for a man who hated to ride), six platoons of National Guard officers wearing crepe, waves of Erie employees, and a stream of carriages. It was an awesome spectacle, and one newspaper understandably compared it to Abraham Lincoln's funeral six years before. From the gaunt, brooding figure of the father-leader to the fat peddler-turned-swindler, fake colonel, debauchee—what a sea change in America's martyred heroes!

The usual explanation is that Fisk had the common touch, meaning that he entertained people, turning his frauds into farce and his outrages into jokes. It meant that he was friendly and generous, albeit with money he had stolen, that his love of show seemed comic, and that he was vulgar in an American way. But perhaps it meant mainly that he was never a hypocrite. In a time of endless social taboos, when any evidence of forbidden behavior was glossed over with cant, everyone knew that Jim Fisk had stolen millions from Erie, that all his grand titles were make-believe, that he had put Erie's offices in an opera house because he liked shows and showgirls, and that he kept the fanciest mistress in the city. Vulgar and flashy though he might be, he was refreshing in his candor. When that old humbug Daniel Drew reproved him, Fisk is reported to have replied:

> No, Uncle, there isn't any hope for Jim Fisk. I'm a gone goose. . . . Some people are born to be good, other people are born to be bad. I was born to be bad. As to the World, the Flesh and the Devil, I'm on good terms with all three. If God Almighty is going to damn us men because we love the women, then let him go ahead and do it. I'm having a good time now, and if I've got to pay for it hereafter, why . . . I'll take what's coming to me.

Perhaps those who looked on him tolerantly did so because they found in him a vicarious release: he flouted the Mrs. Grundys who made them cower, he did what many of them would have liked to do, and he obviously enjoyed it.

Of course, there were a few who now used his life as an object lesson: his violent death, at thirty-six, served them perfectly. Mustering all his sin-shattering eloquence, the pastor of Brooklyn's Plymouth Church, the Reverend Henry Ward Beecher, cried:

> And that supreme mountebank of fortune—the astounding event of his age: that man of some smartness in business, but absolutely without moral sense, and as absolutely devoid of shame as the desert of Sahara is of grass—that this man, with one leap, should have vaulted to the very summit of power in New York, and . . . rode out to this hour in glaring and magnificent prosperity—shameless, vicious, criminal, abominable in his lusts . . . and yet in an instant, by the hand of a fellow-culprit, God's providence struck him to the ground!

How ironic that this ferocious attack should come from a minister who was soon to be arraigned for seducing the wife of a leading member of his congregation.

Although convicted of the murder of Fisk and sentenced to hang, Ned Stokes, with the help of rich relatives, got away with a six-year sentence and served only four years. After his release he became part owner of various restaurants and although repeatedly charged with cheating or ruining his partners, he still owned two restaurants at his death in 1901.

Although Sickles and Fisk flourished, many respectable citizens mistrusted the former and deplored the latter. But the Reverend Henry Ward Beecher was the most popular preacher of his time, a moral guide and, even more, an emotional force. That is why his abandonment of the old religion along with his trial for adultery makes him so significant of the revolution in American standards.

Beecher's father, the Reverend Lyman Beecher, son of a blacksmith, was himself a well-known preacher. In religion a belated Puritan but in character an exuberant and dominating personality, Lyman played a considerable role in the lives of his famous son, his even more famous daughter Harriet, and his other distinguished children. In the views of Lyman, born in 1775, and his son born in 1813, we can see God changing from an implacably righteous and avenging deity into a kind of benevolent old missionary among wayward natives.

Into his first ministry, among oyster catchers and former whaling men in East Hampton, Long Island, from 1800 to 1810, Lyman Beecher poured a furious energy. At ordination meetings of ministers he was so appalled at the amount of liquor served—the sideboard, he said, "looked and smelled like a very active grog shop"—that he began attacking drinking and became a founder of the American temperance movement. He also took a strong stand against circuses, riding on Sunday, the theater, and sundry sects. When Lyman's first wife died, she left him with eight children. To cope with a household that also included various relatives and black "bound girls," Lyman brought home to Litchfield, Connecticut, another wife—dainty, elegant Harriet Porter. Apparently to awe his young bride into piety, Lyman started to read to her Jonathan Edwards's fearful sermon, "Sinners in the Hands of an Angry God." The gulf that separated her generation from his was made clear when she cried, "Dr. Beecher, I shall not listen to another word of that slander on my heavenly father!''

Of his schooldays Henry later declared that he had not a single pleasant recollection. Perhaps he felt that way because he had been a very bashful boy whose speech was so thick that he could scarcely be understood. He could not in later years recall having heard one word in church or school to indicate that there was "any mercy in the heart of God for a sinner like me." The one glimmer of light came from his father's black farmhand Charles Smith: that simple soul gave him his first glimpse of a God of love as well as of religion as joyous.

When his father was called in 1826 to the leading orthodox Calvinist church in Boston, fourteen-year-old Henry was sent to Mount Pleasant Collegiate Institution. There he seems to have found release from the embarrassment that had tied his tongue. In fact, a few years later, at Amherst College, he became known for his gifts as an extemporaneous speaker. Two years before Henry was graduated, his father moved the family to Cincinnati to make the newly established Lane Theological Seminary a Calvinist spearhead in the West. When Henry joined him in 1834, he was twenty-one; a portrait shows him with the prominent nose, large mouth, and full sensuous lips seen in all later views of him. Before he left Amherst, he became engaged to Eunice Bullard, the rather proper sister of a classmate, but it would be seven years before he would bring her west to join him.

Henry found the struggling little seminary facing a grave crisis. Lyman Beecher agreed that slavery was a sin but he opposed emancipation because, he said, one must consider "what is expedient as well as what is right." But at Lane, Beecher's expediency proved the opposite: the entire senior class of forty men, led by Theodore Weld, a passionate abolitionist, walked out of the school. Hardly had the resilient Lyman rebounded from this blow when some narrow, "Old School" Calvinists accused him of taking the heretical "New School" position that man has free will even though supposedly dependent on "God's agency." Beecher was brought to trial before various Presbyterian church bodies and although he was acquitted, Henry found the trials cruel and mean. They left him with a deep distrust of formal theology and church machinery. The whole affair increased his anxieties about his faith and his own future as a minister. In his need he got help from Calvin Ellis Stowe, a professor of biblical literature at the seminary and the future husband of his sister Harriet. Stowe, an immensely learned man, introduced Henry to a Christianity based on love and warmth. Henry responded wholeheartedly.

Soon after his graduation from Lane, Henry received his first call: it came from Lawrenceburg, Kansas, a malarial town with four distilleries, a population of 1,500, and a congregation of twenty. It was here that he finally brought Eunice Bullard as his wife. At this time, too, he went up for ordination before a board of such Old School Presbyterians as had hounded his father, and, like his father, he took advantage of the chance to outwit them. "There he sat," he reported to his brother George, "the young candidate begotten of a heretic . . . but what remarkable modesty . . . and how deferential. . . . The more the lad was questioned the more incorrigibly orthodox did he grow." The willingness to feign orthodoxy did not pass. When his younger brother Charles was about to become a minister in Fort Wayne, he advised: "Preach little doctrine except mouldy orthodoxy. . . . Take hold of the most practical subjects; popularize your sermons. . . . While captious critics are lurking, adapt your mode."

His reputation began to spread and in 1839 he was called to Indianapolis. Its population was only 4,000 but it was the capital of the state. Beecher began to develop a capacity to identify with his audience that would become one of the secrets of his power. In his sermons he concentrated on accepted attitudes thrust home with vivid figures from daily life, along with theatrical impersonations, jaunty humor, a glowing rhetoric, and, borrowing from camp meeting revivals, an uninhibited show of feeling.

He also acquired a reputation for his lectures. A series addressed to young men, warning them against such evils as idleness, gambling, the theater, French novels, and lust was so well received that he published them in book form. Curiously, he was proud that some of his listeners thought his talks showed almost too much firsthand knowledge, especially in his description of the secret thoughts of a lecher. A New York banker who heard him described him as an amazingly eloquent young man with an uncanny knowledge of human nature. It thus came as no surprise when in May 1847, after he had addressed the American Home Missionary Society in New York, he was asked to become the first pastor of Plymouth Church, then being organized by a group of solid Brooklyn citizens. He accepted.

Henry Ward Beecher came east with the confidence of a preacher who had spent ten years on the western frontier, tempered in the fires where the new America was being forged. When the Beechers arrived in Brooklyn it was a city of over 60,000, a quiet, respectable community with some fine residential streets. As in Indianapolis, he insisted on speaking from a platform amid the congregation. This move was based, he said, on "the principle of social and personal magnetism which emanates reciprocally from a speaker and from a close throng of hearers. . . . I want them to surround me . . . and have the people surge about me!" And they did, coming in such numbers that the church was never large enough. "If you want to hear Henry Ward Beecher preach," New Yorkers would say on Sundays, "take the ferry to Brooklyn and then follow the crowd."

His figure was not imposing, his hair hung somewhat thinly to his collar, his voice was neither bell-toned nor organlike, but he had a presence that made him seem large, an inexhaustible fluency, an instinct for chords that would touch and move, the gestures and voices of an actor. Scorning the "holy tone" of most preaching, he could be by turns eloquent, breezy, lyrical, salty, somber, and irreverent, and he was master of a soaring, rapturous climax. "He . . . wears me out with his redundant, superabundant, ever-recovering and ever-reviving energy," admitted Theodore Parker, himself a preacher of no mean power.

Beecher's sermons and lectures were perfect for the time and place. Suddenly America had become the land of boundless opportunity and abundance. After the Puritan dawn and the long morning of the pioneers, noon had come in all its rich warmth. All around him now were countless signs of affluence. Overnight he himself was lapped in success, and the sensuous, self-indulgent part of him bloomed almost rankly.

Like Whitman and with even more fervor, he hailed the future, the prospects of the common people, and the possibilities of brotherhood. To the adulation that soon surrounded him, he responded with uninhibited expressions of love. "Today is goblet day," he chanted in one of the "Star Papers" he wrote for *The Independent,* a religious weekly that he edited. "The whole heavens have been mingled with exquisite skill to a delicious flavor and the crystal cup held out to every lip. . . . It is luxury simply to exist." No wonder Thoreau came away from a Beecher sermon convinced that the man was a magnificent pagan. Beecher conjured up a "perpetual tropical luxuriance of blessed love," and he called for submission—not to God's will but to "the heart's instincts." Intoxicated by his own words, he shouted at his listeners, "Ye are gods!" and "You are crystalline, your faces are radiant!" When they had recovered from their surprise, the prosperous citizens ranged row on row in front of him responded with pleasure and gratitude.

At first he avoided facing the slavery issue squarely, but the tide of events was irresistible. Invited to a meeting to raise funds to buy the freedom of two mulatto girls, the Edmonson sisters, who had fled to escape being sold, Beecher dramatically drove home, not the inhumanity or injustice of the fate they faced, but the sexual depravity of it. "Shall this girl—almost as white as you are—be sold for money to the first comer to do as he likes with?" he cried. By the time he was through, he had the audience throwing money onto the platform simply to save Innocence from Lust. The attention this performance gained him was obviously exciting. He began auctioning off fugitive slaves in Plymouth Church, choosing beautiful young girls as close to white as he could find. When critics called it sensationalism, Beecher retorted that "he is the best fisherman who catches the most fish."

His success at Plymouth Church was rewarded with a handsome salary and a grand tour of Europe. Starved for fine possessions, he began to collect not only paintings and engravings but porcelains, Venetian glass, and even stuffed hummingbirds. Most unusual was his passion for unset gems, which he carried loose in his pockets. He called them his color opiates and, when overstimulated, he would handle them until he felt relaxed.

Although rescued from the malaria, drudgery, and near-penury of her life in Indianapolis, his wife, Eunice, remained something less than happy or ingratiating. She did not age well, and she resented Henry Ward's extravagant tastes and unpredictable emotional commitments. He in turn seems to have regarded her much as an impetuous son might look on a rather strict mother. Meanwhile, his sister Harriet languished in Cincinnati. She was forty years old, had been submerged for fifteen years in marriage to Dr. Stowe, the seminary professor whom she called "my poor Rabbi." She seemed worn out with bearing seven children, with a routine that began at four-thirty in the morning, and with making up for her husband's helplessness in practical matters. *Uncle Tom's Cabin* thus came as such a surprise to everyone, including Harriet herself, that she later solemnly asserted that it had been dictated to her by God. Close as Henry and Harriet may have been as brother and sister, they were, in their campaigns against slavery, even more profoundly allied in their appeal to the emotions.

Although Beecher detested slavery, he had little sympathy for abolitionists. Instead, he at first vaguely advocated relying on God and Christian influences. "All the natural laws of God are warring upon slavery," he declared in 1853. "Let slavery alone. . . . Time is her enemy. Liberty will, if let alone, always be a match for oppression."

But Beecher was acutely sensitive to prevailing views. That is why, when violence broke out in the Kansas-Nebraska Territory, he soon changed his position. Once aroused, his commitment was passionate. Boldly he pledged to send Sharps rifles to the Free Soil settlers. Since some of the rifles were reported to have been shipped in boxes marked "Bibles," all rifles sent to Free Soilers were thereafter dubbed "Beecher's Bibles," and Beecher himself began to be considered a rabid abolitionist. The war broke down all his remaining restraints. If peace, he wrote, means that the North must suppress all sympathy for the oppressed, "Give me war redder than blood and fiercer than fire." He constantly lashed out at the administration for being weak and irresolute, and he called Lincoln "a man without any sense of the value of time." After the Second Battle of Bull Run, he gave up the war as lost, declaring: "Let it be known that the Nation wasted away by an incurable consumption of Central Imbecility." Reading such criticism, Lincoln is reputed to have said only, "Is thy servant a dog?"

When Beecher went to England for a holiday in the summer of 1863, his friends there insisted that the Northern cause desperately needed a champion. So he undertook to address audiences in Manchester, Glasgow, Edinburgh, Liverpool, and London. The audiences were huge and hostile but his speeches, good-humored yet defiant and full of harsh truths, won his listeners completely. It was a great personal triumph and he came home a national hero. At the end of the war, Lincoln chose him to speak at the ceremony on the return of the flag to Fort Sumter.

There was little change in Beecher's home life. Cold and strait-laced, Mrs. Beecher came to be known to her Brooklyn neighbors as "the griffin." Beecher himself described breakfast table conversation in his home as "the vainest, the most vapid, the most juiceless, the most unsaccarine of all things." That was surely one reason Beecher bought fast horses, a townhouse, and one country estate after another, and why he visited Tiffany's regularly to see the latest in precious stones. When he was asked how he reconciled all this with the way of the meek and lowly Jesus, he declared that the belief in a relationship between poverty and sanctity was a medieval notion. And in a lecture on "Moral Uses of Luxury and Beauty," he added that he could not see why a man should not "indulge himself and his family with elements of the beautiful," or why "a man should dress plainly when he is able to dress richly provided he cheats nobody."

Of his income of $40,000 a year, $20,000 came from his church and the rest from his lyceum lecture tours, articles for *The Ledger,* the most popular weekly in America, and testimonials for Chickering pianos, Waltham watches, and even a truss. At one point he accepted an unheard-of advance of $24,000 to do a novel. But writing fiction did not come easily to him. So he turned to sympathetic, worshipful Elizabeth Tilton for encouragement in his creative labors. That was the innocent beginning of what was to become the most sensational domestic scandal that America had known.

When Theodore Tilton first came to Beecher's attention in 1854 he was a twenty-year-old reporter, tall, handsome, with auburn hair, which he wore long. At first he was extremely religious and burned with the kind of perfervid idealism that often consumes itself. His qualities led naturally to an admiration for Henry Ward Beecher that bordered on idolatry. Beecher, charmed by his romantic enthusiasm, promise, and, of course, his admiration, had him made a general assistant on *The Independent.* In the same year, 1856, Beecher officiated at Tilton's marriage to Elizabeth Richards.

"Lib" Tilton was a tiny, dark-eyed, birdlike creature, more appealing than pretty. She had been a devout member of Beecher's congregation since her childhood and had taught in the Sunday school. An ardent reader of the popular novels of Charles Reade and the poetry of Elizabeth Barrett Browning, she mixed a turbid romanticism with religious zeal. In her, as in Beecher, feeling was the controlling agent. It was inevitable that sooner or later she should confuse two major outlets of emotion—the religious and the erotic.

As an editor of *The Independent,* Theodore Tilton secured contributions on lively topics and bold editorials on abolition, women's rights, and religious issues, and, on the side, turned out half a dozen volumes of poetry. Within a few years the circulation of *The Independent* had risen from 17,000 to 60,000, and Tilton was earning ten times more than when he started. From the first, the frankness of his admiration for Beecher was remarkable even in a time when a romantic effusiveness was not uncommon. Once he wrote to Beecher: "My gratitude cannot be written in words, but must be expressed only in love." Beecher shared the feeling. When he visited the Tilton home he found not only exciting visitors—Greeley, Whittier, Phillips, Sumner—but a heady zeal for lofty causes, and warmth. He also found Lib Tilton all aglow at having the great Reverend Beecher as a dear friend. The contrast with the sterile respectability of his own home was overwhelming. "Oh, Theodore," he confessed, "I dread to go back to my own home," and "God might strip all other gifts from me if he would only give me a wife like Elizabeth and a home like yours." Tilton responded in kind, saying, "There is one little woman down at my house who loves you more than you can have any idea of."

Plainly the word "love" was used loosely here. The Tiltons were, like Beecher himself, moving away from the dark old religion of fear into the glowing new religion of love, and along the way love tended to filter into other human relationships, such as that between two men or between a man and his friend's wife. Beecher became a daily visitor at the Tiltons, a part of the family circle. He later spoke of Mrs. Tilton as turning to him with "artless familiarity and with entire confidence. Childish in appearance, she was childish in nature, and I would as soon have misconceived the confidence of her little girls as the unstudied affection she showed me."

Other forces such as the women's rights movement were having their effect on the rigid code governing relations between the sexes. Susan B. Anthony, Elizabeth Cady Stanton, and Beecher's half-sister, Isabella Beecher Hooker, were frequent visitors at the Tilton salon. Beecher became familiar with all of them and even collected money for Anthony at Plymouth Church. One daring soul, Victoria Woodhull, called for equal rights in love.

The first indication anyone had that all was not as it should be between the Reverend Beecher and the adoring women around him at his church was a story that Henry Bowen, a founder of Plymouth Church, and publisher of various religious weeklies, told Theodore Tilton in 1862. Obviously tormented by his secret, he declared that when his wife, Lucy Maria, mother of his ten children, had died at the age of thirty-eight, she had made a deathbed confession so shocking that Bowen could no longer keep it to himself. She had been, she said, sexually intimate with the Reverend Beecher. Biographers who accept Bowen's story believe he did not make it public because he feared it would ruin Plymouth Church. Defenders of Beecher assert that Bowen lied in order to injure Beecher for having withdrawn from *The Independent* in protest against dubious advertising and the paper's "irresponsible" views.

When Beecher returned from Europe as a hero, Tilton seemed to have forgotten the charges. Perhaps when he saw Beecher, now in his fifties, with a paunch and loose jowls but still craving affection, he felt pity for him. Or perhaps he had become tolerant of other men's desires because he had begun to help himself to love wherever he found it. Whatever the reason, he, and of course Elizabeth, welcomed Beecher back into the old intimacy. Beecher took to visiting her even when Tilton was away on lecture tours, and sent her books, pictures, and huge bouquets of flowers. Tilton's concern about his wife's relationship with their pastor is evident in a letter he wrote her during a lecture tour: "Now that the *other* man has gone off lecturing

. . . you can afford to come to see me. . . . You promised the *other* man to cleave to *me,* and yet you leave *me all alone* and cleave to him. 'O Frailty! Thy name is woman!' " The impeachment is direct, but the teasing tone robs it of its sting.

How much Beecher had come to mean to Elizabeth Tilton seems astonishingly transparent in such letters as the one she wrote to her husband in January 1867: "Oh, how my soul yearns over you two dear men! I do love him very dearly, and I do love you supremely, utterly, believe it. Perhaps if by God's grace I keep myself white, I may bless you both. I am striving. God bless this trinity." The depth of her self-delusion is revealed in her application of the sacred term trinity to a relationship verging, in spirit if not in fact, on infidelity. Everything is made acceptable by being dipped in a thick syrup of love. Early in 1868 she begins to protest openly the innocence of her behavior: "About eleven o'clock today, Mr. Beecher called. Now, beloved, let not even the shadow of a *shadow* fall on your dear heart because of this. . . . You once told me you did not believe that I gave a correct account of his visits, and . . . that I repressed much. Sweet, do you still believe this?"

In October 1868, while her husband was away, Elizabeth Tilton went to hear Beecher address a campaign rally for General Grant. The following day she hurried over to her pastor's house to tell him how glorious it had been. He was alone. The fullest account of what happened that evening came from Theodore Tilton in City Court, Brooklyn, more than six years later when he charged Beecher with debauching his wife on October 10, 1868.

In Elizabeth Tilton's diary for October 10, 1868, there was this extraordinary entry: "A Day Memorable." And later that month the following passage leaps from a sermon by Beecher on sin:

The man who has been wallowing in lust . . . and who by God's great goodness has been brought to an hour and moment when . . . his monstrous wickedness stands disclosed in him— that man ought to . . . stand up and say . . . "I confess my sin, and I call on God to witness my determination from this hour to turn away from it." That is the wise course, and you would think so—if it was anybody but yourself.

If he was guilty as charged, such a passage indicates how he was able to reconcile his preaching with his practice: he simply assumed that all men were as inwardly divided as he was.

Although Elizabeth Tilton apparently had mounting qualms about their relationship, they met intimately again and again in the next few months. But after a period of illness in the spring of 1870, according to her husband's testimony, she made—exactly as had Daniel Sickles's wife—a full confession, declaring that her relationship with Beecher had been

> more than friendship; that it had been love, it had been sexual intimacy . . . begun shortly after the death of her son Paul . . . that she had received much consolation . . . from her pastor; that she had made a visit to his house . . . and that there, on the 10th of October, 1868, she had surrendered her body to him in sexual embrace . . . that she had repeated such acts . . . from the Fall of 1868 to the Spring of 1870.

She added that she had been persuaded by Beecher that "as their love was proper and not wrong, therefore it followed that any expression of that love, whether by the shake of the hands or the kiss of the lips, or even bodily intercourse . . . was not wrong."

Tilton was left, he later told a friend, "just blasted" by the confession. After much soul-searching, he decided that his wife had been "trapped up" in her teacher and had followed him blindly. This decision gave him such a feeling of magnanimity as to raise him into a kind of ecstasy. All these feverishly intense letters and statements can only be understood as the emotional excesses that follow an age of repression. Under the Victorian lid, the caldron had come to a boil.

Although Tilton was busier than ever as editor of the *Brooklyn Union,* also owned by Henry Bowen, as well as *The Independent,* as president of the radical suffragists movement, and as a lecturer, he kept brooding on the confession. Then, one night, while Susan B. Anthony kept his ailing wife company at home, he went to dinner with two other leaders of the women's rights movement, Elizabeth Cady Stanton and Laura Bullard, and blurted out his secret to them.

To escape from her troubles, Elizabeth Tilton went to visit friends in Ohio. From there she wrote her husband one of her more self-incriminating letters:

> When, by your threats, my mother cried out to me, "Why what have you done, Elizabeth, my child?" her worst suspicions were aroused, and I laid bare my heart then, that from my lips, and not yours, she might receive the dagger in her heart. . . . For the agony which the revelation has caused *you,* my cries ascend to Heaven night and day that upon mine own head all the anguish may fall.

After returning to Brooklyn, Elizabeth Tilton had a miscarriage. In a letter to a friend she said of this, "A love-babe it promised, you know." It was, as their friend Frank Moulton later observed, a very curious comment from a woman nearly forty years old who had already borne six children, especially when she and her husband had been quarreling bitterly for months.

Bowen was already annoyed by rumors of Tilton's "promiscuity" and "brutality" when Tilton published an editorial in *The Independent* entitled "Love, Marriage and Divorce," including such statements as "marriage without love is a sin against God." Bowen thereupon relieved Tilton as editor of *The Independent.* Soon Bowen heard rumors that Tilton was about to flee to France. He confronted the editor and in the exchange that followed, Tilton revealed his wife's confession. Bowen declared that Beecher must not be permitted to stay another week in his pulpit. Carried away by Bowen's indignation, Tilton wrote to Beecher, "I demand that, for reasons which you explicitly understand, you immediately cease from the ministry of Plymouth Church and quit the city of Brooklyn." It was a melodramatic gesture; when Tilton told his friend Moulton about it, the worldly Moulton at once pronounced him a ruined man. Moulton went straight to Plymouth Church and told Beecher that Tilton wanted to see him at once.

From that point on Moulton was to act as the "Mutual Friend"— patient, self-assured, almost enigmatic. A junior partner in an import-export house, he was characterized by Beecher's critics as a man of conscience determined to see justice done. Beecher's defenders described him as a manipulator who in his business did the "dirty work" of getting favors from the government. Somehow he won the trust of Beecher as well as both Tiltons and held it during the long years he spent trying to settle the quarrel.

When Beecher and Moulton reached the latter's house, Beecher went in alone to see Tilton. Tilton read him Elizabeth Tilton's note, which, he claimed, confessed sexual "intimacy." Beecher, he said, cried, "She could never have made in writing a statement so untrue." He then asked leave to see Mrs. Tilton. As he went down the stairs Moulton heard him moan, "This will kill me." It did not kill him. But it should be said that where Tilton declared that Elizabeth's letter referred to sexual intimacy, Beecher and his defenders behaved as though he were charged not with adultery but with some vague kind of impropriety.

When Beecher entered Elizabeth's room, he found her—as in a painting by a Pre-Raphaelite—lying on a couch, "white as marble . . . with her hands upon her bosom, palm to palm, as one in prayer." He asked her why she had joined in the terrible charges her husband had made. She said that Tilton led her to believe that if she confessed her love for Beecher, "it would help him confess his alien affections." She then gave Beecher what he said was a voluntary statement: "When wearied by importunities, and weakened by sickness, I gave a letter inculpating my friend, Henry Ward Beecher, under assurances that that would remove all differences between me and my husband. That letter I now revoke."

When Tilton returned home, he went up to Elizabeth's room. Soon Elizabeth's nurse heard him shouting; and after a while he emerged with a letter which read:

My dear Husband:
    Mr. Henry Ward Beecher called upon me this evening, asked me if I would defend him against any accusations *in a council of ministers,* and I replied solemnly that I would in case the accuser was any other but my husband. He (H.W.B.) dictated a letter which I copied as my own. . . . I was ready to give him this letter because he said with pain that my letter in your hands . . . "had struck him dead and ended his usefulness."

Elizabeth Tilton's second retraction in a few hours was the beginning of such a bewildering series of recantations that in the end nothing she said was fully believed. Her fault was simply that she yielded to anyone who put pressure on her. When Moulton told Beecher of the second retraction, Moulton testified that Beecher confessed, with much weeping, that he "had loved Elizabeth Tilton very much; that . . . the sexual expression of that love was just as natural in his opinion as the language he used to her." According to Moulton, he also said: "My life is ended. . . . I find myself upon the brink of a moral Niagara with no power to save myself."

When Bowen let Beecher know that he had fired Tilton, Beecher approved. But his remorse increased frighteningly. Finally he called Moulton into his study and admitted he was "mortified" at the part he had played. Moulton wrote down the gist of what he said and then had him sign the account. Although Beecher later testified that he did not read it, it became known as "The Letter of Contrition." It read:

> My dear friend Moulton: I ask through you Theodore Tilton's forgiveness, and I humble myself before him as I do before my God. . . . I will die before anyone but myself shall be implicated. All my thoughts are running toward my friends, toward the poor child lying there. . . . She is guiltless, sinned against, bearing the transgression of another. Her forgiveness I have. I humbly pray to God that he may put it into the heart of her husband to forgive me.

Beecher would always maintain that he was here referring only to having advised Elizabeth to leave her husband and encouraging Bowen to fire Tilton. That he should have damned himself so unreservedly for such minor offences seems wildly excessive even if we allow that he and his coterie had developed a language of emotional exaggeration in which everything was made to seem ten times as agonizing—or blissful—as it actually was.

Beecher now repeatedly met with the Tiltons in an effort at complete reconciliation. Once the two men came upon each other in Moulton's parlor and Beecher impulsively clasped Tilton's face and kissed him on the mouth. At another meeting, which took place in Mrs. Tilton's bedroom, Beecher reported, "I kissed him and he kissed me, and I kissed his wife and she kissed me, and I believe they kissed each other." It was obviously such a statement that caused George Templeton Strong to declare in his diary:

> Plymouth Church is a nest of "psychological phenomena," *vulgo vocato* lunatics, and its chief Brahmin is as moonstruck as his devotees. . . . They all call each other by their first names and perpetually kiss one another. The Rev. Beecher seduces Mrs. Tilton and then kisses her husband, and he seems to acquiesce in the osculation. . . . They all seem, on their own showing, to have been afflicted with both moral and mental insanity.

But Beecher surely indulged in such behavior because it would make all gestures of affection between him and the Tiltons seem harmless.

Astonishingly, Beecher and Elizabeth began to write to each other again. In one letter Elizabeth, as emotional as ever, wrote: "Does your heart bound *towards all* as it used to? So does mine! I am myself again. I did not dare to tell you till I was sure; but the bird has sung in my heart these four weeks." In another she said: "In all the complications of the past years, my endeavor was entirely to keep from you all suffering. . . . My weapons were love, a large untiring generosity and *nest hiding.*"

The illusion that their difficulties were over was soon blasted by Victoria Woodhull. The boldest crusader for sexual liberty in her time, she practiced what she preached, and her unsavory past led such straitlaced women as Beecher's eldest sister, Catharine, to denounce her. Mrs. Woodhull had warned that if these critics did not desist she would shatter them by exposing the monstrous hypocrisy of a certain "public teacher of eminence" who lived in concubinage with the wife of another "public teacher." The critics had not desisted, so Mrs. Woodhull devoted the entire issue of November 2, 1872, of her journal, *Woodhull & Claflin's Weekly,* to exposing the Beecher-Tilton affair.

Overnight it made the Beecher case the domestic scandal of the age. Woodhull gave Beecher the kiss of death, writing,

> The immense physical potency of Mr. Beecher, and the indomitable urgency of his great nature for the intimacy and em-

braces of the noble and cultured women about him, instead of being a bad thing as the world thinks, is one of the noblest . . . endowments of this truly great and representative man. Plymouth Church . . . and the healthy vigor of public opinion for the last quarter of a century has been strengthened from the physical amativeness of Henry Ward Beecher.

Beneath the flourishes the passage contained a genuine insight into the power of Beecher's personality.

When Beecher's half-sister, Isabella Beecher Hooker, demanded the truth from him, he answered, "I tread the falsehoods into the dirt from which they spring." But he thoughtlessly added, "Think of the barbarity of dragging a poor dear child of a woman into this slough"; whereupon Isabella, who was an outspoken feminist, wrote to another brother, the Reverend Thomas K. Beecher, "So far as I can see, it is he who has dragged the dear child into the slough—and left her there." Victoria Woodhull was even less charitable. Forced from her home and hounded from hotel to hotel, she announced, "I will make it hotter on earth for Henry Ward Beecher than hell is below!" She nearly succeeded.

Mrs. Moulton later testified that Beecher, in another fit of despair, had told her he had a powder on his library table that would put him to sleep forever. But Henry Ward Beecher had no intention of using it. Indeed, he remained as popular as before. Great crowds poured into Brooklyn to hear him preach, and he performed without diminution of power. Members of the Plymouth congregation now forced Tilton's expulsion. An "Advisory Council" of sister churches was called to consider this treatment of Tilton. The council administered only a mild rebuke to Plymouth Church, and its moderator, Dr. Leonard Bacon of Yale, referred to Tilton as "a knave" and "a dog." Tilton, furious, published a long reply, including Beecher's damaging "Letter of Contrition."

Hoping to avoid a civil court, Beecher decided that his own church should try him. He himself picked its six members, and his vindication was assured when his followers persuaded Elizabeth Tilton to quit her husband and take her place at Beecher's side. Of the adultery charge, she said pathetically to Mrs. Moulton, "For the sake of Mr. Beecher, for the sake of the influence on the world, for my own position, for my children, I think it is my duty to deny it.'' The one reason conspicuously omitted is that the charge was a lie.

As the first witness before the committee, Mrs. Tilton declared that Beecher had never made an ''indecorous or improper proposal'' to her but had in fact shown her the kind of respect she had failed to get from her husband. Tilton was, she said, madly jealous of Beecher, was himself guilty of ''free love,'' and had become godless as well. At last Beecher himself spoke. He fell automatically into those dramatic postures that had made him famous. He spoke of Elizabeth Tilton as having ''thrust her affections on me, unsought''; and he explained all his acts of contrition as attempts to protect his life work from disaster. ''It is time,'' he thundered, ''that this abomination be buried below all touch or power of resurrection.''

The committee's report, read to the jubilant brethren of Plymouth Church by a professional elocutionist, described Tilton as malicious and revengeful, Elizabeth Tilton as guilty of ''inordinate affections,'' and Henry Ward Beecher as completely innocent but just too trusting. Tilton now instituted suit in City Court again the Reverend Beecher for alienation of his wife's affections. Most New York newspapers still sided with Beecher, apparently believing it more important to save ''the most famous pulpit . . . since Paul preached on the Hill of Mars'' than to arrive at the truth. But the *Chicago Tribune* published a devastating analysis by Elizabeth Cady Stanton that boldly exposed the various church-connected ''rings,'' including the bondholders of Plymouth Church, that would do anything to protect Beecher's name. And the Chicago *Times* spread out the lurid details of Beecher's affair with Lucy Maria Bowen. It smelled to high heaven; and there were still years of it to come.

The trial of *Tilton* vs. *Beecher,* which opened in City Court, Brooklyn, on January 11, 1875, should have been anticlimactic. But it proved to be Ossa piled on Pelion—an uncensored performance of a sex drama, especially titillating in that its main figures were a spiritual leader and a devout matron, one depicted as a sly lecher and the other as a willing victim. While works of art were being emasculated, novels censored into sentimental treacle, and women dared not show their ankles in public, this was a wide-open debate on whether a famous clergyman had cuckolded one of his best friends. The trial lasted almost six months and was given more space in newspapers than any event since the Civil War. The crowds came as though to a fair. The vaunted sanctity of Victorian private life was invaded with fiendish ingenuity and obscene curiosity.

Tilton's case was presented by only a few witnesses, principally Moulton and his wife. Beecher had six lawyers and almost a hundred witnesses. His own answers were often so flippant that the New York *Herald* declared he presented for "scientific man a psychological problem which they must despair of solving." Almost 900 times he said, "I can't recollect" or "I don't know."

Neither Elizabeth Tilton nor Victoria Woodhull was, for obvious reasons, called by either side. In many ways the most impressive witness was Francis Moulton's wife, Emma. Not only was she manifestly a woman of integrity but she had long been one of Beecher's dearest friends. Telling of a meeting with Beecher on June 2, 1873, she said he had expressed his great sorrow that Elizabeth had confessed to her husband and that it would bring only ruin to all. She had answered: "I will always be your friend if you will only go down to the church and confess, because that is the only way out for you. . . . I have never heard you preach since I knew the truth that I haven't felt that I was standing by an open grave. . . . I believed in you since I was a girl, believed you were the only good man in the world. Now . . . I don't believe anybody." Against anyone except Henry Ward Beecher, Emma Moulton's testimony would have proved devastating. But the pastor of Plymouth Church had become the kind of public figure whose fame feeds on all publicity, good or bad.

The jurors stayed out for eight days with reporters watching them through spyglasses from nearby buildings. At last they brought in their verdict: nine to three against Theodore Tilton. That evening, when Beecher arrived at Plymouth Church, a cheering group of worshipers awaited him. But not everyone thought that the split decision had established Beecher's innocence. In England, the novelist George Meredith wrote: "Guilty or not, there is a sickly snuffiness about the religious fry that makes the talk of their fornications absolutely repulsive to read of."

Plymouth Church nevertheless raised a full $100,000 to help pay Beecher's trial expenses. By contrast, Theodore Tilton was financially ruined. But Francis Moulton was unshaken. During the church investigation, Beecher had sworn out a complaint against Moulton for criminal libel. But he now hastily dropped the suit. Moulton thereupon published a letter declaring: "I am indicted of criminal libel in charging Rev. Henry Ward Beecher with criminal intercourse with a female member of his congregation. The charge is true; he knows it . . . [and] the Supreme Ruler will some day reveal the truth." That fall the brethren of Plymouth Church retaliated by dropping Emma Moulton from the church rolls. She immediately requested a council like the one that had reviewed the expulsion of Theodore Tilton. Beecher complied: he called together more than 200 prominent Congregationalists and welcomed them cordially. Beecher was given a vote of complete confidence. After the vote, he cried out: "I have not been pursued as a lion is pursued. . . . I have been pursued as if I were a maggot in a rotten corpse," and "when they rebuke the vine for throwing out tendrils and holding on to anything that is next to it . . . you may rebuke me for loving where I should not love. It is not my choice; it is my necessity." Before an audience he could always speak as though from the heart.

No one can say why Henry Bowen was now moved to face the challenge he had avoided since the deathbed confession of his wife fourteen years before. Perhaps he felt that Beecher was about to escape retribution forever. Going before a special Plymouth Church committee he recalled how he had helped launch the church almost thirty years before and brought Henry Ward Beecher to it as its first pastor. "At last," Bowen said, "there came to my knowledge evidence of his guilt which astounded and overwhelmed me. . . . I received from a lady whom . . . I was compelled to believe . . . full and explicit confession of adultery with Mr. Beecher." The lady, Bowen continued, had a key to Beecher's study in Plymouth Church and met with him there—until she saw another woman enter with a similar key. She never got over the shock, Bowen said, and died shortly afterward. Plymouth Church responded to Bowen's revelation by expelling him.

Beecher soon resumed his career as a lecturer. He was aging now, his hair thin, the skin hanging loosely from his throat. Occasionally at first there was the jeer, or the audience waiting coldly, but before long he was being guaranteed from $600 to $1,000 a night and could write that when he entered a meeting of Congregationalist ministers he was cheered, asked to address it, and had everyone weeping so that it "broke up like a revival meeting."

But the embers of the scandal were not all dead. In April 1878 Elizabeth Tilton, as tormented as ever a decade after the event, published a letter she had written to her legal adviser:

A few weeks since, after long months of mental anguish, I told . . . a few friends whom I bitterly deceived, that the charge brought by my husband, of adultery between myself and the Rev. Henry Ward Beecher, was true, and that the lie I had lived so well the last four years had become intolerable to me. That statement I now solemnly reaffirm. . . . I know full well the explanations that will be sought for this acknowledgment: desire to return to my husband, insanity, malice—everything save the true one—my quickened conscience, and the sense of what is due the cause of truth and justice.

It was the only statement she had ever made without pressure and it had the ring of truth; but it came too late. She went to live with one of her daughters and steadfastly shunned the world until her death in 1897.

Tilton said nothing. He continued to support his children, but after a few years his lecturing opportunities waned. Shorn of wife, causes, and spirit, he drifted to Paris. There he lived in an attic room. When not writing poetry or romantic novels he could be seen playing chess in the Café de la Régence. He died, quite forgotten, in 1907.

After the trial, Beecher resumed his practice of taking sides on political and social questions. But he was erratic, often espousing the right causes but sometimes the wrong men. He favored civil service reform but stubbornly supported Grant and the chief spoilsman, Conkling. He was for unrestricted immigration and the exploited workingman, but in a time of widespread unemployment he could assert that God "intended the great to be great and the little to be little" and that a dollar a day was enough to support a family unless a man insisted on drinking beer and smoking. Any man, he announced in almost perfect unison with Jay Gould, "who cannot live on bread and water is not fit to live." Unhappily for him, the political cartoonists knew that he continued to have an income of about $40,000 a year.

In 1884 he did not actively back Cleveland until the story that Cleveland had an illegitimate son startled the nation. Then, openly referring to his own ordeal, Beecher campaigned with all the ardor of a man seeking vicarious vindication. He even went so far as to say to a youthful YMCA audience, "If every man in New York State tonight, who has broken the Seventh Commandment, voted for Cleveland, he would be elected by a 200,000 majority." What a long way Beecher had come from the *Lectures to Young Men* with its dire warnings to beware the Strange Woman!

He had become equally bold on religious matters. Late in 1877 Canon Farrar of Westminster Abbey created a minor sensation by decreeing that Hell was an obsolete doctrine. This was just what Henry Ward Beecher—and many other people—had felt for a long time. "If now," he proclaimed:

> You tell me that this great mass of men, because they had not the knowledge of God . . . went to hell, then you make an infidel of me; for I do swear, by the Lord Jesus Christ, by his groans, by his tears . . . that the nature of God is to suffer for others rather than to make others suffer. . . . To tell me that back of Christ is a God who for unnumbered centuries has gone on creating men and sweeping them like dead flies . . . into hell, is to ask me to worship a being as much worse than the conception of any medieval devils as can be imagined. But I will not worship cruelty. I *will* worship Love—that sacrifices itself for the good of those who err.

It was not a philosophical or even a theological concept but only an emotion born of a deep personal need and an excruciating experience. Still, it came as a miraculous act of liberation for his listeners, a general amnesty from the fear of eternal damnation. No wonder they loved him.

Nor is it surprising that he welcomed evolution, and especially Herbert Spencer's meliorism, as a reasoned framework for his feeling. Spencer had spun out of Darwin's theory the idea that mankind was automatically moving ever onward and upward. Where many clerics stood aghast at the blasting of the whole biblical version of man's history, Beecher, at seventy, could write boldly: "I am a cordial Christian evolutionist. I would not agree by any means with all of Spencer, nor all of Huxley, Tyndall and their school. They are agnostic. I am not—emphatically. But I am an evolutionist and that strikes at the root of all medieval and orthodox modern theology. Men have not fallen as a race." He resigned from the Brooklyn Association of Congregational Ministers, grandly explaining that he wanted no one to be embarrassed by his views. In the pulpit he had become a law unto himself, a force of nature.

On March 3, 1877, without warning, he suffered a stroke and died a few days later. His body lay in state amid a sea of flowers, and some 50,000 of the curious, mostly women, passed the bier.

Whatever Beecher's sexual passions were, they were only an aspect of his dominant characteristic—what he called love: not platonic love but personal love. That trait explains his attraction for women, his power as a preacher, and the nature of his beliefs. He generated it in almost palpable waves whenever he addressed an audience, mingling amatory and religious appeals in one torrent of ardor. It led him to a faith that discarded hell, infant damnation, and original sin, and offered in their stead a vision of a Christ inspired by compassion for the sinful.

Beecher was far from typical, but neither was he unique. A career remarkably similar to his, at least in its early phases, was that of the Reverend Isaac Kalloch, who is as forgotten today as Beecher is remembered. And Kalloch's career was established, not in commercial, hybridized New York but in Boston, once the hub of the Puritan world, and in the late 1850s, before immigrants had sharply diluted the city's Anglo-Saxon homogeneity.

Like Beecher, Kalloch was the son of a prominent clergyman, his father having been a Baptist minister especially effective in revival meetings in Maine. A child prodigy and a brilliant young preacher in Maine, Kalloch was called in 1855 to the largest church in Boston, Tremont Temple. He soon became, like Beecher, so popular that crowds had to be turned away from his services.

A red-haired giant of a man, and handsome to boot, he was intense and fiery in the pulpit but outside the church was a genial, cigar-smoking, horseback-riding unclerical youth who enjoyed a joke, a glass of whiskey, and the adoration of the ladies. He already had a reputation as a "golden-voiced preacher" when early in 1857 he was accused—exactly as Beecher would be some fourteen years later—of adultery. The woman, Laura Flye Steen, was an old friend and the wife of a respected merchant. The Boston *Times* reported that the Reverend Kalloch had taken Mrs. Steen, an attractive young woman, to a disreputable hotel in East Cambridge before and after the lecture, and had given the impression that she was his wife. The *Times,* a sensational "penny sheet," might have been ignored had it not shocked the entire nation by publishing affidavits from the innkeeper and an omnibus driver claiming that they had seen Kalloch have "sexual connexion" with the lady at the hotel.

Kalloch calmly admitted that he had stopped at the hotel but only to rest before the lecture and after it, and he also pointed out that both Mr. Steen and Mrs. Kalloch had known that Mrs. Steen was accompanying him. The newspaper clamor, however, was so great that Kalloch was indicted and brought to trial. At the trial the two proprietors of the hotel, the wife of one of them, and the bus driver— a seedy crew—testified that they had peeped through a crack and seen Kalloch and the lady embrace and lie down on the floor—mercifully out of sight of the watchers—heard them utter words of love, and saw them rise and rearrange their clothes. One of them even told of seeing the lady lift her dress, after Kalloch had left her, and dry herself with a handkerchief, a detail that newspapers today would consider unprintable.

Demonstrating their confidence in Kalloch, or their gullibility, or simply closing ranks against the common enemy, Mr. Steen and Mrs. Kalloch, in court, sat next to Kalloch, and Steen testified for the defense. Although the judge's summation favored the prosecution, the jury brought in a split verdict, freeing Kalloch. Evidently the sleazy character of the four key witnesses against Kalloch told heavily in his favor.

Many newspapers called the verdict disgraceful and assumed that Kalloch would resign; but his congregation decided that he had "come out of the fire like pure gold, doubly refined" and contributed $1,000 toward his court expenses. Thirty thousand persons tried to get into

Tremont Temple the following Sunday; those who succeeded received his flowery sermon with sobs and cheers. Fortunately for Kalloch, the panic of 1857 soon overshadowed the scandal, and, piety increasing with the hard times, the clergyman was able to launch revival meetings in which sinners repented in squadrons.

Now, however, Kalloch began to display the restlessness that would tear him away from career after career. No one has been able to explain this compulsion to start anew even after his affairs were prospering—unless it was the wealth beckoning from all sides, and especially from the West. Having previously visited Kansas on behalf of the Immigrant Aid Society, Kalloch now made a trial sojourn in the frontier city of Leavenworth. He had begun to raise blooded cattle there and had become a partner in a law firm (he was admitted to the bar almost immediately), when, during a visit he made to Boston, the Tremont Temple offered him $5,000 a year to return. He accepted. Again his fame grew. But again scandal trailed him: the superintendent of the church revealed that female parishioners visited the pastor's study at night and that one had stayed until midnight. Again he was investigated by a church committee and again he was cleared.

But this time he resigned and late in 1860 accepted a call from one of the most fashionable congregations in New York, the Laight Street Baptist Church in lower Manhattan. Notwithstanding the competition of the Reverend Beecher, who deplored him, and other clerical spellbinders, Kalloch soon became known for his preaching and, during the war, for his pro-Union political sermons. But his aristocratic congregation was too sedate for him, and early in 1864 he bade it farewell and again headed for the exhilarating turbulence of Kansas.

Land was still booming in Kansas, so "the famous Rev. Kalloch," presumably acting for the Baptist Home Mission but even more for himself, joined a few other influential citizens in founding the town of Ottawa in the easternmost part of the state. The variety of Kalloch's involvements in the town were astonishing: persuading immigrants to settle there, organizing a church (but not serving in it), starting a newspaper, and even founding a Baptist college. He also awarded himself 900 acres, which after a while were worth $100,000. For four years he was president of the college, resigning after a scandal in which it was said that various trustees, including Kalloch, had made handsome profits on the sale of Indian lands granted to the school. Kalloch also helped to organize a railroad, got federal and state grants of more than 300,000 acres, and became its superintendent. In the course of selling bonds for the road he and others were accused of pocketing some of the proceeds.

Kalloch's activities, even the most admirable, had a tendency to end up in rumors of laxity or self-indulgence—variously concerning a loose way with women, manipulating the truth, and mishandling other people's money. Other newspaper publishers, partly out of envy but surely not without some justification, nicknamed him, in the brutal journalism of the time, the "Sorrel Stallion," and described him as a rogue, an embezzler, and an insatiable lecher. Inured to such attacks. Kalloch merely shifted his center of operations to a larger city, Lawrence. There he took over a leading newspaper, plunged so enthusiastically into stock farming that he was elected president of the state agricultural society, and became active in politics.

Although he dressed like a "sporting man," Isaac Kalloch at forty was a commanding figure, weighing 240 pounds, with broad shoulders, massive head, and clipped, curling beard. He drank heavily, gambled on his racehorses and gamecocks, and gave riotous parties in a stone mansion outside Lawrence. He had clearly broken with the church, and he scoffed at its quarrels and hypocrisies; for their part the Baptist clergy decried him and then prayed for him.

Living so openhandedly, Kalloch was totally unprepared for the panic of 1873. In short order his farm, mansion, prize stock, racehorses, and newspaper were gone, and he barely escaped bankruptcy. Falling back on his voice and platform presence, he went on lecture tours, but the fees were meager. So he chose a much-publicized revival meeting to make a sensational confession of sin and repentance. It was so eloquent that although skeptics warned that he was a shameless opportunist and faker, he was promptly called back to his old pastorate in Leavenworth.

No less than most westward-drifting pioneers, Isaac disliked retracing his steps. Abruptly, at the height of his comeback, he went to San Francisco and persuaded prominent Baptists there to amalgamate several congregations for him, build him a temple, and pay him

$5,000 a year. To his bewildered Leavenworth followers, he announced that he had a mission to convert the wicked in the coast city. But cynics claimed that he was fleeing from large debts.

The Metropolitan Temple built in San Francisco for the Reverend Kalloch in 1876 was the largest Baptist church in the United States. Reflecting new tendencies, it had gymnasiums, day nurseries, and courses in sewing and manual training. Once more Kalloch drew such throngs that he had to repeat his sermons on the street outside the church. He was also distinctly "modern" in doctrine, accepting Darwinism and questioning the infallibility of the Bible. But more and more he devoted himself to politics.

Railroad millionaires and land monopolists ran California like a barony, and during the nationwide railroad strike of 1877, low wages, unemployment, and the competition of Chinese laborers gave rise to the "Sandlotters," a militant workingmen's organization. At first Kalloch denounced them as foreign incendiaries who should be subdued with gun and bayonet. But as they began to elect their men to office he quickly became their champion. The shift was pure demagoguery, but the workingmen jubilantly welcomed Kalloch's eloquence. In no time he had captured the party and was nominated for mayor.

Most newspapers, beholden to businessmen, opposed Kalloch bitterly. He ignored them until the San Francisco *Chronicle*, which the DeYoung brothers, Charles and Michael, had nursed from a blackmailing gossip sheet to the largest circulation on the coast, declared that he was not only still debauching virgins in his study but that his father had been equally lustful. Enraged at last, Kalloch answered in kind, asserting that the DeYoungs were, among other things, monsters born of a whorehouse madam. (They *were* despicable men, but their parents were merely middle-class Jews who had owned a variety store in Cincinnati.) The following day Charles DeYoung waited for Kalloch outside the Temple and shot him twice. For a week Kalloch's doctors claimed that he was dying, and then, on election eve, announced that he would recover. Some observers thought it a pity that both men had not managed to kill each other. But the workingmen of San Francisco voted solidly for the Reverend Kalloch. Told that he had been elected, Kalloch promptly recovered.

If Isaac Kalloch's two years as mayor were not memorable it was partly because Republican aldermen, called supervisors, thwarted him at every turn. In a time of much social unrest, Kalloch advocated social legislation and inveighed against "the accursed spirit of corporate greed and individual selfishness," but achieved little.

Kalloch now learned that Charles DeYoung—still not brought to trial seven months after the shooting—was preparing another "exposé" of him. Isaac's son, Milton, a moody man of twenty-eight who served as an assistant pastor in his father's church, now did what he had long threatened: he shot and killed DeYoung. At the trial he calmly swore that DeYoung had fired first. He was acquitted. Californians were accustomed to the violent settlement of quarrels and the spectacle of the assassin going free. "He had only done what the customary law of primitive people requires," James Bryce observed in *The American Commonwealth*. "It survives in Albania, and is scarcely extinct in Corsica."

The Baptist clergy now tried to unfrock Kalloch but he defied them. When, however, the workingmen's party collapsed and the Democrats spurned him, Kalloch decided not to run again. For a few years he carried on as a pastor, but there was no challenge in the task. He liked the platform the church gave him and his power over audiences, but he had no use for the doctrines and the piety. So one day in July 1883, at age fifty-two, a bit paunchy and his beard streaked with silver, he resigned—this time saying simply that he was bored.

His last move was to the flourishing northernmost part of Washington territory, near Mount Baker, and in the few remaining years of his life he made a great deal of money in railroads, lumber, and large-scale farming. He had quit the church and politics, and his life was at last peaceful, but he told a friend that he now had everything except fun. At his funeral there were, as he had requested, no clergymen and no services. His death went almost unnoticed, and he was soon almost completely forgotten.

Isaac Kalloch was a lecher, gambler, drinker, demagogue, and probably an embezzler. Yet he became a famous preacher in four American cities, a college president, newspaper publisher, railroad superintendent, president of a state agricultural society, and mayor of a great city. He was successful in part because he was a commanding, dynamic, and gifted man, but also because of the era and his circumstances: he profited in religion from the revolt against Puritan austerity and in his sexual conduct from the rejection of Puritan guilt; in Kansas from the frontier with its emphasis on masculinity and rugged independence; and in California from the tolerance of violence, corruption, and slander.

Kalloch was almost too richly endowed, too clearly made for worldly pleasures. The satisfactions he derived from indulgence were plainly greater than any pain or punishment. All his congregations closed their ears to every charge against him. No woman ever accused him of offending her with his advances. Why this pagan sensualist chose the ministry as his profession is something of a mystery, but clearly the reason he remained in it was that it never prevented him from enjoying all the pleasures of this world.

The 1830s saw the rise of various movements—utopian religions, communist experiments, spiritualism, and women's rights—that encouraged, sometimes unintentionally, the practice of free love. At revival meetings, where men and women writhed and moaned and threw themselves about, an occasional by-product of a rapturous seizure was a baby born out of wedlock—a "camp-meetin' child." In the wake of such revivals, visionary and millennial communities sprang up, led usually by men who claimed mystical or divine inspiration and who called upon their followers to reject artificial codes, pool their possessions, and love one another freely. One of these, the "Perfectionist" colony established by John Humphrey Noyes, attracted much attention because it worked well for thirty years despite abusive attacks by "outsiders." It would seem that the more the leaders of utopian communities with exotic sexual codes were accused of lust and immorality, the more their followers saw them as persecuted, God-inspired men.

The son of a wealthy New England family, Noyes acquired a thorough religious education at Andover and Yale, but he soon developed his own conception of a biblical communal Christianity, one that justified a freedom of sexual relations suited to his own roving desires. As early as 1837 he wrote:

In a holy community there is no more reason why sexual intercourse should be restrained by law than why eating and drinking should be. . . . I call a certain woman my wife; she is yours; she is Christ's; and in him she is the bride of all saints. She is dear in the hands of a stranger and according to my promise to her I rejoice.

Noyes set up such a community in 1841 in Putney, Vermont, and in 1848 transferred it to Oneida in central New York. To prevent continual pregnancies among the women, Noyes instituted "male continence," or *coitus reservatus,* in which the man controls himself until detumescence occurs, and then withdraws. Noyes claimed that this was easy to do (there were in fact few unplanned births at Oneida) and that it made sexual intercourse an exquisite "method of ordinary conversation" between man and woman. Understandably some clergymen described the colony as a nest of the darkest sin and depravity.

To curb indiscriminate propagation Noyes later introduced "stirpiculture," a form of eugenics in which he arranged the childbearing of his followers, presumably to produce the best possible offspring. Far from resenting such a monstrous intrusion, fifty-three young women and thirty-eight men signed a statement proclaiming that they had "no rights or personal feelings in regard to childbearing which shall in the least degree oppose or embarrass [Noyes] in his choice of scientific combination." Noyes's critics pointed out that despite "male continence" and his age, fifty-eight, when stirpiculture was introduced, he fathered eight more children. Threatened with a criminal investigation by outsiders in 1879, Noyes hastily retired to Niagara Falls. Without him the colony soon became a joint-stock company, a community business enterprise conventional in almost all its living arrangements and known mainly for the production of silverware.

Although the Oneida women could take the first step in a courtship and were theoretically free to choose their own bedmates, they submitted to Noyes's will and desire with a pliancy that seems utterly incredible in the light of Victorian morality.

As orthodox Calvinism receded during the first half of the nineteenth century and camp meeting revivalism came and went like prairie fires, other more moderate and reassuring forms of faith emerged. One of them was spiritualism. Its central concept was that the living can communicate with the dead. It also treated marriage as a matter of natural affinity and not subject to the laws of church or state. In the 1840s in Ohio, John B. Foot went about the countryside proclaiming the doctrine of "spirit brides," and Francis Barry established a free-love colony near Oberlin. Even though Foot was tarred and feathered and Barry's colony disintegrated, some of their views surely rubbed off on Victoria Claflin Woodhull and her sister Tennessee Claflin.

In both her views of sex and her love life Victoria Woodhull was an astonishing woman. The sexual freedom of her private life may be considered merely bohemian, but her attacks on loveless marriage, hypocrisy, and the double standard anticipate the most enlightened modern opinion. Untrained and undisciplined, there is no doubt that she borrowed almost all her intellectual capital from a few associates and that she espoused crackbrained causes as well as sound ones. Brought up to live by her wits, she threw scruples to the winds whenever it suited her. But on a few subjects, her voice was among the bravest in a time of conformity and cant.

Victoria Woodhull's early life was so sordid that it is a minor miracle that she emerged with so buoyant a view of love and life. Born in 1838 of a disreputable, sometime river gambler, "Buck" Claflin, by a German tavern keeper's daughter, she had grown into girlhood as one of ten neglected children in a hillside shack in Ohio. The Claflins were a queer lot, spiritualist even before spiritualism became popular, the mother going into trances at revival meetings and Victoria talking to spirits by the time she was four. In her teens, Victoria and a younger sister, Tennessee, wandered the Midwest as faith healers, selling a "Magnetic Life Elixir" and, later, a cancer cure that killed at least one patient. Victoria Woodhull tapped both mystical and logical sources, drawing fervor from religious missionaries and reasoned arguments from women's rights crusaders.

Growing up amid the waywardness of the Claflin household, the Claflin girls were destined to become a law unto themselves, especially in their relationships with men. At sixteen Victoria married Dr. Canning Woodhull, something of a fop and a rake but mild and harmless. For the next decade the Claflin clan moved like Gypsies from place to place, practicing "magnetic healing" and giving seances. Having borne Woodhull two children, Victoria matured into a beautiful and mettlesome woman while Tennessee remained high-spirited and coarsely sensual. When Woodhull sank into alcoholism, Victoria left him. She soon took up with a handsome war veteran, Colonel James Blood. A philosophical anarchist and a socialist as well as a spiritualist, Blood supplied Victoria with an intellectual framework for her natural urge to free love and the free life. With him she roved the countryside as a clairvoyant. He adored her and believed in her high destiny, and it was doubtless he who soon directed her great vitality into crusading channels.

At thirty, pert, vibrant, wearing bold, ankle-length skirts and chic Alpine hats, Victoria, along with Tennessee, turned up in New York—sent, she said, by the orator Demosthenes, her spirit-world mentor. Soon they had Commodore Vanderbilt, old, ailing, and an easy prey for "healers," infatuated with their arts and charms, especially with their "laying-on of hands." Outrageously determined to invade a male sanctum, they persuaded the Commodore to set them up as brokers. He not only did so but with a few tips helped the "Bewitching Brokers," as they were dubbed, make a small fortune.

The sisters now established themselves in a glittering Murray Hill mansion. Their ménage included Colonel Blood, Dr. Woodhull (he had been taken back out of pity), numerous Claflins, a crew of servants, and a celebrated visionary, sixty-year-old great-bearded Stephen Pearl Andrews. Andrews, whose father had been an unorthodox Massachusetts Baptist minister, was an immensely learned man. He had practiced law, acquired a medical degree, and had written Chinese and French textbooks. But his passion was the complete reform of society. He had lived in Modern Times, a Long Island community based on socialism and free love, and, under the influence of utopian socialists Charles Fourier and Robert Owen, he advocated a system of world government called the "Pantarchy," with himself as the "Pantarch." The huge book to which he had confided his system, *Basic Outline of Universology,* was monumentally abstruse. He now seized upon Victoria Woodhull as the ideal channel for his ideas. She in turn was deeply impressed by his learning and his vision.

Having come so far, Victoria's ambitions quickly became boundless. In April 1870 she issued her "First Pronounciamento": having matched men in the stronghold of finance, she would challenge them in the arena of politics by becoming a candidate for President. The announcement brought amused but surprisingly tolerant comment—and, of course, much publicity.

Intoxicated by their success, the sisters next inveigled Vanderbilt into helping them establish a newspaper. The first issue of *Woodhull & Claflin's Weekly* appeared on May 14, 1870. A sixteen-page, tabloid-sized journal, it flaunted the motto, "Progress! Free Thought! Untrammeled Lives!" Supplied with arguments by Andrews and Blood, the paper blasted everything from financial fraud to prostitution and crusaded boldly for such causes as birth control, public housing, spiritualism, a universal language named Alwato, and of course Woodhull for President. It was, moreover, the first publication to print the *Communist Manifesto* in the United States. Like Victoria herself it was a catchall of utopian manifestos, muckraking, quackery, free love, and self-advertisement. Andrews and Blood undoubtedly did most of the writing, but Victoria had plainly assimilated their views and could express them, when she wished, in her own way.

Thrusting herself into the struggle for women's rights, Mrs. Woodhull went to Washington during the third annual convention of the National Woman Suffrage Association in January 1871, and to the astonishment of everyone became the first woman to appear before the Judiciary Committee of the House of Representatives. Relishing sensational causes, the ineffable Ben Butler sponsored her. A trim, very attractive woman with a musical voice and what was then called natural magnetism, Woodhull created a great stir with a learned memorial on women's rights. Disregarding her scandalous background and more extravagant views, the tough-minded leaders of the radical suffragists, Anthony, Stanton, and Hooker, welcomed her enthusiastically.

The following day she addressed the women's suffrage convention in Washington and captured it, too. A few months later she startled a suffrage anniversary meeting in New York by calling for secession and the overthrow of "this bogus Republic" if the government did not at once grant women their rights.

She was thus engaged when her mother, a violent, irresponsible creature, went into court charging that Colonel Blood was mistreating her. Nothing came of the charge, but it caused the entire bizarre household on Thirty-eighth Street to be exposed to merciless, hot-eyed publicity. The Cleveland *Leader,* for example, raked up Victoria's past and branded her an "unsexed" and "brazen adventuress" who had thrust herself into the suffrage movement for notoriety and profit. Suffragists in general disavowed her, sensing that she was not interested in any movement but her own. Conspicuous among those who began to harry her were Catharine Beecher, Henry Ward Beecher's domineering eldest sister, and Harriet Beecher Stowe. Unfortunately for them, Mrs. Stanton had told Victoria the "secret" of Theodore Tilton's wife, Elizabeth, and her relations with Henry Ward Beecher. Victoria Woodhull was now ready to document her charges of male hypocrisy.

On May 22, 1871, the New York *World* and *The New York Times* printed the following open letter from Mrs. Woodhull:

> Sir, Because I am a woman, and because I conscientiously hold opinions somewhat different from the self-elected orthodoxy . . . and because I think it . . . my absolute right . . . to advocate them with my whole strength, self-elected orthodoxy . . . endeavors to cover my life with ridicule and dishonor. . . . I do not intend to be . . . offered up as a victim to society by those who cover over the foulness of their lives and the feculence of their thoughts with a hypocritical mantle of fair professions. . . . I advocate free love in its highest, purest sense as the only cure for immorality . . . by which men corrupt and disfigure God's most holy institution of sexual relations. My judges preach against "free love" openly, and practice it secretly. . . . For example, I know of one man, a public teacher of eminence, who lives in concubinage with the wife of another public teacher of almost equal eminence. All three concur in denouncing offenses against morality. . . . I shall make it my business to analyze some of these lives, and will take my chances in the matter of libel suits.

Supremely ironic was the spectacle of Henry Ward Beecher threatened with exposure not by a pillar of morality but by a believer in free love urging him to admit his adherence to her code.

Hastily Tilton, Moulton, and Beecher met and decided that Tilton should try to placate Mrs. Woodhull. Once Tilton met her he found the assignment a pleasure. In another article in *The Golden Age,* he described her as the Joan of Arc of the women's rights movement, and, in a sketch written for her presidential campaign he acclaimed her "mad and magnificent" energies. When they went rowing on the Harlem River and bathing at Coney Island together, it was assumed that he not only admired her theories but practiced them with her. On one occasion, as she was leaving Chicago for New York, "The Woodhull" told a reporter something he was itching to hear—that Tilton had been her "devoted lover for half a year" and had "slept every night for three months" in her arms. But in New York she just as casually denied the story.

When Harriet Beecher Stowe and Catharine Beecher persisted in criticizing her, and Harriet published a novel, *My Wife and I,* in which a brazen "new woman," Audacia Dangyereyes, obviously based on Woodhull, was ridiculed, Woodhull wrote Beecher that if they did not desist, she would strike back disastrously at him; and she summoned him to an interview. He came but refused, he later claimed, to support her views. Woodhull's version of the interview was that he agreed with her on such subjects as divorce and free love but admitted, with tears, that he was too much of a moral coward to proclaim the fact.

Whenever the voices raised against her became too abusive, Victoria Woodhull simply grew more aggressive. In New York's Steinway Hall, during a lecture boldly entitled "Free Love, Marriage, Divorce and Prostitution," someone shouted, "Are you a free lover?" She promptly cried: "Yes! I am a free lover! I have an inalienable, constitutional and natural right to love whom I may, to love as long or as short a period as I can, to change that love every day if I please!" She added that, before long, women would demand the freedom to withhold their bodies from the "demoralizing influence of sexual relations that are not . . . maintained by love."

The lecture stirred such harsh criticism that Woodhull's brokerage business collapsed, and, Vanderbilt having withdrawn his support, she had to suspend publication of her *Weekly.* As her fortunes ebbed, Woodhull grew more and more militant on social and economic questions. In a lecture called "The Impending Revolution," delivered before a huge audience at the New York Academy of Music, she blamed the plight of the workingman on railroad and financial mon-opolists, declaring:

> A Vanderbilt may . . . manipulate stocks or declare dividends by which in a few years he amasses fifty million dollars . . . and he is one of the remarkable men of the age. But if a poor, half-starved child should take a loaf of bread from his cupboard . . . she would be sent to the Tombs. . . . An Astor may sit in his sumptuous apartments and watch the property bequeathed to him rise in value from one to fifty millions, and everybody bows before his immense power. . . . But if a tenant of his whose employer had discharged him because he did not vote the Republican ticket fails to pay his month's rent, the law sets him and his family into the street.

Although fringe groups calling themselves the Equal Rights party now nominated her for the Presidency, she was sinking in a sea of troubles. Along with her family she was forced out of her home, and Susan B. Anthony and other women's rights leaders began to turn their backs on her. Beset on every side, she struck back: at a meeting of spiritualists in Boston she told the whole Beecher-Tilton story. When the story was ignored by the newspapers, she devoted, as we have seen, an entire issue of her weekly to the exposé, declaring that she intended it to fall "like a bombshell into the . . . moralistic social camp."

It did. Over 100,000 copies of the issue were sold, some at ten dollars for a secondhand copy. But the following day Anthony Com-stock, hound dog on the hunt for vice, had the sisters arrested for sending obscene literature through the mail. A month passed before they were released. Twice again they were arrested and twice bailed out. When a speaker at a national convention of spiritualists in Chi-cago asserted that she had prostituted herself with men and then threatened to expose them, she cried:

> A man questioning my virtue! . . . I hurl the intention back in your face, sir . . . and declare that I never had sexual inter-course with any man of whom I am ashamed to stand side by

side before the world. . . . Nor am I ashamed of any desire that has been gratified, nor of any passion alluded to. Every one of them are part of my own soul's life, for which, thank God, I am not accountable to you. . . . And this sexual intercourse business may as well as be discussed now, and discussed until you are so familiar with your sexual organs that a reference to them will no longer make the blush mount to your face any more than a reference to any other part of your body.

With an approach to sexual problems that would not be displayed again in a public discussion for another half century, she pointed out that nothing was so destructive as

intercourse carried on habitually without regard to perfect and reciprocal consummation. . . . Every man needs to have it thundered in his ears . . . that the other party demands . . . that he shall not, either from ignorance or selfish desire, carry her impulse forward only to cast it backward with its mission unfulfilled. . . . This involves a whole science and a fine art . . . now criminally repressed and defeated by the prejudices of mankind. . . . When sexual science is introduced into the schools, as assuredly it will be, sexual ills that now beset the young will vanish.

Although the Equal Rights party soon disintegrated and Grant rode smoothly back into office, Woodhull had become a national figure—the scarlet woman who wore her letter like a badge of honor. Wherever she went she stirred excitement, evoking every reaction from ribald jokes to passionate defense. And always there were the lurid rumors. We would hardly know the truth about such stories were it not for a remarkably candid memoir by Benjamin R. Tucker. More than fifty years later, while living in France after a career as a publisher of libertarian periodicals, Tucker told of his love affair with Victoria Woodhull when she was thirty-five and he was nineteen.

Of an old New England family, Tucker was a studious youth with an acute susceptibility to extremist doctrines ranging from anarchism to free love. Already active at nineteen in reform movements in Boston, he met Victoria Woodhull and was attracted to her. Intimacy between them began when he had occasion to visit her at the Parker House. She greeted him warmly, and as soon as Colonel Blood left the room, she locked the door and, Tucker writes, "marched straight to the chair in which I was seated, leaned over and kissed me, remarking then: 'I've been wanting to do this so long!' Then . . . she gently swung herself around and placed herself upon my knee." She arose just before Colonel Blood came back. When Tucker returned in the morning she was alone, and after some conversation she said, "Do you know I should dearly love to sleep with you?" "Within an hour," Tucker recalls, "my 'ruin' was complete, and I, nevertheless, a proud and happy youth." Abandoning his studies, Tucker followed Woodhull to New York and spent the next seven months with her. But he was disillusioned by the fact that she did no reading or writing and by the "disgraceful" means she sometimes used to gain her ends. "She would have been glorious," he concludes, "if she hadn't been infamous."

Worn out by harassment, suffering from anemia, constantly in need of money, Woodhull, to the dismay of her radical admirers, now retreated into biblical symbolism and rhapsodies on purity, motherhood, and the sanctity of marriage. At this point, providentially, old Vanderbilt died, and his heirs, quarreling over his will, seem to have paid Victoria and Tennessee to dissuade them from testifying at the trial. We do know that the sisters and their entourage suddenly departed for Europe, traveling in style.

When Woodhull arrived in London, the possibility of a totally new life, like another incarnation, suddenly presented itself to her. She was almost forty years old, weary of rebellion and ostracism, and eager for a rest, a conventional husband, and a home. She achieved all of these when John Biddulph Martin of an old English banking family fell in love with her. Martin was a diffident, earnest Englishman who was convinced that his Victoria was a pure, misunderstood spirit, and he spent much of his life defending her from charges that she had had an immoral past. It is interesting to see how Henry James, basing the relationship between the American adventuress Nancy Headway and the rich Englishman Sir Arthur Demesne in his tale "The Siege of London" on the Woodhull-Martin marriage, saw his couple, in characteristic Jamesian fashion, as an attraction between opposites—the overcivilized, rather fatuous European of fine old lineage and the vulgar but vital American. But Mrs. Headway shares none of Victoria Woodhull's social radicalism; she is merely a woman who has been scandalously free with love. Despite James's gift for subtilizing character, Nancy is much more obvious than Victoria and far less challenging.

It was, however, six years before Victoria convinced Martin's family that she had become a model of respectability. She did so by repudiating free love and all other radical doctrines and vilifying Andrews and Blood. So great was the change in her attitude toward love that one biographer suggests that surgery performed on her to correct an ailment may have reduced her sexual drive. Her name was never again linked with that of any man but Martin.

At the turn of the century, some years after her husband's death, Victoria Woodhull moved to the ancient estate he had left her in Worcestershire, and until her own death, in 1927, did everything possible to live down her past—that is, all that had made her unique and significant. As "mistress of the manor," she played at being Lady Bountiful, exuding cheerful sentiments and extolling the genteel virtues. And whenever some newspaper dredged up her past, she charged that it was all lies and blackmail. In the end she was little more than another quaint old lady. Ironically, the obituaries, ignoring all her efforts at proving her conformity, recalled her as a pioneer suffragist, muckraker, and social reformer.

To some of her foes, Victoria Woodhull in her prime was a lamia, glitteringly equipped by the devil to corrupt the innocent; to other detractors she was simply a purveyor of vice for publicity and profit. To her admirers she was a brave crusader, a soaring spirit, liberator of enslaved women and other stifled souls. Circumstances had kept her outside the pale; forced to find her own way, she came to despise the hypocrisy and cowardice of men and to pity the frustration and emotional immaturity of women. It was thus almost by instinct alone that she became the first American woman to publicly denounce loveless intercourse, whether in marriage or prostitution, and to practice and preach freedom in sexual relations. Bomber of the "moralistic camps," shocker of the bourgeoisie, she was in some ways almost a century ahead of her time.

But instincts are not pure, and Victoria Woodhull was almost as much the victim as the beneficiary of her passions and her appetites.

Crucial flaws in her character led her, whenever the pressure mounted, into unconscionable paths. Although the age and the passing years broke and tamed her, much of what she had fought for had become familiar doctrine by the time of her death. Many years before, Elizabeth Cady Stanton had declared, "Victoria Woodhull has done a work for woman that none of us could have done."

# WOMEN WHO BROKE
# THE BARRIERS

Although the nineteenth century in the United States was a period of boundless opportunity, in some ways it had an insidiously narrowing effect on many women. Well into the century, women living on farms and in villages performed a remarkable variety of essential tasks: housekeeping, caring for their children, making clothes, turning out butter, cheese, candles, and quilts, doing a host of farm chores, and often serving in place of teachers, ministers, and doctors. In the maintenance and support of the family they were, in short, the equal partners of men.

But as mid-century approached, industrialization and the subsequent shift in population to towns and cities brought basic changes in family life. As more men went off each day to work in factory, mill, mine, or office, on railroads or steamships, more women, with fewer homemaking functions, became consumers, buying what they needed instead of producing it. Families became more and more dependent on the earnings of man as the "breadwinner."

Because women of the growing middle class or the new upper class had more time for the genteel accomplishments, there was little protest against or even awareness of the erosion of their functions. After two centuries of the straitjacket of Puritanism, Victorian standards of respectability, propriety, and gentility did not seem at all oppressive. The spread of prosperity had made possible some increase in the education of women, but "female seminaries" were still mainly concerned with the polite arts. Besides such traditional women's occupations as teacher, domestic servant, midwife, and seamstress, women could now work in mills and factories, but chiefly in tedious jobs, for as long as fourteen hours a day, and for pitifully low wages.

Like children and idiots, as the early feminists put it, women still had no legal rights: after marriage they could not own property, and a husband could punish his wife almost at will. They were generally considered emotionally unstable and, despite the work done by women on farms, delicate and weak. A surprising number of gentlewomen, it is true, were subject, mainly as a result of psychological and sexual frustration, as well as lack of exercise, to "nervous prostration" or even a semi-invalid existence. In behavior, women were expected to be modest, pious, and accommodating if not submissive. If a woman did not marry, she was likely to become an "old maid," fated to live out her life with relatives.

It was plainly these constraints and age-old prejudices that account for the protests or even rebellion, beginning in the 1830s and 1840s, of a few brave spirits. They had even braver predecessors, principally an Englishwoman, Mary Wollstonecraft, and a Scotswoman, Fanny Wright.

Wollstonecraft was the daughter of a wastrel who had reduced her mother to a household drudge. Her own experiences at home and later as a governess and teacher bred a vein of iron in her. She began to write in the late 1780s, reflecting the great intellectual and political ferment of the time, and published her major work, *A Vindication of the Rights of Woman*, in 1791. Begun as an answer to Rousseau's view that women should be educated to please men, it asserted that men and women were differentiated only by their training; women should not only be given the same education as men but also be prepared for employment that would make them independent. Wollstonecraft was so impatient with sentimental women that she seemed, at thirty-two, already incapable of a romantic relationship. But in the remaining six years of her life, as if desperate to make up for lost time, she had love affairs with two men, bore the first a child out of wedlock, and married the second, the political philosopher William Godwin, only after she became pregnant. (Mary, her child by Godwin, became the author of *Frankenstein* and the wife of the poet Shelley.) Because

231

the young republic was still receptive to revolutionary views, *A Vindication* was widely read in America and was later cherished by the bolder leaders of the women's rights movement.

An equally remarkable spiritual ancestor of the women's rights activists was Fanny Wright. Born in 1795 into a prominent Scottish family, Wright was guided by ideas summed up in such works as Paine's *Rights of Man*. Even as a young woman she condemned social injustice and, under the influence of Byron, romantically saw herself as fated to defy society and its stifling conventions. Seeing America as the Promised Land, she made a long visit there and, on returning home in 1821, gained wide attention with her *Views of Society and Manners in America,* a glowing tribute to the United States and democracy.

But on a second visit she found a hideous defect in the American system—slavery. With the optimism of the utopian reformers of her time she bought a tract in Tennessee and set up a plantation, Nashoba, where slaves could work out their purchase price and be prepared for freedom. But it was a failure from the start—ten confused and indolent blacks and four ill-equipped whites floundering about in a raw wilderness area. Her health failing, Wright visited New Harmony, the utopian commune that Robert Owen, Scottish philanthropist and reformer, was trying to establish in Indiana. Meanwhile, newspapers reported that the whites remaining in Nashoba were advocating the free union of the sexes, and promptly labeled it "Fanny Wright's Free Love Colony."

Deciding that all men and women needed to be prepared for life in an ideal society, Wright now turned to lecturing to make her views more widely known. She drew large and fascinated audiences wherever she went. In Cincinnati, Frances Trollope, an Englishwoman known for her critical view of American life, declared that "all expectations fell far short of the splendor, the brilliance, the overwhelming eloquence of this extraordinary orator." But when Wright moved to New York and began publishing *The Free Enquirer,* a radical weekly that advocated equal rights for women, free nonsectarian education, abolition, birth control, and a workingmen's party, the press and clergy called her the "Princess of Beelzebub."

Then, on a visit to Paris, despondent and finding herself, at thirty-five, without roots or family, she slipped into a relationship with Phiquepal D'Arusmont, a French educator she had met at New Harmony. When she found herself pregnant, they agreed to marry but then gradually drifted apart. Ironically, when she came into a large inheritance in 1846, D'Arusmont laid claim, as was his legal right, to all her property. She had divorced him and was suing to regain her property when she died, virtually forgotten, in Cincinnati in 1852.

Fanny Wright was in principle too literal a rationalist and in practice too naïve an idealist. But she was a pioneer; she groped and she blundered, but she persevered, and her idealism, altruism, and courage left something that would stimulate kindred spirits long after she was gone.

Surprisingly, the women who next became known for resistance to the traditional status of women came from the Deep South: the Grimké sisters were born in South Carolina, Sarah in 1792 and Angelina in 1805. Their disaffection may well have begun when, at the age of five, Sarah, daughter of the chief judge of the South Carolina supreme court and of a mother from a prominent family, saw a black servant whipped. Horrified, she tried to run away from home. At thirteen she experienced another shock when she declared that, like her older brother, she wanted to study law. Her parents, scandalized, made her settle for the usual schooling of a well-bred Southern girl— a little French, embroidery, harpsichord lessons, painting. Although she joined in the busy social life of Charleston in the 1810s, she resented being reduced to "a doll, a coquette, a fashionable fool." As she grew older she tried to find a refuge in religion.

She was twenty-six, plain-looking, and already considered a spinster when, during a visit to Philadelphia, she found a new life for herself, mainly among the Quakers. Their belief in an inner light not only gave women spiritual equality with men but allowed them to serve as ministers. So in 1821 she moved to Philadelphia, a shocking act for an unmarried Southern gentlewoman. For the next fifteen years she would devote herself to Quaker religious and charitable activities.

She was deeply pleased when, a few years later, her younger sister Angelina, an attractive and spirited woman of twenty-three, joined her. Angelina had seen a young black woman slave, who had tried to escape, forced to wear a pronged iron collar and have a front tooth

extracted so she could be identified if she ran away; she needed no
call from religion to go to the North. But she found orthodox Quaker
life stultifying and soon took another radical step, joining the newly
founded Female Anti-Slavery Society of Philadelphia. Before long,
learning that a British abolitionist, George Thompson, whose stand
had moved her profoundly, was being harried by mobs, she wrote a
furious letter to William Lloyd Garrison, editor of *The Liberator*. "If
persecution is the means which God has ordained for the accomplishment of *Emancipation*," she declared, "*let it come!* for it is my deep,
solemn, deliberate conviction that this is a cause worth dying for."
The publication in 1835 of such an outburst by a Southern woman
brought harsh criticism. Her response was a passionate, full-scale
challenge to slaveholders, *An Appeal to Christian Women of the South*. The
Charleston postmaster burned the book, and the police issued such a
threat against her that she never went home again.

The American Anti-Slavery Society immediately saw in Angelina
an ideal advocate of their cause and persuaded her and Sarah to
address a small group of women in New York in 1853. From the
response there, and, soon after, in Boston, the sisters realized that
they were answering a deep urge in women to participate in the affairs of the world. Sarah in particular felt that they had an even
broader cause—equal rights for women. Simply by speaking in public
they were defying an age-old taboo based in part on St. Paul's in-
junction to women to keep silent and not usurp men's authority.

In 1836, after coaching by Theodore Weld, dynamic abolitionist
agitator, the sisters emerged as the first women abolitionist agents.
In Lynn, Massachusetts, over a thousand people came to hear them,
including young women who had been drawn from New England
farms to work in the textile mills and shoe factories. In later talks
Angelina dared to tell her audiences of the seemingly pure-minded
wives of slaveholders living with husbands and sons who used slave
women as concubines. The Congregational clergy now began denouncing the sisters, declaring that a woman who takes man's place
as a reformer earns only shame and dishonor. Even Quaker meet-
inghouses were closed to them. It was Sarah who met the challenge
most defiantly. In a slim book, *Letters on the Equality of the Sexes*, she
focused attention on women's rights, anticipating by a dozen years
the charges made at the first women's rights conventions. "All I ask

our brethren," she wrote, "is that they will take their feet from off our necks and permit us to stand upright on that ground which God designed us to occupy." She demanded not only equal educational opportunities for women but equal pay for equal work. "Whatsoever it is morally right for a man to do," she declared, "it is morally right for a woman to do." Lucretia Mott described Sarah's book as the most important contribution to the women's rights cause since Mary Wollstonecraft's pioneer work. Of even more practical significance was an invitation to the sisters to address the Massachusetts state legislature; Angelina spoke at three successive sessions, winning wide praise for her cogency and grace.

But the emergence of women's rights advocates caused the more rabid abolitionists to see in them a rival in the struggle for emancipation. With characteristic finality Theodore Weld announced that abolition must take precedence over women's rights because such rights were not "a life and death business." Despite this view, the relationship between Angelina Grimké and Weld, who combined great charm with a dark intensity, ripened into love. They were married in May 1838; in the ceremony, attended by leading abolitionists and several former slaves, Weld scrupulously renounced all rights to his wife's property. As soon as they were settled in a small house in New Jersey, Weld decided to document the horrors of slavery from the testimony of slave owners themselves. Aided by Angelina and Sarah, he assembled a mass of evidence, such as ads for runaway slaves, penal codes, and data on breeding slaves, and published *American Slavery as It Is*. It was a devastating indictment.

Soon after bearing her first child, Angelina began to suffer from nervous disorders. These, along with housework, the need to scrimp, and the coming of two more children, ended most of her abolitionist and women's rights activities. At the same time, Weld, exhausted, and his once tireless voice almost gone, began to withdraw from the abolitionist campaigns. Beset by financial problems, they started a boarding school in Eagleswood, New Jersey. In time they built it into a rewarding coeducational and interracial institution with instruction ranging from classical subjects and the arts to crafts, agriculture, housekeeping, and gymnastics for both sexes. But the outbreak of war put an end to this, as to many other enterprises. Although the Welds were pacifists, Theodore Weld made a vigorous tour on behalf of emancipation and Angelina gave a stirring address at a national women's rights convention in 1863. As conscious as ever of her unique position, she declared that although the people of her native region were bleeding and perishing, she felt bound to cry out to the North, "Go on! Go on! Never falter, never abandon the principles which you have adopted."

After the war, the Welds, in their sixties, and Sarah, over seventy, moved to a home near Boston and devoted themselves to teaching and doing whatever they could for women's suffrage. The crowning evidence of the selflessness of the Grimké sisters came when they learned that an Archibald Grimké who had delivered an address at Lincoln University, a school for black men, was one of three sons their brother Henry had fathered on a woman slave in his household. The sisters not only welcomed Archibald and his brother, Francis, into their family circle but supported them with all their means. Their faith was fully justified: Archibald Henry Grimké became a lawyer, an editor, and a distinguished black leader, and Francis James Grimké served for fifty years as a highly regarded pastor in Washington.

Although such later women's rights leaders as Lucy Stone and Elizabeth Cady Stanton acknowledged how much they were inspired by the Grimkés (Stone said they confirmed her resolve "to call no man master"), and although Theodore Weld's *American Slavery as It Is* was the most influential anti-slavery work before *Uncle Tom's Cabin,* the Grimkés were path-breakers destined to be overshadowed by those who followed them.

Women in the mid-nineteenth century were thought to have innate intellectual shortcomings. They could be intelligent, articulate, witty, skillful, charming, and fanciful, but they were believed incapable of profiting from higher education or of engaging in the sustained and analytical thought required by philosophy, the sciences, literary criticism, theological speculation, and the like. As evidence, men could simply point to the fact that women had never distinguished themselves in these fields. Even such works as the novels of Jane Austen, the Brontës, George Sand, Madame de Staël and others could be treated as mere entertainment, romantic flights of the imagination. No one seemed to realize, or to care, that the relatively small number of women noted for their accomplishments was the result of training and conditioning in a social system created exclusively by men.

It remained for Margaret Fuller, born in Cambridge in 1810, to demonstrate that a woman could hold her own among the leading minds of her time. Her father, a lawyer and congressman, was something of a Puritan and even more of a nonconformist. Treating his daughter as though she were a son, he subjected her to so rigorous a classical education that she was often racked by nightmares. He left her with a great pride in intellectual accomplishment but also with a lifelong struggle to free her emotions.

Once out of school, Margaret Fuller began to shine in the intellectual life of Cambridge, making up in wit and learning what she lacked in grace and beauty. In a kind of parallel to the Transcendentalist Club, in which a score of Boston and Concord luminaries, including Emerson, Alcott, Parker, Channing, and Hawthorne, gathered for discussions of Truth, Inspiration, and Individuality and the ideas of such men as Rousseau, Swedenborg, and Fourier, Margaret Fuller in the late 1830s led a select group of women in a series of "Conversations." The conversations were designed to free women from a sense of intellectual inferiority, but they also served as an outlet for some of Fuller's frustrations.

Soon, in a remarkable tribute to a woman, the Transcendentalists chose Fuller to edit a new quarterly, the *Dial*. One of her own contributions to the journal became the core of her *Woman in the Nineteenth Century*. Although diffuse and cloudy, the book has been called "the first considered statement of feminism in this country." Woman, she declared, must put off subservience and be permitted to unfold whatever powers she has. Although she was thirty-three years old and thus an "old maid" by the code of the 1840s, she spoke out boldly on the double standard, prostitution, and sexual passion in women:

> As to marriage, it has been inculcated in women, for centuries, that men have not only stronger passions than they, but of a sort that it would be shameful for them to share or understand; that, therefore, they must . . . submit implicitly to their will; that the least appearance of coldness or withdrawal . . . in the wife is wicked, because liable to turn their husband's thoughts

to illicit indulgence; for a man is so constituted that he must indulge his passions or die!

Her fame spreading, Horace Greeley called her to New York to become the first literary critic of the *Tribune*. In New York, freed from Boston taboos, she visited prisons and asylums as well as theaters and opera houses. And she fell feverishly in love with James Nathan, a German Jew in whom she saw a romantic "Eastern" soul. But after a few months of clandestine meetings, Nathan, taken aback by the intensity of this unorthodox New England sybil, fled to Europe. Seeking emotional fulfillment more than ever, and declaring that only in marriage would the "regions of her being that else had lain in cold obstruction . . . burst forth into leaf and bloom in song," she arranged to go abroad as a correspondent for the *Tribune*.

She landed in Europe just before the revolutions of 1848, and in Rome she found all that she sought: a rich tradition, revolutionary ferment, and a lover. The lover was a penniless noble, Count Giovanni Ossoli, ten years her junior and without any intellectual interests—simply a young Italian who could fulfill her emotional and sexual needs. Within a few months she was pregnant. They married—as belatedly as Mary Wollstonecraft with Godwin, and Fanny Wright with D'Arusmont—but secretly, because Ossoli's conservative Catholic family would have been bitterly opposed.

To their private drama was added a public drama—the defense of Rome by Garibaldi's revolutionaries, with Ossoli fighting in the ranks and Fuller serving in a military hospital. But lack of money forced them to leave for America, resigned to facing malicious gossip and sanctimonious critics. They were spared that ordeal when their ship was wrecked off New York's Fire Island on July 19, 1850.

After Margaret Fuller's death, her admirers prepared a memorial that pictured her as part prophet and part goddess. But many were convinced that she had suffered a moral collapse and gone tragically astray. What such critics resented was that she had wanted something more than the lofty sentiments of the Transcendentalists, the mystic affirmations of an Emerson, or the withdrawal of a Thoreau. Far from suffering a collapse, she had found a place where her long-suppressed desires were freed. "Had I only come ten years earlier!" she cried after arriving in Rome. "Now my life must be a failure, so much strength has been wasted on abstractions, which only came because I grew not on the right soil.''

Margaret Fuller's shortcomings—her egotism, lack of lasting achievements, and the unfulfilled promise of her great gifts—in no way detract from her awareness of the limitations of the New England environment, the needs of women, and the importance of the affections. It was largely her New England breeding that kept her from living life fully. But she never fully resigned herself to that code and had at least one period of emotional fulfillment before she died.

The black woman's experience in the middle of the nineteenth century was a throwback to barbarism. In the land of equality, the refuge of the downtrodden and persecuted, blacks were simply forgotten beings, virtually invisible. More widely than is generally realized, their condition was accepted as a given, a fact of life. If after the coming of the abolitionists, white people gave slavery any thought—very few did—they were told that blacks were an inferior race, that the Bible sanctioned slavery, that they had been saved from the darkness of savagery by the blessings of Christianity, and that most of them were happy with their lot, as witness their singing, dancing, and clowning. Although some historians feel that black women were no worse off than black men, they agree that the woman had the additional burden of being subject to sexual abuse by any white man and of being treated as a mere breeding machine, provider of human livestock.

The war freed blacks, but in most ways it left their situation unchanged. They were almost completely unprepared by education, experience, or knowledge of the free world for emancipation. In the South many simply stayed where they were, continuing to slave as hired workers or sharecroppers. They were free to move about, but many found it easier to endure known burdens and restrictions than risk the unknown. Unable to read or write, for them the outside world was a mystery, dominated in the South by their white masters, and in the faraway North by people who had little use for them except in the most menial jobs.

Like the poor and illiterate in the depths of any society, few American women of color left an autobiography. Of the narratives we have, some—such as Harriet Jacob's *Incidents in the Life of a Slave Girl* (1861)—

concern prewar slave life, while others—such as evangelist Zilpha Elaw's *Memoirs* (1846)—are mainly records of religious experiences. But a woman who lived much of her life in obscurity achieved such fame in her later years that we can get from her recollections as recorded and published by a white friend and the notes of those who knew her a memorable view of what it was like to be a black woman in nineteenth-century America.

She called herself Sojourner Truth. Because her book, *The Narrative of Sojourner Truth: A Northern Slave (1850)*, fascinated those who read it, they persuaded her to attend the first national women's rights convention later that year. She came partly to sell copies of her book— which she herself could not read. In her early fifties, a gaunt, towering figure, dressed in a colorful smock, her head wrapped in a white turban, she stood out like an African queen among the white ladies and gentlemen at the convention. For a while she listened to the earnest speeches, resolutions, and discussions, to Lucretia Mott, Wendell Phillips, William Lloyd Garrison, Frederick Douglass, and others. Then someone announced that she was present, and calls came for her to speak. She rose and began, "Sisters, I aren't clear what ye'd be after. If women want any rights more than they got, why don't they just take 'em and not be talking about it."

After the convention, she joined a group of leading white reformers preaching abolitionism across Massachusetts and into western New York. Despite her total lack of education, she captured audiences with her impressively deep voice, folk wisdom, wit, and rapt, mystical pronouncements.

At another women's rights convention, in Akron, Ohio, when one minister cautioned women not to give up such courtesies as being helped into a carriage or over a ditch, and another minister justified men's special rights on the grounds that Christ was a man, Sojourner pointed to the first minister and said, "That man say that woman needs to be helped into carriages or over mud puddles. Nobody helps me into carriages or over mud puddles—and aren't I a woman?" Baring a well-muscled arm, she added, "Look at my arm! I've plowed and planted and gathered into barns, and no man could head me— and aren't I a woman? I could work as much as a man . . . and bear the lash as well. And aren't I a woman? They talks about this thing in the head—what's this they call it?" Someone called out, "Intellect." "That's it, honey," she continued. "What's that got to do with women's rights or niggers' rights? If my cup won't hold but a pint and your'n holds a quart, wouldn't ye be mean not to let me have my little half-measure full?"

When the crowd stopped laughing, she pointed to the second minister and said, "Then that little man in black there, he says women can't have as much rights as men 'cause Christ waren't a woman. Where did your Christ come from?" She paused and then burst out, "From God and a woman! Man had nothing to do with it." There was silence and then long applause.

Sojourner Truth was born about 1797 to parents who were slaves— slavery would not be abolished in New York State for another thirty years—belonging to a Dutch patroon family, the Hardenberghs, in Ulster County, about eighty miles north of New York City. She, her parents, and ten brothers and sisters lived in the dank cellar of the Hardenbergh manor house. When the "old master" died, the nine-year-old girl, who was known only as Belle and spoke only Low Dutch, was auctioned off, along with a flock of sheep, to the owner of a general store on the banks of the Hudson. "Now," as she later put it, "the war begun." She worked hard, was whipped, and went barefoot even in winter. Sold again, she worked for a tavern keeper for a year or two.

At the age of twelve she was bought by John J. Dumont, who had a great stone house, huge barns, and 700 acres in the Hudson Valley at New Paltz. Dumont treated his slaves fairly well, and Belle was content, especially when Bob, a young slave from a neighboring farm, began to visit her secretly. One day his master caught him with Belle and beat him almost senseless. Belle never saw him again.

She was now a very tall and lithe young woman, and one night when the mistress of the house was away, the master took her to bed with him. Soon, too, an older slave, Tom, who had had two wives sold away from him, laid claim to her. The master decided she was ready to bear children, and she was married off to Tom; in the next ten years she bore five children. She taught them to be honest and to have faith in God. Of the son and three daughters who survived, two of the girls were sold away from her.

She served her master faithfully for sixteen years, yet when she asked for her "free papers" in 1827, a year before the state officially emancipated slaves, he would not release her. Prompted, she said, by the voice of God, she fled, carrying only her last baby. She was taken in by a devoutly religious couple, the Van Wagenens. They gave her a full name, Isabella Van Wagenen, as well as her freedom, and astonished her by declaring, "Before God, all of us are equal." They read to her from a big book that, they said, came from God. When they reached the words, "I am the Way, the Truth, and the Life," she said simply, "I knew that, God told me." And when they took her to church, she sat in a corner and listened to the hymns until she could sing all of them.

Then, shatteringly, she heard that her youngest boy, Peter, had been sold, illegally, by the Hardenberghs to an Alabama slaveholder. Ignoring jeers at her concern for a "paltry nigger child," she set out to get him back. With the help of Quakers, she found a lawyer, carried the case to court, and won the child back, beaten and scarred. That night a light filled her room and with it a vision of Jesus such as would guide her forever after.

Aided by a white woman, Isabella now took a great step, moving to New York City with her two young children and hiring out as a servant. Soon she attached herself to a fanatically religious couple, Elijah and Sarah Pierson, and accompanied them in missionary work in the slums and brothels of the city. She also began to talk to God openly, capturing attention at prayer meetings.

Religious cults had begun filling the gap left by the retreat of Calvinism, and now another visionary, a former carpenter, calling himself Matthias and making Christlike pronouncements, joined the Piersons. Gathering several disciples and appointing Pierson his John the Baptist, he declared a new kingdom of God on earth. Having persuaded his followers, including Isabella, to turn over all their savings to him, Matthias began to indulge in bizarre extravagances. Although he sometimes mistreated Isabella, she clung to her faith in a communal way of life.

Becoming uncomfortable in the city, the cult moved to a rich disciple's estate, Zion Hill, north of Tarrytown. There Matthias, like several other prophets of the religious utopias of the time, took what he called a "match wife"—others would have called it free love—choosing the wife of one of his followers, Ben Folger. Folger in turn took the cook to bed. Soon the prophets in this paradise proved mortal as well as sinful: Pierson sickened mysteriously and died. The local authorities, responding to rumors of strange goings-on at Zion Hill, began to harass the group. Their suspicions were confirmed when Folger charged that Matthias was an impostor and a swindler and even hinted that he and "the black woman" had poisoned Pierson. Brought to trial as a charlatan and thief, Matthias was sentenced to three months in jail. Although Isabella was not charged with any crime, she was pictured as a kind of sorceress, and one newspaperman referred to her as "the most wicked of the wicked." At that point a man of conscience, Gilbert Vale, came to Isabella's defense, and in a pamphlet published in 1835 showed how grossly she had been maligned. She was even persuaded to sue Folger and, supported by a dozen character witnesses, astonished everyone by winning the case, including an award of $125 in damages.

But she had sunk all her savings in the Kingdom, and she now had to work harder than ever to support herself and, for a time, her son Peter. Increasingly she was oppressed by a sense of a city riddled by greed and vice, devoted to the worship not of God but of Mammon. So, one day in 1843, the Voice having spoken to her again, she told her mistress that she was leaving. "I must," she declared, "be on my father's business." The Lord, she added, had given her a new name, Sojourner, because she would have to travel "up and down the land." And her second name, she said, would be Truth because that was now her master.

An imposing, masculine-looking woman, carrying her possessions in a bundle over her shoulder, she made her way through Long Island and Connecticut, and into Massachusetts, talking and singing of a kind and loving God and bringing a message of hope. Along the way she picked up letters of recommendation such as the one from a man in Bristol, Connecticut, who wrote to his sister in Hartford: "I send you this living messenger as I believe her to be one that God loves. . . . Let her tell her story . . . and you will see that she has the leaven of truth, and that God helps her to see where but few can. She cannot read or write but the law is in her heart." So in more and more towns she was made welcome.

At Northampton, Massachusetts, she came upon a utopian commune, the Northampton Association of Education and Industry. It was crowded into a huge old building that served both as a silk-making factory and a boardinghouse. At first it repelled her because it was such a confusion of industrial activity and communal living. But it was also a revelation, introducing her to that remarkable breed, the abolitionists. There she met and heard a thin-faced, angular man named William Lloyd Garrison declare that the Constitution and the laws legalizing slavery were "the most bloody arrangement" ever made to protect "the most atrocious villainy ever exhibited on earth."

She also met Frederick Douglass, a young, powerfully built, almost white-looking black man. She heard him tell, in white men's English, how his master had let him learn to read, but when he began to "think too much" had sent him to a slave trainer for "breaking-in." The trainer's method was to work and whip him relentlessly. He survived by thinking, "He will not kill me. Dead, I'd be worthless." He escaped to the North, miraculously educated himself, was discovered by the abolitionists, and became the first man of color to serve as a full-time agent of the Massachusetts Anti-Slavery Society. At one of his talks, hearing him declare that "once you know how to read the Bible, you will be forever unfit to remain a slave," Isabella sang out, "You read, but God himself talks to me."

Sojourner remained in the Association because it warmed her to see how everyone shared in even the most disagreeable tasks. It was another "kingdom" but one not ruled by sinful or tyrannical men. But after a few years it disintegrated—another dream gone. She tarried for a while in a little house of her own, delaying her return to her "Father's business" partly because religious revivals were waning. At this point, Olive Gilbert, a selfless laborer for abolition, met Sojourner and was so impressed by her that she decided to record her story and publish it. The result, *The Narrative of Sojourner Truth,* with a preface by Garrison, is a stark account of Sojourner's trials and triumphs, her perceptions and her abounding faith.

Sojourner now took to the road again. After the lecture tour with the leading abolitionists, she made her way to Ohio. There, Marcus Robinson persuaded her to help sell subscriptions to his *Anti-Slavery Bugle.* Because she now used a cane, wore glasses, and could no longer walk from town to town, he lent her a horse and buggy. When asked how old she was, she would answer, "Gone sixty," but she was probably about fifty-five.

The first time Sojourner regretted that she had never learned to read was when she heard everyone talking about a book, *Uncle Tom's Cabin, or The Man That Was a Thing,* by a woman named Harriet Beecher Stowe. When parts of it were read to her, she saw that its appeal, like her own, was deeply emotional, and she decided to see Mrs. Stowe. The opportunity came when she returned to Massachusetts and learned that the author was in Andover, where her husband was teaching at the theological seminary.

Harriet, having heard only vague stories about Sojourner, thought the visit would be brief. But when the lank figure with the dark, careworn features under the turbanlike kerchief turned up, Harriet was fascinated. And when she began to speak, Harriet was spellbound. Asked about her lectures, Sojourner answered, "The Lord has made me a sign unto this nation, and I go around a-testifying and showing them their sins against my people." Sitting down, she sank into a kind of trance, and then burst out, "Oh, Lord! Oh, the tears and the groans, and the moans, Lord!" Soon Harriet called in her father, the celebrated Reverend Lyman Beecher, to meet her visitor. Learning who he was, Sojourner said she was a kind of preacher herself, but when he asked her whether she drew her texts from the Bible, she answered, "No, honey, can't read a letter. I has just one text to preach—When I found Jesus!" In the end, they kept Sojourner there for days, listening raptly to her stories, visions, and songs. They never saw her again, and Harriet would write, "Sojourner has passed away from among us as a wave of the sea."

Later in the 1850s, Sojourner turned west again. Repeatedly she visited the little town of Battle Creek amid the forests and lakes of Michigan. She found Quakers there who welcomed all the antislavery leaders. They were so sympathetic that in 1857 she sold her house in Northampton and bought another, hardly more than a cabin, in Harmonia, a village near Battle Creek. In time, her daughters and a few of her grandchildren moved nearby. But as the Midwest, and especially Kansas, became a testing ground for the coming conflict, abolitionist speakers faced hostile audiences—people who labeled slaves a lazy, lecherous tribe of baboons and threatened to tar and feather all "nigger lovers." In such confrontations Sojourner's plain-speaking and barbed rejoinders proved far more effective than the civil responses of most white speakers. Once, in a United Brethren meetinghouse in northern Indiana, a doctor charged that Sojourner was a man and challenged her to show her breasts to some lady in the audience. Without hesitating, she bared her breasts, crying, "It's to your shame I'm doing this, not to mine," and added that her breasts had suckled many a white babe.

After the Dred Scott decision and the hanging of John Brown, the contrast between her views and those of Frederick Douglass became more marked, he turning more militant while she clung to her faith in God and the power of truth. At a huge protest rally in Boston's Faneuil Hall, when Douglass declared that the slaves could have no hope except in their right arms, Sojourner rose in the front row and stunned the audience by crying out, "Frederick, is God dead?"

The differences between them remained even after the war began, Douglass criticizing Lincoln for putting off the emancipation while Sojourner counseled patience. Not that she was in any way submissive. When she insisted on holding meetings in Indiana after that state, torn by anti-war and anti-Negro sentiment, barred nonresident black persons, she was repeatedly arrested. Each time, her staunch abolitionist friend, Josephine Griffing, had to convince the judge that the law was unconstitutional. Again and again, as late as the fall of 1862, she held meetings despite jeers and even blows. Just before emancipation, she returned home exhausted, ill, and penniless. Her friends made an appeal for her, and contributions came in from far and wide.

Then, in April 1863, the *Atlantic Monthly* printed an article, "Sojourner Truth, the Libyan Sybil," by Harriet Beecher Stowe. The title came from an impressive statue, *Libyan Sybil,* created by the sculptor William Wetmore Story after he had heard Mrs. Stowe's account of Sojourner's visit. But Sojourner, baffled by the title and unable to read the article, was far more excited by the enlistment of a grandson, James Caldwell, in a black regiment from Massachusetts. "He's gone forth," she said, "to redeem the white people from the curse that God sent upon them."

Her health returning, she went back to her travels, this time with a special goal: to meet Abraham Lincoln. Slowly, lecturing as she went, she made her way to Washington, accompanied by a grandson, Sammy Banks. There she was overwhelmed by the number of ragged and destitute runaway slaves, many of them living in sickeningly filthy shacks in an area called "Murder Bay." As more and more of them poured in, they were shunted into various camps, including one in Arlington Heights called Freedmen's Village. Sojourner worked in the camps, urging the people to keep clean; they listened to her as to an oracle.

At last, on October 29, 1864, Lucy Colman, another abolitionist friend of Sojourner's, led her into Lincoln's office. The former slave and the Emancipator made a strange pair, both tall and gaunt, both showing signs of age and countless trials. She would never forget how cordial and kind he was. As she left, he said he hoped to see her again. But his days were numbered.

For a while, Sojourner stayed on in Freedmen's Village, teaching the refugees from slave hovels how to adapt to freedom. When slave-holders from Maryland, where emancipation was still being fought in the courts, abducted black children from the camps, Sojourner told the frantic mothers they could bring the raiders to justice; they were astonished. The frustrated Marylanders threatened to have Sojourner put in the guardhouse. "If you try to put me in the guardhouse," she announced, "I'll make the United States rock like a cradle."

When the war ended, the Freedmen's Villagers went wild with joy. A week later the bullet of an assassin plunged them into bottom-less grief. Oppressed by the desolate future faced by the refugees, Sojourner left Washington and went home. But soon she became convinced that the best hope for dispossessed blacks was grants of western land with buildings erected especially for the old and feeble. She went forth with a petition and then turned again for support to the white gods in Washington. Grant received her in his characteristic low-keyed way, and in the Senate chamber a dozen influential polit-icos came forward to greet the onetime slave. But Charles Sumner, the truest friend of the Negro in that body, warned her that Congress would turn over western lands far more readily to veterans, railroads, and industry than to former slaves. Sumner did join her in getting a ban on segregated, "Jim Crow" public transport in Washington, but time and again she had literally to fight conductors who sought to eject her. Once when she and Laura Haviland, beloved benefactor and teacher of poor blacks, boarded a trolley, the conductor tried to force Sojourner off. When Mrs. Haviland protested, the conductor exclaimed, "Does she belong to you, lady?" "No," was Haviland's answer. "She belongs to humanity." But in the South, Jim Crow would continue to rule until another black woman, in Selma, Alabama, almost a century later would refuse to sit in the back of a bus.

During the next four years, Sojourner moved through twenty-one states with her petition, but when in 1875 Sammy Banks died, she gave up that forlorn mission. As late as 1878 she gave talks all over Michigan and attended a women's rights convention in Rochester. To her pleas for trust in God and love she had added not only women's rights but temperance and penal reform. Finally, in November 1883, although her spirit still burned bright, her body failed.

Many newspapers carried tributes to her, but it remained for a leading black editor, T. Thomas Fortune, to point out that she had been the only black woman to fight for abolition. Frederick Douglass, by then an influential political figure living in a fine house in Washington, praised her for her courage, devotion to her people, and insights into human nature. But he had long been critical of her as one of the "Garrison school of nonresisters," and of her attempt to get freedmen to relocate rather than fight for their rights. He also resented the way this "quaint old sister" had ridiculed his speaking and acted like "a person of cultivation," and even more, her challenge to his call to arms with her call to faith—"Frederick, is God dead?"

As a Northern Negro, Sojourner Truth's life was not typical of the vast majority of black women, but it is just as significant because it illustrates how widespread was the oppression of black women in America. Because at times she lived on an otherworldly plane and was guided by mystical voices and visions, she was never a leader of her people or a political force. But to many she was an inspiring example of how independent, wise, and high-minded a black woman could be.


No discrimination against white women in the Gilded Age compares with the mistreatment of black women. But a few sects did reduce all women to a categorically inferior status. By far the largest of such groups was the Latter-day Saints—the Mormons. Their fanatical sectarianism as well as their industry and discipline had aroused the hostility of their "Gentile" neighbors in Illinois even before rumors of their practice of polygamy reached the rest of America. This hostility led to the murder by a Gentile gang of their founder and prophet, Joseph Smith, in 1844, and to violent attempts to drive them out of Illinois.

In that same turbulent year a Mormon couple, Chauncey and Eliza Webb, celebrated the birth of their fifth child, Ann Eliza. Thirty-one years later, that same Ann Eliza, then the apostate wife of Brigham Young, successor to Joseph Smith, published an intimate and bitter account of life in an American harem. It would help bring about the final abolition of polygamy in America but only after many thousands of women from 1840 to 1890 had lived their entire lives as little more than concubines.

Ann Eliza's father, a wagon-builder, and her mother, an obsessively devout girl, were both brought up in central New York State, an area swept, as we have seen, by revivalist sects. When the leader of one such sect, Joseph Smith, proclaimed himself a messiah, Chauncey Webb and his future wife were among the first to be converted by him. In search of a refuge from their Gentile enemies, they followed him to Ohio, and then to Missouri and Illinois. Declaring that he was following the example of the Old Testament patriarchs, Smith had apparently taken additional wives as early as 1835. By 1843 he had persuaded others in the Mormon hierarchy that such "celestial marriages" were divinely ordained and would guarantee the admission of the wives into the heavenly kingdom. But Smith and, after his death, his successor, Brigham Young, practiced it privately until Young made it public in 1852.

Shortly before he was slain, Smith included Chauncey Webb among those whom he urged to take additional wives. Webb was shocked and his wife was horrified. But when Young renewed the pressure, Webb declared that he would leave the decision to his wife. After untold torment, prayers, and a fear that she was "fighting against the Lord," she gave way. With her approval, Webb chose a nineteen-year-old boarder of theirs, Elizabeth Taft, as his second wife.

After years of harassment in Illinois, Young in 1846 finally ordered his 20,000 adherents to abandon their homes and follow him to a new Zion in the West. Their astonishing trek took two years and carried them, guided by Frémont's maps and charts, a thousand miles across the plains and into the desert area around Utah's Great Salt Lake. It was a fearsome experience for many of the adults, but Ann Eliza, who was two years old at the outset, remembered it only as a kind of long outing.

Within a few years Young, a master organizer and a tremendously forceful personality, had carried off the double miracle of making the desert bloom and establishing a thriving community, Salt Lake City. No longer afraid of opposition within the community or revulsion outside, he announced "plural marriage" as a divine command. The wrath this aroused among non-Mormons would last for forty years.

Although Mrs. Webb seemed, in time, to be reconciled to the presence of a second wife, her patience was sometimes tried to the breaking point, expecially when the younger woman retired with her husband at night or showed affection for him in her presence. By contrast, Webb's original qualms concerning plural marriage soon vanished. As a prosperous Mormon, he was urged in 1856 to take still another wife. Astonishingly, he responded by taking not one but three, choosing them from a group of converts brought from England by Mormon missionaries. So, overnight, there were five Mrs. Webbs, and Mr. Webb, at forty-four, could enjoy three more wives, each less than half his age. Apparently inured to sharing her husband, Mrs. Webb declared she was as satisfied with a fifth of him as with a half. As for the new wives, fresh from mid-Victorian England, it is hard to imagine how they reconciled themselves to a relationship that the outside world considered concubinage or simply legalized adultery.

Developing into a slender, beautiful young woman, Ann Eliza soon attracted the attention of Young himself. When a friend of hers surmised that he might be thinking of marrying her, Ann Eliza was outraged. The friend was right. Young began by inviting Ann Eliza to join the acting company in what was dubbed Brigham's Theatre. Realizing that the Mormons were cut off from all the amusements of American society, Young had supervised the building of a large and splendid theater to provide what was called "holy fun." The company he assembled played mostly comedies and musicals, Young disliking romantic dramas because, he claimed, they made "such a cussed fuss over one woman."

Since Ann Eliza lived at a distance from the theater, Young persuaded her to remain on weekdays with his daughters in the "Lion House," a three-story building that housed a dozen of his wives. Far from being, as the scandal sheets hinted, a kind of caliph's palace, with concubines lolling on pillows in scented boudoirs, the Lion House was more like a female dormitory. Ann Eliza came to hate its almost institutional routine and especially the monotony of its skimpy meals.

Perhaps it was the more glamorous aspects of her experience as an actress that led her to fall in love with, and marry, another amateur actor, a ruggedly handsome young Englishman, James Dee. Ann Eliza soon quit the stage to devote herself to her husband. He did not reciprocate: within a month, she later claimed, he was paying court to other women. When she protested, furious arguments resulted, concluding with Dee threatening to bring home another wife. During a quarrel late in her first pregnancy, he knocked her to the floor. Afterward he was so contrite that she forgave him and even became pregnant again. But another argument ended with his choking her until her parents came to her rescue. Her father immediately ordered Dee out of the house.

With Brigham Young's approval, Ann Eliza won a divorce and the custody of her children. She would later refer bitterly to Dee as a man who believed that ''woman was made to be a slave of her lord.'' But the evidence of Dee's second marriage and his respectable later career in Ogden, Utah, hardly bears this out. His children by his second wife assert that he never struck them, was not a polygamist, and even saw to it that his two sons by Ann Eliza shared in his estate. They claimed that Ann Eliza's mother, craving a high-placed husband for her daughter, promised that she would get Young to marry Ann Eliza if her daughter divorced Dee.

For a time Ann Eliza enjoyed ''a sweet restfulness.'' But this ended one day in 1867 when Young, after a revival meeting in which he attacked Mormon women for copying the ''whorish'' styles of the Gentiles, surprised Ann Eliza by walking her home. He joined her family for dinner and then spoke to her father privately. After he left, her father gave her what she described as the most shocking message she would ever get. Young, he said, wanted her as a wife. ''I thought,'' she later wrote, ''Father had gone crazy. . . . When I realized that it was a fact, I could do nothing but cry.'' The thought of becoming the wife of an old man who had a score of wives sickened her.

But descendants of Young have insisted that Ann Eliza and her mother maneuvered Young into the marriage. In any event, Young decided to take his time, especially since he had just acquired two young wives. After a while he gave Ann's oldest brother, Gilbert, a contract for installing telegraph poles, but he put off paying him till Gilbert went bankrupt. He then threatened to excommunicate Gilbert if Ann Eliza did not marry him. Since Gilbert had two wives, excommunication would have made him a bigamist by American law. It was this threat along with the fear that she was opposing the will of the Lord, Ann Eliza later wrote, that finally made her give way. The sixty-eight-year-old Prophet and the twenty-four-year-old divorcée were married in April 1869.

When Ann Eliza refused to live in the Lion House, Young bought a private house for her. But she complained that it was unbearably small and meanly furnished, and that the monthly quota of food was totally inadequate. During the first year Ann Eliza did attend meals, prayer meetings, and social events at the Lion House. Young's wives were a curiously mixed lot, ranging in age from the early twenties to the late sixties, from refined and well-educated to ordinary women. Some worshiped Young, others disliked or feared him, while still others were indifferent to him. Some he visited regularly and got with child over a period of ten, fifteen, or more years; others he avoided or virtually banished. On one he lavished endless attention and favors. Another went mad with guilt, remorse, and jealousy.

Young, a shrewd governor who combined arbitrary benevolence with despotic control, worked hard, attending to official business and seeing callers all day long. Meanwhile, the women in the Lion House were busy cleaning their quarters, sewing, making quilts, and taking care of their army of children. They dressed well, generally in homespun but in fashionable silks on Sundays. Each day at five o'clock the Prophet would lead his families into the huge dining room. The wives and children filled two long tables. Young and his latest favorite, Amelia Folsom, an elegant and haughty young woman, sat at a small head table. While the wives dined on common fare, Brigham and his Amelia enjoyed a variety of delicacies. At seven, Young would lead a prayer meeting followed by a period of informal conversation. As a father—he had fifty-six children—he was a strict disciplinarian. Ann Eliza claimed that he treated her sons by Dee as "interlopers," neglected his own children, and hardly knew some of them. But several of his daughters later insisted that he was a loving and devoted parent. He remained a remarkably virile man, fathering three children, each with a different mother, in one month in his sixty-third year, and his last child when he was sixty-nine.

There was, if anything, more immorality in the prurient curiosity of many Americans about the sexual activities of Mormons than in what went on in Mormon bedrooms. Aside from the fact that less than 25 percent of Mormon families are said to have been polygamous, many Mormon wives came from middle-class New England homes and shared the common view that sexual activity in women was intended for procreation, not pleasure. Many of the women defended the system, and a number of Young's wives even petitioned Congress to reject new anti-polygamy legislation. Such wives, along with Young, asserted that polygamy ended prostitution, abortion, and foundlings, and reduced adultery to a minimum.

But unquestionably polygamy was a completely man-favoring system in a man-dominated society. In the first official statement on plural marriage, Orson Pratt, an "Apostle," advised each wife to obey her husband "with meekness and patience in all things." The system permitted a man to take a succession of ever younger women and to put aside any wife who did not please him. Men did not hesitate to marry several sisters or a mother and her daughter. One Apostle, Orson Hyde, married women who could serve him, such as a cook, a laundress, and a dairymaid, since that was cheaper than hiring them. For a woman it banished the hope of being the sole object of a husband's love or the sole mistress of her household. Many wives accepted the practice as a holy duty. But a few rose up in wrath: when one Mormon elder announced that he had a divine command to take another wife, his wife announced that she had a command to shoot such a woman.

Ann Eliza continued to complain about her cramped quarters, and Young moved her with her sons and mother to a large farmhouse outside the city. Ann Eliza liked the rural setting, but after three years she and her mother were, she complained, overworked and worn out. Again Young moved them, this time to a spacious house in the city. But again she found herself without even the basic necessities. She now began, she writes, to hate Young.

Constantly short of money, Ann Eliza finally asked Young's permission to take in borders. He consented readily and she soon rented all her spare rooms. Her boarders, all Gentiles, included Albert Hagan, a lawyer, and Major James Pond, a reporter on the anti-Mormon Salt Lake City *Tribune*. They gave Ann Eliza her first favorable view of the outside world. She also met a Methodist minister, the Reverend C. C. Stratton; he and his wife were so sympathetic to her plight that she began discussing with them and with Hagan how she could gain her freedom. They urged her to seek a divorce. She agreed. On July 15, 1873, she was secretly taken by the Strattons to the Walker House, a well-known Gentile hotel. In the morning the *Tribune* broke the story of her flight. It created a nationwide sensation, with reporters from California, Chicago, and New York calling for interviews. Every newspaper, except for a few pro-Mormon journals, greeted her move as a long-awaited blow to Mormon polygamy and Brigham Young.

At first Young thought her move an act of pique. But he realized how serious it was when she filed a bill of divorce declaring that after they had "cohabited" for a year, he had subjected her to "cruel and inhuman treatment, ending in an absolute desertion." Asserting that Young had an income of $40,000 a month, derived from the tithes collected from church members, and was worth $8 million, Ann Eliza asked for alimony of $1,000 a month.

Young's first response was an offer to settle with her for $15,000, and, significantly, safe passage out of Utah. She admitted that she was tempted, but she turned down the offer when she thought of how many lives would be affected by the decision in her case. Far more disturbing was a dreadful letter from her mother filled with such statements as "Your death would have been preferable to the course you are taking. How gladly would I have laid you in your grave had I known what was in your heart. . . . The Lord, my Father, grant that you may . . . flee from your present dictators, as you would from the fiends of darkness." But Ann Eliza had gone too far to be able to turn back.

Now a celebrity, hailed by some as a heroine of morality but deplored by others as a scarlet woman, Ann Eliza was bombarded by lecture offers from such famous promoters as P. T. Barnum and James Redpath. At first, she shrank from the very idea of exposing her private life and being paid to do so, but when her divorce hearing was put off until May 1874, her lack of money and, she later insisted, her desire to end polygamy, caused her to reconsider the offers. As a test of her abilities she gave a talk in the Walker House. It went remarkably well. Much encouraged, she allowed Major Pond—it was the beginning of his career as a leading lecture agent—to arrange a few engagements for her. Faced by threats of violence from Mormons, she had to be spirited out of the city, taking a nerve-racking, forty-mile ride at night to a distant railroad station.

Ann Eliza was scheduled to give her first lecture in Denver, but popular interest led her to speak in Laramie and at other stops along the way. So cordial was the response everywhere that even though a snowstorm struck Denver on the night of her lecture, the audience packed the largest church in town. The crowd was spellbound by the simple facts of her life and her account of the evils of polygamy. Afterward both men and women came up to shake her hand. She repeated her success all across Kansas—the posters there billed her as "The Rebel of the Harem"—Iowa, Illinois, and Wisconsin.

But these were only a preliminary to the address, in Boston's renowned Tremont Temple, that would decide whether she would become a truly successful lecturer. Fortunately, Pond had joined forces with Redpath, the agent who had raised lecturing from a poorly paid activity to the overflow audiences and handsome fees gathered by such performers as Beecher, Charles Dickens, and Mark Twain. Sensing the strong appeal of a beleaguered, genteel, and attractive young woman talking frankly about polygamy, Redpath arranged front-page newspaper advertisements and strategic interviews for her.

Everything seemed wonderfully promising until the day before the lecture, when the Chicago *Times* published an article purporting to reveal Ann Eliza Young's love life with her "amorous" manager, Major Pond. It described in the most suggestive terms how the clerk in a hotel in Bloomington, Illinois, had learned that the "oily-tongued" Pond had spent the night in Mrs. Young's room and how a conductor on the train to Jacksonville found that the couple had shared a berth.

Ann Eliza was stunned and bewildered. But after desperate conferences with Pond and Redpath, she agreed that she must go on with the lecture. She entered Tremont Temple as though going to her doom; to her astonishment she found a huge and obviously friendly audience awaiting her. At the conclusion of her talk, the response was overwhelming. The next day the Boston papers were equally enthusiastic. In the next few weeks the friends of Ann Eliza and Pond investigated the sources of the scandalous article. When the conductor and the hotel clerk were tracked down, they both denied that they had started the rumors. Several newspapers, as well as organizations that had sponsored her, blasted those who had spread the story.

Buoyed by a contract from Redpath guaranteeing her $2,000 for four weeks of lectures, she went on to engagements in Philadelphia, New York, and other eastern cities. But now her main objective was to reach Washington and strike a blow for the strongest anti-polygamy bill ever presented to Congress. Once in the Capital, she was escorted by a friend, a General Maxwell, to the House of Representatives. She was promptly invited into the House chamber, introduced, and roundly applauded. But she had one bitter opponent there, English-born George Q. Cannon, a Mormon who had been admitted to Congress as the delegate from Utah even though he was a polygamist and not a naturalized American citizen. The next day, addressing a gathering of prominent officials and their wives, Ann Eliza challenged them for coming to see her mainly out of curiosity and despite their tolerance of a delegate with four wives. So effective was her talk that at her second lecture President Grant attended and sat in the front row. She began by declaring that polygamy among the Turks or savages might not shock them, but in a Christian civilization it was incredible:

> Polygamy in the United States! Polygamy among Anglo-Saxons! . . . Has it, in truth, an existence among us, or have stories . . . from Utah described monsters of the imagination. . . . Polygamy in the United States is no figment of the fancies. . . . It is a prevailing social custom among 100,000 of your citizens. . . . It originated with a man of Puritan ancestry and born in the State of Vermont. Its greatest exemplar . . . is another native of Vermont.

Among those who came up to congratulate her after her lecture was Grant himself. A few weeks later the Poland Bill banning polygamy was passed by Congress.

Ann Eliza would later declare that the most arresting discovery she made about Gentile life was that women were generally "cared for tenderly, cherished, protected, loved and honored." She had been taught she writes, that

> my sex was inferior to the other; that the curse pronounced upon the race in the Garden of Eden was woman's curse alone, and that heaven was inaccessible to her, except as she might win it through some man's will. I found, to my surprise, that woman was made the companion and not the subject of man. . . . Her husband's God was her God as well, and she could seek him for herself. . . . Motherhood took on a new sacredness, and the fatherly care and tenderness . . . seemed sadly sweet to me . . . used as I was to see children ignored by their fathers.

In spite of her successes, Ann Eliza, cut off from the certainties of the Mormon religion, found herself spiritually adrift. But with the aid of several sympathetic Methodist ministers, she apparently achieved peace of mind. She also experienced a sense of vindication when her mother, sickened by the way Young and his cohorts were besmirching Ann Eliza's character, began to repudiate Mormonism. At the age of fifty-eight, Mrs. Webb left her husband and returned to live in central New York State where she had grown up. Ironically, she soon found that there was as much fanaticism and as many skeletons in the closets of monogamous families as in polygamous unions. She was eventually so disgusted by the "religious nonsense" she saw everywhere that when a man she respected said it was time that the Old Testament was thrown into the stove, she added that the New should go with it.

Ann Eliza scored a special triumph when, a year after fleeing from Salt Lake City in fear and desperation, she returned to it and was greeted at the Walker House by a cheering crowd and a band. When her divorce suit finally came to trial, Young boldly claimed that she had never been legally divorced from Dee and was therefore an adulteress. He asserted that he had treated her with great generosity and that she had deserted him. Even more unexpected was his declaration that all his wives except the first were "celestial concubines." The final verdict was that Ann Eliza, like all of Young's wives after the first, was a concubine and therefore not entitled to alimony. Young had won the battle, but in branding his wives concubines he had lost the war. It may no longer have mattered to him because he was gravely ill and would die a few months later.

Publishers had long urged Ann Eliza to put her story into a book. She finally consented, and in 1875 published *Wife No. 19, or the Story of a Life in Bondage, Being a Complete Exposé of Mormonism.* A 612-page work, it was a vivid account, marred only by too many virulent attacks on Young and sensational stories of polygamists' excesses. There is, however, little doubt that Mormonism under Young was not the completely evil system Ann Eliza made it out to be. The average Mormon family was at least as proper, God-fearing, law-abiding, industrious, and well-cared-for as its Gentile counterpart. Most of the Mormon men who became polygamists had only two wives and most of them were not lecherous old men corraling nubile adolescents. Mormon women also claimed that the system gave every woman a better chance to find a husband. Although the anti-polygamy laws were constantly being strengthened, they were rarely enforced because of the fear that they were unconstitutional and infringed on Mormon religious rights. When the Edmunds Bill in 1882 specified fines and prison terms for polygamists and barred them from voting or holding office, the Mormons protested that they were being persecuted while libertines, strumpets, and brothel-keepers among the Gentiles were relatively unmolested. But the end of polygamy was in sight.

By 1883, after ten years and 2,000 lectures, after constant travel, uncomfortable trains, hasty meals, and depressing hotel rooms, Ann Eliza was worn out and beset by nervous disorders. Even more discouraging, the Edmunds Bill left her beating a dead horse. Just as she was preparing to retire, she met and became intimate with a big, hearty, fifty-three-year-old lumber tycoon, Moses R. Denning. He was married and had five children, but he soon divorced his wife, and in May 1883, a month after Ann Eliza's farewell lecture, they were married. She went to live in his imposing, thirteen-room home in Manistee, a boomtown in the Michigan lumber country.

During the next few years Ann Eliza led a quite private life. Although a goodly number of Mormons were still practicing polygamy more or less secretly, the church leaders were tired of the conflict, and they officially banned the practice in 1890. The ban should have given Ann Eliza a tremendous sense of accomplishment and vindication. But her satisfaction was marred by serious marital problems. Denning, she later claimed, was driven by such "unreasonable passion and lust" that her health was impaired and she was forced to deny him sexually. He responded by charging that she was frigid, and he turned for sexual satisfaction to their maids and other women. After nine years, finding a monogamous marriage as unsatisfactory as her polygamous experience, she sued for divorce. A few years later she left Michigan and rented a bungalow in Denver near her sole surviving son. When he died, she moved to El Paso where her brother Gilbert was engaged in engineering work. Only once did she emerge from the obscurity of her later years. Because of evidence that some Mormons were still practicing polygamy, she published in 1908 a revised edition of her autobiography. But polygamy was a dead issue and the book was ignored.

The end of the story of Ann Eliza's life is a mystery: at the age of sixty-four she disappeared from view. There is no reliable record after 1908 of the fate of this once famous woman. Did she welcome obscurity after a life of such notoriety? Or did she wish to live alone after three failed marriages?

The answers to such questions hardly matter. She had done her work. Almost alone of a legion of Mormon women she had fought unremittingly in lectures, interviews, books, and letters to end what she considered a relic of barbarism and an insult to womankind. And what she sought had come to pass.


Few episodes in the history of reform movements in America are more surprising than the one in 1848 in which five women in an upstate New York community organized a convention attended by a hundred women and men and issued a "Declaration of Rights" that might have come from a group of latter-day women's liberationists. The declaration charged that throughout history man had sought by "repeated injuries and usurpations" to establish "an absolute tyranny" over woman, deprive her of her legal rights, profitable employment, access to education, the professions, divorce and the custody of her children, and the right to vote. It proclaimed that woman is man's equal, and its most provocative statement was that it was grossly insulting to deny women the vote and yet grant it to "drunkards, idiots, horseracing rumselling rowdies, ignorant foreigners, and silly boys." It was the first example of Elizabeth Cady Stanton's use of shocking language to shatter inertia and complacency.

Church leaders and conservative citizens assailed the declaration, and the convention organizers were caricatured as sexless old maids, radicals, and heretics. Actually all five were married and had children, and three were Quakers. The moving force behind the convention, Mrs. Stanton, was a thirty-two-year-old mother of four. It was the beginning of a career that established her, side by side with Susan B. Anthony, as the most forceful, stimulating, and original-minded figure in the women's movement of the next half century.

There is no easy way to explain why the daughter of a wealthy family in a village northwest of Albany became the most militant critic of a male-dominated society that prevented women from owning property after marriage, testifying in court, serving on juries, attending college, entering the professions, admitting sexual desire, denouncing the double standard, speaking at public meetings, wearing anything but ankle-length garments, and resisting physical punishment by a husband, and that even proclaimed that women had smaller brains than men. One may perhaps find clues to her development in the fact that her mother, who came of a distinguished old family, was strong-willed and self-reliant, or that her father, Daniel Cady, was a farmer's son who became a lawyer, a congressman, and finally an associate justice of the New York Supreme Court.

But Elizabeth Cady seems to have remembered her mother only distantly in later years, and if her father influenced her, it was through the challenge he presented as a self-made man. That challenge was driven home in 1826, when she was eleven years old: her father, needing a male heir who could keep his fortune intact, suffered a devastating blow with the death of the last of his five sons, Eleazer, who had just graduated from college. Daniel Cady still had five daughters, but when Elizabeth tried to console him, his response was "Oh, my daughter, I wish you were a boy!" Throwing her arms around his neck, she cried, "I will try to be all my brother was."

She carried out her promise, excelling in Greek and mathematics, in debating with her father's law clerks and in outdoor games and "equestrian competitions." At first her father encouraged her but in time he came to disapprove of such unfeminine accomplishments. As she told Susan Anthony many years later, "To think that all in me of which my father would have felt a proper pride had I been a man is deeply mortifying to him because I am a woman."

After graduating at the top of her class at the local academy in 1830, Elizabeth wanted to go on to college, but aside from the fact that no college admitted women, her father was appalled at the thought. He was finally persuaded to let her enter Emma Willard's Troy Female Seminary. She disliked the atmosphere of an all-female school, but Mrs. Willard had replaced traditional women's courses with a more rigorous program resembling that of men's colleges. Just as important, Elizabeth found in Mrs. Willard a role model—a woman who was feminine and yet energetic, self-directed, and eminently competent.

Another influence, in the long run negative, was a revival led by that fireball of an evangelist, Charles Grandison Finney. It swept through Troy, as Elizabeth puts it, like an epidemic, and made her, with her "gloomy Calvinist training," one of its first victims. The ordeal of confessing sins and being "converted" at fiercely emotional revival meetings was so unsettling to fifteen-year-old Elizabeth Cady that she became ill and had to go home. But a skeptical analysis of the entire experience by her brother-in-law, Edward Bayard, a lawyer and her closest older friend, not only restored her peace of mind but would eventually lead her to reject all religious authority.

As a spirited young woman and a member of a socially prominent family, Elizabeth led a life during the next few years filled with parties, dances, horse racing, and other social amusements. When the Bayards moved to Seneca Falls, west of Syracuse, in 1834, Elizabeth visited them more and more frequently until, so the story goes, Edward Bayard fell in love with her. Although he was ten years older than she and still married to her sister Tryphena, he urged her to run away with him. She wisely refused to do so, but she would always speak of him in the warmest terms.

Late in the 1830s Elizabeth Cady began making the visits to her cousin Gerrit Smith that would prove to be the most influential of her youth. Eighteen years older than Elizabeth and immensely wealthy, Smith was not only a prominent abolitionist but also a generous supporter of an extraordinary variety of reforms and philanthropies, ranging from the American Bible Society to equal rights for women and opposition to capital punishment, drinking, smoking, and eating meat. His mansion in Peterboro, New York, was a station in the underground railroad, and he would be one of the "Secret Six" who supplied the arms for John Brown's raid at Harper's Ferry. He was elected to Congress in 1852 but soon resigned because of its resistance to abolition.

An extreme individualist, Smith refused to accept the Bible as infallible truth and hung a plaque proclaiming "God is Love" over his bedroom door. At his house Elizabeth met male and female abolitionist agents, fugitive slaves, politicians, and every kind of reformer. "The rousing arguments at Peterboro," she recalled, "made social life seem tame and profitless elsewhere." Smith, she said, gave her "a new inspiration in life . . . new ideas of individual rights." And finally, it was there in 1839 that she met Henry Stanton, a renowned abolitionist agent, and within a month became engaged to him.

Ten years her senior, a tall, handsome man and an eloquent speaker, Stanton seemed to her a heroic figure. Originally intending to prepare for the ministry, he had joined his friend Theodore Weld at the Lane Theological Seminary in Cincinnati. When the seminary ordered the student anti-slavery society to disband, Weld and Stanton led a walkout of fifty rebels. Both of them were soon hired by the American Anti-Slavery Society for the hazardous job of roving agents.

So great was the opposition to her engagement, especially from her father, who had no use for abolitionists and particularly one who at thirty-five had no reliable income, that she broke it off. But when she learned that Stanton was going to a World Anti-Slavery Convention in London and would be gone for eight months, they decided to elope. Before they sailed they visited Angelina and Theodore Weld in New Jersey. They shared with the Welds not only abolitionism but also Sylvester Graham's health program: a vegetarian diet— Emerson called Graham "the poet of bran bread and muffins"— avoiding caffeine and alcohol, and bathing in cold water. Judging from later evidence, they ignored Graham's advice to limit sexual intercourse to twelve times a year.

In London, Elizabeth Cady Stanton was shocked by the refusal of the convention to recognize women delegates. "It was really pitiful," she wrote long afterward, "to hear narrow-minded bigots pretending to be teachers and leaders of men, so cruelly remanding . . . womankind to absolute subjection to the ordinary masculine type of humanity." But far more important to her was her meeting with Lucretia Mott, Quaker minister, abolitionist, and feminist. Although Mrs. Mott was twenty-two years older than Mrs. Stanton, they formed a deep bond. A soft-spoken but resolute woman, with a husband who shared her convictions, Mrs. Mott had become a Quaker but soon joined the Hicksite faction in rejecting rigid rule by orthodox elders and in believing that women and men had equal spiritual gifts. An advocate of immediate emancipation of slaves, she had refused as early as 1825 to use any product of slave labor, and in 1833 had organized the Philadelphia Female Anti-Slavery Society. She introduced Stanton not only to the Friends' belief in an inward light but to the radical views of such writers as Mary Wollstonecraft. "Mrs. Mott was to me an entirely new revelation of womanhood," Stanton recalled. "I had never heard a woman talk what, as a Scotch Presbyterian, I had scarcely dared to think." When the convention declined to seat them, they left the hall together and resolved to form in America a society for the rights of women. Eight years would pass before they could carry out this plan.

When the Stantons returned home, Henry, realizing that as an abolitionist agent he could not support a family or achieve the political career he now wanted, resolved to become a lawyer. He spent fifteen months studying law in Judge Cady's office and then decided to practice law in Boston. By the time they moved in 1842, Elizabeth Stanton had borne two sons and a third child was on the way. She plunged into her duties as a mother with characteristic verve and learned, as she said, "another lesson in self-reliance."

Life in Boston was tremendously stimulating, allowing the Stantons to mingle with a remarkable array of reformers and writers, including William Lloyd Garrison, Elizabeth Peabody, Frederick Douglass, Theodore Parker, Lydia Maria Child, Bronson Alcott, Emerson, Whittier, Lowell, and Hawthorne. But the city left Henry disappointed in his political expectations, and in 1847 he moved his growing family to Seneca Falls. The town had only 4,000 inhabitants, and while Henry could carry on much of his business in Albany and Washington, Elizabeth suddenly found herself a rural housewife. The novelty of housekeeping had passed away and left her feeling lonely, depressed, and finally angry. "The general discontent I felt with woman's portion," she wrote in her autobiography forty years later, "as wife, mother, housekeeper, physician and spiritual guide, the chaotic conditions into which everything fell without her constant supervision, and the wearied, anxious look of the majority of women impressed me with a strong feeling that some active measures should be taken to remedy the wrongs of society in general, and of women in particular."

So, in the summer of 1848, when Lucretia Mott came to upstate New York for a Quaker meeting, Elizabeth Stanton visited her and several other women and poured out a "torrent of my long-accumulating discontent with such vehemence and indignation that I stirred myself as well as the rest . . . to do and dare anything." The result was that four Quaker women, believing that salvation required good works, joined Stanton in calling the Seneca Falls convention that marked the start of the women's rights movement. But Stanton had four more children in the next ten years—although she approved of birth control, she seems not to have practiced it—and these, together with housekeeping, prevented her from attending any of the national women's conventions in that period. Instead, she sent a vigorous message to each and corresponded with many feminists. But the lack of a strong leader and the tendency of the reformers to spend their energies on a variety of causes such as temperance, foreign missions, and abolition left the movement floundering.

For a time Henry Stanton did quite well politically as well as financially. In 1849 he was elected to the New York State Senate and gained a reputation as an able politician but, as a result of several shifts from party to party, something of an opportunist.

One of Stanton's less successful assertions of independence occurred when her cousin Libby Smith began wearing baggy pantaloons under a knee-length skirt, a costume soon popularized by Amelia Bloomer. Stanton promptly adopted the outfit, finding it more comfortable and practical, especially during pregnancy. She even made dress reform a part of her feminist program, arguing that women's clothes had been designed to arouse men's passion and that the endless yards of skirts, petticoats, and hoops were unhealthy and wasteful. But the costume evoked such relentless ridicule that after two years she gave up wearing it in public.

In the spring of 1851, Stanton met a bright, energetic, earnest young reformer, Susan B. Anthony, and began a collaboration that would last fifty years. The daughter of Hicksite Quakers, Anthony, born in 1820, had been a teacher for fifteen years and then had resigned to take over management of the family farm near Rochester. She was already active in temperance and other reform movements. Rather severe in appearance and dress, she had not married. The two women soon developed a profound affection and expressed it in almost amatory terms, a way in which women often found release for suppressed sexual emotions. In their collaboration as reformers, Stanton would provide the ideas, strategy, and rhetoric while Anthony organized, recruited, circulated petitions, rented halls, and delivered speeches.

Although Stanton now had a full-time housekeeper, the birth of her fifth child left her overwhelmed by her responsibilities. In a letter to Anthony she burst out, "Men and angels, give me patience! I am at the boiling point! If I do not find some day the use of my tongue on this question, I shall die of intellectual repression, a women's rights convulsion! . . . How much I long to be free of housekeeping and children, so as to have time to think and read and write." It did not help matters that Henry was away for ten months of every year throughout the 1850s and did not return even for the birth of his children.

Such was Elizabeth Cady Stanton's growing reputation that the New York State women's rights group, meeting in Albany in 1854, chose her to present their case to the state legislature. Passionately summing up all the rights women should have at every stage in their lives, the address established her as the most effective exponent of women's rights in America. Yet it would be six years before she made another public address. "My whole soul is in work," she wrote to Anthony, "but my hands belong to my family."

Despite her impatience with mothering, Stanton had a sixth child in 1856. So she contented herself with writing articles for reform journals and various newspapers, including Horace Greeley's New York *Tribune*. Beyond that, Anthony prodded her relentlessly to prepare speeches for her. Typical was Anthony's request for a speech to be delivered at a state teachers' meeting. Stanton's answer was, "I will do what I can . . . if you will hold the baby and make the puddings." Anthony did just that. Stanton came through with a speech recommending that the teachers demand the same wages as men. When Anthony reported that the women had rejected such a demand as unseemly, Stanton exploded: "What an infernal set of fools these school-marms must be!! Well, if in order to please men they wish to live on air, let them. The sooner the present generation of women die out the better. We have jackasses enough in the world without such women propagating any more."

In 1858, after accepting invitations to make speeches in Philadelphia and Washington, Stanton canceled both because, at the age of forty-three, she was having a miserable pregnancy with her seventh child. Much upset, Anthony wrote to another reformer, the Reverend Antoinette Brown Blackwell, America's first female minister:

Ah me!!! Alas!! Alas! Mrs. Stanton!! is embarked on the rolling sea—three long months of terrible nausea are behind and what the future has in store, the *deep* only knows. . . . But her husband, you know, does not *help* to make it easy for her. . . . Mr. Stanton will be gone most of the Autumn, full of *Political Air Castles.* . . . He was gone 7 *months* last winter. . . . I only *scold now* that for a *moment's pleasure* to herself or her husband, she should thus increase the *load of cares* under which she already groans.

The letter is startling in its candor not only on the part played by sexuality but in its shrewd characterization of Henry Stanton's activities.

Returning to the forefront of women's rights agitation, Stanton made three major speeches in 1860. In the first she addressed the New York State Assembly on married women's property rights. Calling it "A Slave's Appeal," she asserted that the ultimate protection for women and their property was the right to vote. To the argument that women should not be exposed to the coarseness of public life, she answered that any wife who has lived with a brutal man or a drunkard is thoroughly acquainted with all the revolting facts of life.

But it was in the third address, at the Tenth National Women's Rights Convention at New York's Cooper Institute, that she struck the most controversial note: women's right to divorce—a scandalous subject in the Gilded Age since it was assumed that only adulterers divorced and that liberalizing the law would in effect license free love. As early as 1856, referring to familiar stories of sexual abuse in marriage, Stanton had boldly declared: "Man in his lust has regulated this whole question of sexual intercourse long enough. Let the mothers of mankind set bounds to his indulgence." Marriage, she contended, was a man-made institution in which a husband "gives up no right, but a woman, every right, even the most sacred of all, the right to her own person. . . . So long as our present false marriage relation continues, which in most cases is nothing more or less than legalized prostitution, women can have no self-respect." Marriage, she went on, should be a simple contract that could be quickly ended in cases of "drunkenness, insanity, desertion, cruel and brutal treatment, adultery, or mere incompatibility." It would be divorce without guilty parties. The public reaction was harsh, and Stanton soon realized that many women, even if unhappily married, would reject divorce because it would tarnish their reputation and deprive them of home, children, and financial support. Women, she saw, would have to become independent before they could be free to choose divorce.

The presidential campaign of 1860 and the rise of abolition and anti-Southern sentiment soon drained off interest in the women's rights issue. After shifting his allegiance several times, Henry Stanton finally campaigned for Lincoln. He expected an important post as his reward but had to settle for the position of deputy collector of the New York Customs House. Elizabeth, however, after eighteen years in Seneca Falls, looked forward to living in the city.

New York in the spring of 1862 was alive with the war spirit and full of feverish activity. Believing that their support of the war effort would gain equal rights for women as well as blacks, Stanton wrote: "The war is music to my ears. It is a simultaneous chorus for freedom," and backed the war effort wholeheartedly. It came close to home when one of her sons, Henry, not yet eighteen, ran off and became a volunteer. Anthony had no faith that the women would be rewarded and she fiercely opposed giving up their own campaigns. She would prove entirely right. Meanwhile, both Stanton and Anthony were sharply critical of Lincoln's delay in proclaiming emancipation. Together they established the National Woman's Loyal League and collected 400,000 signatures to prove that emancipation had popular support.

Henry Stanton was not happy with his job, and as early as 1862 his superior, the chief collector, reported unfavorably on his performance. His troubles came to a head disastrously when certain bonds put up by shippers disappeared from his office. The culprit proved to be the Stantons' eldest son, Daniel, always an unmanageable youth, whom Stanton had made a clerk in his office. The incident became a headline scandal and Stanton was forced to resign. He eventually joined the staff of Dana's *Sun* and remained there until his death.

The Stantons and Anthony agreed with the abolitionists and radical Republicans in viewing Lincoln's reelection as a setback for the nation. Such was their distrust of his reconstruction policies that when he was assassinated they viewed it as a "terrible exhibition of God's wrath." Later Mrs. Stanton would see the wisdom of Lincoln's course and be conscience-stricken at having worked for his defeat.

Even as Henry, sixty years old in 1865, faded into the background, Elizabeth became increasingly prominent. More and more independent of him, especially after she came into a sizable inheritance on her father's death, she bought a spacious country house and garden in Tenafly, New Jersey. She and Henry also acquired a brownstone in New York, which Henry came to prefer, so that after a while they maintained separate households.

The postwar period proved to be the most divisive for the women's movement. When the Fourteenth Amendment, giving blacks citizenship and thus the vote, was proposed in 1865, Stanton was infuriated because it used the word "male" in defining citizens. When the abolitionists, led by Wendell Phillips, endorsed it, she exclaimed, "Do you believe the African race is composed entirely of males?" But Phillips insisted that including women would "lose for the Negro far more than we should gain for the woman." It was, most reformers declared, "the Negro's hour." Provoked to the limit, Stanton resorted to such nativist and elitist statements as "The best interests of the nation demand that we outweigh this incoming pauperism, ignorance, and degradation, with the wealth, education, and refinement of the women of the republic.'' Even her friends were shocked, and Garrison privately characterized her as ''a female demagogue.''

In desperation, Stanton, claiming that nothing in the Constitution prohibited women from holding office even if they could not vote, nominated herself as an independent candidate for Congress from New York City's Eighth District. Sadly limited in her campaign by her duties as mother and homemaker, not to mention her work as speechwriter for Anthony, she received only twenty-four votes.

Failing to win suffrage on the national level, Stanton and Anthony now made several efforts on the state level, most notably in Kansas in 1867. That state was voting on two propositions, one to give the vote to women and the other to give it to blacks. The two women toured the state separately, Stanton speaking two or three times daily, enduring dirt, poor food, and unclean beds. In log cabins, churches, barns, and the open air, she faced audiences that ranged from contemptuous or amused men to appreciative women. Often she won them over with her matronly appearance, lively wit, and respect for their pioneer role. But the state Republican machine opposed them and both referendums were defeated.

Eastern reformers blamed Stanton and Anthony's failure on their close association in Kansas with George Francis Train, a rich promoter and flamboyant showman with a scandalous past and grandiose political ambitions. They made a strange trio: Train in a colored waistcoat and lavender gloves, Stanton in black silk and lace, and Anthony plain and prim. Lucy Stone called Train a lunatic, and Garrison wrote him off as a ''crack-brained harlequin,'' but Stanton insisted that, aside from a few ''idiosyncrasies,'' he was a ''pure, high-toned man,'' and added, with her usual brass, that she would accept aid from the devil himself as long as he did not tempt her to lower her standards. But probably Train's greatest appeal for the two women was his promise to help them start a newspaper.

Returning to New York, they plunged into publishing the paper, boldly naming it the *Revolution*. ''A journal called the *Rosebud*,'' Stanton observed, ''might answer for those who come with kid gloves and perfumes to lay immortal wreaths on the monuments which in sweat and tears others have hewn and built, but for us . . . there is no name like the *Revolution*.'' In January 1868, with Stanton as senior editor and Anthony as business manager, they put out their first issue, a six-page paper featuring the motto "Men their rights and nothing more; women their rights and nothing less." It covered most aspects of women's lives and needs, with Parker Pillsbury, a minister turned reformer, reporting on politics, and Train adding notes favoring organized labor, the abolition of armies, and open immigration. A friendly critic thought it a keen and wide-awake paper, but others considered it irresponsible and demagogic. The paper's association with Train, its unpopular editorials, and its rejection of certain types of advertising, particularly for patent medicines, cut its revenue and circulation. Soon Train went off, unceremoniously severing his ties to the paper; after two and a half years, it folded, Stanton leaving Anthony burdened with a debt of $10,000.

At a meeting of the American Equal Rights Association in New York in 1868, Stanton and Anthony opposed a Fifteenth Amendment because it gave voting rights to blacks but not to women. Provoked, Douglass declared that when women are "hunted down . . . in New York and New Orleans; when they are dragged from their houses and hung upon lamp-posts; when their children are torn from their arms . . . then they will have an urgency to obtain the ballot equal to our own." So Stanton, speaking in Washington at a convention of state suffrage groups, called for a Sixteenth Amendment to enfranchise women. A popular novelist, Grace Greenwood, reported that Stanton's speeches were models of composition,

> clear, compact, elegant and logical . . . and there is no denying or dodging her conclusions. . . . [She is] now impassioned, now playful, now witty, now pathetic. . . . Mrs. Stanton has the best arts of the politician and the training of the jurist, added to the fiery, unresting spirit of the reformer. . . . Yet she is in an eminent degree womanly, having an almost regal pride of sex.

It was such a tribute as Stanton must have dreamed of.

Ignoring a conservative New England group, Stanton now called together delegates who favored a federal amendment for women's suffrage and organized the National Woman Suffrage Association. Alienated by Stanton's belligerence, her racist position on the Fifteenth Amendment, and her exclusion of men, the New Englanders, led by Lucy Stone, soon founded a rival group, the American Woman Suffrage Association. It chose a man, Henry Ward Beecher, as its president, and began a conservative publication, the *Woman's Journal.* Disillusioned by the dissension, Stanton later admitted that "at times a sense of utter loneliness made the bravest of them doubt the possibility of maintaining the struggle." Hoping to influence public opinion, she turned more and more from conventions to lecture tours.

At the January 1870 meeting of the national group, the more conservative members, led by a new recruit, Isabella Beecher Hooker, half-sister of Henry Ward Beecher and Harriet Beecher Stowe, took control. She had helped Lucy Stone found the New England association but had sided with Stanton in the major split. Her assertiveness had irked Stanton: inviting women to a meeting in Rhode Island, she had included instructions, as Stanton reported to a friend, concerning

> dress, manners, and general display of all the Christian graces. I did my best to obey orders, and appeared in a black velvet dress with real lace, and the most inoffensive speech I could produce; all those passages that would shock the most conservative were ruled out, while pathetic and aesthetic passages were substituted. . . . I believe I succeeded in charming everyone but myself and Anthony, who said it was the weakest speech I ever made. I told her that was what it was intended to be.

But when Hooker, who had undertaken to organize and underwrite the 1871 convention of the national group in Washington, did not invite her, Stanton was shaken. She did not attend.

Another challenge to the leaders of the movement came, as we have seen, from that master of shock treatment, Victoria Woodhull. She had so impressed Anthony and Isabella Hooker that they had asked her to address the National's 1871 convention. Any qualms Stanton may have had about Woodhull's disreputable past were apparently swept aside when in a rousing address Woodhull struck such notes as "We will overthrow this bogus republic and plant a government of righteousness in its stead." Ignoring Anthony's protests, Stanton refused to condemn Woodhull. "Man," she wrote to a friend, "creates the public sentiment . . . and then makes us hangmen for our sex. Women have crucified the Mary Wollstonecrafts, the Fanny Wrights, the George Sands. . . . Let us end this ignoble record. . . . If Victoria Woodhull must be crucified, let men . . . plait the crown of thorns."

Throughout the 1870s Stanton spent as much as eight months a year on the lecture circuit. Although she was in her late fifties and getting uncomfortably stout, she was clearly glad to be free of family responsibilities. Despite her maternal aura, the thought of what she had endured as a woman, she wrote to another feminist, was enough to arouse her to a

> white heat of rebellion against every "white male" on the continent. When I think of all the wrongs that have been heaped on womankind, I am ashamed that I am not forever in a condition of chronic wrath . . . my eyes a fountain of tears, my lips overflowing with curses, and my hand against every man and his brother. Oh! How I repent of the male faces I have washed . . . the pants mended, the cut fingers . . . I have bound up . . . and then to think of these lords and lackeys strutting . . . dear, oh dear, it is too much!"

Finally, in 1879, exhausted by a long tour, Stanton quit the lecture circuit and turned to a project she and Anthony had talked about for years, a history of the women's suffrage movement in America. Working in Stanton's Tenafly home, they completed the first three volumes by 1885; three additional volumes would take later contributors another twenty-four years. The *History* was a massive compendium of personal reminiscences, biographical sketches, speeches, state reports, and photographs. Such was the continued indifference to the subject, even among women, that when Stanton donated a set to the Vassar College library, it was returned.

In the 1880s Stanton began long sojourns abroad, staying in England with her daughter Harriot, an active feminist married to a wealthy Englishman, and in Paris with her son Theodore, a journalist. In England she reveled in her reception as a celebrated reformer and feminist. In 1887, while on one of these trips, she received word of her husband's death. They had maintained a friendly relationship, but their children believed that in their later years they were estranged. She may well have resented how belatedly she had achieved the freedom from domestic responsibilities he had enjoyed throughout their forty-five years together.

Although hampered by illness, failing eyesight, and obesity, Stanton remained active and as militant as ever. When Anthony began wooing conservative and religious groups such as temperance societies in order to make suffrage look respectable, Stanton found this too confining. "I cannot . . . sing suffrage evermore," she wrote to a friend: "I am deeply interested in all the questions of the day." She proceeded to endorse coeducation, better housing for the poor, an end to capital punishment, and free kindergartens. When Anthony started merger talks with Lucy Stone and the American Woman Suffrage Association, Stanton remained aloof. But when the two groups were united in 1890 as the National American Suffrage Association, Stanton was made its president.

After her husband's death, Stanton sold the Tenafly house and, along with a son and a widowed daughter, moved into a large apartment on New York's West Side. Despite their disagreements, Anthony asked her to speak at the 1892 convention of the merged associations. At seventy-seven, a grandmotherly figure dressed in black silk, with white curls under a lace cap, she delivered a moving statement of her credo as a woman. Called "The Solitude of Self," it dwelt on woman's need for absolute self-reliance to prepare her for the "awful solitude" in which she must face life's crises—childbirth, widowhood, catastrophe, old age, and death. "No matter how much women prefer to lean, to be protected and supported . . . ," she declared, "they must make the voyage of life alone." The strongest reason, she went on, that woman asks a voice in government, in religion, equality in social life, and a place in the trades and professions is her "birthright to self-sovereignty." She delivered the speech again before the Senate Committee on Woman Suffrage, and everyone agreed that it was her finest effort. But in its stoic view and its emphasis on the isolation in which a woman faces crises, it may be seen as reflecting her own peculiar experience as Henry Stanton's wife and as a lifelong crusader for an unpopular cause.

Scornful of the timidity and conservatism of most of the new recruits to the suffrage movement, Stanton refused reelection to the presidency. Instead of demanding equality as their natural right, the younger feminists resigned themselves to claiming that they were morally superior to men and more devout, virtuous, and respectable. More and more confined to her apartment, Stanton devoted herself to articles and columns for a dozen periodicals. On her eightieth birthday, in 1895, 6,000 of her admirers crowded into a flower-bedecked Metropolitan Opera House to hear three hours of tributes and give her ovation after ovation. Only two weeks later she published the most daring and controversial of her works, *The Woman's Bible.*

Stanton had long before stopped attending church regularly and resented deeply the clergy's hostility to women's rights, especially since women were their main support. Believing in a male-female deity, she addressed her mealtime grace to "Mother and Father God." Endlessly bitter over the inferior status assigned to women in all religions, she set out to show how all passages in the Bible concerning women had been used to prove that woman was an afterthought in the Creation, the source of original sin, doomed to subordination in marriage, and unfit to serve as a minister, and how other passages were interpreted as sanctioning slavery and capital punishment. All this, she declared, represented not Holy Writ but the bias of male authors in an ancient patriarchal society.

Moderate as many statements in *The Woman's Bible* may now seem, it created a sensation: hostile critics branded it heresy and yet it became a best-seller. The violence of that reaction may explain why Stanton's autobiography, *Eighty Years and More,* skirts party dissension, avoids recrimination, and plays up her role as friend, mother, shrewd observer, and wise guide, seeking perhaps to offset any conception of her as a contentious or unhappy radical.

The challenging character of *The Woman's Bible* had widened the gap between Anthony and Stanton, but when Stanton died in 1902 Anthony was grief-stricken. Months later she said: "How lonesome I do feel. . . . It was a great going out of my life when she died."

Long before Stanton's death, leadership in the women's movement had passed to Anthony and her "girls." Although a less appealing personality than Stanton and in no way such a bold and original thinker, Anthony was more of an organizer and more conciliatory toward conservative women and new recruits. She has reaped the reward—celebration on stamp and coin as the pioneer leader of the women's movement. But one may question whether her concentration on suffrage warranted the energies it drained from feminists for over seventy years. By contrast, Stanton's hammering away at all the ways men have subordinated women anticipated by a century the "consciousness-raising" of women's liberationists. As a well-known editor wrote to her in her last years,

> Every woman who seeks the legal custody of her children; who finds the door of a college or university open to her; who administers a post-office or a public library; who enters upon a career of medicine, law or theology; who teaches school or tills a farm or keeps a shop or rides a bicycle—every such woman owes her liberty largely to yourself and to your . . . earliest co-workers.

Although the women's rights leaders mounted a broad assault on domination by man, most of them did not attempt to break into the professions or callings traditionally filled by men: they remained subject to a male God and clergy, male legislators and government officials, male police and soldiers, and male doctors, lawyers, merchants, and editors. It took a few indomitable and remarkably competent women, each acting alone, to breach the wall around the age-old male domains. Among the most respected, well-rewarded, and well-guarded of these professions were law and medicine.

Hebrew, Greek, Roman, and later European societies all contributed to the idea that courts of law were the sacred precincts of man. Beyond that, English common law, which the first colonists brought to America, established the principle that a husband was lord of the household and that a woman had virtually no legal status: it declared, in effect, "Husband and wife are one and he is the one."

In 1873, when Belva Ann Lockwood, at the age of forty-three, became one of the first two women to graduate from the National University Law School in Washington, she was appalled to learn that women would not receive a degree because it would hurt the reputation of the institution. Frustrated beyond enduring, Mrs. Lockwood wrote a stinging letter to President Grant, titular head of the university, literally demanding her diploma. Meanwhile the vice-chancellor of the university, privately sympathizing with the two women, included their diplomas among those he submitted for President Grant's signature. All the diplomas came back signed, probably because no one paid any attention to the names on them. A few months later, when Mrs. Lockwood was admitted to the bar in the District of Columbia, one justice in the court was heard to remark, "Bring on as many women lawyers as you choose; I do not believe they will be a success." Insofar as his statement included Belva Ann Lockwood, he was completely wrong.

Belva Ann Bennett was an outstanding pupil in the school in Royalton on the Niagara frontier of western New York. After graduating, she paid her way through the Royalton Girls Academy by teaching in summer sessions at the local school. At eighteen, a slim, quite pretty girl, she married Uriah McNall, who worked at a local sawmill. But an accident at the mill struck him down and he died a few years later. Left a widow at twenty-three, with a three-year-old child, Belva met the crisis firmly: refusing to retreat to her parents' home, she turned to the only professional work open to a woman, teaching. She was offered a position in the district school, but when she learned that she would be paid only seven dollars a week while male teachers received between ten and fifteen dollars a week, she rejected the offer indignantly. She then hurried to the Methodist minister's wife, a friend of hers, hoping to get that good woman to intercede for her. But the lady's answer was: "I can't help you. And you can't help yourself. It is the way of the world."

Belva's response was to equip herself with more education. Leaving her daughter with her parents, she went off to Genesee College, near Rochester. For a tuition fee of $8.50 a term she took the "Scientific Course," studying geometry, electricity, magnetism, and political economy. She also attended a class in law given by a lawyer in the village. In her spare time she devoted herself to the student antislavery and temperance movements. She graduated with honors and soon found a position as director, called "preceptress," of the Union School at Lockport. Lockport was a key transportation and manufacturing center on the Erie Canal, and its high school had an excellent reputation. Mrs. McNall herself taught advanced mathematics, logic, and natural science. She disturbed many parents by introducing a course in public speaking for the girls and even more by gymnastic exercises that she herself led. A few parents protested, but the school board supported her, and most of the girls responded enthusiastically. Small as such victories were, they taught her that many taboos were based on prejudice or ignorance. Outside of school, Belva served on various committees of the women's rights movement. Once she helped arrange a lecture by Susan B. Anthony. Miss Anthony stayed in the same house as Belva and they found each other so stimulating that they talked all night.

The end of the war brought a great surge of commerce and growth to such cities as New York and ever-increasing political activity in Washington. To thirty-six-year-old Belva McNall, Lockport began to seem provincial and confining. So in 1866 she boldly moved to Washington with her seventeen-year-old daughter. After a period of teaching in a boarding school, she opened her own school in a Union League hall. But not content with teaching, she kept looking for a way of entering another field.

She had meanwhile become friendly with Ezekiel Lockwood, an elderly dentist who shared her advanced views, and finally married him in 1868. Relieved of the need to continue teaching, Belva became more active in the women's suffrage and peace movements. Among the first efforts of the Lockwoods on behalf of women was an attempt to establish a Washington chapter of the equal rights association, but the response was not encouraging. Recalling her humiliation when the Royalton school trustees offered her half of what they paid men, she then circulated a petition urging that women in federal service receive the same pay as men. When several congressmen suggested that she incorporate the petition in a bill, she was annoyed because she had to hire a lawyer to formulate it. The more she thought about this, the more she was convinced that legal training was the path to influence and authority.

Wasting no time—she was forty years old—she applied to two law schools. Both told her that they did not accept women, one adding that women would be an "injurious diversion" for the male students. Fortunately, the newly established National University Law School opened its doors to women, and in 1870 Belva Ann Lockwood and fourteen other women matriculated. After graduating, she was licensed to practice in Washington. At first, most of her clients were women. More than once she won cases for them by using their inferior status to their advantage. Thus, when a poor young woman was accused of wounding a constable who came to her home to search for goods allegedly stolen by her husband, Mrs. Lockwood noted that the woman's husband had given her a pistol and told her to shoot anyone who tried to enter their house. Undaunted by an all-male jury, she pointed out that under the common law prevailing in the District of Columbia a wife must obey her husband. The blame in this case, she concluded, must be placed on the husband. The jury acquitted the woman.

Taking all kinds of cases, including those of clients who could not afford to pay her, Belva Ann Lockwood gained a reputation as a concerned as well as competent attorney, a keen and confident woman who knew the law and was an effective speaker. She won national recognition when she drafted and steered through Congress a soldiers and sailors' bonus bill. But when she tried to present a claim against the government in a federal court of claims, the chief justice simply said, "Mistress Lockwood, you are a married woman," signifying that she could not serve as an attorney there because her husband might be liable for her actions.

She promptly applied to the U.S. Supreme Court for permission to practice before it. But that august body, "in accordance with immemorial usage," denied her application. She then set about getting Congress to pass a bill to enable women attorneys to practice in the Supreme Court. She also applied for admission to the Maryland bar. Her rejection there was even more absurd, the judge declaring, incredibly, that he could find no feminine pronouns in the statutes, only "he, him and his." Carried away by his wisdom, he added that a woman's place was in the home, waiting upon her husband and bringing up her children. A few years later, Mrs. Lockwood was admitted to the bar in both Maryland and Virginia, and her bill to gain women attorneys admission to the Supreme Court was passed by both houses of Congress. On March 3, 1879, Belva Ann Lockwood, a slender, self-assured woman of forty-eight, became the first woman to be admitted to the U.S. Supreme Court. Her only regret was that her husband had not lived to share her triumph: he had died two years before. But there were other compensations: she now had a twenty-room house that would serve as her office as well as her home for the next thirty years.

Accustomed to doing things her own way, Mrs. Lockwood rode around the capital on a tricycle, stirring waves of attention as she passed. Assisted by her daughter, she took on a great variety of cases—divorce actions, pension claims, and every crime from common assault to murder. But she remained particularly sympathetic to the claims of wives and widows, and she constantly strove to make marriage a civil contract in which both parties had property rights. The most notable case she brought before the Supreme Court was the claim of the Cherokee Indians for the payment promised them when their people had long before been forced off their native lands in North Carolina. Her passionate plea, made when she was seventy-five years old, won $5 million for the Cherokees and a sizable fee for herself. But as evidence of what a woman attorney could accomplish, she won far more.

Belva Ann Lockwood's commitment to women's suffrage diverted her in 1884 into the most widely publicized but ill-advised undertaking of her career—running for President. It began when she was sent to the Republican National Convention in Chicago in 1884 as a representative of a national equal rights organization. At the convention she urged the resolutions committee to include an equal rights plank in its platform, but it simply brushed the request aside. She was therefore astonished when Elizabeth Cady Stanton and Susan B. Anthony recommended that women support the Republican candidate, James G. Blaine. She sent off an irate letter to the *Woman's Herald of Industry*, organ of the so-called Woman's Republic, the brainchild of a Mrs. Maretta Stow. In her letter Lockwood argued—as Stanton had in New York—that although women could not vote, no law prohibited them from running for office. They must simply put up their own candidate for President. As a model of a great woman ruler, she pointed out, they need look no further than Queen Victoria.

Mrs. Stow, a zealot who believed, among other things, in electricity as a cure for all illnesses, hailed the letter, and within a few weeks the Equal Rights party, meeting in California, nominated Belva Ann Lockwood for President and Maretta Stow for Vice President. It would have been an empty gesture had not Lockwood taken the nomination seriously and drawn up a strong platform for the party. In her acceptance speech in a "convention" in Maryland attended by only sixty people, she promised to seek equal rights for all, a fair share of public offices for women, and a national system of laws. On speaking tours to a dozen cities, accompanied by bands and banners, she proclaimed, "In this free republic, contrary to the Bill of Rights, we are governed without our consent." She attracted nationwide attention but much of it was scornful. The Washington, D.C., *Morning Journal* mocked her with

> *When our votes for you are cast,*
> *Belva, dear; Belva, dear;*
> *Will you tax the bustle vast,*
> *Belva, dear; Belva, dear?*
> *Will you place a tariff high*
> *on the hosiery we buy?*
> *We await your calm reply,*
> *Belva, dear; Belva, dear!*

Even the women's rights leaders thought her candidacy unwarranted and brought ridicule on the entire suffragist movement. She received 6,161 votes, all necessarily cast by men.

To her other commitments Lockwood now added international peace and labor reform. As early as 1885 she managed to get Congress to consider a bill for an international court to maintain world peace, and from 1889 to 1911 she was a delegate to every international peace congress, ranging from London and Bern to Milan and Budapest. Everywhere her rallying cry was: "No one can be called a Christian who gives money for the building of warships or carrying on a conflict."

She remained just as busy in her professional capacity, noting at the age of eighty-one that she was coping with three weighty cases. Although she had suffered severe financial reverses, including the loss of her house, apparently at the hands of an "unscrupulous admirer," and a spiritual setback when war broke out in Europe, she worked for the reelection of Woodrow Wilson not long before her death in 1917. And she had the satisfaction of knowing that after seventy years of struggle, women were about to win the right to vote. She herself had done more than anyone to enable women to become lawyers: by 1900 over 1,000 women had followed in her footsteps. She had, beyond that, broken down another barrier that the Gilded Age had sought to maintain against the participation of women in the affairs of the world.

If it was difficult for mid-nineteenth-century Americans to imagine a woman as a lawyer, it was nearly impossible for them to conceive of a woman as a physician or surgeon. Although women nursed the sick and served as midwives, that was very far from dissecting cadavers and operating on both men and women.

But Bethenia Owens decided as a young girl that she could do anything a boy could do. Perhaps she decided this when she outwrestled her brother Flem or lifted loads as heavy as he did on their coastal farm on the Clatsop plains of northern Oregon. Or perhaps it was a matter of emulating her father, who had been a sheriff in Kentucky of whom it was said, "Tom Owens is not afraid of man or devil." Or perhaps it was that her parents were pioneers who had made a perilous crossing of the plains in a covered wagon in 1843 when she was three years old.

Kept busy doing farm work and tending baby sisters and brothers, Bethenia had almost no time for schooling. Then big, strong Le-Grand Hill came calling when she was little more than fourteen, and before she realized what it would mean, she was married. Excited by the fact that LeGrand had managed to buy a 320-acre farm—on credit—she was not dismayed at having to live temporarily in a twelve-by-fourteen-foot cabin "chinked" with mud and grass, with only one small window, no floor or chimney, and a bed frame of wooden rails thrust into holes in the wall. They had only eight head of stock, Bethenia's riding mare, a cow, a calf, some tinware, Le-Grand's horse and gun, and twenty dollars left from a down payment on the property. But she had faith in her husband and a buoyant nature. And she was in love.

Her faith in her husband dwindled steadily when he delayed in starting to build a new house and then constantly left the work to go hunting or to camp meetings. In the fall, rains flooded the cabin and skunks roamed nightly among the pots and pans. When they could not meet the payments on the new house, the owner of the land took it over. For a time they lived with Bethenia's parents in Roseburg in southern Oregon, but when LeGrand heard of a gold strike in Yreka,

California, he sold their cows and persuaded a very reluctant Bethenia to move to Yreka and live there with one of his aunts.

Fortunately, Aunt Kelley and Bethenia liked each other. But she added to Bethenia's mounting disappointment in her husband when she revealed that LeGrand had lived with her for six years and left her convinced that he would not amount to anything. He will never get anywhere, she warned Bethenia, and he will "fool away" your money. A month after arriving in Yreka, Bethenia gave birth to a baby boy.

The aunt, an able woman who supported herself by selling milk, eggs, and pies, and by sewing, soon taught Bethenia how to make and sell shirts. She was right about LeGrand: he drifted from job to job and idled away the time in between. Losing patience, Bethenia insisted on moving back to Roseburg. There LeGrand promptly put all their modest savings into starting a brickyard; it soon failed and her father had to come to their rescue. Far more disturbing was the way LeGrand, ignoring the fact that little George was a sickly baby, spanked him unmercifully when he cried. Once, when Bethenia protested, they quarreled violently and LeGrand struck her. As soon as he left the house, she took the baby and fled to her parents' home. LeGrand tried repeatedly to get her to return to him, but she was adamant, declaring, "LeGrand, I have told you many times that if we ever did separate, I would never go back, and I never will."

In her parents' home, surrounded by affection, Bethenia soon recovered her spirits and little George his health. Her marriage had been a mortifying experience, but, she later wrote, it taught her to rely on herself and call no man master. When an older woman whom she respected urged her to return to her husband because Scripture forbade divorce except for adultery, she answered that there were other acts that were just as unforgivable. After a court battle, she won a divorce, custody of her son, and the right to resume her maiden name.

Because, at eighteen, she could scarcely read or write, Bethenia went back to primary school side by side with her younger brothers and sisters. She ignored, as she always would, the head-shaking of her friends and neighbors. Eager for more education, she moved to Astoria on the northern Oregon coast and spent several years taking more advanced courses. Living in rented rooms with her son, she rose at 4:00 A.M. and paid her way by doing sewing and washing for several families, earning barely five dollars a week. "Nothing," she later recalled, "was permitted to come between me and this, the greatest opportunity of my life."

At the close of her courses, she had made so much progress that she was asked to substitute for a teacher who was ill. She went on to serve as a full-time teacher in several western Oregon communities, beginning at $25 a month and the expense of "boarding round." When she reached $40 a month, she ventured to have a small house built for her in Astoria. At one point LeGrand Hill returned and pleaded with her to rejoin him. But she no longer was, as she said, the little child-bride he had abused but "a full-grown, self-supporting woman who could look upon him only with pity."

She returned to Roseburg and encouraged by her experience in sewing and aided by a brother-in-law, Hyman Goldberg, a dry goods merchant, she started a millinery and dressmaking business. It went well for a few years, and despite competition from a milliner who opened up next door, she eventually cleared more than $1,500 a year.

Her success in business as well as in teaching, and her disgust with the way even drunken men were allowed to vote in elections, stirred Bethenia Owens into actively supporting such causes as temperance and women's suffrage. She began doing articles on these issues for the Roseburg paper and for a women's newspaper published in Portland by a well-known reformer, Abigail Scott Duniway. While helping an elderly local doctor with his nursing, she found not only that the work was deeply rewarding but that she could perform some of his functions as well as he could. She began to think of becoming a doctor. In 1870 any other woman would have dismissed such an idea as a pipe dream, especially if she was thirty-one years old and the sole support of a fourteen-year-old son. But Bethenia Owens's reaction was to begin studying Gray's *Anatomy* and other medical books of her doctor friend. When she mentioned her intention to the prominent lawyer who had helped her win her divorce, he cheered her tremendously by declaring: "Go ahead. It is in you; let it come out. You will win." Susan B. Anthony, for whom she had arranged a lecture in Roseburg, was equally encouraging. Bethenia enrolled her son in the University of California at Berkeley and began exploring the possibility of going east to a medical school.

When they learned of her plans, her family and friends were incredulous. Typical was a woman who exclaimed: "Well, this beats all! You must have gone stark crazy to leave such a business as you have and go off on such a wild goose chase." Even her son opposed the plan. But Bethenia had long since learned to disregard the automatic opposition aroused by any attempt to break out of "woman's sphere." Friends had given her leads to doctors in Philadelphia, which was known for its medical schools, but she later admitted that when she finally found herself, one rainy night in 1871, on a train headed across the continent, she was overwhelmed by fear and loneliness.

When Bethenia Owens disclosed to a doctor in Philadelphia how little formal education she had, he warned her that she would probably be admitted only by the Eclectic School of Medicine, a primitive institution that concentrated on the use of plants and drugs and ignored surgery. He also advised her to take a summer course in anatomy with a Dr. Samuels. She enrolled for the course, and she never forgot the look of disbelief on the faces of the other students, all male, when she entered the doctor's dissecting room. Their astonishment mounted when, amid the nauseating odor of decomposing flesh, she watched, without recoiling, the dissection of a human foot. But by the end of the course they were admiringly referring to her as "Mrs. Anything-a-Man-Can-Do"—part of the answer she had given to every challenge.

At the Eclectic School, Owens's training consisted of five months of lectures followed by four months of work in the dirty, ill-smelling clinics and the autopsy room of Blockley Hospital. After her graduation, she paused in New York for instruction in a new treatment utilizing electrified and medicated vapor baths.

On her return to Roseburg, the other doctors in the area refused to take her seriously. Mainly to embarrass her, they sent her an invitation to an autopsy of an old man that would take place in a barn. To their consternation, she came. As a crowd of men and boys gathered to watch the performance, one of the doctors asked her whether she realized that the old man had died of a chronic bladder infection and that the dissection would therefore involve the genital organs. They were astonished when she answered, "One part of the human body is as sacred to the physician as another," and before they could recover, added, "What is the difference between the attendance of a

man at a female autopsy and a woman at a male autopsy?'' Determined to confound her, a doctor thrust a case of dissecting instruments into her hands. She calmly accepted the case and proceeded to
perform the dissection. At the close she diagnosed the cause of death
as a malignant growth blocking the passage through the peritoneum.
The crowd burst into cheers.

But the townspeople were aghast at this "woman who dared,"
and she realized then that they would never accept her as a doctor.
With her son still at the University of California, she moved to Portland. Besides following standard practice, she equipped two rooms
with electrified medicated baths. These proved particularly attractive
to patients with rheumatism or neuritis. She also became known for
her competence in maternity cases and the treatment of children. She
soon had a steady flow of patients, and doctors who had at first re-
buffed or slighted her now accepted her. Tired of living alone, Owens
gladly adopted the fourteen-year-old daughter of a patient who was
facing death. When her son graduated from the university and decided that he too wanted to be a doctor—he was now very proud of
his mother—she was able to send him to the Medical College of Wil-
lamette University in Salem, Oregon.

Bethenia Owens's hunger to improve herself professionally increased with the years. At thirty-eight, having amassed the impressive
sum of $8,000, she decided to take a full-length medical course and
become a surgeon. By that time no one thought she was foolish to
undertake such a daunting program. Instead, when she went off to
Philadelphia in 1878, she carried letters from senators, governors, and
other doctors. But when she told a famous surgeon at Philadelphia's
renowned Jefferson Medical College, Dr. Samuel Gross—he had been
the subject of Thomas Eakins's masterpiece *The Gross Clinic,* whose
realism would soon shock the art world—of her wish to enter the
school, he predicted that she would not be accepted. But he also
convinced her that she could do just as well at the University of
Michigan. She went at once to Ann Arbor and was welcomed there.
For two years, she put in sixteen hours a day at her tasks, rising
before dawn and, after a cold bath, plunging into a round of lectures,
clinics, and laboratory work. After receiving her degree, she devoted
a year to hospital work in Chicago and then returned to the university
as a resident physician.

Following a tour of Europe and especially its hospitals, Dr. Owens opened an office in Portland. Becoming known as the first woman graduate physician on the Pacific Coast—she had given up being a "bath doctor"—she was soon earning as much as $7,000 a year. Despite her growing reputation, her clientele was made up chiefly of women. Challenged by the strict limits still put upon women, she often gave lectures and wrote articles on women as physicians and on women's suffrage. That period, she later recalled, was one of the busiest and most satisfying of her life.

With her son practicing medicine in Washington and her adopted daughter attending medical school, Owens was once again living alone. She had often declared that she was married to her profession. But when she met Colonel John Adair, a land developer whom she had known in her childhood, she changed her mind; they were married in 1884. Probably influenced by Lucy Stone, the feminist who had retained her maiden name after marriage, but also by pride in her accomplishments, she thereafter signed herself Bethenia Owens-Adair.

Her husband's plan to reclaim a section of coastal lowland led them to move to a farm on the northernmost Oregon coast. But making night calls to distant farms, helping with farm work in a region often shrouded in fog, spending long hours in the saddle, and taking care of two small sons left Owens-Adair with a chronic rheumatism. After visits to the high, dry climate of North Yakima, Washington, where her son had his practice, she persuaded her husband to move there. Once again she established a thriving practice, and with it a reputation as a surgeon who could operate, if necessary, on a kitchen table in an outlying farmhouse. A lifelong habit of pushing others, as well as herself, to the limit made her bedside manner, as her son put it, "mighty abrupt." As late as 1905, during a diphtheria epidemic, she answered calls for sixty hours with only a few intervals of rest.

Finally, at the age of sixty-five, having accumulated $25,000, she retired from active practice and joined her husband at their seaside farm. In that same year she was a speaker at a banquet arranged by the American Medical Association to honor women physicians. "I thank God," she said, "that I have been spared to see this day, when women are acknowledged before the world as the equal of men in medicine and surgery.''

Dr. Owens-Adair never gave up advocating causes, however controversial, that she considered worthwhile. As early as the 1880s, after seeing what went on in an Oregon state insane asylum, she began urging the sterilization of the insane. She resumed her campaign in 1906, emphasizing ''eugenic improvement,'' and hailed the passage of a modified sterilization law in 1922, two years before she died.

The most remarkable aspect of Bethenia Owens-Adair's career was that an uneducated farmgirl was able to overcome the prohibitions and prejudices of the age and the limitations of life on the Pacific frontier. She not only opened the way for future women physicians but also exploded another myth about the competence and adaptability of womankind.

# 9

## CRITICS
## AND CASSANDRAS

There were of course many Americans who were not content with their lot in the Gilded Age. Some languished on worked-out New England farms, others in the slums of cities and towns, in the hovels of poor whites and freed blacks in the South, in the log cabins of backwoodsmen or on homesteads on the prairie. Some were resigned to their fate or clung stubbornly to hopes and dreams. Others simmered with unfocused resentment or vented their grievances at local meetings or in petitions to their legislators. Only a few began, in farmers' granges, the early labor unions, or in the abolitionist or women's rights movement to join in some form of organized protest.

If such people were discontented, it was the discontent of the economically or socially deprived. But there were others, admittedly few, who enjoyed all or most of the benefits of the social system yet were deeply disturbed by the values and practices that were reshaping American life. Such critics, faced by the prevailing conviction that America was the best of all possible worlds, hardly achieved anything like the scope or influence of such European radicals as Marx, Engels, or Louis Blanc, and somewhat less than such English dissidents as Carlyle, Ruskin, and William Morris. The Americans were for the most part voices crying out not in a wilderness but in something like a county fair.

The most famous of the political economists was Henry George. His campaigns against the increasing concentration of wealth and on behalf of working people were the most systematic and intense of any American critic of his time. Although almost entirely self-educated, George achieved a grasp of economic problems and an acquaintance with history that would have done credit to a university-trained authority.

Although George's parents were people of some education, Henry, a bright, energetic youth, left high school after only a few months. He was scarcely sixteen when, in 1855, fascinated by the great sailing ships in the Philadelphia wharves, he left home and, like a number of Victorian youths of good families, went to sea. He sailed as a cabin boy on a merchant ship bound for Australia and India and was away for fourteen months. In Melbourne, when members of the crew asked for a discharge—they wanted to go prospecting in the goldfields—the captain had them arrested. Such incidents explain why, years later, as an editor of a San Francisco newspaper, George became known for his defense of seamen's rights. The rough life of deck and forecastle and what he saw in India of the extremes of poverty and riches sowed the seeds of many of his later views. On his return to Philadelphia, George found work as an apprentice typesetter, a training that was as much of an education to him as it would be to Walt Whitman and Mark Twain. But after his independence as a sailor, the restrictions put upon him at home, especially by his puritanical mother, led him, in December 1857, to ship out as a storekeeper on a steamer going around Cape Horn to San Francisco.

George found San Francisco alive with excitement over reports of gold in the Fraser River across the Canadian border. Infected by the gold hunters' fever, he hurried north but soon found that little gold was being brought out. Drifting back to San Francisco, he moved from job to job, setting type, working in a rice mill, and, although far from robust, doing farm labor. Returning to typesetting, he was admitted to the local typographical union and began earning a journeyman's wages. But he now wanted to work for himself, and in April 1861 he and several other printers bought the San Francisco *Evening Journal*. Although they worked tirelessly, they could not compete with newspapers that received dispatches by the new transcontinental telegraph. After only eight months the partnership was dissolved.

He was now faced by another crisis: he had fallen in love with Annie Fox, an eighteen-year-old Australian girl who had been orphaned and was living with an uncle in California. The uncle, a prosperous, strong-minded man, was understandably opposed to his niece's penniless suitor. But George was an ardent wooer and the couple, defying Uncle Matthew, eloped, with Henry dressed in a borrowed suit and Annie bringing only a packet of books. Despite such a troubled beginning, the marriage would be marked by a lifetime of love and mutual respect.

Years of intermittent employment and chronic debt followed. George became so desperate when his wife was pregnant with their second child and they had no food in the house that he decided one morning to somehow get money from the first person he met. As he recalled many years later, "I stopped a man—a stranger—and told him I wanted $5. He asked what I wanted it for. I told him that my wife was confined and that I had nothing to give her to eat. He gave me the money. If he had not, I think I was desperate enough to have killed him."

At twenty-six, an insatiable reader and stimulated by what he had learned in printing shops, he began to write. Among his first efforts was a long letter to a labor journal warning against the tendency of the press to "pander to wealth and power" and of society "to resolve itself into classes who have too much or too little." Although strongly opposed to slavery, family obligations kept him from enlisting in the Union army. But the assassination of Lincoln moved him to write so impassioned a eulogy on the fallen President that a paper for which he had set type, the *Alta California,* featured it, and then engaged him to write several special articles. Almost overnight he was launched on his career as a journalist, serving as an editorial writer on the San Francisco *Times* and then as its managing editor.

Soon he found his major theme as a writer. In an article in *The Overland Monthly,* a journal edited by that new star on the western literary horizon, Bret Harte, he pointed up the widening gap between rich and poor, writing,

One millionaire involves the existence of just so many proletarians. . . . We need not look far from the palace to find the hovel. When people can charter special steamboats to take them to watering places . . . build marble stables for their horses, and give dinner parties which cost . . . a thousand dollars a head, we may know that there are poor girls on the streets pondering between starvation and dishonor.

George also began the first of his many battles against entrenched interests. The San Francisco *Herald,* unable to compete against the monopolistic news service run jointly by the Associated Press and Western Union, sent George to New York to set up an independent service. But Western Union soon raised its rate on dispatches from George's service and forced him out of business. The episode added a bitter personal note to his quarrel with all monopolies.

A blot on George's growing record as a defender of human rights was an article in which he joined the West Coast chorus, led by labor, against the admission of Chinese immigrants. To George, both as a union member and a student of economics, the immigrants, mostly men who came to work on contract for "coolie wages" and then returned home, were simply a disruptive factor. He conceded that as individuals they might be intelligent and teachable, but he echoed the most bigoted nativists when he said that as a group they were "utter heathens," treacherous, cruel, and filthy. He later acknowledged that this attack was crude, but he never repudiated it.

While in New York, George was appalled by the contrast between "monstrous wealth and debasing want." In his travels across America he was also struck by the tremendous rise in land values. Once, while riding through the California hills on his mustang pony, he was astonished to learn that a landowner was asking $1,000 an acre. In a flash, as he describes it, he concluded that "with the growth of population, land grows in value, and the men who work it must pay more for the privilege." Inspired by this conclusion, he wrote a pamphlet, *Our Land and Land Values,* printed a thousand copies, and gave away most of them. It contained the kernels of his future masterwork, *Progress and Poverty:* all land is the gift of nature and should belong to all; increases in the value of land are unearned; therefore the fairest tax is a tax on land values.

Determined to spread the message, George and two other news-papermen established the San Francisco *Evening Post* in 1871. It at-tacked corrupt officials and monopolies and called constantly for an exclusive tax on land. It was only a four-page paper, but it lasted four years and earned George the post of secretary of the California delegation to the Democratic National Convention in Baltimore in 1872. He added to his influence by helping elect William S. Irwin governor of California. When, after leaving the *Post,* he sought a state job that would leave him time for the major work he was planning, the governor appointed him state inspector of gas meters.

At home George was a devoted father and husband, close to his children and confiding constantly in his wife. Although he belonged to no church—perhaps a reaction to the excessive piety of his mother—he was in spirit a religious man, insisting that social injus-tice, not a vengeful God, was responsible for mankind's burdens.

A speech George made at a major rally for Samuel Tilden in the 1876 presidential race went off so well that he became the principal speaker in the California campaign. Even more remarkable was his emergence as the leading candidate for the first professorship of po-litical economy at the University of California. But when he delivered a lecture at the university in which he referred to the "learned fools" produced by colleges and criticized political economists for opposing every effort of working people to increase their wages and reduce their hours of work, he failed to get the appointment. The university au-thorities evidently did not relish being told that

> the blasphemous dogma that the Creator has condemned one portion of his creatures to lives of toil and want, while he has intended another portion to enjoy "all the fruits of the earth and the fullness thereof" has been preached to the working classes in the name of political economy, just as "cursed-be-Ham" clergymen used to preach the divine sanction of slavery.

But he was deeply disappointed when he was denied the position.

With each article and speech, George cut deeper and wider. His concern with the larger economic problems was spurred by the nationwide depression and violent railroad strikes that staggered America in the late 1870s. It was also a difficult time personally for George: a fourth child, Anna, was born in 1877—she would become the mother of Agnes de Mille, the famous dancer and choreographer—and income from his gas meter inspections declined as hard times reduced the number of meters.

It was in this atmosphere that he began writing *Progress and Poverty*. Working feverishly, he finished it in eighteen months. Several publishers in the United States and England turned it down because they thought it too "aggressive" or not salable. Finally he had a printer friend set it in type and plated. With this major expense covered, D. Appleton & Company agreed to publish it. *Progress and Poverty* had an extraordinary impact because of its immense conviction, moral fervor, patient detail, and its aim, at least in tone, at the common reader. Its main point, that landowners reaped unearned profit from every rise in the value of land and that a single tax on land would make all other taxes unnecessary, struck most readers as a revelation, even though the French Physiocrats, Herbert Spencer, and others had proposed it many years before. The weakness in George's approach was that he focused more on the agrarian society that was passing away than on the industrial society that was emerging. Thus he spoke of land as the source of all wealth and the private ownership of land as the chief obstacle to ending poverty. He deplored the "insane desire to get rich at any cost," and asserted that what drove men to "working, scheming, striving . . . long after every possible need is satisfied . . . [is] the sense that their wealth . . . makes them men of mark in the community."

Noting that Darwin's theories were encouraging an unlimited confidence in mankind's progress, he insisted that there were signs everywhere of corruption, imminent chaos, and decay: "The pillars of the state are trembling . . . and the very foundations of society quiver with pent-up forces that glow underneath! The struggle that must either revivify, or convulse in ruin, is near." Like a revivalist preacher, he terrified his audience with threats of doom and then lifted them up with a vision of a masterly economic solution.

The ultimate success of *Progress and Poverty* was astonishing, the publishers claiming that it had the largest circulation of any nonfiction work before 1900 except for the Bible. Not only were millions of readers with no previous interest in political economy captured by his arguments but in the coming years large audiences would welcome George on his lecture tours in America, England, and Australia, and such world figures as Sun Yat-sen, George Bernard Shaw, and Leo Tolstoy would testify to his influence.

Curiously, among both George's supporters and critics were people of distinctly conflicting views. Some conservatives went along with George because of his laissez-faire views of government control, his defense of businessmen's profits, and his opposition to all taxes except the one on land. But they attacked his land-tax scheme as confiscation and saw it as a first step toward the expropriation of all commercial property. They also pointed out that some land was owned by workingmen who had earned it by toil and sweat.

Radicals hailed George's plan because it was a tax on "unearned increment." But they faulted his program for not seeking to take over all the means of production and for not using a tax on wealth to reduce the gap between the rich and the poor. Some of George's basic assumptions and prophecies have, moreover, not stood the test of time. Challenging his prediction that wages would continue to fall, economists have argued that labor's share of the national income has remained fairly stable. They have also rejected his claim that a land tax alone would pay for all the services of governments and have challenged his charge that strikes are destructive and that a graduated income tax would lead to bribery and evasion.

When George, a year after publishing *Progress and Poverty,* moved to New York with the hope of getting a newspaper post there, he wrote to a friend, "I am afloat at 42, poorer than at 21." Despite the huge sale of his major work, he made only a few hundred dollars a year from it—many copies were sold in very cheap editions—and not much more from his lectures.

Long troubled by the plight of the Irish people in their struggle with poverty and English rule, George published a pamphlet, *The Irish Land Question,* in 1881. It described Ireland as a conquered nation suffering from the same baneful land system that "prevails in all civilized countries." One result of the pamphlet was his engagement by the *Irish World,* a New York newspaper, to make a lecture tour in Ireland. Arriving in Ireland late in 1881, George and his wife became so friendly with Michael Lavitt, the militant rebel leader, that he was repeatedly detained and questioned by the police. Crossing over to England—it was the first of six increasingly successful tours he would make there between 1882 and 1890—George attracted much attention by openly encouraging the radical land nationalization movement. On his return to New York he was welcomed by labor unions at Cooper Union and was the guest of honor at a banquet given by prominent citizens at Delmonico's.

Greatly encouraged, George pressed his attack on poverty, asserting, in *Social Problems* (1883), that there would be enough for everyone were it not for the failure of America to make full use of its labor resources. Carried away by his own fervor, he indulged in such sensational generalizations as:

> The experiment of popular government in the United States is clearly a failure. . . . Our government by the people has in large degree become . . . government by the strong and unscrupulous. . . . In some sections bribery has become chronic, and numbers of voters expect regularly to sell their votes. . . . In many places it [the party machine] has become so strong that the ordinary citizen has no more influence . . . than he would have in China. . . . In our national Senate, sovereign members of the Union are supposed to be represented; but what are more truly represented are railroad kings and great moneyed interests. . . . And the bench . . . is being filled with corporate henchmen.

So great had George's reputation grown by 1886 that the labor unions of New York City invited him to become their candidate for mayor. Many years later George revealed that the Tammany bosses in New York, seeing a grave threat to their rule, guaranteed him a seat in Congress if he would withdraw. They declared that he could not win the mayoralty race but that his participation in it would "raise hell." George answered that he did not want the mayor's office but did hope to raise hell.

The campaign was a hectic one, with George making as many as fourteen speeches a day. His platform featured a steep tax on all unused land. All the major newspapers opposed him, calling him an "apostle of anarchy" and a dangerous fanatic who preached socialism, communism, and nihilism. The Democratic candidate, Abram Hewitt, a respected congressman, won the race with 90,000 votes, but George received 68,000 votes and came in ahead of a young politico named Theodore Roosevelt.

Annoyed by the charges that he was a socialist, George made clear how much he disagreed with socialism in his response to a papal encyclical, "The Condition of Labour." In his *Open Letter to Pope Leo XIII* (1891), he protested that the encyclical "gives the gospel to the labourers and the earth to the landlords," and then added:

> We differ from the socialists in our diagnosis of the evil and . . . as to remedies. We have no fear of capital, regarding it as the natural handmaiden of labor; we look on interest as natural and just; we would set no limit to accumulation, nor impose on the rich any burden that is not equally placed on the poor; we . . . deem unrestricted competition to be as necessary . . . as the free circulation of the blood. . . . We would simply take for the community . . . the value that attaches to land by the growth of the community.

Such statements left radicals confirmed in their view that George advocated only a slightly modified form of capitalism.

In 1890 George agreed to go on a lecture tour in Australia, drawn to it by its progressive government. It was a triumphal jaunt, but it lasted over three months and so exhausted him that on his return to America he suffered a stroke. He recovered quickly and soon plunged into his last major work, *The Science of Political Economy*. Left unfinished at his death, it is a massive patchwork summary of his economic and philosophic views. One of its most aggressive passages is another attack on professors of political economy. He accuses them of misrepresenting *Progress and Poverty* or treating it as beneath contempt, but he stoops to gratuitous insult when he charges that their criticism results from their loyalty to the "pecuniary interests" that support them.

It seemed to George, as to many progressive-minded individuals, that the century was closing in darkness and that the democratic principles that had triumphed with the election of Jefferson in 1800 were being overwhelmed a century later by the Hamiltonian faith in plutocracy and aristocracy. As his health failed, and especially after the death of Jennie, his thirty-year-old daughter, he came to feel that "life was a strife" filled with as many defeats as victories.

In a surprising display of confidence in George's leadership, several Democratic factions urged him in 1897 to run once again for mayor of New York. Despite warnings by his physician that a major campaign could prove fatal, he felt that it was his duty to run. His motive, he confided to his wife, was that his election would thrust his doctrines into the arena of world politics. At the height of the campaign he made thirty speeches in twelve days. The result was another stroke and his death five days before the election.

Henry George was an evangelist preaching faith not in a religious creed—although he would say, "There never was a holier cause"—but in a single economic measure. A visionary in the guise of an economist, he was dedicated to convincing mankind that the poor could be freed from their bondage and that governments could be financed entirely through one master stroke of legislation.

George's influence came from the seeming simplicity of his proposal and his passionate sympathy for the working classes. Most of all it came at a time when America had been confronted with a race of plutocrats who seemed able to subvert the system to their own advantage. But George's proposals, like most panaceas, were based on unsupported assumptions and an oversimplification of the problems of an industrial society.

Perhaps it was his very lack of formal education along with his experience of toil and poverty that enabled him to perceive the inequity in one of the oldest and most common economic arrangements—the private ownership of land—and to communicate with a larger audience than had been reached by any other social critic except Thomas Paine.


Speaking from a totally different sphere but often equally sharp in their censure were certain descendants of old American stock, especially in New England. Inheritors of the Puritan imperative and the standards of the heroes of the early republic, they saw themselves as defenders of the faith, keepers of the flame, preservers of culture and tradition. In general, they deplored the spread of the acquisitive spirit, political corruption, social injustice, and the ostentation of the new rich.

Although Americans outside of New England, such as Walt Whitman and Mark Twain, occasionally mounted shattering attacks on the idols of the age, the nerve center of most of these critics was Boston. For them that old city was, or had been, the American Athens, with Cambridge the sanctuary of poets and men of letters, and Harvard the mother of scholars and teachers. It was the Olympus where those aging giants Emerson, Thoreau, Longfellow, Lowell, Holmes, Hawthorne, and Whittier still dwelt, the forums where Wendell Phillips, Charles Sumner, and the latest Adams still debated, the pulpits where many of the leading spokesmen of the church held forth, where such master teachers as Louis Agassiz, Asa Grey, John Fiske, Francis James Child, and Charles Eliot Norton passed along their learning, and where such reformers as Thomas Wentworth Higginson, Julia Ward Howe, Lucy Stone, and George William Curtis worked for peace, universal suffrage, and women's rights. It was where *The Atlantic* and the *North American Review* published some of the best writing in America, where authors such as Howells, Mark Twain, Thomas Bailey Aldrich, Hamlin Garland, and the Jameses came as to a sacred shrine, and from which Bronson Alcott, father of Louisa May, sent out his orphic message to the world. It was a region where a farmer might discuss democracy with a college professor, and a blacksmith quote Shakespeare and the Bible.

But the climate in which such men and women flourished had begun to change even before the Civil War. The Boston area itself had been transformed not only by the tremendous influx of Irish and other immigrants, and the spread of factory districts and surrounding mill towns, but by the decline of the clergy, the rise of bankers and businessmen, and the shift in power to New York and other cities. It was out of this setting that the voices of the Brahmin critics rose, sometimes harshly, sometimes righteously or haughtily, sometimes wistfully.

Although a Boston Brahmin brought up in a Beacon Street mansion, Wendell Phillips was so radical in his views that he was long considered a traitor to his class. Because he became, along with Garrison, the most fierce and uncompromising of the early abolitionists, his later career as a critic of American political and social standards has generally been overlooked.

As early as the 1850s, Phillips attacked the "commercial interests" and the materialism of the age. But only when the war was won and the man long reviled as a "ferocious ranter" and a "nigger-stealer" was acknowledged as the most influential figure outside official circles did he concentrate on such issues as the rights of women, Indians—he called Custer a "ruthless savage"—and, most of all, workingmen. The real danger, he wrote in 1869, is that "our laws will be made not by Congress but in the gambling hells of Wall Street."

As keynote speaker at the 1871 convention of the Labor Reform party, he shocked the nation by asserting that the party was willing to accept such a principle as "the overthrow of the whole profit-making system, the extinction of all monopolies, [and] the abolition of the privileged classes." It was hardly surprising that he was labeled a dangerous radical. Undeterred, he insisted that the major threat to republican institutions was the new economic force—big corporations. "Rich men die," he observed, "but banks are immortal and railroad corporations never have any diseases." Ignoring political realities, he advocated a graduated tax that could "crumple up wealth by making it unprofitable to be rich."

After the financial panic of 1873, Phillips, claiming that the government had allowed the banks to control the currency, wrote:

> If corruption seems rolling over us like a flood, mark, it is not the corruption of the humbler classes. It is millionaires who steal banks, mills, and railways; it is defaulters who live in palaces and make away with millions; it is Money Kings who buy up Congress; it is demagogues and editors in purple and fine linen who bid fifty thousand dollars for the Presidency itself.

When the Labor Reform party nominated him for governor of Massachusetts, he advocated making legal tender as good as gold, an inflationary measure aimed at helping the debtor classes. It was a simplistic solution to an extremely complex problem. He was roundly defeated.

Despite his affinities with the Cambridge academic community, its members deplored his radical views and involvement in violent controversies. So when he was invited to give the Phi Beta Kappa address at Harvard in 1881, he retaliated, charging the educators with a "fastidious scholarship that shrinks from rude contact with the masses." It is "very pleasant," he said, "to sit high up in the world's theatre and criticize the ungraceful struggles of the gladiators," letting it be known that but for the ugly smell of gunpowder they would have joined the battle.

A Puritan soldier of conscience, Phillips was unstinting in his sense of responsibility and courage, tireless in his dedication, and merciless in his righteousness. On pure principle he gave up a promising career as a lawyer to devote himself to a dozen causes that often earned him the bitterest vilification and contempt. Trite as the figure may seem, he was a knight forever riding out, sometimes quixotically, to the aid of the disadvantaged.


Charles Eliot Norton came from much the same background as Phillips, but whereas Phillips was a rabid champion of equality, Norton was a rearguard defender of caste and culture. Even in his boyhood Norton was a proper Bostonian. More interested in books than in boys' games—he was never robust—and well-behaved and precocious, he was capable by the time he was ten of passing judgment on sermons and lectures. A clear augury of his concern with class and cultivation was his comment on an aunt's servants: "They are very neat, obliging, and have much more refinement than is common among country people."

The son of Andrews Norton, Dexter Professor of Sacred Literature at Harvard Divinity School, and Catharine Eliot, daughter of a wealthy Boston merchant, Charles grew up at Shady Hill, a mansion on a fifty-acre tract only a mile from Harvard. The Nortons were sufficiently well off to afford a carriage, a luxury in the village of Cambridge, and in 1828, when Charles was one year old, to spend six months in Europe. In England they managed to visit Wordsworth, Southey, and other famous writers. When Charles entered Harvard at fourteen he was already a connoisseur and collector of rare books, coins, engravings, and art objects.

By the time Charles's father graduated from Harvard, in 1807, the Calvinists, still believing in innate depravity, hellfire, and a wrathful God, had been displaced by Unitarians, who saw God as a kind of benign father and Christ as a great teacher. A man of strong opinions—Carlyle called him the "Unitarian Pope"—Andrews Norton was increasingly embroiled in defending Unitarianism against a set of beliefs even further removed from the old orthodoxy—Transcendentalism.

In contrast to Andrews Norton's public conflicts, his family life was one of harmony and attachment. Hardly a week passed without social visits from such Cambridge luminaries as the historian Bancroft, poet and professor Longfellow, and the president of Harvard, Josiah Quincy. Their talk of people and places, of literature and politics was at least as stimulating to young Charles as his college classes. They left him with a love of learning, a sense of duty to society, and a deep respect for the views of an educated elite. The result was a youth with a rarefied set of standards and a patrician code of conduct.

For a young man with such ideals, it may seem surprising that after graduating from Harvard he joined a firm of East India merchants on a Boston wharf. His duties included the warehousing and shipping of merchandise and keeping accounts. Obviously not yet ready to choose a permanent career, he stayed in the India trade for nine years. Although it moved him out of the academic setting, he was surely the only one in the trade who contributed learned articles on archaeology and other subjects to the *North American Review.*

A welcome interruption in his work came in 1849 when his firm put him in charge of a cargo bound for India. During his six-month stay in India he was at first shocked by the gap between the poverty-stricken masses and their lordly British rulers. But in the end he decided that in introducing schools, hospitals, railroads, and similar improvements, English rule had been highly beneficial. On the way home he stopped in Europe and, aided by glowing letters of introduction, was able to meet with Tocqueville, Alfred de Vigny, Alphonse de Lamartine, and other prominent writers and political figures in Paris. But the high point of his trip was a series of intimate talks with Elizabeth and Robert Browning in Florence. It was an early example—he was only twenty-two—of his gift for winning the confidence and friendship of some of the most interesting men and women of his time.

After his return to Cambridge, Norton began to press for trade schools and better housing for the working class. His motives were not entirely humanitarian: the revolutions of 1848 had persuaded him, as he declared in the *North American Review,* that "benevolence is not simply a duty, it is a necessity" dictated "by the most refined selfishness as well as by virtue." Appealing to businessmen, Norton argued that such reforms were cheaper than the cost of coping with pauperism or the vice and crime bred by poverty. On a visit to New York, he found a vivid illustration of this in the contrast between the "reckless wastefulness" of the luxurious new St. Nicholas Hotel and the abysmal squalor of the nearby Five Points slum. "In the heart of a Christian city," he wrote in *Putnam's Magazine,* "it is a shame worse than barbarism."

The horrors of a Five Points "tenement" were hardly a secret. Charles Dickens in his *American Notes* (1842) had described how he had crept up the pitch-dark, crumbling stairs of such a house; and he had written:

> Open the door of one of these cramped hutches full of sleeping negroes. Pah! They have a charcoal fire within; there is a smell of singeing clothes, or flesh, so close they gather round the brazier; and vapours issue forth that blind and suffocate. From every corner . . . some figure crawls, half-awakened, as if the judgment-hour were near at hand, and every obscene grave were giving up its dead. Where dogs would howl to lie, women, and men, and boys slink off to sleep, forcing the dislodged rats to move away in quest of better lodgings.

Eager for action, Norton now drew up a plan for model lodging-houses and persuaded businessmen to invest $40,000 in the venture. Within two years he arranged for the construction of two five-story brick houses in Boston, each building accommodating twenty families at a rent between two and three dollars a week. Although the experiment eventually failed, Norton was understandably proud of it. In its dependence on being economically sound, the undertaking contrasts with that of socialists and other reformers who believed that such enterprises should be supported by society.

Norton had little or no sympathy for such reformers. Indeed, his first book, *Considerations on Some Recent Social Theories,* published anonymously in 1853—evidently to avoid responsibility—is a sweeping attack on the panaceas offered by Charles Fourier, Claude Saint-Simon, and Robert Owen, and such idols of revolutionaries as Lajos Kossuth and Giuseppe Mazzini. They disregard, he asserts, the immutable laws of nature and with blind enthusiasm battle for "misty visions." Sharing a fundamental belief of the evangelicals of his time, he insists that social change must come through the moral improvement and religious convictions of individuals, not through revolutionary action. Believing that the masses still lack the necessary "counsel, restraint and education," he even doubts that a republic is the best form of government. The people, he declares, will grope blindly unless they are guided by the few who have been blessed with the rare genius fitting them to lead. Protected by anonymity, he dares to add, "The old doctrine of the divine right of kings has been supplemented by one not less absurd—the divine right of the people."

Subscribing to a kind of *noblesse oblige,* Norton thought that the revolutions of 1848 would teach the rich to acknowledge their obligations to the people. Despite this insistence on social responsibility, Norton, identifying with a native-born Anglo-Saxon Protestant elite, welcomed the newly formed Know-Nothing party with its blatant nativism and its hostility to new immigrants—in the Boston area mostly Irish—and to Catholics.

Although Norton's book represented a conservative view, it was the work not of an aging cynic but of a well-meaning young man. Its criticism of radical solutions, moreover, came only after numerous utopian communes, ranging from New Harmony in Indiana to Brook Farm in Massachusetts and the Fourierist "phalanstery" in New Jersey, had all failed, some of them disastrously. But the book, appearing at a time when the nation was glorying in its growing power and achievements, was virtually ignored.

Young Norton's views were a curious mixture of a sense of obligation to the people, but with little respect for their intelligence or capacity for self-government, and an utterly unrealistic faith in the altruism and leadership qualities of the affluent and well-born.

After the death of his father in 1853, Norton, financially independent, began a transition from the world of business to social criticism, editing, and teaching. Having published a book, articles, and reviews, he had become known in a circle that included Lowell, Longfellow, Emerson, Parkman, Whittier, and Hawthorne—all kindred New Englanders whose works were in familiar literary traditions. It is therefore surprising that *Putnam's Magazine* should have asked him to review a book of poems by an unknown New Yorker named Walt Whitman. It is even more surprising that a critic of such refined tastes should have described *Leaves of Grass* as "this gross yet elevated, this superficial yet profound, this preposterous yet somehow fascinating book," and declared that the most incongruous elements in it "seem to fuse and combine with the most perfect harmony." His summary of it as a union of "Yankee transcendentalism and New York rowdyism" reveals as much about Norton as about Whitman. A month later he wrote to Lowell that although it had passages that are "disgustingly coarse," and that no woman should read it, it contained the "most vivid and vigorous *writing* . . . [and] great stretches of imagination." It was a prime example of the way Norton's judgment could sometimes overcome his conservative tastes.

Soon after, troubled by poor health, Norton turned over his business affairs to his brother-in-law and left for Europe. Together with his mother and two sisters he went to Italy, drawn not only by the congenial climate but, like so many nineteenth-century English and American expatriates, also by Italy's spiritual and artistic heritage. During this visit, Norton, influenced by John Ruskin's view of art as a reflection of a nation's morality, began to see in Gothic cathedrals an ideal fusion of art and spirituality. Only a supreme combination of faith and fervor, he decided, could have inspired the painting and sculpture of the Middle Ages and moved an entire people to build such magnificent structures. But he also believed, as he tells us in *Notes of Travel and Study in Italy* (1859), that in the Renaissance an increase in opulence, papal corruption, and despotism led to a sharp decline in morals. The result, he said, again echoing Ruskin, was that art, instead of revealing "the beauty of God . . . was degraded to the service of ambition and caprice, of luxury and pomp, until it became utterly corrupt and false." Rome, he wrote, "still stagnates under the superstitious priests."

In his descriptions of the freshness, innocence, and "rough sincerities" of life in the twelfth and thirteenth centuries, Norton appears untroubled by the evils of feudalism, the fierce bigotry of the clergy, and what he himself refers to as "the burnings and the massacres." Like his Puritan ancestors, he seems to have taken the evil in human nature for granted and was simply pleased to find a people who retained "a spark of sweetness and humanity."

Seeing the Renaissance as a gilded rather than a golden age of art because its artists looked to wealthy patrons rather than to God, Norton in effect disqualified all art not inspired by religious faith. But he scorned the religion of America's camp-meeting revivalists because it lacked great leaders and inspired no architecture besides the "bare boards of a Methodist meeting-house."

Drawn to writers and artists guided by moral and spiritual values, he managed on his visits to London to become intimate with John Ruskin, Matthew Arnold, and those fellow devotees of the Middle Ages, the Rossettis, William Morris, and other Pre-Raphaelites. Some even considered him one of Ruskin's so-called satellites. But Ruskin, although eight years older than Norton, thought of his American friend as somehow wiser than himself and certainly his intellectual equal. The extraordinary intimacy of their relationship is evident in his description of Norton as a bright-eyed man with "the sweetest smile," and especially in letters addressed to "Darling Charles" and signed "From your loving J.R."

Returning to the United States after two years in Europe, Norton was struck by the "haste, novelty and restlessness of America," the low level of taste, and the poverty of the arts. So he began, several years before Matthew Arnold's similar challenge to the British, his high-minded effort to persuade Americans to devote more attention to the cultural side of life. Exempt from need, Norton could afford to be contemptuous of what he described as "getting on" in "a ten per cent stockbroking age." With a kind of Puritan belief in the purifying effect of suffering, he saw the depression of 1857 as "hard but wholesome." For a few years financial troubles will, he wrote, "check the social extravagance which had reached a ridiculous excess." It apparently did not occur to him that a depression would hardly seem wholesome to those who were struggling to survive.

Like many otherwise democratic Americans, Norton had an ambivalent attitude toward slavery. He considered it a curse and was outraged by the return to a Southern master of a fugitive slave caught in Boston in 1854. But he also shared the common belief that blacks were an inferior race and not ready for freedom or equality. When he visited a South Carolina cotton plantation in 1855 he found slavery a "moral miasma" as degrading to masters as to slaves. "If I ever write against slavery," he declared, "it shall be on the ground not of its being bad for blacks but of its being deadly to the whites." As usual, he came to a moral conclusion: he saw no remedy but the

> slow progress of the true spirit of Christianity, bringing together black and white . . . and by degrees elevating both classes, the one from the ignorance and brutality in which it is now sunk, the other from the indifference and the blindness of mind in which it rests content. But this is a work of ages. I am losing all confidence . . . that any immediate, compulsory measures would improve the conditions of either masters or slaves.

To abolitionists this must have seemed a resignation to evil, and to slaves an abandonment to their miserable fate.

At the close of 1860, aroused at last by the arrogance of the South, Norton declared that there was no longer time for compromises. Once convinced that war alone could end slavery as well as the rebellion, he became surprisingly militant. "The discipline of steel," he announced, "is what we need to recover our tone." He feared that the "commercial spirit" as well as prosperity had undermined the will to fight, but after the attack on Fort Sumter, he was reassured by the patriotic ardor that swept the North.

Kept by poor health from active service, he began writing articles calling, with Puritan rigor, for discipline, loyalty, and self-denial. He welcomed an appointment as editor of the New England Royal Publications Society, which distributed weekly articles, mainly on war issues, to a few hundred local journals. Even more gratifying was an invitation in 1863 to join Lowell as co-editor of the influential *North American Review*. He proved to be an enterprising editor and even sought to broaden the magazine's audience by encouraging a lighter tone in the contributions.

Norton was thirty-five when he married young Susan Ridley Sedgwick, daughter of a New York lawyer. Although he would always be reticent about his private life, we know that his relationship with her as well as with the six children born to them in the next ten years was close and affectionate.

At first, like many of his class, Norton was made uneasy by the election of Abraham Lincoln. The Illinois country lawyer, he thought, lacked stature, culture, and breeding. But by the summer of 1863, he was praising Lincoln's honesty, simplicity, and goodness of heart. Still later he hailed him as "on the whole the greatest gain from the war." Throughout the war, Norton clung to a conviction that the people would emerge tempered by the ordeal. Provoked by Ruskin's contemptuous dismissal of America's problems, Norton protested to another English friend that Ruskin simply failed to understand that

in spite of all that is wrong and base in our present conditions . . . [and] all the selfishness and conceited over-confidence generated by our marvelous prosperity . . . I believe that we have made an advance in civilization, that the principles upon which our political order rest are in harmony with the moral laws of the universe.

As the nation faced postwar reconstruction, Norton turned to social criticism. He took a leading role in establishing a new weekly, *The Nation,* edited by E. L. Godkin and dedicated to reform. His own contributions in the next few years reveal an ambivalence on several basic issues: he valued social equality but deplored the lowered standards of culture, he appreciated the increased opportunities to amass wealth but decried the extravagance of the rich, and he acknowledged the benefits of democracy but bemoaned the character of its leaders.

There were also ambivalences in Norton's private life. Despite his pleasure in the amenities enjoyed by the Cambridge elite, he was drawn to the simpler life of an earlier, agrarian America. He seems to have found the answer in long summers spent in an old-fashioned country house—it had neither gas nor electricity—in Ashfield, a village in rural northwest Massachusetts. There he enjoyed the country life without its hardships or reponsibilities.

The pressures of editorial duties, writing, and lecturing undermined his health, and in 1868 he again turned to Europe for rest and refuge. He went with his wife, their four young children, and his mother and two sisters, and this time, lulled by the relaxed life on English country estates and in spacious Italian villas, he stayed abroad for five years. In England he established stimulating friendships with Dickens, Darwin, and George Eliot, communed with Carlyle, despite that old man's quirks and violent prejudices, and introduced young Henry James to circles of society that James would explore in a dozen novels.

But Norton was disturbed in England by the gap between the upper classes and the poor, and in an article he sent to the *North American Review* he assailed the cynical attitudes of British capitalists. At the same time, after attending a peace congress in Switzerland, he scoffed at the blind faith in democratic institutions displayed by the radicals at the meeting. There were distinctly Calvinist undertones in his view that as long as man's "moral disposition" remained "vicious," political change could hardly guarantee liberty and peace, no less end selfishness and "evil passions."

Although he lamented the dirt and disease in Italy, he regretted even more the way people were replacing the "delightful individuality" of old houses with the "commercial and trading taste" of New York and Paris. "Happy country! Fortunate people!" he added scornfully. "Before long they may hope for their Greeleys, their Beechers and their Fisks." But in Italy he could still take refuge in his studies of medieval architecture, art, and Dante.

Norton's doubts about social progress were heightened by reports of President Grant's inept appointments. This was particularly discouraging since he had welcomed Grant as a strong, sensible, and magnanimous leader. Soon he was referring to Grant's blunders as "offensive to every right-thinking man." More and more disappointed in Europe as well as America, he sometimes sounded a profoundly cynical note, as when he asserted that anyone "who knows what society . . . really is . . . must agree that it is not worth preserving." But the felicity of his private life could dispel such moods and enable him to declare, "I believe cheerfulness to be part of godliness . . . and of all men I have the least excuse for sadness." A year later, in Europe, that cheerfulness was cruelly shattered when his wife, only thirty-four years old, died a few days after giving birth to their sixth child. We get a touching glimpse of his grief when in a letter to his old friend Professor Child he tells how much he cherished his wife's youthful freshness and how full of promise their life together had been. When he sailed for home in 1873, his record of his many conversations with Emerson, who was also returning on the same vessel, reveals his deep sense of loss. To Norton, oppressed by private tragedy as well as public corruption, Emerson's boundless optimism seemed to belong to another age. His soul, Norton writes,

> received its bent from the innocent America before 1830. He breathed in the confident, sweet, morning spirit of a time when America believed that the 4th of July, the Declaration of Independence [and] the common school . . . were finalities in political and social happiness . . . when our institutions and our progress were the wonders of . . . the Old World . . . when there were Peace Societies, and it seemed to the youth uninstructed by the past as if the Millennium were not so very far off. His philosophy was of necessity one of hope; the gospel of prosperity . . . before General Jackson was chosen President and we had entered on the new and less child-like epoch of our modern democracy.

When he tried to talk to the older man of misery and crime in society and of disorder and ruthlessness in nature, Emerson would not listen. Such a persistent optimism, Norton observed, might be agreeable in an Emerson but was dangerous in a people. "It degenerates," he wrote, "into a fatalistic indifference to moral considerations . . . [and a] disregard for honour in our public men."

On his return to Cambridge, Norton cast about for a post that would utilize his knowledge of the arts. Learning of his quest, the new president of Harvard, Charles W. Eliot, invited him to become professor of the history of fine arts, the first appointment of its kind in America. One member of the Harvard board opposed the choice because he suspected, quite shrewdly, that Norton would preach a "disintegrating skepticism." He did not realize, Norton remarks, "how conservative, how respectful of the old I was." Eliot, an innovative administrator, had already begun to recruit a group of teachers and scholars that would usher in Harvard's "golden age."

So, at the ripe age of forty-seven, Charles Eliot Norton began a career at Harvard that would last almost thirty years and, in his influence on several generations of students, constitute his own golden age. The appointment revived Norton's conviction that he had a cultural mission—to show his students how lacking in the creative spirit America had been and inspire in them "a love of things that make life beautiful and generous." Revealing his shortcomings as much as his gifts as a critic, he told Eliot that the fine arts had in general been the domain of dilettantes who too often approached art from the purely aesthetic side. Much that they wrote, he asserted, was "foolish and ignorant" and neglected the far more important relationship of the arts to political, spiritual, and social conditions. It was the view of a man who needed both a moral and utilitarian justification for his interest in the arts: beauty and sensory delight were not enough. Guided by such convictions, Norton concentrated on the great age of Athens and on medieval Florence and Venice, including their handicrafts. By contrast, in America, he asserted, machinery was reducing every product to a dull uniformity. The crippling effect of such generalizations was evident in Norton's neglect of the Italian Renaissance and in his lack of interest in any later period of art.

In time, Norton's course became one of the most popular in the college, with attendance increasing from a handful of students in 1874 to over 400 in 1895. As he himself knew, many students elected it because it was considered a "snap" course. But a considerable number took it because they enjoyed Norton's caustic comments on American society or because he was a famous scholar and, after a while, the last of the "Cambridge Immortals." "One had to be a hard-headed Philistine, indeed," a student later recalled, "to resist the charm of his stoop-shouldered, husky-voiced but supremely urbane and gentle presence; and a high purity and resolution . . . that flashed through his gentleness at times must have awed even the slothful lowbrow." Others were not so kind. Josephine Preston Peabody, at Radcliffe in 1895, noted in her diary:

Professor Norton lectured in Italian 4 this afternoon. The dear old man looks so mildly happy and benignant while he regrets everything in the age and the country—so contented while he gently tells us it were better for us had we never been born in this degenerate and unlovely age . . . that I remain fixed between wrath and unwilling affection.

Norton was equally critical of contemporary American literature, and especially the new realism. Clinging to an outworn Puritan morality and Victorian standards of propriety, he decried not only novelists who depicted what he considered the degraded aspects of American life but also women poets who "bared their souls to the greedy eyes of the public." But nowhere is his judgment more warped by his prejudices than in his conviction that ignoble qualities in a writer result in ignoble works. He thought that Pope was a liar, Swift simply a cynic, and that Byron, Shelley, Swinburne, and Trollope lacked the "instincts of gentlemen." As might be expected, Wordsworth, Keats, Tennyson, Arnold, Dickens, Browning, and above all Scott passed his character test.

Over the years Norton often lamented the dull conformity in the intellectual life of America. But he was even more discouraged by the low state of politics. Of the seven Presidents between 1865 and 1900, admittedly an unimpressive array, he disapproved of all but Cleveland. He came to dread presidential campaigns. At such times, he wrote to his English friend, Leslie Stephen, he read the newspapers with an "ever increasing dislike of my fellow-countrymen."

Mainly because he viewed the growing labor unrest of the 1880s and 1890s as unruly mob action, he was deeply disturbed by it. He urged employers to improve working conditions, but he bitterly opposed unions and advocated force to break industrial strikes. Similarly, his faith in the principles of democracy was mixed with alarm at its practices. "I have as strong a conviction as you that 'democracy' will work," he wrote to Lowell in 1884, "but it may work ignobly, ignorantly, brutally." His bitterness grew boundless when jingoism swept the country in the 1890s. He saw the declaration of war against Spain over Cuba's struggle for independence as "the growth of a barbaric spirit of arrogance." When a newspaper reported that he was advising students not to enlist, he was harshly attacked in the press and pulpit. One politician declared that he deserved to be lynched; but the cruelest blow was a public rebuke by a former Harvard classmate and a leading senator, George Hoar. When Norton wrote Hoar that he had been misquoted, Hoar replied: "All

lovers of Harvard and . . . of the country have felt for a long time
that your influence [is] bad for the college and bad for the youth of
the country. . . . I am afraid that the habit of bitter and sneering
speech about persons and public affairs has so grown upon you that
you do not yourself know always what you say."

Hurt but unrepentant, Norton's indignation was soon refueled by
what he described as the "bastard imperialism" of the "miserable
war with the Philippines." Characteristically finding a parallel in the
ancient world, he said he could now understand "the feeling of a
Roman as he saw the Empire breaking down and civilization dying
out." The following year, making his own doleful contribution to the
*fin de siècle* mood, he wrote: "The old century is flickering out in ugly
fashion."

Charles Eliot Norton's darker views of American life came not
from any innate pessimism—even his recurrent illnesses seem never
to have affected his disposition—but from a commitment to the hopes
and ideals of the Cambridge circles of his youth and the leaders of
the early Republic. That was why he continued to believe that conscientious citizens must do what they could to raise the cultural and
spiritual standards of the people. There is no reason, he wrote to a
friend, why "we who feel the present darkness should not use every
effort . . . to dispel such part of it as our poor torches can light up."
And much as he deplored the rampant materialism, he acknowledged
that "the spread of comfort, the superb . . . spectacle of fifty millions
of human beings living in peace and plenty compensate in certain
measure for the absence of high culture, of generous ideals and of
imaginative life."

Unfortunately, such concessions were sometimes marred by a note
of condescension. Considering that all but a few Americans, he wrote
to an Indiana newspaper editor, belong by descent to "the oppressed,
ignorant and the servile class, or peasantry," and have "no traditions
of intellectual life, no power of sustained thought, no developed rea-
soning faculty. . . . They constitute . . . as good a community on a
large scale as the world has ever seen."

It is hardly surprising that Norton looked back wistfully to the
New England of his youth. Scarcely a trace remains, he wrote, of the
ideas of those days. "I fancy," he added, "that there has never been
a community on a higher or pleasanter level than that of New En-

gland during the first years of the century, before the coming of the Jacksonian democracy and the invasion of the Irish.'' In the troubling days at the end of the century, he mourned the passing of ''our Emersonian June,'' and the decline from the level of those who created the *Dial* to that of ''this football generation.'' For him, the Emersonian June had given way to Grant's November.

If Norton's intellectual escape was his studies of medieval cathedrals and Dante, his country place at Ashfield was his physical refuge. With a patriarchal benevolence he gave the town a library, sponsored exhibitions of traditional crafts, and collected funds for the local academy by organizing an annual harvest festival. Norton's scorn for the spirit of his time may seem in part an aging man's nostalgia for a world that never was, but his complaints against what industrialization was doing to the countryside were increasingly justified. Long before the rise of conservation movements he joined that master creator of parks, Frederick Law Olmsted, in a long-drawn-out but successful campaign to save Niagara Falls and the Adirondacks, where he had hiked in his youth, from industrial exploitation.

He was equally zealous in promoting the studies he loved, founding and becoming the first president of the Archaeological Institute of America and soon afterward establishing the School for Classical Studies in Athens and its counterpart in Rome. But his principal labors, aside from his teaching, were literary. These yielded a finely wrought prose translation of Dante's *Divine Comedy,* editions of the poetry of John Donne and Anne Bradstreet, and articles on many cultural issues. Because of Norton's respect for the privacy of authors as well as his editorial judgment, Ruskin, Lowell, and Carlyle entrusted the editing of their letters to him. Surprisingly, in view of his distaste for frank sensuality, he also prepared an edition of Donne's love poems. He did expurgate some of the poems, but he anticipated most remarkably the modern homage to Donne, finding in the poems such a ''combination of passion with delicate sentiment; of sensualism with spirituality; of vivid imagination in conception and expression with lively wit and charming fancy, as to set them above all others of their kind.'' Like his response to Whitman, it was proof of a submerged capacity to appreciate genius even when in some respects it offended his moral code.

Norton's nostalgia for an earlier America did not extend to the old religion. His father had taken a major step away from Calvinism when he became a Unitarian. Thus freed, Norton, along with the skeptics among his English friends, turned to agnosticism. In an article in 1868 he called the church an anachronism and boldly urged Americans to become freethinkers and adopt a religion based not on dogma and ceremony but on social service and brotherly love. When Leslie Stephen, the "Godless Victorian," as one biographer has labeled him, sent him a copy of an essay, "Free Thinking and Plain-speaking," Norton called it the most powerful statement of "the rectitude and superior manliness" of those who reject the old faith. Many years later he explained that it was the manliest position because it threw men back on their own resources. Once an intelligent man left God and immortality out of his reckoning, Norton wrote shortly before his death, his motives for virtuous conduct depended entirely on the highest quality in his nature. A call for each individual to rely on his own sense of responsibility, it was a stoic conclusion to an individualist's credo.

After Norton's death in 1908, he was memorialized with affection and respect—and only a few reservations—by Howells, Henry James, and others. But his reputation, dependent on his personal relations and a scattering of books, articles, and translations, has faded. As a worshiper of things of the spirit among a people preoccupied with property and success, he was fated to be seen by some as an anachronism, overly fastidious, and a carping or even sanctimonious critic.

But his admirable qualities are clear enough: a capacity for close friendship with distinguished men and women, a commitment to social service, especially as a teacher, lofty standards of morality, a belief in a religion of brotherhood rather than of ritual, and an active hostility to the commercialization of all values, to the wastefulness of the rich, to unregulated industrialization, and to chauvinism.

But there were, as we have noted, certain ambivalences in his views. He deplored the materialism of the age but hailed the spread of abundance; he criticized democracy for giving rise to mediocre leaders but cherished the freedom and individual development it permitted; he encouraged an appreciation of the arts but was blind to almost all art after the Middle Ages and to works that lacked moral significance.

Torn by conflicting loyalties, he paid his dues to social democracy, but his deepest allegiance was to an intellectual aristocracy.

It was this combination of qualities that accounts for his dual role as critic of the Gilded Age and pioneer missionary of culture. It also makes many of his criticisms of American society as valid today as they were a hundred years ago. In his discontent with what he felt was the spiritual aridity of American life he has been seen as a fore-runner of such alienated spirits as T. S. Eliot, who was himself at Harvard while Norton's influence was still at work there. As a champion of the humanities, he is an ancestor of those who speak out for that aspect of our culture today.

It was a far cry from the patrician scorn aimed at the Gilded Age by a few Boston Brahmins to the saber thrusts of Walt Whitman and Mark Twain. Indeed, both Whitman and Twain repeatedly ex-pressed disdain for the gentility and inhibitions of the Brahmins. Al-though as critics both men were supreme individualists, they shared an antipathy to Puritan morality, Victorian taboos, and the Protes-tant work ethic, and each in his own way celebrated the "natural" and unsophisticated man and the pleasures of the senses. Certainly in their background as sons of relatively poor parents, brought up in country households, with little formal education, and sent to work at an early age, they were of a totally different breed from the Nortons, Longfellow, and Adamses.

But there the parallel between the two men ends: Whitman was born in a house built by his father, a carpenter, in a Long Island farming community. In a family of eight children he was the favorite of his mother, a vigorous woman of Dutch and Quaker ancestry. He would always remain deeply, too deeply, attached to her. When Walt was four, his father, hard-pressed, moved the family to the small market town of Brooklyn. There Walt learned carpentry from his father, but far more important in his development was the fact that Walter Sr. was a freethinker and an admirer of Tom Paine. It would leave Walt Whitman forever free of the sense of sin and damnation that haunted many children of orthodox parents. Thus one of Walt's most cherished memories was of being taken to hear a lecture by that passionate feminist, radical, and veteran of utopian communities, Fanny Wright. "She possessed herself," he recalled, "of my body and soul."

Like most of his peers, Walter left school when he was twelve. But he soon became an apprentice in a printing shop, a liberal education for any alert youth. After a spell as a compositor in New York, he spent four undemanding years as a schoolmaster in various parts of rural Long Island. A tall, large-bodied youth, rather indolent, and unfocused in his aims, he liked to wander on the wide Long Island beaches. But he also enjoyed visiting Manhattan and mingling intimately with workmen, ferryboat pilots, and omnibus drivers, always with a much greater interest in young men than in young women.

Whitman was barely twenty when he began contributing poems and prose to a Long Island newspaper. Still far from the image he would create of a homespun-clad "rough" and a writer of uninhibited, free-form poetry, he dressed carefully and his verse was banal in theme and conventional in manner. After a halfhearted attempt at publishing a weekly newspaper on Long Island, he worked as an editor and reporter for various local newspapers. When the spirit moved him, he was an able editor, but he still often took time off to sample the pleasures of the city. Dressed in a frock coat and swinging a cane, he would saunter along Broadway, fascinated by the surge of traffic, the elegant shops and grand hotels. He could already have said, as he later put it, "I loaf and invite my soul."

As an editor he supported a variety of worthy causes but occasionally he gave way to the prejudices of his time, as when, like the Know-Nothings of the Native American party, he attacked Catholics and the Irish. Pressed for money, he turned to writing fiction, selling to magazines dozens of short stories loaded with sentiment, melodrama, and moral messages. He even ground out a trashy temperance novel, *Franklin Evans; or, The Inebriate,* in which a farmboy falls prey to the gin mills and prostitutes of the big city but finally saves himself from a drunkard's death by swearing off all vices. Although he later termed the book "rot of the worst sort," he praised it effusively in an anonymous review in the *Sun,* a self-puffery he would practice shamelessly again and again. Ironically, the book had a large sale.

Whitman's career as a journalist reached a peak in 1845 when he was appointed editor of the *Daily Eagle,* Brooklyn's leading newspaper. Although he still found time for loafing, he turned out a well-edited paper. Revealing his wide reading, he even managed to substitute excerpts from the work of such writers as Carlyle, Coleridge, Goethe, and George Sand for the advertisements that had cluttered the front page.

After getting a taste of politics while electioneering for the Democrats in the early 1840s, Whitman became active in the party. He took part in patriotic rallies, and, beginning his love affair with the United States as the standard-bearer of freedom and democracy, he approved of the war with Mexico and America's expansionist activities. Like many other Americans in the 1830s and 1840s, he was divided on slavery. Disturbed by what he called the "abominable fanaticism" of the abolitionists, he asserted in an editorial in 1842 that the lives of English laborers starving in their hovels were far more wretched than those of blacks on Southern plantations. But when slavery threatened to spread into the new territories in the West, he campaigned with anti-slavery Whigs in 1848 to elect Martin Van Buren President on a Free Soil platform. Van Buren was badly defeated, and the publishers of the *Eagle*, retreating into conservatism, fired Whitman—because of his radical views, he claimed; because of his sheer laziness, they claimed. Both were probably right.

Providentially, another publisher offered Whitman a post as editor of a New Orleans newspaper, the *Crescent*. Whitman accepted gratefully. Although he held the job for only a few months, it enabled him to savor a city famous for its exotic atmosphere and sensuous pleasures. It also allowed him to hint at a liaison in which, he claimed, he had fathered, then or later, six children. Even if the story was a wild exaggeration or, more likely, a total fabrication, it served as a basis for the poems in which he dwells on passionate relationships with women as well as men.

Whitman returned to New York in June 1848. In that year of European revolutions, he was radical enough to be chosen a delegate to the national convention of the Free Soil party. He also established the Brooklyn *Freeman*, a paper dedicated to preventing the addition of "a single inch of slave land" to the Union. But this foray into political journalism ended within a year, when the most radical supporters of the cause, the "Barnburners," accepted compromises.

A variety of influences, reinforcing his own inclinations, now led

Whitman to create the image of himself as both man and poet for which he would become famous. Filtering down from his mother's Quaker forebears was the belief that each human being is guided by an Inner Light emanating from the Divine Spirit and can speak from "inspiration." From Emerson as early as 1837, in his memorable declaration of cultural independence, "The American Scholar," had come a clarion call for a poet who would express "the spirit of the American freeman," "embrace the common," and explore "the familiar and the low." Even closer to home was one of Emerson's lectures in New York in 1842, which Whitman attended. Emerson declared that the American poet would "worship" in America not as an immigrant but as "Yankee born." He would visit, Emerson went on, "without fear, the factory, the railroad, and the wharf. When he lifts his great voice, men . . . forget all that is past . . . and immediately the tools of their bench, and the riches of their useful arts, and the laws they live under, seem to them weapons of romance. As he proceeds . . . they are filled with cheer and new faith." For the twenty-three-year-old Whitman, this was a prophecy he would forever seek to fulfill.

Finally, there was for Whitman, as for many thoughtful readers, the unsettling works of Thomas Carlyle. Whitman reviewed no less than six of his books in 1846 and 1847 and was deeply impressed by his denunciations of materialism and "mammonism," and even more by his mystical conviction that certain gifted individuals were the spiritual leaders who shape the destiny of mankind. Even though Whitman would later turn away from him because of his attacks on democracy, Carlyle's vision enabled him to see himself as one whose inspired utterances would speak for the people.

Partly because there was much illness, mental as well as physical, in his family, along with his notion that physical well-being was the way to an exalted spiritual state, Whitman subscribed to such fads as hydropathy, or water cure, animal magnetism—whence his famous "I sing the body electric"—and phrenology. He was completely won over by the latter when the Fowler brothers, the leading experts on cranial "bumps," declared that Whitman's head showed him very strong in Friendship, Sublimity, Self-Esteem, Benevolence, Amativeness, and Adhesiveness (fraternal love), only moderately endowed with Acquisitiveness, and at fault only in Indolence, Voluptuousness, Alimentativeness (love of eating), and Animal Will (disregard for the opinions of others). He was particularly struck by the Fowlers' contention that a man could reshape his life by exercising the faculties on his "chart." Pseudoscientific though these theories were, they encouraged Whitman's deliberate transformation of himself into a man he would later describe as "one of the roughs, large, proud, affectionate, eating, drinking and breeding, his costume manly and free, his face sunburnt and bearded, his postures strong and erect, his voice bringing hope and prophecy." It was surely more of an idealized conception of a virile American male than a description of Whitman himself.

Whitman struck corresponding notes about himself in the poems he began to write in the early 1850s. They revealed that, like Emerson and Thoreau, he had come under the spell of the literature of the East. Although neither a mystic nor religious, Whitman began to see great poets as the agents of a transcendent power. He repeatedly experienced what he described as flashes of illumination and a sensation of having created poems in a trance. This may be why he sometimes seems to have recorded a poem just as it first came to him, as though editing and shaping would compromise its authenticity. Such poems must be appreciated, he wrote, as "one enjoys music, flowers and the beauty of men and women."

It is easier to list such influences than to explain how Walt Whitman—as he now called himself—fused them in 1855 into the unique poetic personality he unfolded in the first edition of *Leaves of Grass*. A volume of only ninety-five pages—it would eventually swell to more than 400 pages—it was an unprecedented mélange of rapturous chants, carols, incantations, confessions, catalogs, lullabies and threnodies, self-advertisements, frontier brag, and undigested digressions. It was a spillway of emotions celebrating Walt Whitman as the incarnation of "the divine average" and the democratic spirit, the body no less than the soul, and his love, sexual no less than spiritual, for men as well as women. He wrote as though no poetry had ever been written before. The result was a work that has not lost its aura of freshness and originality and that would free poets, for better or worse, from many of the conventions of their art.

As every student of literature knows, the book was greeted as vulgar, obscene, pretentious, and not poetry at all. We can hardly imagine the reaction of genteel Victorians to such expressions as "Soft-tickling genitals," "love flesh swelling and deliciously aching," "limpid jets of love," and "bellies press'd together and glued together with love." Or, on a broader subject, how could they cope with a poem that, speaking of animals, declared:

> They do not sweat or whine about their condition,
> They do not lie awake in the dark and weep for their sins,
> They do not make me sick discussing their duty to God,
> Not one is dissatisfied . . . not one is demented with the mania of
>     owning things,
> Not one kneels to another nor to his kind that lived thousands of years
>     ago,
> Not one is respectable or industrious over the whole earth.

In six lines he repudiated not only guilt for so-called sins but self-pitying discontent, unbridled acquisitiveness, the religion of the churches, respectability, and the work ethic. Whether it was dedication to his newfound mission as poet and prophet or simply a matter of temperament, he himself was content with the barest necessities, along with the freedom to live as he pleased.

A few years later, in the preface to *Leaves of Grass,* he goes a step further, deploring those who abandon themselves to "the toss and pallor of years of moneymaking with all their scorching days and icy nights and all their stifling deceits and underhanded dodgings," meanwhile missing all "the bloom and odor of the earth and of the flowers . . . and of the sea," and in the end facing death "without serenity." This, he concludes, is "the great fraud upon modern civilization."

The paradox in such eruptions of scorn is that they occur amid his overflowing confidence in American democracy and the common people. Fully aware of this, he makes his famous declaration:

> Do I contradict myself?
> Very well then I contradict myself,
> (I am large. I contain multitudes.)

A disarming but confusing attitude, it would give rise to much of the disagreement concerning his nature as well as his beliefs.

The most remarkable exception to the barrage of condemnation and abuse was Emerson's reaction. Having long hoped for a truly American poet, he hailed *Leaves of Grass* in a letter to Whitman unsurpassed in its generosity and open-mindedness. "I find it," he wrote, "the most extraordinary piece of wit and wisdom that America has yet contributed. . . . I give you joy of your free and brave thought. . . . I greet you at the beginning of a great career . . . and have felt much like striking my tasks, and visiting New York to pay you my respects."

His ego swollen to bursting, Whitman published the letter without Emerson's permission. He then wrote glowing, unsigned "reviews" of the book for three different publications. His justification for such behavior would surely have been that a writer who defies both literary traditions and social taboos must gain recognition as best he can.

Perhaps because Whitman found poetry best suited to chanting the joys of life, love, and freedom, he channeled most of his criticisms of his fellow Americans into his prose. His earliest sustained outburst at corruption, misgovernment, and greed occurs in "The Eighteenth Presidency," a campaign pamphlet prepared in 1856, which he circulated but which was not published until long after his death. Aiming at public officials, he wrote:

Not one in a thousand has been chosen by any spontaneous movement of the people . . . all have been nominated and put through by . . . caucuses of the politicians, or appointed as rewards for electioneering . . . every trustee of the people is a traitor, looking only to his own gain, or to boost up his party. The berths, the Presidency included, are bought, sold . . . and filled with prostitutes. In the North and East swarms of . . . office-vermin, kept editors, clerks . . . aware of nothing further than the drip and spoil of politics. . . . In the South no end of blusterers, braggarts, windy, melodramatic . . . altogether the most impudent persons that have yet appeared in these lands, and with the most incredible successes, having pistol'd, bludgeoned . . . and threatened America into one long train of cowardly concession.

Readers familiar only with the sympathy and love for all kinds of men and women expressed in *Leaves of Grass* will be even more amazed at the scurrility of the attacks he leveled at a President who had made concessions to the South. "Never," he wrote, "were more publicly displayed more deformed . . . snivelling, unreliable, false-hearted men. . . . The President eats dirt and excrement for his daily meals, and tries to force it on the States. The cushions of the Presidency are nothing but filth and blood." Scarcely less savage is his characterization of the delegates to party nominating conventions. They are, he charges, "robbers, pimps . . . conspirators, murderers, fancy-men . . . contractors, kept editors, spaniels . . . jobbers . . . slave-catchers . . . lobbyists, sponges, ruined sports, expelled gamblers . . . crawling, serpentine men . . . the born freedom-sellers of the earth."

Despite Whitman's unauthorized publication of his letter, Emerson visited him repeatedly in New York and referred to him familiarly as "our wild Whitman." In a somewhat less sympathetic vein, he wrote to Carlyle in the spring of 1856; "One book, last summer, came out in New York, a nondescript monster, which yet had terrible eyes and buffalo strength, and was indisputably American. . . . After you have looked into it, if you think . . . it is only an auctioneer's inventory of a warehouse you can light your pipe with it." Later, Whitman, promoting, as usual, his own claims to virility, belittled Emerson as lacking "red blood, heat, brawn, animality."

Two other high-minded New England worthies, Bronson Alcott and Henry Thoreau, also visited Whitman. They were taken aback at finding him sharing a dismal attic room with a mentally retarded younger brother. The room had only a few makeshift pieces of furniture, an unmade bed, and prints of Hercules, Bacchus, and a satyr—a curious trio even if chosen half in jest—on the bare walls. Despite Thoreau's feeling that some of Whitman's poems were "disagreeable, to say the least . . . as if the beasts spoke," he thought him "a great fellow." Whitman in turn found Thoreau an admirable person but, like most literary New Englanders, supercilious and anti-democratic. Emerson shrewdly observed that Thoreau's fancy for Whitman arose from his "taste for wild nature, for an otter, a woodchuck or a loon."

Whitman joined the staff of the Brooklyn *Daily Times* in 1857 and for two years wrote on a great variety of subjects. In the end, a few of his editorials took such a tolerant view of prostitution and of un-married women who breached the sexual barrier that the protests of local clergymen, it was said, forced him to resign. Meanwhile, he was publishing in various magazines a few of the poems that would go into the next edition of *Leaves of Grass*. Of one of them, the incomparable "Out of the Cradle Endlessly Rocking," a Cincinnati newspaper declared that it was "unmixed and hopeless drivel," while a gifted young English poet, Algernon Charles Swinburne, called it "the most lovely and wonderful thing I have read in years."

Whitman now did his loafing at Pfaff's, a beer cellar located under the Broadway pavement at Bleecker Street. Writers, editors, sportsmen, merchants, actors, and actresses, including such sexually liberated women as Ada Clare and Adah Isaacs Menken, gathered there amid a haze of cigar smoke and the odors of Rhine wine, wurst, and sauerkraut. Half a century before the rise of bohemianism in Greenwich Village, it was an expression of protest against the reign of gentility and the philistines.

Although Whitman continued to frequent Pfaff's even after the war began, the days for such dalliance were numbered. He did not enlist—besides being forty-two years old, he was appalled by the thought of firing a gun at anyone. But when his brother George, a captain, was listed among the wounded, Whitman hurried south in search of him. He found George in a Virginia field hospital, recovering from a minor injury. But what he saw of the wounded young men there made him decide to do whatever he could to help and solace them.

Settling in Washington, he supported himself with hack writing and eventually, after pulling political strings, as a clerk in the Interior Department. But he spent all his free time visiting, as a YMCA "soldiers' missionary," the sick and wounded in the scores of hospitals, mostly makeshift, in the city and nearby camps. In the next three years he made, he estimated, 600 such visits and ministered to over 80,000 soldiers from both sides. He brought them everything from fruit and beer to underwear, small change, and reading matter. But just as important was the tenderness and sympathy with which this large, full-bearded, pink-cheeked man waited on lonely, helpless, dying youths, sponging them and dressing their wounds, feeding and comforting them. When he kissed them at parting, as he often did, they clung to him and kissed him in return. The descriptions of suffering and fortitude he later included in his autobiographical *Specimen Days* are among the most memorable that came out of the war.

Whitman's long stay in Washington—it lasted over ten years—was a deeply disturbing experience on two levels, both leading to the realization that American democracy faced many perils and pitfalls. On one level was the agony, physical and spiritual, of the war itself, heightened by the fact that those on one side were defending the right to enslave their fellowmen. On another level was life in the Capital in wartime and afterward. By 1863 Washington had become a vast troop depot surrounded by camps and fortifications. Its population was a bewildering mixture of average citizens, office seekers, profiteers, lobbyists, politicians, prostitutes, good Samaritans, deserters, and the anxious relatives of wounded or missing men. The constant movement of wagon trains, inflation, shortages, and the alternately cheering and frightening news of battles combined at times to reach, in Whitman's words, a "hellish intensity."

In more than forty poems written during the war and assembled in *Drum-Taps* in 1865, Whitman registered the anguish and sacrifice of what he summed up as "America brought to hospital in her fair youth." Compared to the conventional glorification of war, it was a somber and sensitive, if uneven, collection, capped by that profoundly moving lament for the murdered President, "When Lilacs Last in the Dooryard Bloom'd." A peculiarly interesting reaction to the book was an unsigned review in the *Nation,* describing it as "the effort of an essentially prosaic mind to lift itself by a prolonged muscular strain, into poetry . . . a medley of extravagances and commonplaces . . . [with] art, measure, grace, sense sneered at on almost every page." It was written by a twenty-two-year-old critic, Henry James; in later life James referred to the review as an "atrocity" perpetrated in "the gross impudence of youth."

Hardly had Whitman published *Drum-Taps* when a newly appointed Secretary of the Interior, James Harlan, declared that he would cleanse his department of anyone who had disregarded "the decorum and propriety described by a Christian civilization." Obviously alerted to Whitman's poetry, Harlan found a copy of *Leaves of Grass* on the poet's desk and promptly fired him. It was not entirely a misfortune, for Whitman's friends soon got him a more agreeable post in the Attorney General's office.

With his ever-renewed faith in the common people, Whitman was convinced that much good had come out of the Civil War, most of all a renewed sense of national unity. The conflict had demonstrated, he said, that "the unnamed, unknown rank and file" could fight and die for a great principle. Although he detested slavery, the main issue, he insisted, was the survival of the union and the triumph of democracy, the one system that combined "perfect individualism" with control by "the aggregate."

But he had much more difficulty in drawing an optimistic conclusion from the atmosphere of postwar America. Carlyle, in a typically crabbed article in the New York *Tribune* in August 1867, dismissed the Civil War as having been fought for what he described as the empty purpose of freeing "three million absurd blacks." The article aroused Whitman to a long rejoinder, which he expanded into an eighty-four-page pamphlet, *Democratic Vistas,* in 1871. In this long and wandering essay he once again held up democracy as the best hope of mankind, but he also repeatedly erupted into furious attacks on corruption, extravagance, and lack of moral integrity. Although he rejoiced at the spread of prosperity and material comforts, he declared that the soul of man would not be satisfied with these alone. Despite all such advantages, "society in these States," he wrote, is "canker'd, crude, superstitious and rotten. . . . The underlying principles of the States are not honestly believ'd in. . . . We live in an atmosphere of hypocrisy throughout." Bitterly he reported that a friend in the government Revenue Department, who visited cities to investigate fraud, had confirmed his belief that

> the official services of America . . . are saturated in corruption, bribery, falsehood, maladministration; and the judiciary is tainted. The great cities reek with respectable as well as non-respectable robbery and scoundrelism. In fashionable life, flippancy, tepid amours . . . small aims or no aims at all, only to kill time. In business, the one sole object is, by any means, pecuniary gain. . . . The best class we show is but a mob of fashionably dress'd speculators and vulgarians. . . . I say that

our New World democracy, however great a success . . . in materialistic development . . . is, so far, an almost complete failure in its social respects, and in really grand religious, moral, literary and esthetic results.

Turning to New York, he is, as always, enthralled by its "splendor, picturesqueness, and oceanic amplitude," the tumultuous streets and rich shops, but where, he asks, are the manners and arts worthy of a free, rich people? On all sides, he answers, there is "flippancy and vulgarity, low cunning, infidelity . . . everywhere an abnormal libidinousness, unhealthy forms, male, female, painted, padded, dyed, chignon'd—with a range of manners probably the meanest . . . in the world."

His contempt is even greater when he considers America's writers and artists: "Do you call these genteel little creatures American poets? Do you term that perpetual, pistareen, paste-pot work, American art, American drama, taste, verse? I think I hear, echoed as from some mountaintop far in the West, the scornful laugh of the Genius of these States."

These tirades were surely so harsh because Whitman himself was temperamentally unprepared for the threat to the democratic ideal by venal politicians and freewheeling tycoons. Despite such attacks, his faith in the people remained unshaken. They have, he wrote, a latent power and capacity far surpassing that of all the vaunted, history-book heroes. Despite the evils, the misery, and the meanness, there was in every soul "an immortal courage" that would not capitulate. Coming of age in the heyday of utopian and religious visionaries and the afterglow of Jacksonian enthusiasm, Whitman never adjusted to the fact that human nature in America would not prove endlessly perfectible.

The legend of Whitman as a uniquely American genius, a poet of Homeric stature, champion of the common man, prophet of democracy, and celebrant of love in all its forms began with the emergence after the war of several passionate supporters. The first was William O'Connor, novelist, editor, and advocate of abolition and other radical causes. In 1866 he published *The Good Gray Poet*—Whitman was actually only forty-seven—which portrays Whitman not only as a great poet and prophet but also as a noble human being. Almost at the same time John Burroughs, a young clerk in the Treasury Department and later a famous naturalist, published his *Notes on Walt Whitman as Poet and Person,* as worshipful a work as O'Connor's but more discriminating. In England extravagant praise from William Michael Rossetti and other Pre-Raphaelites, from Swinburne, and in France from Turgenev brought Whitman his first international attention. If it seems ironic that such early and unreserved recognition of Whitman came not from the average man whom he championed but from European intellectuals and aesthetes, the explanation in part is that they were culturally and aesthetically free to accept his sensuality and defiance of genteel standards and to see in him a peculiarly American genius.

Whitman's concern with official corruption was now overshadowed by personal calamity: he was laid low by a stroke in February 1873. A few months later he suffered another blow: the death of his mother. How deeply he was still attached to her was evident when he left Washington and moved into the rooms she had occupied in his brother George's house in Camden, New Jersey. There he surrounded himself with her possessions in a pathetic effort to recapture her presence. The episode goes far toward explaining his failure to marry or love any other woman.

Soon Whitman's absence from Washington led to his discharge from his government clerkship. He was now forced to rely mainly on the meager revenue from the sale of his books. This, along with hostile critics who still described his work in such terms as "nauseating," led him to place an unsigned, typically manipulative article in a Camden newspaper in which he spoke of himself as "old, poor and paralyzed," and a victim of persecution and neglect that had wrecked his life. The article set off a strident international debate, with vigorous defenders, many of them British, picturing him as a martyred genius, a golden eagle pursued by crows. His critics retorted that his poetry was garbage and that, far from being an eagle, he was a dirty bird with unclean habits. Although he would never be free from abusive criticism, the debate marked the beginning of a steady growth in his reputation and in a circle of devoted admirers.

His health stabilizing, Whitman was able to give public readings.

At the same time his long liaison with Peter Doyle, a horsecar conductor, having come to an end, he now took up with Harry Stafford, a barely literate New Jersey farmboy, not to mention fleeting associations with other young men. Although in an exchange with an English historian, John Addington Symonds, who was known to have intimate relationships with men, Whitman expressed horror at the imputation that he was a homosexual, the evidence suggests that whether or not the love was consummated, Whitman loved men sexually. The subject is important because the skewed pattern of his life experiences, ranging from his affairs with young men to his intimate nursing of soldiers in wartime, is reflected in scores of erotic passages in his poems. Beyond that, his paeans to universal love and brotherhood were as often amatory as fraternal. It was certainly this vein that caused *Leaves of Grass* to be banned in Boston in 1881 and long made many readers recoil from both the man and his work.

At sixty-five, finding life in the household of his brother George, an inspector in a pipe foundry, no longer tolerable, Whitman at last acquired a home of his own, a run-down house in a working-class district of Camden. There he lived his last years, relying heavily on Horace Traubel, a half-Jewish, half-Quaker youth, as his companion, secretary, and disciple. Whitman dressed in homespun, with a wide-brimmed sombrero, open-collared shirt—trimmed with lace on festive occasions—and the great white beard of his later and most familiar image. Seated in an old chair, surrounded by ragged piles of books and papers, he radiated an air of meditative serenity, a man fully prepared, as many of his poems declared, to welcome death as he had welcomed life.

It is a measure of the Gilded Age that the most eloquent champion of America and democracy, and the most confident prophet of the capacity of the New World to produce a New Man, should have been stirred to some of the harshest denunciations of the aims and spirit of the age. These outbursts may seem to have been only brief lapses from his profound faith in the American character and the American system. But they betray a deep anger at the many who, seduced and corrupted, were disappointing him. These are the protests of a dreamer who cannot bear to be awakened from his dream.

An outwardly indolent man who rarely earned more than a bare living, Whitman was a complete anomaly, a "loafer," albeit an inspired and inspiring one, in a world dedicated to making money, acquiring property, and achieving respectability. Whether by temperament or principle, or both, he himself was satisfied with little better than rags in a time when the hero was one who climbed from rags to riches. He lived, in short, as though he truly believed there was no profit in gaining the world if you lost your soul. In an age that became a byword for prudery and pretense, he was astonishing in his free expression of his innermost urges, and especially his sexuality. Even his approach to democracy was not so much political as emotional and sexual—a longing for a loving brotherhood, a universal embrace. A hundred years later his hopes and prophecies are as far as ever from being fulfilled. But Whitman will be remembered, perhaps more and more wistfully, because in an era marked by the rise of spoilsmen, speculators, and parvenus, he devoted his life to singing of leaves of grass, the joys of lovers, and a dream of democracy.

Mark Twain is perhaps the most striking example of the acute contradictions fostered by the Gilded Age. Samuel Langhorne Clemens was born into a respected but hard-pressed family in a Mississippi River hamlet in southern Missouri in 1835. His mother came of old Kentucky Presbyterian stock and his father began as a lawyer but ended up as a storekeeper. The death of his father sent Sam out to work at the age of thirteen. He spent the next fourteen years as an itinerant printer in New York, Philadelphia, and Cincinnati, and as a riverboat pilot, a footloose western miner, and a journalist in California, becoming, as one editor put it, a "sagebrush Bohemian." But for the remainder of his life he was an eminently successful author and lecturer, living in splendid homes in Hartford and on New York's Fifth Avenue, as well as in European villas and on a huge Connecticut estate.

The contradictions were most conspicuous in his involvement in get-rich-quick schemes and in intimate friendships with a few of the most predatory plutocrats of his time even as he was writing *The Gilded Age,* a book that skewered rapacious speculators and corrupt politicians.

For most of his career Mark Twain was not considered a serious social critic, partly because his humor defused indignation: readers and audiences were amused, not aroused, by it. He was enjoyed as a wit and jester in the tradition of such western humorists as Artemus Ward and Josh Billings. It was also easy to write him off with laughter because his fiercest satires and most pessimistic messages were not published until his later years and after his death in 1910.

Only in those last years did some observers recognize that he had always been such a critic but that his outrageous exaggerations, incongruous digressions, colloquial style, comic dialect, and self-mockery, and, as a lecturer, his deadpan demeanor, drawling delivery, and delayed "snappers" had made him seem simply a humorist and, to the literati, something of a buffoon. Thus, although he first attracted national attention, in 1865, with what he later called "a villainous backwoods sketch," "The Celebrated Jumping Frog of Calaveras County," he was already known in California for his journalistic exposés of corrupt officials. Soon afterward he revealed his satiric gift in reporting on a four-month assignment in the Sandwich (later Hawaiian) Islands, describing them as a Pacific Eden where the gentle natives were happy despite their lack of the white man's commerce, work ethic, "civilization and other diseases." But it was in a travel letter on the islanders to the New York *Tribune* that he gave full rein to his satiric impulse:

> We must annex these people. . . . We can introduce the novelty of thieves, all the way up from street-car pickpockets to municipal robbers and Government defaulters, and show them how amusing it is to arrest them . . . and then turn them loose—some for cash and some for "political influence." . . . We can give them some Barnards [a corrupt New York judge] to keep their money corporations out of difficulties. . . . We can give them railway corporations who will buy their Legislatures like old clothes. . . . We can furnish them some Jay Goulds who will do away with their old-time notion that stealing is not respectable. . . . We can give them lectures! I will go myself.

Just as withering was his "Disgraceful Persecution of a Boy," a "defense" of a youth who had engaged in the California sport of stoning Chinese immigrants. So, too, his first full-length work, *The Innocents Abroad,* covering five months as a correspondent with a group of middle-aged, prosperous American tourists in the Mediterranean and Near East, mixes glowing but more often scoffing descriptions of historic places with gibes at the provincialism and gullibility of the tourists and revulsion at the widespread proverty and religious su-perstition. He erupts constantly into the irreverent humor that would be his benchmark. Thus when an Arab boatman demands eight dol-lars to take the tourists for a sail on the Sea of Galilee, he remarks, "Do you wonder now that Christ walked?" or when, on finding the Holy Land a wilderness, he says, "No Second Advent—Christ been here once, will never come again." Some critics thought *Innocents* crude, but most readers, accustomed to travel books full of decorous clichés, found it completely refreshing.

On his return to America, Mark Twain served briefly in Wash-ington as a private secretary to William Stewart, a senator from Ne-vada, but long enough to develop a view of congressmen that was summed up in his description of them as the only "distinctly native American criminal class." The experience also furnished him with material for the merciless indictment of politicians in *The Gilded Age.*

Mark Twain's transition from a journalist who lodged in boarding-houses and indulged freely in drink and bohemian liberties to a propertied citizen abiding by middle-class conventions began with the success of *Innocents* and his lecture tours, but even more distinctly with his marriage in 1870 to Olivia Langdon. "Livy" was the protected, gentle, high-minded daughter of a wealthy family in Elmira, New York. Her father had built a fortune from a coal and iron business and become a pillar of provincial society. Weary, at thirty-five, of his unsettled existence, Sam Clemens clearly welcomed the guidance of a wife born into the gentry; he was charmed by her caresses and endearments and tickled at being "dusted off" by her, and later, by his three daughters. Although he venerated the purity of well-born women ("I wouldn't have a girl that *I* was worthy of"), the view of a few critics that Livy bowdlerized his works as well as his behavior simply does not square with the evidence: even after their engage-ment, angered by the intensive inquiries the Langdons were making into his past, he wrote to Livy, "I have been through the world's 'mill' . . . and I know it through and through . . . its follies, its frauds, and its vanities—all by personal *experience* and not through dainty *theories* culled from nice moral books in luxurious parlors where temptation never comes." Whatever Livy's influence was, Mark Twain would never give up mocking most of the idols of his time or indulging in whiskey, profanity, ribaldry, and other legacies of his life as a sagebrush bohemian. Indeed, he would not only draw Livy into a more active life despite her frequent illnesses but, with his skepticism, also erode her religious faith.

Even after he had been accepted by the Langdons and attached to their coal barony, Mark Twain made clear that he had not changed his views. In an "Open Letter to Commodore Vanderbilt," he called on Vanderbilt to surprise the country by "doing something right." I don't remember, he wrote, "ever reading anything about you which you oughtn't to be ashamed of," and concluded, "how unfortunate and how narrowing . . . for a man to have wealth who makes a god of it instead of a servant."

Any question about how early Mark Twain arrived at his cynical conclusions about the gods of his time was surely answered by his "The Revised Catechism," which appeared in the New York *Tribune* in September 1871:

What is the chief end of man?—to get rich. In what way?—dishonestly if we can; honestly if we must. Who is God, the one only and true? Money is God. Gold and Greenbacks and stock—father, son and the ghost of the same—three persons in one; these are the true and only God, mighty and supreme: and William Tweed is his prophet.

He spoke with authority, for he himself was already caught up, and would be again and again, in the scramble for quick wealth.

The Clemenses began their married life in an elegant Buffalo home bestowed on them by Livy's father. But they soon moved into an exotically ornate, nineteen-room Victorian mansion—it is still standing—built for them in a suburb of Hartford, a city already known for its prosperous insurance companies and manufacturers of armaments. Their neighbors included Harriet Beecher Stowe, two of Harriet's well-to-do sisters, and the co-editors of the Hartford *Courant*,

Charles Dudley Warner and General, formerly Governor, Joseph Hawley.

At about the same time he published another full-length work, *Roughing It,* an anecdotal, self-mocking chronicle of his adventures and misadventures during the Nevada silver boom and the flush times in San Francisco. It added greatly to his reputation as a humorist, but its very humor made it easy for readers to underrate it as a record of a significant American experience and as a disillusioning picture of the feverish pursuit of instant riches.

Perhaps because Mark Twain's writings seemed to English readers to confirm their conception of America as still a colonial society with a frontier culture, they enjoyed his work as much as did his fellow Americans. Thus his first visit to England was a triumphant one. A distinctive figure with his full shock of reddish hair, huge, down-curling mustache, and western drawl, he was lionized everywhere. He in turn was impressed by the orderliness of English society and its government by a dedicated elite. On his return home he was struck by the contrast between what he had seen in England and an America in the grip of unprecedented political corruption and economic exploitation. In Hartford he discussed these impressions with Charles Dudley Warner. Warner, who had been a surveyor in Missouri and a lawyer in Chicago before becoming editor of the *Courant,* responded so sympathetically that the two men, encouraged by their wives, decided to collaborate on a novel about the new era and the men and women who characterized it.

The result, *The Gilded Age*—it was impressive enough to lend its name to the age—is far more successful as a satire on the spirit of the times than as a novel. Its principal targets were the men and women of postwar America who lived in perpetual expectation that some magical scheme would make them rich. Virtually every major character is the victim of such a delusion: the members of the genteel Hawkins clan live in a miserable Missouri log cabin but dream of the day when a desolate Tennessee mountain tract that "Squire" Hawkins once bought for a song, much as had Mark Twain's father, will be found to contain coal, iron, and precious metals; the Boltons, a highly respected Philadelphia Quaker family who find themselves ever deeper in debt because Mr. Bolton is taken in by every glib swindler who approaches him; Philip Sterling, an upright New England youth who is lured into coal-mining ventures; and Laura Hawkins, a beautiful country girl who, seduced and abandoned by a villainous Southerner, Major Selby, develops all the "feminine wiles" and makes her way as a lobbyist to the glamorous heights of Washington society. But the supreme example of unquenchable optimism, archetype of the "promoter," is Colonel Beriah Sellers, whose glittering schemes bewitch everyone while his family dines on turnips and water.

No one is spared: the politicians in Washington are venal, logrolling, high-living hypocrites; the midwestern settlers wallow in ignorance and squalor; the Quakers, Southerners, and New Yorkers are equally avaricious. Mesmerized by the new financial hocus-pocus called "credit," a speculator brags: "I wasn't worth a cent a year ago, and now I owe two millions of dollars." *The Gilded Age* is a bitter dose only faintly relieved by a conventional romance and stock melodrama. Although often close to caricature, it makes such other novels of the political scene as Henry Adams's *Democracy* (1881) and F. Marion Crawford's *An American Politician* (1884) seem tame and detached. Only *Honest John Vane* (1875), by that pioneer realist in American fiction John De Forest, outdoes *The Gilded Age* in its portrayal of corrupt politicians and speculators.

Even in private Mark Twain declared that he had lost all faith in democratic government and, perhaps recalling the British elite, he inveighed obsessively against "this wicked, ungodly suffrage, where the vote of a man who knew nothing was as good as the vote of a man of education and industry." A similar elitism marked his support of women's rights. In an unpublished piece, "The Temperance Crusade and Woman's Rights," he observed that temperance prayer meetings in front of whiskey shops might seem pathetic, but he understood completely the frustration of women who were allowed no voice in elections or making laws and had long endured jeers and insults in their struggle for their rights while "every ignorant whiskey-drinking foreign-born savage in the land may hold office." He called not only for women's suffrage but for a women's party to wrest control from "the loafers, thieves, and pernicious politicians." If that fails, he wrote, there will be time enough for prayer.

Mark Twain's exasperation with the democratic system would subside from time to time, but meanwhile, as he told his good friend William Dean Howells, "A man can't write successful satire unless he be in a calm judicious humor. I don't ever seem to be in a good enough humor with ANYTHING to satirize it." His solution as a writer was to turn back to the past, to life in the 1840s and 1850s, as in *Tom Sawyer, Huckleberry Finn,* and *Life on the Mississippi,* and to that romanticized refuge of disillusioned American and British writers, the Middle Ages, as in his *The Prince and the Pauper, A Connecticut Yankee in King Arthur's Court,* and *Joan of Arc.*

By the mid-1870s Mark Twain's books, articles, and lectures were yielding a handsome income. This encouraged him not only to live on a scale that put an "almost ghastly" pressure on him but also to begin making risky investments. As though his life were imitating the fiction of *The Gilded Age,* he allowed an inventor named Bowers to gull him into backing the development of a "domestic still" for desalinating water and an "improved steam generator" for tugboats. Bowers, an alcoholic, eventually took off with whatever was left of the investments.

The paradox here is that even as he was enjoying every bourgeois comfort, he was celebrating in his most memorable books, and especially *Huckleberry Finn,* the freedom of his young heroes from the bonds of Victorian respectability. What greater contrast could there be than that between Mark Twain affectionately gentrified by a well-born wife, living in a mansion among the elite of Hartford, served by a coachman, butler, and maids, and a slave to deadlines, and Huck Finn, a homeless, ragged, wayward but self-sufficient young scamp who has fled from all restrictions of family, school, and church in a midwestern village to the boundless liberty of a raft drifting down the Mississippi?

Mark Twain may well have been vicariously challenging all unjust social codes when he has Huck, who is helping a slave escape, face the fact that he is not only committing a crime but also depriving kind old Miss Watson, owner of the slave, of her property. Letting, as Mark Twain puts it, his heart overcome his conscience, Huck decides not to betray the slave, and in a memorable moment declares, "All right then, I'll *go* to hell."

Huck is almost illiterate, but whenever he talks of life, he is as articulate and worldly-wise as Mark Twain himself. It is hardly a crude country boy speaking when Huck tells Tom Sawyer that even though the Widow Douglas is good to him, he can't stand living with her because she makes him go to school and church and talk nice, won't let him smoke or go fishing, prays over him all the time, and gets up, eats, and goes to bed by a bell. It is hardly Huck who concludes, "Looky here, Tom, being rich ain't what it's cracked up to be. It's just worry and worry, and sweat and sweat, and a-wishing you was dead all the time." And there is surely more than a little of Mark Twain in the Huck whose famous closing line is, "But I reckon I got to light out for the territory ahead of the rest, because Aunt Sally she's going to adopt me and sivilize me, and I can't stand it. I been there before."

If *Huckleberry Finn* was an expression of nostalgia for the freedom of an untamed twelve-year-old in the Midwest of the 1840s, Mark Twain's other masterpiece, *Life on the Mississippi,* was a romanticized recollection of the independence, daring, and heroic stature of a pilot in the golden age of the steamboat. From 1857 till the Civil War began, Mark Twain was such a pilot, realizing the dreams of countless youths who had thrilled daily to the arrival of that embodiment of power and glamor, the riverboat. Looking back from the pressures and prohibitions of his life in the 1880s, Mark Twain filled his book with memories of "the grace and poetry" of the great river, the mysteries of a pilot's craft, and tales of legendary river men and remarkable passengers. But he left nostalgia behind when he hailed the progress and "go-ahead atmosphere" of the upper-river towns and poured scorn on a backward South. It was Sir Walter Scott, one of his favorite targets, who set the world, Mark Twain charged, "in love with dreams and phantoms; with decayed and swinish forms of religion; with degraded systems of government, with . . . sham grandeurs, sham gauds, sham chivalries of a brainless and worthless long-vanished society." Only in the South, he goes on, is a "genuine and wholesome civilization" confused with Scott's "Middle-Age sham civilization," and only there is practical common sense and progressive ideas and works "mixed up with the duel, the inflated speech, and the jejune romanticism of an absurd past."

Paradoxically, Mark Twain's humor was motivated as much by sorrow or bitterness as by joy or jocularity. Adding to the paradox, he was troubled by melancholia—in his western days he had even contemplated suicide—and yet he thoroughly enjoyed the pleasures of life. By his middle forties a variety of frustrations left him subject to fits of depression and outbursts of rage sufficient to frighten his children: blocks in his writing regimen, mounting expenses, the conflict between his contempt for the Beriah Sellerses and his itch to make a fortune quickly, and an almost paranoid distrust of business associates. Some of these may explain why a man known as a cordial host and a ready companion in drinking, billiard playing, and poker games should have fallen out with many of his friends and associates. It is just as hard to understand why in later years he often referred to them in the vilest terms, as when he declared that Bret Harte was "a liar, a thief, a swindler, a snob, a sot, a sponge, a coward." Even his reliance on wild exaggeration in his humor hardly explains such assaults.

Mark Twain's sense of frustration was aggravated by the riots and pillage that marked the coal and railroad strikes of 1877. They were evidence, he felt, of the breakdown in democratic government. His response to these events as well as to his personal problems was to flee to Europe for longer and longer periods. A stay in Germany in 1878 left him full of admiration for the respect for law and order and the industriousness and frugality of the people. By contrast, his travels in Italy and France called forth striking examples of his dual view of sex. In Italy his comments on the "indecency" of many paintings and sculptures reached a pitch of prudery when he termed a Venus by Titian in the Uffizi palace "the foulest, the obscenest picture in the world." But it was the sexuality of the French that evoked his most outrageously insulting thrusts. They are, he declared, a filthy-minded people governed by prostitutes, and the "two great branches of French thought are science and adultery." The implication that Americans, and particularly American women, were morally purer required that he block out the licentiousness he had surely observed in his years as miner, pilot, and reporter.

Nor is it easy to reconcile such opinions with the acceptance of the "double standard." This bit of Victorian hypocrisy allowed him to condone prostitution as a necessary evil, regale his male friends with dirty jokes and smoking-car stories, give a men's club in Paris an unprintable talk on masturbation, and circulate in manuscript a work called *1601,* a bawdy "fireside conversation" among prominent Elizabethans. All this may not have been so much an expression of his own sexuality as a challenge to the Victorian effort to deny all sexuality. But the challenge did not extend to what was permissible in literature and art; thus, he declared that *Tom Jones* was disgusting and that *Gulliver's Travels* and *Don Quixote* were unfit for such readers as his Livy. Brought up amid the stale Puritanism of a Missouri village and surrounded after his marriage by Victorian taboos, he responded by deploring any open display of sexuality and by reserving his own forays into bawdry for all-male company. He also kept sexual experiences out of all his books except for the story of Roxy, a slave woman in *Pudd'nhead Wilson* who is a victim of her master's lust, and Laura, whose passion, in *The Gilded Age,* is punished with pain and death.

The irony in Mark Twain's position is that *Huckleberry Finn* was banned by the Concord library—and in other communities down to the present—and that Louisa May Alcott, model author of books approved for young readers, would declare, "If Mr. Clemens cannot think of something better to tell our pure-minded lads and lasses, he had best stop writing for them." Mark Twain's response was to point out that the "moral icebergs" of Concord banned his book but accepted the unexpurgated Bible and a New York *World* strewn with accounts of prostitution, adultery, and abortion.

Late in 1877 Mark Twain stopped work on *Huckleberry Finn* and set out to create a work for young people that would meet the highest moral standards. The result, *The Prince and the Pauper,* set in sixteenth-century England, is a fairy-tale–like story of a prince and a pauper who exchange places. Because no one detects the exchange, it teaches an elementary lesson in the injustice of such class distinctions. But it also demonstrates that when Mark Twain retreated into historical romance he lost much of the bite and exuberance that had made him famous.

He also allowed himself to be distracted from *Huckleberry Finn* by much more alien enterprises. Believing that his books would appeal to readers who never entered a bookstore, he turned to Frank Bliss, a Hartford subscription book publisher. Bliss's door-to-door salesmen reached people who had few books of any kind. Although almost all of Mark Twain's books had been phenomenally successful—*The Innocents Abroad* sold 100,000 copies within two years—Mark Twain was not satisfied with his share of the profits. So he became a director in Bliss's company, and finally, under the delusion that an author would know how to sell books, he established his own subscription company headed by his nephew, Charles L. Webster. His major publishing achievement was securing the rights to Grant's memoirs. After meeting Grant in 1877, he was especially proud that he, a Confederate irregular who had quit after two weeks of utmost misery, had become an intimate of the greatest American military hero. When he finally won the rights, he was overwhelmed by his success. But it was a triumph that would not only cause him to overexpand his publishing company but also deflect him from his own writing.

Far more disastrous was his conviction that he could make a fortune by investing in some new mechanical marvel. Enthralled, like almost everyone else, by such man-made miracles as the telegraph, telephone, locomotive, sewing machine, rotary press, and typewriter, he allowed this obsession to waste not only his finances but his time and spirit. His worst misjudgment was a fifteen-year infatuation with a typesetting machine. Spurred by his own experience with the tedium of typesetting by hand, he began his ill-fated commitment in 1880 by investing $5,000 in a typesetter being developed by James M. Paige, a gifted but erratic inventor. Fascinated by its sensitivity and complexity—it had 18,000 parts—on the rare occasions when it worked, he was forever estimating the millions it would earn. Despite his sympathy with workingmen, he boasted, only half in jest, that the Paige machine would do the work of a crew of men and would, moreover, not get drunk or join a union. The result was that in the next dozen years he was constantly involved in seeking capital for the project and in arranging demonstrations, which usually failed because too many parts were too fragile. Only after he had sunk no less than $190,000 in it and drained his publishing house did he admit that he had made a fearful mistake. With the bitter wisdom of experience he later observed that there were two occasions when a man should not speculate: "When he can afford it and when he can't."

In 1891, seeking a treatment for Livy's ailments, the Clemenses again went off to Europe. They would remain away for much of the next nine years, generally sojourning in fashionable spas and elegant villas. As Mark Twain left America in body, so in *A Connecticut Yankee in King Arthur's Court* he left it in spirit. On the surface it is an amusing fantasy about Hank Morgan, a superintendent in the Colt arms factory in Hartford who is knocked unconscious, wakes up in sixth-century England, and through his mastery of mechanical wonders becomes King Arthur's prime minister. Mark Twain uses the Yankee's viewpoint for a merciless scourging of kings, nobles, churchmen, and knight errantry as well as a stark picture of the misery of the masses. In the first note he made for the book, in 1884, he had a typically comic vision of it:

> Dream of being a knight errant in armor in the middle ages. Have the notions and habits of thought of the present day mixed with the necessities of that—No pockets in the armor. No way to manage certain requirements of nature. Can't scratch. Cold in the head—can't blow—can't get at handkerchief, can't use iron sleeve. Iron gets red hot in the sun—leaks in the rain, gets white with frost and freezes me solid in winter. Suffer from lice and fleas. Make disagreeable clatter when I enter church. Can't dress or undress myself. Always getting struck by lightning. Fall down, can't get up.

But by the time he finished the book five years later, the humor had petered out. The Yankee, frustrated by the subservience of the people, abandons his effort to introduce democracy and social justice, wrecks the mechanical systems he had installed, and declares that what he has seen has made him ashamed of the human race. Bitter as the Yankee's conclusion may seem, it was as nothing, Mark Twain wrote to Howells, to what he would say if he were to write the book over again. Such thoughts, he said, "burn in me; and they keep multiplying; but now they can't ever be said. And besides, they would require a library—and a pen warmed up in hell." It was only a sample of the pessimism that increasingly marked his outlook in the last twenty years of his life.

Taking the line of least resistance, Mark Twain now set still another tale, *Pudd'nhead Wilson,* in the Missouri of his boyhood. The story of a sensitive slave woman who substitutes the baby she has borne her master for one of his own, it strikes at the monstrous injustice of slavery based on skin color. But its picture of the inhumanity, arrogance, and greed of the master race leaves little room for the humor and spirit that distinguish *Tom Sawyer* and *Huckleberry Finn*. Its dark undertones are reinforced by such pronouncements under the chapter heads as "All say, 'How hard it is that we have to die'—a strange complaint to come from the mouths of people who have had to live," and "It was wonderful to find America, but it would have been more wonderful to miss it."

Mark Twain wrote *Pudd'nhead Wilson* between trips he made back to America in attempts to stave off bankruptcy. He would have failed, particularly during the financial panic of 1893, had not Henry H. Rogers, next to Rockefeller in the mighty Standard Oil trust, helped him out. Rogers was an oil baron who eliminated competitors ruthlessly—they called him "Hell-Hound Rogers"—but a cultivated man and a generous friend. He not only liked Mark Twain but admired him, and the writer in turn would later say, "He is not only the best friend I ever had, but is the best man I have ever known." Realizing that Mark Twain was worrying himself sick, Rogers persuaded him to declare himself bankrupt. Livy was appalled at the prospect even though her husband's business friends assured him there was little of the disgrace that was still associated with bankruptcy in Europe. But Livy, with Rogers agreeing, did insist that her husband, as a world-famous author, must make every effort to pay off his creditors.

Mark Twain's failure in business, along with illness, advancing age, and deaths in his family, seems to have led to a deepening loss of purpose and hope. His critics also believe that his hobnobbing with Rogers, Carnegie, John Mackay of Comstock-lode fame, and other moguls in their exclusive clubs and on their yachts led to a muffling of his outbursts against the business buccaneers. In support of this they could quote his own repeated observation: "Tell me where a man gets his cornpone and I'll tell you what his opinions are." But his defenders have pointed out that Rogers saved him from ruin. They also could contend that he continued, albeit mostly in private, to lash out at Gould, Rockefeller, and their like, and to say to his friend Joseph Twichell, "Money-lust has always existed, but not in the history of the world was it ever a craze, a madness, until your time and mine."

Of the three works Mark Twain completed in this period, two, *Tom Sawyer Abroad* and *Tom Sawyer, Detective,* were uninspired attempts to cash in on the fame of earlier books. In view of his increasing cynicism, the third, *Personal Recollections of Joan of Arc,* may seem, in its glorification of a peasant girl's piety, purity, and self-sacrifice, surprising. But the very magnification of Joan's virtues underscores the cruelty of the degenerate nobles and priests who betray her. It is an inverted fairy tale in which a saintly maiden, instead of being saved by a handsome prince, is destroyed by wicked witches. It is also a Victorian tribute to an ideal, but quite sexless, woman.

Since paying off his creditors had become a matter of honor, Mark Twain started in 1895 on a year-long lecture tour around the world. Everywhere, from Australia to India to South Africa, he drew capacity audiences. It was an immensely exhilarating experience, but by the time he reached London on his way home he was exhausted. In London, too, he got word that his beloved daughter Susy was ill. He and Livy sailed at once but were still at sea when a cable informed them that Susy had died of meningitis. She was twenty-four years old.

Mark Twain never got over that blow. With masochistic intensity he blamed himself for neglecting her. He asserted that he had long hated life but that now he was indifferent to it. "It is a horrible world," he insisted. "It is hell; the true one." Coupled with the fact that Jean, his youngest daughter, had been diagnosed at the age of twelve as having epilepsy, it convinced him that an evil spirit was pursuing his family. Livy, declining into invalidism, often refused to see anyone, including her husband. He felt guilt for having shaken her faith, but when she wanted to turn to God for help, he burst out that the universe was ruled by some malign thug. But such moods would pass and he would then tell her not to mind anything he said except that he loved her.

His principal relief from attacks of despondency was writing. One result was *Following the Equator,* an elaborate account of the tour. Its touches of humor are counterbalanced by sardonic descriptions of the efficiency with which whites had killed off the aborigines in such places as Australia and Tasmania, and by such statements as "No tribe, however insignificant, and no nation, however mighty, occupies a foot of land that was not stolen," and "The secret source of humor itself is not joy but sorrow. There is no humor in heaven."

But these were only hints of the nihilistic views and nightmarish visions he was recording in sketches and stories, some of which he himself thought were too shocking to publish. In one of these, "Man's Place in the Animal World," he declares that of all animals only man is guilty of making war, of hypocrisy, envy, slaughter for religion's sake, killing for sport, oppression of the poor, accumulating, if he is rich, more than he can use, and, worst of all, a "moral sense" that enables him to distinguish good from evil and therefore to do evil consciously. In our evolution, he concludes, we have degenerated from the "higher animals" till we have reached "the bottom stage of development. . . . Below us—nothing." It may well have been the morbid examples he gives of man's cruelty and of the diseases that make man "a basket of festering offal" that kept him from publishing it.

But it was a step toward *What Is Man?*, a dialogue in which a wise "Old Man" tells a naïve "Young Man" that man is a machine, entirely determined by heredity and environment. Man seeks only to secure his own approval and displays such qualities as self-sacrifice, heroism, and kindness only for his own spiritual comfort. When the youth protests that this degrades man to a "nobody" and makes life not worth living, the Old Man denies it and asserts, surprisingly, that "inborn temperament" ultimately determines whether one will be happy or not. Although *What Is Man?* jolts and challenges, its view of man as a machine is a reduction to absurdity, and its turnabout conclusion that individual temperament can overcome external influences virtually cancels its determinist thesis. Despite this conclusion, Livy detested the work so thoroughly that he did not publish it until after her death, and then privately.

As the century drew to a close and the United States took on more of the "white man's burden," Mark Twain found that what he had said of the atrocities committed by whites in Australia and Tasmania applied just as well to their racist counterparts in America. In "The United States of Lyncherdom," he lashed out at the lynch mobs of the South and described, with shock, the way women and children flocked to see the burnings and the butchery. He was equally disturbed by the actions of American missionaries in China and American soldiers in the Philippines. He created a furor when, in "To the

Person Sitting in Darkness,'' he derided a respected missionary who reported how lenient he had been in extracting a thirteenfold indemnity from Chinese peasants for the Chinese who had been killed by Boxers rebelling against foreign intruders. And he quoted American soldiers who boasted of bayoneting wounded Filipino guerrillas. "Extending the Blessings of Civilization to our Brother who Sits in Darkness," he wrote, "has been a good trade and has paid well. . . . And there is money in it yet, if carefully worked. . . . The Blessings-of-Civilization Trust . . . is a Daisy. . . . But Christendom has been playing it badly of late years."

But Mark Twain's most chilling comment on both American and British expansionism was the greeting to the twentieth century he published in the New York *Herald* on December 30, 1900: "I bring you the stately maiden named Christendom, returned bedraggled from pirate raids in Kiao-Chou, Manchuria, South Africa and the Philippines, with her soul full of meanness, her pocket full of boodle, and her mouth full of pious hypocrisies. Give her soap and towel but hide the looking-glass."

Not long afterward, when Theodore Roosevelt decried the use of the motto "In God We Trust" because coins carried the name of God into improper places, Twain observed: "It was a beautiful motto. . . . I don't believe it would sound any better if it were true," and, he went on, since the Civil War, the country has not trusted in God but in "the Republican Party and the dollar—mainly the dollar." A parallel kind of cynicism filtered into his fiction, most conspicuously, among his published works, in "The Man that Corrupted Hadleyburg" and "The $30,000 Bequest." In the first, a stranger seeking revenge for a rebuff he had suffered in Hadleyburg uses a ruse to make all the town's leading citizens reveal their shameless greed. In "The $30,000 Bequest" a respected couple learn that they will come into a $30,000 legacy on the death of a relative who lives at a distance, but only if they never inquire about him. Their hopes and plans soar uncontrollably. They make imaginary investments that lead them to live far beyond their means. Years later they learn that the relative died penniless. Shamed and shattered, they waste away. Like the Hadleyburg story, it is a sermon by a man who knows how corrupting is the lure of easy money and believes that everyone is susceptible to this infection.

But it was in *The Mysterious Stranger,* not published until 1916, that Mark Twain fused fantasy with an utterly nihilistic view of man and life. In a town in Germany in the 1590s, an attractive young stranger approaches a boy, Theodor, and his friends, medieval counterparts of Tom Sawyer, and convinces them by miraculous feats that he is an angel, nephew of that fallen angel Satan. He fascinates the boys with his supernatural powers and his insights into the follies of mankind. He uses the townspeople as examples of much the same faults and vices Mark Twain describes in *What Is Man?* No sane person can be happy, the stranger asserts, when he sees what a fearful thing life is. But the stranger's last words are the most desolating: life is only a grotesque dream; there is no God, no universe, no human race, only vacant space. And you, he says to Theodor, ''are but a thought . . . wandering forlorn among the empty eternities.'' As the stranger vanishes, the boy is appalled, knowing that ''all he had said was true.'' So intense had Mark Twain's pessimism become that where his alter ego in *What Is Man?* was simply a worldly-wise old man, here his spokesman is more like a god. His standards are meant for angels, not earthlings, and a sensitive youth would surely have been more impressed by his powers than his message.

When Mark Twain came home in 1900, he was greeted as a genius who was also that rarity in a commercial age, a man of utmost honor in business. Because his Hartford home now had too many heartbreaking associations, he moved his family to an apartment in New York and then into a mansion overlooking the Hudson at Riverdale, just north of the city. Although he still could not resist sinking a fortune in Plasmon, a protein food concentrate promoted as a cure for a dozen ailments, or investing in a ''spiral hatpin,'' he was buoyed by an income of $100,000 a year and a flood of lecturing offers. With Livy's health somewhat improved, and Clara, his second daughter, pursuing a career as a concert singer, he felt free to indulge in a round of banquets and speeches, vacations in Bermuda, and cruises on Rogers's yacht. A magnificent fete on his seventieth birthday and honorary degrees from various universities, including one that brought the onetime mining-camp bohemian to Oxford, cheered him immensely, but family problems and illness continued to plague him:

Livy's health declined again in 1902 and she died two years later. Clara suffered a nervous breakdown, and Jean went from sanatoriom to sanatorium before her death in 1909.

Reports of new and old imperialist outrages added to Mark Twain's alienation. He attracted wide attention in 1905 with a blast at King Leopold's exploitation and massacres of his black subjects in the Belgian Congo and a call for a holy war to end Czar Nicholas's "insane" enslavement of the Russian people. But in a few instances prudence won out. Thus when he wrote "The War Prayer," asserting that a people who prayed for victory were begging God to help in bringing death and desolation to other human beings, he did not publish it for fear that it would prove too shocking. "I have told the whole truth in that," he remarked to a friend, "and only dead men can tell the truth in this world."

Less understandable was his behavior when Maxim Gorki, Russian short-story writer and playwright, came to America in 1906 to win support for Russian revolutionists. Mark Twain began by speaking at a dinner for Gorki and announcing plans for a fund-raising banquet. But when he learned that the woman with Gorki was his mistress—Gorki was separated from his wife—he hastily abandoned his sponsorship of the visitor. "I am a revolutionist—by birth, breeding, principle, and everything else," he told reporters, but whereas laws can be evaded, "an openly transgressed custom brings sure punishment."

Despite this conclusion, in his last important work, *Letters from the Earth,* written in 1909, he was mercilessly critical of conventional attitudes toward sexuality. He may seem to have again bowed to prejudice when he did not publish the work, but it was a frontal attack not only on prudery but on religion, the Bible, and the traditional conception of God. The spokesman for Mark Twain in these pages is the archangel Satan. Having heard that God has created a place called Earth, Satan visits it in order to report on a creature called man. The first strange practice he notes is that man prays daily to God even though his prayers are never answered. Although God visits every kind of affliction on them, Christians call him "our Father." In addition, religious wars have spilled more innocent blood than all political wars. Can you therefore believe, Satan asks, that this "moral bankrupt" is a teacher of meekness and righteousness? The deity, Satan continues, brought life and death to the world. Life was "a fever-dream made up of joys embittered by sorrows, pleasure poisoned by pain. . . . No intelligent person would consent to live his life over again. His or anyone else's.''

Restrictions imposed by Mark Twain's surviving daughter, Clara, held up publication of the book until well after his death in 1910, perhaps as much because of its startlingly candid comments on sexuality as on religion. The "Gay Nineties" had brought a relaxation of sexual prohibitions among sophisticates and a few bohemians, but Clara was no more willing than her father to challenge lingering taboos. Satan challenges such a taboo when he observes that man has imagined a heaven lacking "the supremest of all delights . . . sexual intercourse.'' The very thought of it, he says, sets a man wild. Although God grants each individual his own temperament, the Bible forbids adultery indiscriminately. It makes no distinction, Satan writes, between "the excitable goat . . . that has to have some adultery every day or fade and die; and the tortoise, that cold calm puritan, that takes a treat only once in two years and then goes to sleep in the midst of it.'' Such sweeping prohibitions, Satan reports, also fail to consider that woman's capacity for sex is unlimited: from the age of seven till she dies she is "ready for action and competent. As competent as the candlestick is to receive the candle . . . [and] she wants that candle—yearns for it . . . as commanded by the law of God in her heart.'' But man is competent only from about sixteen to sixty. Finally, even though man "never sees the day he can satisfy more than one woman, [whereas] no woman ever sees the day she can't . . . put out of commission any ten masculine plants . . . put to bed to her,'' man comes to this astonishing conclusion: "The Creator intended the woman to be restricted to one man.''

If *Letters from the Earth* sometimes seems too brash and too flippant to be taken seriously, the fact that Mark Twain did not intend to publish it in his lifetime freed him to write as frankly as he pleased. What it does demonstrate is that even though it was written only a year before his death, he was still in command of a devastating skepticism and an endlessly imaginative sense of humor.

The secrets of Mark Twain's enduring appeal are many: in the face of prohibitions and taboos, especially among the genteel, he celebrated the free and venturesome life and the pleasures that, he asserted, were sanctioned by the laws of our nature; he expressed even his darkest views with an infectious exuberance, making millions laugh even as he burlesqued their faults and delusions and championed their victims, whether blacks, Chinese, Jews, or Pacific Islanders. He gave average Americans the satisfaction of seeing one of their own explode the pomp, cruelty, and corruption of kings, congressmen, and Carnegies. How gratifying it was for an ordinary citizen to laugh through a lecture or book in which an aggrieved stranger showed up the leading citizens of Hadleyburg, or a Connecticut Yankee outwitted King Arthur's chief wizard!

To those who are troubled by the inconsistencies in his views, we may point out that he himself said, "We all do no end of feeling and we mistake it for thinking." It is pointless to challenge the logic or the contradictions in such works as *What Is Man?* or *The Mysterious Stranger.* They are the protests of a sensitive and idealistic man against the shortcomings of mankind, the indifference of God, and the miseries of the world. If he had totally despaired, he could hardly have written so provocative and spirited a book as *Letters from the Earth* at the age of seventy-four. These are not studies in philosophy but cries of the heart.

If Mark Twain seems more and more to have magnified the disappointments and misfortunes that other people as well as he himself suffered, that in a way is a measure of his sympathy with a world of men and women who, he felt, were in the grip of circumstances beyond their control. He insisted that this view gave him no sense of intellectual or spiritual superiority. Thus when he declared, "The human race is a race of cowards," he immediately added, "and I am not only marching in that procession but carrying a banner."

But we should not be misled: he was the master of a very special power—to riddle folly with ridicule and to light up the darkness with laughter. The Mark Twain who began as "the wild humorist of the Pacific slope" had become half a century later the most famous of American writers, compared by critics to Voltaire, Cervantes, and Swift.

# EPILOGUE

By 1890 the Gilded Age had wrought far greater changes in American life than any other period in the nation's history. Even those in rural areas whose daily life seemed much like that of their forefathers were affected by it, sometimes in ways too subtle to measure. Politically they had long since learned the virtues and advantages of democracy, but the revelations of corruption, especially after the Civil War, made them aware that their system had its own pitfalls and problems.

In religion the age displaced the unyielding Puritanism of a Cotton Mather with the flexible creed of a Henry Ward Beecher. It substituted the goal of success for a hope of heaven, and it banished the fear of hell but bowed to the force of social approval, propriety, and respectability.

In the world of work, the rise of industry and commerce moved the majority of Americans from country to city and from work on farms and in crafts to factories and offices. It spread prosperity but widened the gap between Millionaires Row and the Five Points slum. It gave rise to captains of industry, the moving force behind the phenomenal growth of railroads, foundries, mines, oil wells, and mills, but it also let loose those masters of cutthroat competition, the robber barons.

In many fields it let men, women, and children labor like slaves, but it also heard the first cries of protest from unions, reformers, and a few forerunners of the muckrakers and radicals of the Progressive

Era. Its get-rich-quick spirit lured many into a feverish scramble for gold and an unchecked exploitation of natural resources, but the Gold Rush petered out and a few brave souls began a call for conservation. It introduced the machines that made goods and services more available to almost everyone, but it sometimes found them as much masters as servants.

To the violence of frontiersmen and desperadoes, it added the violence of mining-town roughs, vigilantes, city gangs, and street rioters. In the name of manifest destiny, it made war on Mexico and annexed Texas and California. It tolerated lynchings, savaged the Indians, and discriminated against Chinese, Jews, and others. But it also made an immeasurable sacrifice to free the slaves. And it opened wide its gates to the oppressed and disadvantaged everywhere. It fused a hundred different peoples into a new breed. It nurtured a ''Boss'' Tweed but also an Abraham Lincoln.

It sought to supplement charity with social services and humanitarian reforms, and it replaced the one-room schoolhouse with a multitude of public schools, colleges, museums, and libraries. It treated women as household servants or as idols on pedestals, denying both their abilities and their sexuality, letting men rule the world and, when they chose, go off to saloon, brothel, or, as sensational scandals revealed, trysts with willing women. But it also saw the brave beginning of a century-long struggle for women's rights.

It censored books, paintings, and sculpture while favoring sentimental romance and derivative art, yet gave rise to Whitman, Emerson, Thoreau, Melville, Henry James, Howells, Emily Dickinson, and Mark Twain as well as Homer, Inness, Ryder, Eakins, and Whistler. It fell for a P. T. Barnum but also made room for a William James. In building it inspired gimcrackery and imitation palazzos but also the soaring majesty of the Brooklyn Bridge and the beauty of Frederick Olmsted's parks.

In sum, America in the Gilded Age blundered and triumphed, forged forward and staggered back, grew great but with formidable flaws. As anyone can see, it marked the beginnings of much that is America today, for better or for worse.

# SELECT
# BIBLIOGRAPHY

Adams, Charles Francis, Jr. *An Autobiography*. Boston, 1916.

Adams, Charles Francis, Jr., and Henry Adams. *Chapters of Erie and Other Essays*. Boston, 1871.

Adams, Henry. *Democracy: An American Novel*. New York, 1880.

——. *The Education of Henry Adams*. Privately printed, 1906; Boston, 1918.

Andrews, Kenneth R. *Nook Farm: Mark Twain's Hartford Circle*. Cambridge, Mass., 1950.

Andrews, Wayne. *Architecture, Ambition and Americans*. New York, 1955.

Andrews, William L. *Sisters of the Spirit: Three Black Women's Autobiographies*. Bloomington, Ind., 1986.

Banner, Lois W. *Elizabeth Cady Stanton: A Radical for Woman's Rights*. Boston, 1980.

Bari, Valeska, ed. *The Course of Empire: First-hand Accounts of California in the Days of the Gold Rush*. New York, 1931.

Barker, C. A. *Henry George*. New York, 1955.

Beecher, Henry Ward. *Autobiographical Reminiscences,* ed. T. J. Ellinwood. New York, 1898.

——. *Lectures and Orations,* ed. N. D. Hillis. New York, 1913.

——— . *Twelve Lectures to Young Men.* New York, 1879.

Beecher, Lyman. *The Autobiography of Lyman Beecher,* ed. Barbara M. Cross. Cambridge, Mass., 1961.

Bernard, Jacqueline. *Journey Toward Freedom: The Story of Sojourner Truth.* New York, 1987.

Boardman, Fon W., Jr. *America in the Gilded Age, 1876–1900.* New York, 1972.

Boynick, David K. *Pioneers in Petticoats.* New York, 1959.

Brandon, William. *The Men and the Mountain: Frémont's Fourth Expedition.* New York, 1955.

Brooks, Van Wyck. *New England: Indian Summer.* New York, 1940.

Broun, Heywood, and Margaret Leech. *Anthony Comstock: Roundsman of the Lord.* New York, 1927.

Browder, Clifford. *The Wickedest Woman in New York: Madame Restell, the Abortionist.* Hamden, Conn., 1988.

Brown, Rollo Walter. *Lonely Americans.* New York, 1929.

Bruff, J. Goldsborough. *Gold Rush: The Journals, Drawings and Other Papers,* ed. G. W. Read and Ruth Gaines. New York, 1944.

Bryce, James. *The American Commonwealth.* New York, 1888.

Buck, Franklin A. *A Yankee Trader in the Gold Rush: The Letters of Franklin A. Buck.* Boston, 1930.

Carnegie, Andrew. *The Gospel of Wealth.* Cambridge, Mass., 1962.

Carpenter, Francis, ed. *Carp's Washington.* New York, 1860.

Cashman, Sean Dennis. *America in the Gilded Age.* New York, 1984.

Catton, Bruce. *The Centennial History of the Civil War,* 3 vols. New York, 1961, 1963, 1965.

Chapman, John Jay. *Memories and Milestones.* New York, 1915.

Chesnut, Mary Boykin. *A Diary from Dixie,* ed. B. A. Williams. Boston, 1969.

Clark, Clifford E., Jr. *Henry Ward Beecher: Spokesman for a Middle-Class America.* Urbana, Ill., 1978.

Clews, Henry. *Fifty Years on Wall Street.* New York, 1908.

Curtis, George William. *The Potiphar Papers.* New York, 1853.

Dana, Charles A. *Recollections of the Civil War.* New York, 1898.

De Forest, John W. *Honest John Vane.* New York, 1875.

——— . *Miss Ravenel's Conversion from Secession to Loyalty.* New York, 1867.

DeVoto, Bernard. *The Year of Decision: 1846.* Boston, 1943.

Dickens, Charles. *American Notes.* London, 1842.

Dorsey, Leslie, and Janice Devine. *Fare Thee Well: A Backward Look at Two Centuries of Historic American Hostelries, Fashionable Spas and Seaside Resorts.* New York, 1964.

Douglas, Ann. *The Feminization of American Culture.* New York, 1977.

Egan, Ferol. *Frémont: Explorer for a Restless Nation.* New York, 1977.

Eggleston, Edward. *The Hoosier Schoolmaster.* New York, 1871.

Flexner, Eleanor. *Century of Struggle: The Woman's Rights Movement in the United States.* Cambridge, Mass., 1959.

Fox, Mary Virginia. *Lady for the Defense: A Biography of Belva Lockwood.* New York, 1975.

Frederickson, George. *The Inner Civil War: The Change in the Outlook of Intellectuals in the Gilded Age.* New York, 1965.

Frémont, Jessie Benton. *Memoirs of My Life.* Chicago, 1887.

———. *Souvenirs of My Time.* Boston, 1887.

———. *A Year of American Travel.* New York, 1878.

Frémont, John Charles. *Expeditions of John Charles Frémont,* ed. Donald Jackson and Mary Lee Spence. Urbana, Ill., 1973.

———. *Narratives of Exploration and Adventure,* ed. Allan Nevins. New York, 1956.

Garland, Hamlin. *Main-Traveled Roads.* Boston, 1891.

———. *A Son of the Middle Border.* New York, 1917.

———. *Trail-Makers of the Middle Border.* New York, 1926.

Garraty, John. *The New Commonwealth, 1870–1890.* New York, 1968.

Geismar, Maxwell. *Mark Twain: An American Prophet.* Boston, 1970.

George, Henry. *Progress and Poverty.* New York, 1879.

George, Henry, Jr. *The Life of Henry George.* New York, 1900.

Goodwin, Cardinal L. *John Charles Frémont: An Explanation of His Career.* Stanford, Cal., 1930.

Grant, Ulysses S. *Personal Memoirs of Ulysses S. Grant.* New York, 1885.

Gray, Dorothy. *Women of the West.* Millbrae, Cal., 1976.

Green, Martin. *The Problem of Boston: Some Readings in Cultural History.* New York, 1966.

Griffith, Elisabeth. *Extraordinary Woman: The Life of Elizabeth Cady Stanton.* New York, 1984.

Grodinsky, Julius. *Jay Gould: His Business Career.* Philadelphia, 1957.

Handlin, Oscar. *This Was America: As Recorded by European Travelers.* Cambridge, Mass., 1969.

Harris, Charles Townsend. *Memories of Manhattan in the Sixties and Seventies.* New York, 1928.

Hesseltine, William P. *Ulysses S. Grant, Politician.* New York, 1935.

Hibben, Paxton. *Henry Ward Beecher: An American Portrait.* New York, 1927.

Hill, Hamlin. *Mark Twain: God's Fool.* New York, 1973.

Holbrook, Stewart H. *The Age of the Moguls.* New York, 1953.

Holzman, Robert S. *Stormy Ben Butler.* New York, 1954.

Hopkins, C. D. *The Rise of the Social Gospel in American Protestantism.* New Haven, Conn., 1940.

Howe, Edgar W. *Plain People.* New York, 1929.

———. *The Story of a Country Town.* Atchison, Kans., 1883.

Howells, William Dean. *A Hazard of New Fortunes.* New York, 1890.

———. *The Rise of Silas Lapham.* New York, 1885.

Hoyt, Edwin P. *The Vanderbilts and Their Fortunes.* New York, 1962.

James, Henry. *The American.* Boston, 1877.

Johnston, Johanna. *Mrs. Satan: The Incredible Saga of Victoria Woodhull.* New York, 1967.

Josephson, Matthew. *The Politicos, 1865–1896.* New York, 1938.

———. *The Robber Barons: The Great American Capitalists, 1861–1901.* New York, 1934.

Kaplan, Justin. *Mr. Clemens and Mark Twain.* New York, 1966.

———. *Walt Whitman: A Life.* New York, 1980.

Keller, Allan. *Scandalous Lady: The Life and Times of Madame Restell.* New York, 1981.

Kirkland, E. C. *Charles Francis Adams, Jr. 1835–1915: The Patrician at Bay.* Cambridge, Mass., 1955.

Kirkland, Joseph. *Zury, the Meanest Man in Spring County.* Boston, 1882.

Klein, Maury. *The Life and Legend of Jay Gould.* Baltimore, Md., 1986.

Larkin, Oliver. *Art and Life in America.* New York, 1949; rev. 1960.

Lerner, Gerda. *The Grimké Sisters from South Carolina, Rebels Against Slavery.* Boston, 1967.

Leslie, Anita. *The Remarkable Mr. Jerome.* New York, 1934.

Lewis, Lloyd. *Captain Sam Grant.* Boston, 1950.

Litwack, Leon F. *Been in the Storm So Long: The Aftermath of Slavery.* New York, 1979.

Lynes, Russell. *The Tastemakers.* New York, 1954.

McAllister, Ward. *Society As I Have Found It.* New York, 1890.

McDowall, J. R. *Magdalen Facts.* Privately printed, New York, 1832.

McFeely, William S. *Grant: A Biography.* New York, 1981.

McLoughlin, William G. *The Meaning of Henry Ward Beecher: An Essay in the Shifting Values of Mid-Victorian America.* New York, 1970.

Macrae, David. *The Americans at Home.* London, 1871.

Marberry, M. M. *The Golden Voice: A Biography of Isaac Kalloch.* New York, 1947.

Margo, Elizabeth. *Taming the Forty-Niner.* New York, 1955.

Martin, Edward W. *Behind the Scenes in Washington.* Philadelphia, 1873.

Martin, Frederick Townsend. *The Passing of the Idle Rich.* New York, 1911.

Marx. Leo. *The Machine in the Garden: Technology and the Pastoral Ideal in America.* New York, 1964.

Medbury, J. K. *Men and Mysteries in Wall Street.* New York, 1871.

Miller, Helen Marley. *Woman Doctor of the West.* New York, 1960.

Morgan, H. Wayne, ed. *The Gilded Age: A Reappraisal.* Syracuse, N.Y., 1963.

Morris, Lloyd. *Incredible New York, 1850–1950.* New York, 1957.

Muzzey, David Saville. *James G. Blaine: A Political Idol of Other Days.* New York, 1934.

Nevins, Allan. *The Emergence of Modern America.* New York, 1927.

——— . *Frémont: Pathmarker of the West.* New York, 1939; rev. 1960.

——— . *Hamilton Fish: The Inner History of the Grant Administration.* New York, 1936; rev. 1957.

Nies, Judith. *Seven Women.* New York, 1977.

[Norton, Charles Eliot.] *Considerations on Some Recent Social Theories.* Boston, 1853.

——— . *Letters of Charles Eliot Norton,* with biographical comment by Sara Norton and M. A. DeWolfe Howe. Boston, 1913.

——— . *Notes of Travel and Study in Italy.* Boston, 1859.

Oberholtzer, E. P. *Jay Cooke: Financier of the Civil War.* Philadelphia, 1907.

O'Connor, Richard. *Gould's Millions.* New York, 1962.

——— . *The Scandalous Mr. Bennett.* New York, 1962.

Olmsted, Frederick Law. *A Journey in the Seaboard Slave States.* New York, 1861.

Parker, Robert A. *A Yankee Saint, John Humphrey Noyes and the Oneida Community.* New York, 1935.

Parrington, Vernon Louis. *Main Currents in American Thought.* New York, 1927.

Pauli, Hertha. *Her Name Was Sojourner Truth.* New York, 1962.

Phillips, John Graham. *The Great God Success.* New York, 1901.

Poore, Ben Perley. *Reminiscences of Sixty Years in the National Metropolis.* Philadelphia, 1886.

Rammelkamp, J. S. *Pulitzer's Post-Dispatch.* Princeton, N.J., 1967.

Royce, Josiah. *California from the Conquest in 1846 to the Second Vigilance Committee in San Francisco, 1856: A Study of American Character.* Boston, 1886.

Royce, Sarah. *A Frontier Lady: Recollections of the Gold Rush and Early California,* ed. R. H. Gabriel. New Haven, Conn., 1932.

Rugoff, Milton. *The Beechers: An American Family in the Nineteenth Century.* New York, 1981.

——— . *Prudery and Passion: Sexuality in Victorian America.* New York, 1971.

Sabin, E. L. *Kit Carson Days.* Chicago, 1914.

Sachs, Emanie. *The Terrible Siren: Victoria Woodhull.* New York, 1928.

Sarnoff, Paul. *Russell Sage: The Money King.* New York, 1965.

Scharnhorst, Gary, with Jack Bales. *The Lost Life of Horatio Alger, Jr.* Bloomington, Ind., 1985.

Sears, Lorenzo. *Wendell Phillips: Orator and Agitator.* New York, 1909.

Seitz, Don C. *The James Gordon Bennetts, Father and Son.* Indianapolis, Ind., 1928.

Sherwin, Oscar. *Prophet of Liberty: The Life and Times of Wendell Phillips.* New York, 1958.

Smith, F. Hopkinson. *Colonel Carter of Cartersville.* New York, 1891.

Smith, Henry Nash. *Virgin Land: The American West as Symbol and Myth.* Cambridge, Mass., 1950.

Smith, Matthew Hale. *Sunshine and Shadow in New York.* Hartford, Conn., 1868

Sojourner Truth. *Narrative of Sojourner Truth: A Northern Slave Emancipated by the State of New York in 1828* (by Olive Gilbert). Privately printed, New York, 1853.

Sproat, John G. *The Best Men: Liberal Reformers in the Gilded Age.* New York, 1968.

Stanton, E. C., Susan B. Anthony, and M. J. Gage. *History of Woman Suffrage.* Rochester, N.Y., 1887–1922.

Stern, Madeleine. *We the Women: Career Firsts of Nineteenth Century America.* New York, 1963.

Stone, Candace. *Dana and the Sun.* New York, 1938.

Strong, George Templeton. *Diary of George Templeton Strong,* ed. Allan Nevins and M. H. Thomas. New York, 1952.

Swanberg, W. A. *Jim Fisk: The Career of an Improbable Rascal.* New York, 1959.

——— . *Pulitzer.* New York, 1967.

——— . *Sickles the Incredible.* New York, 1956.

Taylor, Bayard. *Eldorado, or Adventures in the Path of Empire.* New York, 1850.

Thomas, Lately. *Sam Ward: King of the Lobby.* Boston, 1965.

*Tilton vs. Beecher: Action for Criminal Conversation.* Verbatim Report. New York, 1875.

Twain, Mark. *The Autobiography of Mark Twain,* ed. Charles Neider. New York, 1959.

——— . *The Mark Twain Papers.* Berkeley and Los Angeles, 1967.

——— . *A Pen Warmed-up in Hell: Mark Twain in Protest,* ed. Frederick Anderson. New York, 1972.

——— . *The Writings of Mark Twain.* New York, 1906.

Vanderbilt, Kermit. *Charles Eliot Norton: Apostle of Culture in a Democracy.* Cambridge, Mass., 1959.

Wade, Mason. *Margaret Fuller: Whetstone of Genius.* New York, 1973.

Wallace, Irving. *The Twenty-seventh Wife.* New York, 1961.

Wecter, Dixon. *The Hero in America: A Chronicle of Hero-Worship.* New York, 1941.

Weisberger, Bernard A. *They Gathered at the River: A Story of the Great Revivalist.* Boston, 1958.

Welles, Gideon. *Diary of Gideon Welles.* Boston, 1911.

Wharton, Edith. *The Age of Innocence.* New York, 1920.

——— . *A Backward Glance.* New York, 1934.

Whitman, Walt. *Complete Poetry and Collected Prose.* Notes by Justin Kaplan. New York, 1981.

Wikoff, Henry. *The Reminiscences of an Idler.* New York, 1880.

Wilson, Forrest. *Crusader in Crinoline: The Life of Harriet Beecher Stowe.* Philadelphia, 1941.

Young, Ann Eliza. *Wife No. 19, or the Story of a Life in Bondage, Being a*

357

*Complete Exposé of Mormonism . . . by Brigham Young's Apostate Wife.* Hartford, Conn., 1875.

Young, Kimball. *Isn't One Wife Enough? The Story of Mormon Polygamy.* New York, 1954.

Zweig, Paul. *Walt Whitman: The Making of the Poet.* New York, 1984.

# INDEX

Abert, Colonel, 110–11
Abortion, 174–75
Acton, Sir William, 172
Adair, John, 286
Adams, Charles Francis, Jr., 4, 13, 42–43, 55, 65, 298
Adams, Franklin P., 170
Adams, Henry, 25–26, 37–38, 334
Adams, John, 2
Agassiz, Louis, 71, 298
Age of Innocence, The (Wharton), 81, 84–85, 182
Albany and Susquehanna, 61
Alcott, Amos Bronson, 150, 237, 263, 298, 322
Alcott, Louisa May, 298, 338
Aldrich, Thomas Bailey, 298
Alger, Horatio, Jr., 8–12, 165
  books of, 8–9, 10, 11–12
  life of, 9–12
Allen, John, 178
Alta California, 290
American, The (James), 80
American Anti-Slavery Society, 234, 262

American Commonwealth, The (Bryce), 217
American Equal Rights Association, 270
American Fur Company, 40
American Home, The (Macrae), 174, 182–83
American Home Missionary Society, 194
American Jockey Club, 74, 77, 145
American Medical Association, 286
American Notes (Dickens), 302
American Politician, An (Crawford), 334
American Slavery as It Is (Weld), 235, 236
American Union, 63
American Unitarian Association, 11
American Woman Suffrage Association, 271, 273
America's Cup, 76
Ames, Oakes, 31
Anderson, Sherwood, 103
Andrews, Stephen Pearl, 221, 222, 228

359

Anthony, Susan B., 199, 201, 222, 225, 260, 261, 265–75 *passim,* 277, 279, 283

*Anti-Slavery Bugle,* 244

*Appeal to Christian Women of the South, An* (Grimke), 234

*Appleton's Journal,* 90

Archaeological Institute of America, 313

Arnold, Matthew, 305, 311

Associated Press, 65, 291

Astor, Caroline (née Schermerhorn), 81, 83, 91–92

Astor, Carrie, 71

Astor, Emily, 17

Astor, Henry, 48

Astor, John Jacob, 17, 27, 40–41, 89

Astor, John Jacob, III, 90

Astor, Mrs. John Jacob, 71, 81, 89

Astor, William, 90–91, 92

Astor, William B., 25, 89

Astor House, 69

Astor Library, 88

*Atalanta* (yacht), 73

*Atlantic, The,* 298

Atlantic & Pacific, 63

*Atlantic Monthly,* 246

Austen, Jane, 236

Babcock, Orville E., 28, 29, 30, 34

Bacon, Dr. Leonard, 206, 209

Badeau, Adam, 28, 29

Bagioli, Teresa. *See* Sickles, Teresa

Baltimore and Ohio Railroad, 94

Bancroft, George, 112, 114, 301

Banks, Nathaniel P., 119

Banks, Sammy, 246, 248

Baptist Home Mission, 214

Bar Harbor, Maine, 72, 166, 168

Barnard, George, 56, 58, 61

Barnum, P. T., 8, 87, 136, 254

Barry, Francis, 220

*Basic Outline of Universology* (Andrews), 221

"Battle Hymn of the Republic, The," 20

Bayard, Edward, 261

Bayard, James A., 26

Beale, E. F., 134

Bear Flag War, 113

Beckford, William, 86

Beecher, Catharine, 205, 223, 224

Beecher, Eunice (née Bullard), 192, 193, 195, 197

Beecher, Harriet (née Porter), 191–92

Beecher, Henry Ward, 122, 130, 190, 191, 192–212, 214, 271
    Elizabeth Tilton and, 197–210, 223, 225

Beecher, Reverend Lyman, 191–92, 245

Beecher, Reverend Thomas K., 206

Belknap, General, 28

Belmont, August, 71, 74, 78, 89

Belmont, Mrs. August, 71

Bennett, Belva Ann. *See* Lockwood, Belva Ann

Bennett, James Gordon, Jr., 75, 76, 142, 144, 145–49, 180

Bennett, James Gordon, Sr., 141, 142, 143–44, 145, 149, 154

Benson, John, 131–32

Benton, Jessie. *See* Frémont, Jessie

Benton, Thomas Hart, 105–6, 108, 109, 110, 111, 112, 115, 118

Bigelow, John, 29

Billings, C. K. G., 70

Biltmore (mansion), 89

Bingham, William, 40

Black Friday, 60–61

Blackwell, Antoinette Brown, 266

Blaine, James G., 27–28, 33, 65, 279

Blair, Frank, Jr., 120

Blair, Montgomery, 121
Blanc, Louis, 288
Bliss, Frank, 338, 339
Blood, James, 221, 222, 227, 228
Bloomer, Amelia, 264
Boldini, Giovanni, 94
Boone, Daniel, 2
Borie, Adolph E., 29
Boston *Times,* 213
Boswell, James, 173
Bouguereau, Adolphe, 94
*Bound to Rise* (Alger), 8
Bowen, Henry, 199, 201, 202, 204
Bowen, Lucy Maria, 199, 207, 209
Bowles, Samuel, 57
Bradstreet, Anne, 313
Brady, "Diamond Jim," 73
Breckenridge, Tom, 116–17
Brevoort family, 90
Brewton, Miles, 85
Bridger, Jim, 106
Bristow, Benjamin, 34
Brook Farm, 1, 3, 143, 150–51, 152, 158, 303
Brooklyn Association of Congregational Ministers, 212
Brooklyn *Daily Eagle,* 316–17
Brooklyn *Daily Times,* 322–23
Brooklyn *Freeman,* 317
*Brooklyn Union,* 201
Brontë sisters, 336
Broun, Heywood, 170
Brown, Charles Brockden, 85
Brown, John, 246, 262
Browne, William M., 20
Browning, Elizabeth Barrett, 301
Browning, Robert, 301, 311
Brownlow, William G., 26
Bruff, J. Goldsborough, 133–36
Bryan, William Jennings, 167
Bryant, William Cullen, 154
Bryce, James, 217
Buchanan, James, 108, 113, 185
Buck, Franklin, 128–33

Buck, Mary, 128, 131, 132, 133
Buckingham, James Silk, 79
Buckingham, William A., 26
Bullard, Eunice. *See* Beecher, Eunice
Bullard, Laura, 201
Burroughs, John, 52, 327
Butler, Benjamin F., 28, 32–33, 156, 222
Butterfield, General, 28, 60
Butterworth, Samuel, 184
Byron, George Gordon, 85, 232, 311

Cady, Daniel, 260
Caldwell, James, 246
California, 111–15
  Gold Rush, 82, 117, 125–31, 133–40
Calvinism, 2, 301, 308, 314
Cambridge Theological School, 10
Cameron, Simon, 26
*Campaigning on the Oxus, and the Fall of Khiva* (MacGahan), 147
Candy, Captain, 145
Cannon, George Q., 256
Carlyle, Thomas, 288, 313, 317, 318, 322
Carnegie, Andrew, 5, 27, 341
Carroll, Charles, 40
Carson, Christopher "Kit," 106, 109, 111, 115
Casanova, 173
Casey, James F., 31
Castro, Don José, 112, 113
"Celebrated Jumping Frog of Calaveras County, The" (Twain), 330
Central Park, New York City, 70, 75
Chandler, Mrs. Winthrop, 92
Chandler, Zachariah, 26
Channing, William Ellery, 237
Chase, Salmon P., 15, 50

Cherokee Indians, 279

Chesnut, Mary Boykin, 179

Chicago *Times,* 255

Chicago *Tribune,* 207

Chicago World's Fair of 1893, 88–89

Child, Francis James, 298

Churchill, Jennie (née Jerome), 76

Churchill, Lord Randolph, 76

Churchill, Winston, 76

Civil War, 4, 99, 120–22, 142, 144, 153–54, 160, 185, 196, 267–68, 306, 307, 325

    fortunes made during, 43, 45, 49–50, 54–55, 68

    Grant's service in, 24, 153–154

    social life during, 14–15

Claflin, Tennessee, 47, 220, 221, 222, 225, 227

Clare, Ada, 323

Clark, William, 106

Clarke, Joseph I. C., 146

Clay, Henry, 72

Clemens, Clara, 345, 346, 347

Clemens, Jean, 342, 346

Clemens, Olivia (née Langdon), 331–32, 339, 341, 342, 343, 345, 346

Clemens, Samuel Langhorne. *See* Twain, Mark

Clemens, Susy, 342

Cleveland, Grover, 27, 65, 156, 164, 211, 311

Cleveland, *Leader,* 223

Clews, Henry, 41, 68, 71

Clough (hunter), 135–36

Club-House, 73

Coaching Club, 75

Cobb, Howell, 14

Coleridge, Samuel Taylor, 317

Colfax, Schuyler, 31

Colman, Lucy, 247

*Colonel Carter of Cartersville* (Smith), 44

Colton, Walter, 134

Columbia College, 16, 17

Columbia University, 170

Comstock, Anthony, 175–76, 225

Conkling, Roscoe, 26, 210

*Connecticut Yankee in King Arthur's Court, A* (Twain), 335, 339–40

*Considerations on Some Recent Social Theories* (Norton), 302

Contraception, 173–74

Cooke, Henry, 50

Cooke, Jay, 49–52, 87

Cooper Institute, 267

Cooper, Peter, 43, 72

Cooper Union, 295

Corbin, Abel, 59

Corey, Bromfield, 41–42

Cox, Jacob Dolson, 20, 29, 30

Cramer, M. J., 29

Crawford, F. Marion, 22, 148, 334

Crawford, Thomas, 18

Crédit Mobilier affair, 31

Creutzfeldt, Frederick, 116

Crèvecoeur, St. John de, 96

Crocker, Charles, mansion of, 87, 133

Crockett, Davy, 2

Currier & Ives, 102

Curtis, George William, 28, 151, 298

D'Adjuria, Gregorio, 180

*Daily Chronicle,* 49

Damrosch, Walter, 79

Dana, Charles A., 33, 142, 143, 146, 149–59

    Pulitzer and, 161, 164, 165–66

D. Appleton & Company, 293

D'Arusmont, Phiquepal, 232–33

Darwin, Charles, 308

Darwinism, 211–12, 216, 293

Davis, Alexander Jackson, 86–87

Davis, Bancroft, 33

Davis, Jefferson, 161

Davis, Kate. *See* Pulitzer, Kate
Davis, William Worthington, 161
Day, Benjamin, 141
Dead Rabbits, 76–77
*DeBow's Review,* 180
Debs, Eugene V., 83
Dee, James, 251, 257
De Forest, John W., 26, 181–82, 183, 334
Delavan House, 56
Delaware & Hudson Canal Company, 61
Delmonico, Charles, 70
Delmonico's, 70, 295
Demidoff, Paul, 19
de Mille, Agnes, 293
*Democracy* (Adams), 26, 334
*Democratic Vistas,* 325
Denning, Moses R., 258–59
Dent, Colonel, 29
Dent, Fred, 29
Dent, General, 33
DeYoung, Charles, 216, 217
DeYoung, Michael, 216
*Dial, The,* 151, 237, 313
Dickens, Charles, 302, 308, 311
"Disgraceful Persecution of a Boy," (Twain), 330–31
*Divine Comedy* (Dante), 313
Divorce, 182–83, 267
Dodge, William B., 25
Dominican Republic, 30
Donne, John, 313
Douglass, Frederick, 240, 244, 246, 248, 263, 270
Downing, Andrew Jackson, 86
Doyle, Peter, 328
Dred Scott decision, 246
Drew, Daniel, 44, 46–47, 48–49, 54, 93, 190
    Erie Railroad and, 48, 55–58
*Drum-Taps* (Whitman), 324
Duffey, Eliza Bisbee, 174
Dumont, John J., 241

Duniway, Abigail, 283
Dwight, Timothy, 7

Eakins, Thomas, 285
Eckert, Thomas, 63
Eclectic School of Medicine, 284
École des Beaux Arts, 87
*Education of Henry Adams, The* (Adams), 37–38
Edwards, Jonathan, 2, 191
Eggleston, Edward, 103, 104
Eidlitz, Leopold, 87
"Eighteenth Presidency, The," (Whitman), 321
*Eighty Years and More* (Stanton), 274
Elaw, Zilpha, 240
Eliot, Charles W., 309
Eliot, George, 308
Eliot, T. S., 315
Elssler, Fanny, 181
Emerson, Ralph Waldo, 42, 150, 151, 237, 263, 298, 304, 309
    Whitman and, 318, 321, 322
Engels, Friedrich, 288
English common law, 275
Enlightenment, 3
Equal Rights party, 225, 226, 279
Erie Railroad, 48, 55–58, 61–62, 188, 189, 190
E. W. Clark and Company, 49

Fabens, J. W., 30
Fahnstock, H. C., 51
Family Circle Dancing Class, 83
Female Anti-Slavery Society, 234
Field, Cyrus W., 64–65, 126
Field, David Dudley, 126, 127
Field, Stephen J., 126–27
Fifth Avenue Hotel, 69
Fink, Mike, 2
Finney, Charles Grandison, 261
First Unitarian Church of Brewster, 10

Fish, Hamilton, 13, 25, 29, 33, 155, 186
Fish, James D., 36
Fish, Mrs. Hamilton, 28
Fish, Mrs. Stuyvesant, 70
Fisk, Jim, 45, 52, 54, 74, 187–91
  corner on gold and, 60–61
  Erie Railroad and, 55–58, 61, 188, 189, 190
  Josie Mansfield and, 56, 187, 188–89
Fisk, Mrs. Jim, 56, 187
Fiske, John, 298
Flagler, A. M., 27
Folger, Ben, 242–43
*Following the Equator* (Twain), 342–43
Folsom, Amelia, 252
Fonthill Abbey (mansion), 86
Foot, John B., 220
Fortune, T. Thomas, 246
Fourier, Charles, 221, 237, 303
Fowler brothers, 318
Fox, Annie. *See* George, Annie
*Frank Leslie's Illustrated,* 72
Franklin, Benjamin, 2, 7
*Franklin Evans; or, The Inebriate* (Whitman), 316
*Frank's Campaign* (Alger), 10
*Free Enquirer, The,* 232
Free love, 218–19, 220, 223, 224, 225–26, 228, 232, 242
"Free Thinking and Plainspeaking," (Stephen), 314
Frémon, Charles, 107
Frémont, Jessie (née Benton), 18, 108–9, 110, 111, 112, 114, 118, 119, 120, 123, 124, 125
  Lincoln and, 121–22
Frémont, John Charles, 18, 23, 106–25, 134, 136, 249
Freniére, Louison, 108
Free Soil party, 317
Fruitlands, 3

*Fruits of Philosophy* (Knowlton), 173–74
Fugitive Slave Law, 118
Fuller, Margaret, 151, 237–39
*Functions and Disorders of the Reproductive Organs, The* (Acton), 170

Gamble, Jane, 181
Gardner, Isabella Stewart, 45
Gardner, John L., 45
Garfield, James A., 31, 35, 156, 158
Garland, Belle, 101
Garland, Hamlin, 97, 98, 99–102, 105, 298
Garland, Harriet, 100
Garland, Isabel (née McClintock), 98
Garland, Richard, 97–101
Garrison, William Lloyd, 234, 240, 263, 269
Gates, John W. "Bet-a-Million," 73
"Gay Nineties," The, 347
Genesee College, 276
George, Annie (née Fox), 290, 294, 297
George, Henry, 39, 289–97
Gibson, Charles Dana, 83
Gilbert, Olive, 244
*Gilded Age, The* (Twain and Warner), 16, 26, 43, 329, 331, 333–34, 338
Gillespie, A. H., 113
Godey, Alexis, 111
*Godey's Lady's Book,* 73
Godkin, E. L., 156–57, 164, 168, 307
Godwin, William, 231
Goelet, Robert, 89
Goethe, Johann Wolfgang von, 317
*Going to the Bath* (Bouguereau), 94
Goldberg, Hyman, 283
*Golden Age, The,* 224

Gold Rush, 82, 117, 125–31, 133–40

*Good Gray Poet, The* (O'Connor), 326–27

Gore Place (mansion), 85

Gorki, Maxim, 346

Gould, Anna, 93

Gould, George, 73, 92, 180

Gould, Helen (Jay's daughter), 92–93

Gould, Helen (née Miller) (Jay's wife), 54

Gould, Jay, 27, 52–54, 58–67, 73, 78, 87, 92, 149, 163, 341
  corner on gold, 59–61, 62
  Erie Railroad and, 55–58, 61–62, 189

Government Relief Company, U.S., 137

Graham, Sylvester, 262

Grant, Jenny, 59, 60

Grant, Jesse, 35

Grant, Mrs. Ulysses S., 28, 35, 60

Grant, Ulysses, Jr., 36

Grant, Ulysses S., 1, 22–25, 26, 28–38, 74, 91, 143, 160, 185, 200, 210, 226, 247, 275–76
  administration of, 28–35, 308
  before the Civil War, 22–24
  Civil War record, 24, 153–54
  Charles Dana and, 153–54, 155–56, 158
  Jay Gould and, 50, 51, 59, 60, 62
  Twain and, 339
  Ann Eliza Young and, 256

Grant & Ward, 36

*Great God Success, The* (Phillips), 169

Greeley, Horace, 25, 31, 142–43, 146, 149, 151, 153, 154, 155, 238

Greenwood, Grace, 270

Grey, Asa, 298

Griffing, Josephine, 246

Grimes, James, 26–27

Grimké, Angelina. *See* Weld, Angelina

Grimké, Archibald Henry, 236

Grimké, Francis James, 236

Grimké, Sarah, 233–35, 236

Gross, Dr. Samuel, 285

Grymes, John Randolph, 18

Grymes, Medora. *See* Ward, Medora

Gwin, William, 14, 20, 117

Hagan, Albert, 254

*Harbinger, The,* 151

Harlan, James, 324

Harmsworth, Alfred (Lord Northcliffe), 166

*Harper's,* 130, 132

*Harper's Weekly,* 33

Harrison, William Henry, 23, 106–7, 112

Harte, Bret, 132, 290, 337

Harvard *Courant,* 332–33

Harvard University, 9, 150, 298, 300, 301, 309–10, 311–12, 315

Hassler, Ferdinand, 108

Haviland, Laura, 247

Hawley, Joseph, 333

Hawthorne, Nathaniel, 15, 85, 143, 151, 237, 263, 298, 304

Hayes, Rutherford B., 32, 35, 156, 158, 161

Hayward, Ned, 78

*Hazard of New Fortune, A* (Howells), 42

Hearst, William Randolph, 142, 154, 167–68, 170

Heth, Jorce, 8

Hewitt, Abram, 296

Higginson, Thomas Wentworth, 298

Hill, LeGrand, 281–82, 283

*History of Prostitution* (Sanger), 170

*History of Woman Suffrage* (Stanton and Anthony), 272
Hoar, E. R., 29
Hoar, George, 311–12
Hoffman House, 70
Holmes, Oliver Wendell, 298
Homestead Act of 1862, 43
Hone, Philip, 86–87
*Honest John Vane* (De Forest), 26, 334
Hooker, Isabella Beecher, 199, 206, 222, 271
*Hoosier Schoolmaster, The* (Eggleston), 103
Hotel Brunswick, 77
Howe, E. W., 103, 104–5
Howe, Julia Ward, 18, 19, 20, 70, 298
Howe, Dr. Samuel Gridley, 18, 20
Howells, William Dean, 41–42, 298, 314, 334, 340
*Huckleberry Finn* (Twain), 335–36, 338
Hudson, Silas A., 29
Hudson and Harlem railroad, 93
Hudson's Bay Company, 40
Hunt, Richard Morris, 87–89
Hunt, William Morris, 87
Huntington, Collis P., 25, 78, 124
*Hunt's Merchants' Magazine*, 41
Hyde, Orson, 253

Ide, William, 113
*Incidents in the Life of a Slave Girl* (Jacob), 239–40
*Independent*, 90
*Independent, The*, 194–95, 198, 199, 201, 202
Ingalls, General, 28
Ingersoll, Robert, 27
*Innocents Abroad, The* (Twain), 331, 338
*Irish Land Question, The* (George), 294
*Irish World*, 294
Irving, Henry, 22, 72

Irving, Washington, 85
Irwin, William S., 292
Isabella, Queen of Spain, 186

Jackson, Andrew, 23, 309
Jackson, Claiborne, 120
Jacob, Harriet, 239–40
James, Henry, 12, 22, 71, 80, 88, 148, 227–28, 298, 314, 324
Jefferson, Thomas, 85
Jekyll Island, 166
Jerome, Catherine, 77
Jerome, Clara, 75, 76, 77, 80
Jerome, Leonard W., 74–77, 78, 145, 180
Jerome Park, 74, 75, 145
Johnson, Andrew, 21, 25, 185
Jordan, Eben, 54, 55
Jordan, Marsh & Co., 54–55
Josephson, Matthew, 88
*Journalist, The*, 164
Journalists, 141–70

Kalloch, Milton, 217
Kalloch, Reverend Isaac, 212–18
Kansas Pacific, 62
Kearny, Stephen Watts, 114–15, 124
Keats, John, 311
Keene, James, 21, 64
Kennedy, John A., 177
Key, Philip Barton, 184–85, 186
King, Captain, 116, 117
Kingdom, Edith, 92
Kirkland, Joseph, 102
Knickerbocker Club, 77
Knights of Labor, 65, 157
Knowlton, Dr. Charles, 173–74
Know-Nothing party, 119, 303, 316
Kossuth, Lajos, 303

Labor Reform party, 299
*Ladies of the First Empire* (Boldini), 94
Lamartine, Alphonse de, 301

Lane Theological Seminary, 192, 193, 262
Langdon, Olivia. *See* Clemens, Olivia
Larkin, Oliver, 90
Larkin, Thomas O., 115
Latham, Milton S., 20
Lavitt, Michael, 294–95
*Leaves of Grass* (Whitman), 304, 319–20, 321, 322, 323, 324, 328
*Ledger, The,* 197
Lee (lawyer), 53
Lefeul, Hector Martin, 87
Lehr, Henry, 91
Lenox, Massachusetts, 72
Leopold, King of Belgium, 346
*Letters from the Earth* (Twain), 346–47, 348
*Letters on the Equality of the Sexes* (Grimke), 234
Leupp, Charles, 53
Lewis, Meriwether, 106
Lewis, Sinclair, 103
Liberal Republican party, 30–31
*Liberator, The,* 234
*Life on the Mississippi* (Twain), 335, 336
Lincoln, Abraham, 32, 120, 125, 127, 143, 144, 160, 185, 196, 267–68
assassination of, 290
Beecher and, 196, 197
Jenny Frémont and, 121–22
Norton on, 307
Sojourner Truth and, 246, 247
Lippmann, Walter, 170
Little Rock Railroad, 27
Livingstone, David, 146
Lloyd, Henry Demarest, 90
Lobbyists, 15–16, 19, 21
Lockwood, Belva Ann (née Bennett), 275–81
Lockwood, Ezekiel, 277, 278
Logan, John Alexander, 28

London *Daily News,* 46, 147
Longfellow, Henry Wadsworth, 17, 71, 85, 298, 301, 304
Lowell, James Russell, 23, 263, 298, 304, 311, 313
Lowell, Massachusetts, 3, 32
Luckemeyer, Edward, 70
Lyndhurst (mansion), 58, 86–87
Lyon, Nathaniel, 120–21, 125

McAllister, Hall, 18, 19, 82
McAllister, Ward, 19, 68, 71, 81–84, 91, 92
McClellan, George B., 23
McClintock, Isabel. *See* Garland, Isabel
Macrae, Reverend David, 174, 182–83
McCulloch, Hugh, 21
MacGahan, Januarius Aloysius, 147
McGuffey, William Holmes, 7
McGuffey's *Reader,* 7–8, 99, 165
Mackay, John W., 148–49, 341
McKinley, William, 167
McNall, Uriah, 276
Madison, Dolly, 14
Magdalen Society, 177
Maillard, Adolph, 18
*Maine* (battleship), 168
*Main Street* (Lewis), 103
Manhattan Company, 64, 66
Manifest destiny, 30, 157
Mann, Horace, 41
Mansfield, Josie, 56, 58, 187, 188
"Man's Place in the Animal World" (Twain), 343
"Man that Corrupted Hadleyburg, The" (Twain), 344
Marcy, William, 112
Marine National Bank, 36
Martin, John Biddulph, 227–28
Martineau, Harriet, 79
Marx, Karl, 288

Mason, Colonel, 114–15

Massachusetts Anti-Slavery Society, 244

Masters, Edgar Lee, 103

Mather, Cotton, 96

Matthias, 242

Maury, Matthew Fontaine, 64

Maxwell, Lucien B., 109

Mazzini, Giuseppe, 303

May, Caroline, 147–48

Meade, General, 185

Medbury, J. K., 44

Medill, Joseph, 142

Mellon, James, 45

Mellon, Thomas, 45

Melville, Herman, 130

*Memoirs* (Elaw), 240

Memphis and El Paso Railroad, 123

*Men and Mysteries in Wall Street* (Medbury), 44

Menken, Adah Isaacs, 323

Men's clubs, 77–78

Meredith, George, 208

Merritt, Ezekiel, 113

Metropolitan Club, 77

Metropolitan Museum, 88

Metropolitan Opera House, 78–79, 274

Metropolitan Temple, 216

Mexican War, 23, 37, 49, 142

Milan, King of Serbia, 77

Mill, John Stuart, 172

Missouri Compromise, 118, 152

Missouri Pacific Railroad, 92

*Miss Ravenel's Conversion from Secession to Loyalty* (De Forest), 183

Monroe, James, 40

Monticello (mansion), 85

*Moral Physiology* (Owen), 173

Morgan, J. P., 45, 78, 169

Mormons, 248–59

Morris, William, 288, 305

Morrissey, John, 73, 76–77

Morton, Oliver P., 26

Mott, Lucretia, 235, 240, 263, 264

Moulton, Emma, 206, 208, 209

Moulton, Frank, 202–3, 208–9, 223

Mount Airy (mansion), 85

Mulligan, Colonel, 122, 125

Mulligan, James, 27

Myers, Gustavus, 66

*My Secret Life,* 175, 176

*Mysterious Stranger, The* (Twain), 345, 348

*My Wife and I* (Stowe), 224

Napoleon III, 87

*Narrative of Sojourner Truth: A Northern Slave, The* (Sojourner Truth), 240, 244

Nast, Thomas, 33

Nathan, James, 238

*Nation, The,* 31, 156, 159, 307

National American Suffrage Association, 273

National University Law School, 275–76, 277

National Woman's Loyal League, 268

National Woman Suffrage Association, 222, 270

Native American party, 119, 303, 316

Nevins, Alan, 4

New England Royal Publications Society, 306

New Harmony, 3, 303

New Orleans *Crescent,* 317

Newport, Rhode Island, 17, 71, 72, 73, 82, 89

Newsboys' Lodging House, 11

*New Year's Day* (Wharton), 182

New York Academy of Music, 78, 79, 224

New York Central, 95

New York *Evening Post,* 147, 149, 154, 156, 164, 168

New York *Evening Telegram*, 145, 149

New York *Herald*, 126, 141, 142, 144, 145, 146–47, 148, 149, 156, 208, 344

New York *Journal*, 167–68

New York Society for the Suppression of Vice, 176

New York State Assembly, 266

New York State Guard, Ninth Regiment of, 188, 189

New York Stock Exchange, The, 44

New York *Sun*, 10, 141–42, 146, 154, 155–59, 316

  Pulitzer and, 161, 162, 165–66

New York Sunday *World*, 167

*New York Times, The*, 64, 149, 154, 156, 223

New York *Tribune*, 25, 117, 143, 144, 146, 151, 152, 153, 156, 238, 265, 325, 330, 332

New York *World*, 63, 65, 66, 146, 223, 338

  Hearst and, 167, 169

  Pulitzer and, 163–64, 165, 167–68, 169, 170

New York Yacht Club, 77, 144

Nicaragua, 46

Nicholas, Czar of Russia, 346

Nicollet, Joseph, 107, 108, 109

*North American Review*, 298, 301, 302, 306, 308

Northampton Association of Education and Industry, 243–44

Northern Pacific, 50–51

*North Star* (yacht), 46, 75

Norton, Andrews, 300, 301, 304, 314

Norton, Catharine Eliot, 300, 308

Norton, Charles Eliot, 298, 300–315

Norton, Susan Ridley (née Sedgwick), 306–7, 308–9

*Notes on Travel and Study in Italy* (Norton), 304

*Notes on Walt Whitman as Poet and Person* (Burroughs), 327

Noyes, John Humphrey, 218–19

O'Connor, William, 326

Ogontz (mansion), 50, 51, 87

Olmsted, Frederick Law, 70, 313

"Open Letter to Commodore Vanderbilt, An" (Twain), 332

*Open Letter to Pope Leo XIII* (George), 296

Oregon Trail, 109–11, 126

Ossoli, Giovanni, 238

*Our Land and Land Values*, 291

Outcault, R. F., 167

"Out of the Cradle Endlessly Rocking" (Whitman), 323

*Overland Monthly, The*, 290

Owen, Robert Dale, 173, 177, 221, 232, 303

Owens, Bethenia, 281–87

Owens, George, 282, 283, 284, 285, 286

Pacific Mail Steamship Company, 21, 62

Paget, Sir James, 170

Paige, James M., 339

Paine, Thomas, 315

Palmer, Potter, 87

Panama Canal, 169

Panic of 1837, 17, 33, 150

Panic of 1857, 53, 214

Panic of 1873, 51, 77, 215

Paraguay, 19, 20

Parker, Reverend Theodore, 173, 237, 263

Parkman, Francis, 106, 304

Patriarchs, 83

Patti, Adelina, 76

Paulding, William, 86

*Paul the Peddler* (Alger, Jr.), 8

Peabody, Elizabeth, 263
Peabody, Josephine Preston, 310–11
Pendleton's, 16
Pennsylvania Railroad, 95
People's party, 161
Perry, Caroline Slidell, 78
*Personal Recollections of Joan of Arc* (Twain), 336, 342
Philadelphia Female Anti-Slavery Society, 263
Philadelphia *Ledger,* 50
Phillips, David Graham, 168–69
Phillips, Wendell, 98, 100, 240, 268, 298–300
Pierson, Elijah, 242
Pierson, Sarah, 242
Pike, Zebulon, 106
Pike's Opera House, 58, 61, 187
Pillsbury, Parker, 270
*Plain People* (Howe), 104
Plymouth Church, 194, 195, 199, 202, 205, 206, 207, 208–9
Pocaho (mansion), 123
Poe, Edgar Allan, 85
Poinsett, Joel R., 107
Polk, James, 112, 115
Polygamy, 248–59
Pond, James, 254, 255
Poore, Ben Perley, 16, 28
*Poor Richard's Almanac* (Franklin), 7
Pope, Alexander, 311
Pope, John, 122
Populists, 167
Porter, Fitz-John, 28
Porter, Harriet. *See* Beecher, Harriet
Pratt, Orson, 253
Pratt, Colonel Zadock, 53
Prentiss, Benjamin M., 121
Price, General, 122
Prime, Ward & King, 17, 18
*Prince and the Pauper, The* (Twain), 335, 338

*Progress and Poverty* (George), 39, 291–92, 293–94, 296
Prostitution, 16, 172, 176–80, 337
Provôt, Etienne, 108
*Pudd'nhead Wilson* (Twain), 338, 340–41
Pulitzer, Joseph, 65, 142, 146, 154, 159–70
Pulitzer, Kate (née Davis), 161, 162, 163, 165, 168
Pulitzer Building, 166
Puritanism, 2, 7, 42, 83–84, 85, 89, 171, 172, 176, 217–18, 230, 297
*Putnam's Magazine,* 302, 304

Quakers, 2, 233, 234, 245
Quincy, Josiah, 85, 301

Racquet and Tennis Club, 77
Radcliffe, Ann, 86
*Ragged Dick,* 8
Randolph, John, 14
Rawlins, John Aaron, 28, 29
Raymond, Henry, 149, 154
*Recollections of the Civil War* (Dana), 153–54
Redpath, James, 254, 255, 256
Reid, Whitelaw, 156
*Reminiscences of an Idler, The* (Wikoff), 181
Renville, Joseph, 108
Republican National Committee, 25
"Restell, Madame." *See* Trow, Anna
Reuter, Baroness de, 149
"Revised Catechism, The" (Twain), 332
*Revolution,* 269–70
Robinson, Marcus, 244
Richmond *Dispatch,* 14
Ripley, George, 143, 150, 151
Ripley, Sophia, 151

*Rise of Silas Lampham, The* (How-
ells), 41
Rockefeller, John D., 5, 46, 78, 341
Rogers, Henry H., 341, 345
Roosevelt, Theodore, 169, 296, 344
Roseberry, Lord, 21–22
Rossetti, William Michael, 305,
327
Rothschild, Salomon de, 20
Rothschild family, 62, 74
*Roughing It* (Twain), 333
Rousseau, Jean Jacques, 237
Royce, Josiah, 124, 138, 139, 140
Royce, Sarah, 136–40
Ruskin, John, 288, 304, 305, 307,
313

Sage, Russell, 27, 62, 64, 180
St. Louis *Post-Dispatch,* 162–63, 170
St. Louis *Times,* 161
St. Nicholas Hotel, 69, 302
Saint-Simon, Claude, 303
Salt Lake City *Tribune,* 254
Samuels, "Bully," 144
Sand, George, 236, 317
"Sandlotters," 216
San Francisco *Chronicle,* 216
San Francisco *Evening Journal,* 289–
90
San Francisco *Evening Post,* 292
San Francisco *Herald,* 291
Sanger, Dr., 178
Sanger, William W., 170
Saratoga Springs, New York, 71,
72–73
Schenck, Robert C., 28, 34
Schermerhorn, Caroline Webster.
*See* Astor, Caroline
Schermerhorn family, 90, 91
School for Classical Studies, 313
Schurz, Carl, 28, 31, 160, 161, 164
*Science of Political Economy, The*
(George), 296
Scott, Sir Walter, 85, 336

Scott, Winfield, 23
Scripps-Howard chain, 170
Sedgwick, Susan Ridley. *See* Nor-
ton, Susan Ridley
See's Exchange, 130
Selover, A. J., 64
Sembrich, Marcella, 92
Senate Committee on Woman Suf-
frage, 273
Seneca Falls convention, 259–60,
264
*Serpents in Doves' Nests* (Todd), 174
Seward, Frederick W., 14
Seward, William, 20, 122
Shaw, George Bernard, 294
Shelley, Mary, 231
Shelley, Percy Bysshe, 231, 331
Sherman Anti-Trust Act of 1890,
95
Sherry's, 70–71
Sickles, Daniel, 61, 183–87
Sickles, Teresa (née Bagioli), 184–86
Simpson, Bishop, 177
*Sink or Swim* (Alger), 8
*1601* (Twain), 337–38
Slidell, John, 14
Smith, F. Hopkinson, 44
Smith, Gerrit, 261–62
Smith, Henry Nash, 96
Smith Jedediah, 106
Smith, Joseph, 248
Smith, Libby, 264
Smith, William "Baldy," 33
Smith, Gould & Martin, 54
*Social Problems* (George), 295
*Society as I Have Found It* (McAllis-
ter), 83
Sojourner Truth, 242–48
*Son of the Middle Border, A* (Garland),
97
Southhampton, New York, 72
Spanish-American War, 168, 311
Specimen Days (Whitman), 324
Spencer, Herbert, 41, 211, 293

Spiritualism, 219–20, 225
Spoils system, 28
*Spoon River Anthology* (Masters), 103
Sprague, Kate Chase, 15
Sprague, William, 15
Springfield *Republican,* 14, 57
Staël, Germaine de, 236
Stafford, Harry, 326
Stanford, Leland, 133
Stanley, Henry Morton, 146–47
Stanton, Daniel, 268
Stanton, Elizabeth Cady, 199, 201,
    207, 222, 223, 229, 236, 259–
    75, 279
Stanton, Harriot, 272
Stanton, Henry, 262, 263–64, 265,
    266, 267, 268, 272–73
Stanton, Theodore, 272, 273
Staten Island Railway, 93
Steen, Laura Flye, 213
Stephen, Leslie, 311, 314
Stewart, A. T., 25, 43
Stewart, William, 331
Stillman, James, 148
Stockton, Robert, 114
Stokes, Edward Stiles, 188–89, 191
Stone, Lucy, 236, 269, 270, 273,
    298
Story, William Wetmore, 246
*Story of a Country Town, The* (Howe),
    103, 104–5
Stow, Mrs. Maretta, 279
Stowe, Calvin Ellis, 193, 196
Stowe, Harriet Beecher, 191, 193,
    196, 223, 224, 245, 246, 332
Stratton, C. C., 254
Strong, George Templeton, 47,
    189, 205
Stuart, James, 126, 127–28
Sullivan, Louis, 88
Sumner, Charles, 26, 30, 247, 298
Sun Yat-sen, 294
Supreme Court, 127, 169, 278, 279
Swedenborg, Emanuel, 237

Swift, Jonathan, 311
Swinburne, Algernon Charles, 314,
    323, 327
Symonds, John Addington, 328

Taft, Elizabeth, 249, 250
Tayloe, John, II, 85
Tayloe family, 14
Taylor, Bayard, 117
Taylor, Zachary, 23, 40
Taylor Hotel, 56
"Temperance Crusade and Wom-
    an's Rights, The" (Twain),
    334
Tennyson, Alfred, 22, 311
Tenth National bank, 59
Terry, Ellen, 22
Texas, 112
Texas & Pacific, 65
"$30,000 Bequest, The" (Twain),
    344
Thomas, Lorenzo, 122
Thoreau, Henry David, 1, 96, 195,
    298, 322
Tilden, Samuel Jones, 35, 161, 292
Tilton, Elizabeth, 197–210, 223,
    225
Tilton, Theodore, 197–210, 223–24
Tocqueville, Alexis de, 301
Todd, Reverend John, 174
Tolstoy, Leo, 294
*Tom Sawyer* (Twain), 335
*Tom Sawyer Abroad* (Twain), 342
*Tom Sawyer, Detective* (Twain), 342
Topographical Corps, U.S., 107,
    110
"To the Person Sitting in Dark-
    ness" (Twain), 343–44
*Trail-Makers of the Middle Border*
    (Garland), 97
Train, George Francis, 269, 270
Transcendentalists, 3, 150–51, 237,
    301
Traubel, Horace, 328

*Travels* (Frémont), 136
Travers, William, 74
Tremont Temple, 212, 213–14, 255–56
Trollope, Frances, 89, 232, 311
Trow, Anna (Madame Restell), 174–75
Troy Female Seminary, 261
Trumbull, Lyman, 26, 27
Tryon, Constance, 94
Tucker, Benjamin R., 226–27
Turgenev, Ivan, 327
Twain, Mark, 16, 36–37, 43, 289, 298, 329–48
Tweed, "Boss," 57, 58, 61, 74, 76, 149, 189
*Twelve Temptations, The,* 187, 188
Twichell, Joseph, 341
Tyler, John, 80
Tyler, Mrs. Robert, 80
*Typee* (Melville), 130

*Uncle Tom's Cabin* (Stowe), 196, 236, 245
Union Club, 77
Union Pacific Railroad, 27, 31, 62, 65, 124
Union School, 276–77
Unitarians, 301, 314
"United States of Lyncherdom, The" (Twain), 343
University of California, 292
University of Michigan, 285
University of Tübingen, 17
Utopians, 1, 3, 232, 243–44, 303

Vale, Gilbert, 243
Van Buren, Martin, 108, 317
Vanderbilt, Alva, 71, 81, 88, 183
Vanderbilt, Cornelius B., 25, 45, 45–48, 73, 76–77, 93, 94, 180
  Erie Railroad and, 55–57
  Woodhull and, 221, 222, 224, 227

Vanderbilt, Cornelius Jeremiah, 93
Vanderbilt, George Washington, 89, 93
Vanderbilt, Mrs. Cornelius B., 81
Vanderbilt, William H., 47, 63, 93–95
Vanderbilt, William Kissam, 81, 88, 93, 183
Vanderbilt family, 78, 89
Van Rensselaer, Mrs. John King, 182
Van Wagenen, Isabella. *See* Sojourner Truth
Vassar College, 272
Vaux, Calvert, 70
Veblen, Thorstein, 83
Victoria, Queen of England, 82, 279
*Views of Society and Manners in America* (Wright), 232
Vigny, Alfred de, 301
Villard, Oswald Garrison, 147
*Vindication of the Rights of Women, A* (Wollstonecraft), 231–32

Wagner, Richard, 79
Wales, Prince of, 22, 80
Walker, Joe, 106
Walker, William, 46
Wall Berry, 73
Ward, Annie, 18
Ward, Ferdinand, 36
Ward, Julia. *See* Howe, Julia Ward
Ward, Louisa, 18
Ward, Medora (née Grymes), 17–18, 19, 20–21, 180
Ward, Sam (son), 16–22, 82, 122, 180
Ward, Samuel (father), 82
Warner, Charles Dudley, 16, 43, 333
"War Prayer, The" (Twain), 346
Washburne, Elihu, 24, 29
Washington, George, 8, 23

Washington City and California Mining Association, 134
Washington *Daily National Intelligencer,* 134
Washington, D.C. *Morning Journal,* 280
Webb, Ann Eliza. *See* Young, Ann Eliza
Webb, Chauncey, 249
Webb, Eliza, 249, 250, 251, 252, 253, 257
Webb, Gilbert, 252, 259
Webster, Charles L., 339
Webster, Daniel, 72
Wecter, Dixon, 11
Weld, Angelina (née Grimke), 233–36, 262
Weld, Theodore, 192, 234, 235–36, 262
West, expansin to the, 2–3, 96–140
Westchester Polo Club, 145
Western Union, 63, 64, 65, 66, 92, 291
*Westliche Post,* 160
Wharton, Edith, 81, 84–85, 88, 181–82
*What Is Man?* (Twain), 343, 345, 348
Whiskey Ring, 34
Whistler, James McNeill, 148
White, Fanny, 184
White, Stanford, 168
Whiting, Beverly, 107
Whitman, George, 323, 327, 328
Whitman, Walt, 289, 298, 304, 315–29
Whitney, William C., 78
Whittier, John Greenleaf, 263, 298, 304
*Wife No. 19* (Young), 258, 259
Wikoff, Henry, 180–81
Willard, Emma, 261
Willard's, 54

Williams, Bill, 106, 116–17
Wilson, Henry, 31
Wilson, Woodrow, 280
*Winesburg, Ohio* (Anderson), 103
Wise, Henry, 119
Wollstonecraft, Mary, 231–32, 263
*Woman in the Nineteenth Century* (Fuller), 237–38
*Woman's Bible, The,* 274
*Woman's Herald of Industry,* 279
*Woman's Journal,* 271
Woman's Republic, 279
Women
 black, 239–48
 first, in traditionally male professions, 257–87
 lobbyists, 15–16
 Mormon, 249–59
 women's rights movement, 199, 205, 218, 222, 223, 225–26, 231–32, 234–35, 236, 237–38, 259–87, 298
Wood, Annie, 187
Woodhull, Dr. Canning, 220, 221
Woodhull, Victoria Claflin, 47, 199, 205–6, 208, 220–29, 271
*Woodhull & Claflin's Weekly,* 205–6, 222, 224, 225
Woods, Josie, 74, 177–78
Woollcott, Alexander, 170
Wordsworth, William, 311
World Anti-Slavery Convention, 262–63
Wright, Fanny, 231, 232–33, 316

Young, Ann Eliza (née Webb), 249–59
Young, Brigham, 111, 249, 250–54, 257–58

Zion Hill, 242–43
*Zury: The Meanest Man in Spring County* (Kirkland), 102